ENCYCLOPAEDIA OF MODERN MURDER

Colin Wilson, a biographer, historian and novelist, is the author of some fifty books, many of which are studies of criminology and sexuality past and present. The best known of these are the *Outsider Cycle*, *Origins of the Sexual Impulse* and *A Casebook of Murder*. His research for this encyclopaedia has been aided by an enormous library of books and articles covering criminal cases amassed by him over the last twenty years.

Donald Seaman was on the staff of the *Daily Express* for twenty-five years, working variously as a crime reporter, feature-writer and foreign correspondent, before moving to Cornwall, where he is a near neighbour of Colin Wilson. He has written six thrillers and one exposé of the intelligence network, *The Great Spy Scandal*.

Also by Colin Wilson in Pan Books

ENCYCLOPAEDIA OF MURDER (with Pat Pitman)
THE PSYCHIC DETECTIVES

ENCYCLOPAEDIA
OF
MODERN MURDER
1962–82

COLIN WILSON
and
DONALD SEAMAN

Pan Books London and Sydney

The authors and publishers are grateful to the following
for permission to reproduce illustrations: Associated Press Ltd,
John Topham Ltd, Press Association Ltd, Syndication International
Ltd, S. & G. Press Agency Ltd.

First published 1983 by Arthur Barker Ltd
This edition published 1986 by Pan Books Ltd,
Cavaye Place, London SW10 9PG
9 8 7 6 5 4 3 2
© Colin Wilson and Donald Seaman 1983, 1986
ISBN 0 330 28299 9
Scanned and phototypeset by
Datasolve Information, London
Printed and bound in Great Britain by
Cox & Wyman Ltd, Reading

CONTENTS

CONTENTS

ACKNOWLEDGEMENTS

Many good friends in the media helped with the considerable research involved in preparing the *Encyclopaedia of Modern Murder*. Especial thanks are due to: Percy Hoskins, CBE, doyen of Britain's crime reporters and chief crime consultant to Express Newspapers; James Nicoll, foreign editor of the *Daily Express*; Ross Mark, Washington correspondent of the *Daily Express*; Roy Walters, deputy editor, BBC Radio News; Stephen Claypole, editor, News and Current Affairs, BBC, Northern Ireland; W. D. Flackes, former BBC Northern Ireland political correspondent; Dr Frank Goble of the Thomas Jefferson Research Foundation; K. L. Gunderson, head of the BBC News Information department and Miss Wendy Honeysett, also of News Information; and Brian McConnell, QGM, the author and journalist. We also wish to thank the following: A. E. Van Vogt, Dan McDougald, Dr James Rentoul, John Dunning, Alfred Reynolds, Ludovic Kennedy, Stephen Spickard, Dennis Stacy, Dr A. L. Rowse, Ted Harrison, Kenneth Moyer, Richard Neville and Grethe Nordhelle.

The book owes its final form to the many suggestions and editorial work of Marcia Fenwick, to whom both authors express their gratitude.

THE AGE OF MURDER

An introductory essay by Colin Wilson

Since the *Encyclopaedia of Murder* was completed in 1960, there
has been a strange and frightening change in the patterns of violence
in the civilized world. An increasing number of crimes are characterized by a kind of motiveless viciousness. In October 1982 an unknown
psychopath went round Chicago druggists, slipping capsules containing cyanide into bottles of a pain-relieving drug called Tylenol.
A twelve-year-old girl was the first to die, and within days, the total
had risen to seven. A week later, a man bought a bottle of eye lotion
in Grand Junction, Colorado, and collapsed in agony when he tried
to use it – someone had substituted pure hydrochloric acid. Within
weeks of the original incident more than a hundred imitative cases
had occurred in America. The authorities issued a warning to children
playing 'trick or treat' on Hallowe'en, pointing out that in past years
children had been injured by psychopaths who put poison in sweets,
or needles and razor blades in apples. The warning proved to be
sadly justified when a record number of children had to be rushed
to hospital after eating doctored treats.

Of course, 'motiveless' aggression is not new. In 1951 there was a
series of explosions in public places in New York. Fortunately no
one was killed. The 'mad bomber' wrote to the police denouncing
the Edison company for causing his tuberculosis; this enabled them
to track down a man called George Metesky, who had left the Edison
company with TB in 1931. Metesky was found to be insane, and was
sent to an asylum.

But insanity or paranoia no longer provide an adequate explanation
for crimes of sick violence. There seems to be more often an element
of sadism that springs out of a kind of boredom. In November 1980
two teenage gunmen went out on the streets of Los Angeles and
casually killed four people in twenty minutes. Three days later, three
youths walked up to a car that had halted at a traffic light, and shot
the driver, David Rudnick, in the head; then they ran away, laughing.
A burglar broke into the home of Dorothy Aquilar, and killed both
her and her baby in his playpen. Two young muggers held up a girl

1

and her escort outside a restaurant in Venice, near Los Angeles, and took their money; then, without reason, they shot the girl, Sarah Rubicoff. Three men drove down a quiet street in a Los Angeles suburb, and one of them leaned out of a window and killed a child, Joyce Huff – a total stranger – with a shotgun. In 1978, fifteen-year-old Mary Vincent accepted a lift near San Raphael, California; the driver throttled her unconscious, raped her, then hacked off both her arms below the elbow; when arrested, Larry Singleton, aged fifty-one, could give no reason, except that he had been drinking.

Psychologically speaking, it would be inaccurate to describe any crime as motiveless. Metesky had a motive; so did the various killers mentioned above – police described the shooting of Joyce Huff as a 'thrill killing, like deer stalking or partridge shooting'. But in the past, a crime usually brought the criminal some *advantage*. We call a crime motiveless if it seems to do no one any good. Before 1960 such crimes were rare, and the few that occurred belong to the end of the decade: Norman Foose, who in July 1958 shot two children as they stood beside their mother in Cuba, New Mexico, and later explained that he wanted to do something about the population explosion; and Penny Bjorkland, who went for a ride with a man she knew slightly, and killed him with a revolver, explaining: 'I was curious to see if I could commit a murder and not have it on my conscience'. By the mid 1960s there was a steady and perceptible rise in such crimes. In November 1966, eighteen-year-old Robert Smith walked into a beauty parlour in Mesa, Arizona, made five women and two children lie on the floor, then shot them all in the back of the head. He explained, 'I wanted to become known, to get myself a name.' His teacher described him as an exemplary student who had never shown any sign of hostility or aggression. Dozens of similar cases will be found in the pages that follow.

If we look back into the history of human violence, we discover that there *is* a precedent for such crimes. But the men who committed them were tyrants or men of great wealth. The Greek tyrant Phalaris is reputed to have roasted men alive; Alexander of Pherae amused himself by having men torn apart by dogs; Caligula ordered a bridge of ships to be constructed over the Bay of Baiea, then went along it pushing people into the sea. The crimes of Gilles de Rais, Ivan the Terrible, Vlad the Impaler, are too well known to need description. The problem here seems to be that the ruler has the power of life and death, which he uses against enemies or wrongdoers; then he begins to use it as casually as someone scratching his nose. When the African explorer Speke presented a gun to King Mutesa of Uganda in 1861, he was horrified when the king ordered an urchin to go and kill someone to see if it worked; the urchin obeyed the order, killing a bystander, and the king laughed with satisfaction. In the past, a few robbers and brigands also acquired a reputation for sadistic violence – like the legendary robber chief in *Ali Baba*. Hans Schmidt, the Nuremberg hangman, writing at the end of the sixteenth century, mentions several such cases – like the bandits who broke into a mill, raped the wife and maidservant, then forced the wife to eat fried eggs off the corpse of her husband.

Crimes like these were rarities. Most criminals were not sadistic; their crimes were simply a matter of necessity, of keeping body and soul together. Throughout his long history, man has found life a continual uphill struggle – against danger, climatic fluctuations, food shortages. We find it very difficult now to imagine what life was like before public welfare: how, for example, thousands of families were allowed to starve to death in the great potato famine in Ireland in the nineteenth century. The advance of civilization has raised the general level of comfort so that large numbers of people have a security that was almost unknown in the ancient world. Millions of people are now able to enjoy the kind of leisure and comfort that would have been envied by Greek tyrants or Roman emperors. The trouble is that leisure and comfort also produce boredom, a desire for sensation, and this seems to explain why an increasing number of criminals have come to behave like Caligula or Gilles de Rais.

We can see the Roman emperor syndrome in many cases in this book – Melvin Rees, Norman Collins, Dean Corll, Ted Bundy, Wayne Gacy: men who treated their victims as 'throwaways'. But there are hundreds of other cases that have been left out because they are too commonplace to deserve presenting in detail – cases like the murder of two teenagers, Chris Barber and Linda Bosteder, in San Bernardino, California, in February 1966. The police were so shocked by the medical evidence that they worked overtime for months until five youths were finally arrested and charged. It emerged that the five had been driving around aimlessly, drinking vodka out of the bottle, when they saw the teenagers near a bus station and offered them a lift. In a remote spot, the youths tore off the girl's clothes. Her boyfriend managed to kick one of them, which so enraged them that they told him they would 'show him what it was really like to be raped'. The boy was forced to watch while the girl he intended to marry was raped by three youths at the same time –

3

orally, anally and vaginally. After this the couple were killed. This crime is of the kind that was committed by wealthy young thugs in Nero's Rome or Justinian's Constantinople – or, for that matter, eighteenth-century London, where a society called the Bold Bucks specialized in rape and mutilation. The difference is that the California thugs were not rich – merely bored.

How can we begin to understand this sudden increase in sadistic violence? Recent advances in our knowledge of the physiology of stress provide a partial explanation. Stress can be produced by overcrowding, and overcrowding has different effects on different animals. The Sika deer on James Island, in Chesapeake Bay, began to feel overcrowded when the population exceeded one to an acre, and began to die of fatty degeneration of the liver and overproduction of adrenalin. Lemmings panic when they become overcrowded and commit mass suicide by drowning. But experiments on overcrowded rats by John B. Calhoun at the National Institute of Mental Health in Maryland showed that rats react more aggressively. The overcrowded rats formed gangs and roamed around raping females and eating babies, acts which are unknown under natural conditions.

The source of aggressive behaviour lies in a small nucleus in the brain called the amygdala. A mild old lady whose amygdala was electrically stimulated in the laboratory became foul-mouthed and aggressive. When the current was switched off, she was horrified and apologized. But she could not control her reaction when the current was switched on. Some people are affected in this way by alcohol, and this could help to explain a case like that of Larry Singleton, the rapist who mutilated his victim. It is also interesting to note that Charles Whitman, the sniper who shot eighteen people from the university tower in Texas, was terrified by his inability to control his rages, and that a post mortem revealed a brain tumour. Richard Speck, killer of eight nurses in Chicago, had been knocked unconscious by a swing as a child. Many other killers are found to have suffered head injuries. Kenneth Moyer in America has added enormously to our knowledge of these areas in recent years.

But such physiological factors can only offer a partial explanation. There is no evidence that most mass killers have anything wrong with their brains. The disorder lies in the realm of the personality. Robert Smith, who shot the women in the beauty parlour, admitted to being 'inspired' by Whitman and Speck; in order to know why he should admire two deranged criminals, we need to know what it was in his personality that responded to the idea of mass murder. What seems puzzling is the *casualness* of it. After all, the killer is virtually throwing away his own life as well as that of the victim.

In my *Criminal History of Mankind* I point out that André Gide anticipated this type of crime in 1914 in his novel *The Vatican Cellars*, in which a young aesthete decides to push a fellow traveller out of the door of a train for no particular reason. Gide called it 'the gratuitous act', and the *Oxford Companion to French Literature* defines this as an 'inconsequent action performed on impulse, possibly to gratify a desire for sensation'. That still leaves us with the psychological riddle of why anyone should want to do anything so preposterous.

One interesting clue is that so many of these 'motiveless' killers are of average or above average intelligence – although the stupidity of their crimes often seems to belie it. It applies to Charles Manson, Ian Brady, Melvin Rees, John Frazier, Harry Lanham, Ted Bundy, and many other cases in this book. The common factor here is that none made any active use of the intelligence; this, in turn, seems to have been due to the criminal's *low opinion of himself* – a defective self-image. And this leads again and again to a state of unmotivated resentment. Such men feel – quite correctly – that they are as intelligent as many people who have achieved success. So there must be something rotten and corrupt about a society that gives them no opportunity to use their talents. The crimes spring out of this resentment.

And here we are coming close to the heart of the problem of 'motiveless' crime. In most cases we can trace a feeling of resentment, that 'somebody deserves the blame'. This is a concept that has been developed by the English novelist Brian Marriner. Marriner, who has himself served a term in prison for robbery with violence, argues that throughout most of his social history, the average man has been a conformist, accepting miseries and disasters with the stoicism of a cow standing in the rain. Education and the rise in living standards have changed all that; he has come to feel that he deserves justice and a degree of consideration as an individual. Even in prison he knows he has certain rights, and some of the most violent prison riots of the past half century have been due to a feeling that those rights have been violated. Where in the past he was passive, modern man has become *reactive*. Marriner suggests that this explains a great deal about the rise in violence and 'motiveless' crime.

This is undoubtedly true; but it is still important to recognize that the crimes of 'reactive man' are not necessarily justified. In 1976 three men held up a school bus in Chowchilla, California, drove twenty-six children and the bus driver a hundred miles, and forced them to climb down into an underground prison, a removal van that had been buried. The prisoners managed to escape, and the $5 million ransom was never paid. The three kidnappers proved to be rich young men, and one of them felt he had 'some reason for revenge' against another small town in Madera County (where Chowchilla is situated.) But how could kidnapping a busload of children from Chowchilla 'punish' the inhabitants of another town? The Roman emperor Theodosius once took revenge for the murder of a Roman garrison by inviting all the inhabitants of the Greek town where it had taken place to a public festival, then had them all slaughtered. That makes a kind of gruesome sense; but the kidnapping of a busload of schoolchildren seems virtually senseless, an act of insanity. But the kidnappers were not insane. What we are encountering here is what Sartre called 'magical' thinking, meaning completely illogical thinking that cannot possibly accomplish its object – like an ostrich burying its head in the sand. And magical thinking is a vital clue to the psychology of crime.

An old joke tells of an Arab in the Sahara asking another Arab why he is carrying an umbrella. 'I bought it in England. It has magical properties. If you want it to rain, you leave it at home.' Magical thinking can also be seen in Patrick Byrne, the man who killed and mutilated a girl at the Birmingham YWCA in 1959: 'I did it to get my revenge on women for causing me sexual tension.' The means has no logical connection with the end. But magical thinking is not confined to stupid people and criminals. The Nobel Prize winner Elias Canetti was reported in the newspapers in August 1982 as having decided not to publish his latest book – a volume of memoirs – in England because the English had proved themselves unappreciative of his earlier books. But if this is true, who is to blame, and how can the revenge accomplish any possible object except to diminish his royalties? This is again a case of magical thinking, like a man who has stubbed his toe against the bed and swears at his wife.

The working of the magical process can be seen clearly in many 'reactive' crimes. Charles Manson had built up a furious resentment against the bourgeoisie, the 'pigs', the people who were denying him the success he deserved. The 'motive' behind the murders committed by the Manson family was the belief that they would cause a race war between blacks and whites. We can see that Manson's whole neo-fascist mythology was pure magical thinking. He was lashing out, expressing a bottled-up resentment *which had no proper object*. The same was true of the Zebra murders committed by five members of a black militant organization in San Francisco in 1973–4. The twenty-three victims were chosen at random and included men, women and children. The Death Angels, of which the five men were members, had a rule that a man could not become a full member until he had killed either four white children, five women or nine men. It could be argued that this kind of thinking does not qualify as magical because the Death Angels regarded themselves as engaged in a race war. But a normal war has an object, and armies fight to achieve it. Hit and run killings cannot achieve any object. To understand the workings of the magical process in such crimes, we need to know what 'reactive man' is reacting *against*. The answer seems obvious: authority. But what is not so obvious is that the authority may be entirely illusory. There was no possible connection between Manson and his victims; it would have been as logical to express his resentment by throwing stones at cats.

A textbook on hypnosis describes a case in which a medical student hypnotized a female patient in a mental home and told her that she had to kiss the head physician. It proved to be completely impossible to cancel the order, even by counter-hypnosis; the head physician had to submit to being embraced before the patient would relax. The 'order' had reached a level of her subconscious mind in which it became a kind of instinct. And it should be clear that the process by which 'reactive man' comes to resent authority is also akin to hypnosis.

When we try to pinpoint the exact nature of the thought process that leads to violence and crime, we see that it consists in looking around for somewhere *to lay the blame*. This is what Karl Marx and Charles Manson have in common: a belief that other people are to blame for the troubles of humanity – and, incidentally, for their own misfortunes. They have totally blinded themselves to the idea that they themselves might be partly to blame. So the solution to their problems lies out there, in the external world, and in a group of people labelled capitalists or bourgeoisie or 'pigs'.

Why has magical thinking burst its bounds and expanded into crime in the second half of this century? To understand this we need to grasp that the nature of crime tends to change in a changing society. Societies, like individuals, evolve through a hierarchy of values or needs. It was the late Abraham Maslow, an American psychologist, who observed that animal – and human – behaviour is governed by a 'hierarchy of needs'. The basic need is for food and drink, and until this is satisfied, nothing else much seems to matter. When a man has achieved a regular food supply, he begins to think about security, a roof over his head. A tramp who had never owned a home might well feel that if only he could live in a country cottage, he would be perfectly happy. But in fact, the next 'level' of need would soon emerge: the need for love, for sex, for a close human relationship. And when human beings have satisfied this level, they become concerned with self esteem, with being liked and respected by the community – being recognized. According to Maslow, if all these levels of need are satisfied, a man is likely to develop a need for creative activity – for what Maslow calls 'self-actualization', some form of expression of his creative urges.

A little over two centuries ago, most crime concerned that basic level of need: food and drink. People stole or murdered to stay alive. Sex crime was almost unknown. By the mid nineteenth century, society in Europe and America had evolved to a point where very large numbers of people could feel secure about their food supply and a roof over their heads, and sex crime began to make its appearance as a distinctive criminal phenomenon. By the mid twentieth century, the most basic type of crime – crime merely to stay alive – had become a rarity, since most civilized countries were welfare states and a man was no longer likely to starve; but sex crime had become commonplace.

The emergence of motiveless crime in the 1950s was actually the emergence of the 'self-esteem' level of Maslow's hierarchy. Robert Smith killed because he wanted to 'become known'. We suddenly encounter the phenomenon of the high IQ criminal. Charles Manson was inspired by a science fiction novel about a superman, *Stranger in a Strange Land* by Robert Heinlein; Ian Brady, the Moors murderer, preached the ideas of de Sade. In the mid nineteenth century, the typical murderer was a drunken illiterate; a hundred years later the typical murderer regards himself as a thinking man. So he is; the problem being that his thinking tends to be magical. He uses ideas as a vehicle for emotions; they help him select someone on whom he can lay the blame. The scapegoat may be a group or an individual. Ian Brady decided that humanity itself was contemptible, and made this his rationale for murder. The Manson family and the Death Angels selected a racial group. Another type of killer – the loner – may select some celebrity – the Pope, the President, a famous pop singer. He feels that in killing them, he is correcting the balance between them and his own lack of celebrity. All three types are using magical thinking as an instrument to bolster self-esteem.

Before we leap to the conclusion that our modern world is rushing into decadence and decay, it may be as well to bear in mind that this kind of ruthlessness has characterized the human race for at least the last three thousand years. The Assyrians, who dominated the Middle East from 1200–700 BC, boasted on their monuments of slaughtering whole nations and impaling women and children. Genghis Khan and Tamerlane did even worse things; so did the Spanish Catholics who tried to convert the Dutch Protestants with fire and sword. Man is certainly no worse now than he has ever been. In fact, there is more altruism, more generosity, more social concern, than at any previous time in history. Our problem is that modern society is placing certain individuals under peculiar stresses. It can hardly be accidental, for example, that so many of the nastiest crimes mentioned in this introduction have taken place in California, and that of all the states of America, California has the largest and steadiest influx of population. An area that is subject to an unending population explosion is bound to become what John B. Calhoun calls 'a behavioural sink'.

That this 'crime reaction' is taking place at all suggests that nature is engaged in solving the problem in her own ruthless and wasteful manner. Overcrowded lemmings commit suicide; overcrowded deer die of stress. Man's reaction to stress is violence. The obvious way to reduce the violence would be to reduce the stress; but in our highly complex civilization this seems impossible. Instead we are forced to consider piecemeal solutions, to most of which there are objections. A ban on privately owned firearms would certainly have a dramatic effect on America's crime figures; but as the crime rate rises, most Americans feel an increased need to keep a gun to defend themselves; so the chance of a ban continues to recede. Television violence can lead to crime – as in the case of Norman Smith, who shot a woman after watching a programme called *The Sniper*; but television producers argue that it is their job to reflect a violent society, not to tell fairy stories about it; here again is a vicious circle. Pornography presents the same kind of moral dilemma; in certain cases, like that of Ted Bundy, we know that sex crime has been inspired by pornography. But since the end of the Victorian era, society has been moving in the direction of sexual frankness, and it is difficult to believe that repression and censorship can be long-term answers.

9

It is equally difficult to decide how far crime can be reduced by increasing severity in the laws. There is a tendency on the part of the public to feel that sentences are too light. In 1981 a German rapist who killed nine girls with a lump hammer told the court frankly that he would do it again even if he was not released for twenty years; but under West German law, 'life' imprisonment means seven years. In America savage sentences in the 1970s led to a remarkable decrease in the crime rate, and a scheme for sentencing habitual offenders to long prison terms – a 'three-time' rapist or burglar can be sentenced to life – has proved equally effective. Judges point out that most habitual offenders commit dozens – sometimes hundreds – of crimes every year, so that keeping them permanently in jail is bound to benefit the community. Yet the notion of locking a man away for life is bound to raise the same kind of moral misgivings as the arguments for the return of the death penalty. In the long run, no community can benefit from the sacrifice of justice to expediency, because injustice has the effect of producing more resentment, and therefore more crime.

One of the few practical solutions to which none of these objections apply is the idea of involving the whole community in crime prevention. In certain American cities, patrols of citizen vigilantes have cut the burglary rate dramatically. So have neighbourhood 'watch' schemes in which everyone is asked to pay more attention to what goes on in the street, and to report anything suspicious to the police. The success of these schemes underlines a vital point: that the crime problem is partly the fault of the attitude of respectable citizens. In the mid 1950s a *Life* photographer took a series of photographs of a man lying bleeding on a New York pavement, and commuters carefully walking around him, taking care not to look down. In 1964 the murder of Kitty Genovese was witnessed by thirty-seven people, none of whom attempted to interfere or to apprehend the killer; all explained that 'they didn't want to get involved'. It could be argued that every one of these shared the murderer's guilt. 'Citizen watch' schemes not only prevent crime; they destroy the negative attitude that makes crime possible.

Yet all these pragmatic solutions leave us with a feeling that we are somehow missing the central point. Reading about Corll and Manson and Brady leads to a recognition that they are not laboratory rats, driven to violent behaviour purely by social pressures. They are free individuals who have *decided* to kill by following a certain thought-process. It is because the thought-process is magical –

because it contains a fallacy – that they end as killers. Magical thinking, as we have seen, is the attempt to avoid the effort of self-control at all costs, based on the spoilt child's assumption that he 'deserves' freedom, and that all his desires ought to be satisfied more or less immediately. All of which suggests that the increase in motiveless crime since 1960 reflects an increase in magical thinking. Long-term solutions demand a deeper understanding of the nature of magical thinking.

The roots of the present lie in the past. The historian Lewis Mumford remarked: 'Unhappily for mankind, the release of nuclear energy had been preceded by an even more devastating kind of liberation: a release from moral inhibitions and salutary taboos it had taken civilized man four or five thousand years to build up.' For practical purposes, we could say that the origin of this devastating liberation could be traced back to 1762, the year Rousseau's *Social Contract* appeared, with its famous opening sentence: 'Man is born free but he is everywhere in chains.' And over the next century, as the dogmas of Christianity gradually loosened their hold, moral philosophy was dominated by this idea that man is born free – with its corollary that he is *not* free because various wicked authorities have entered into a conspiracy to deprive him of his freedom. Proudhon gave the revolutionary bandwagon another push with his dictum, 'Property is theft'. By the end of the century, Rousseau's philosophy of freedom had virtually replaced the religious philosophy of earlier centuries.

There can be no doubt that this religious philosophy deserved to take a beating. It was based on dogma and authority, and was horribly repressive. But it was also based on a realistic vision of human nature. It saw man as a bundle of miseries and ailments, a battleground of physical and emotional problems, who is in trouble from the moment he is born. It recognized that man's chief problem is desire – or, as the Church would say, temptation – and that this applies to kings as much as to beggars. No one stands any chance of happiness unless he can achieve some degree of self-knowledge and self-discipline.

Rousseau's assertion that man is born free is quite simply untrue. The sad truth is that very few people ever feel free – whether they happen to be free in the political sense or not. We all know people who ought to feel free, because they have money and leisure, and yet who are miserable and neurotic. We all know people who ought to be miserable – because they are overworked and poor – yet who

11

remain remarkably cheerful. The very nature of freedom seems paradoxical.

Rousseau ignored this paradox because he himself was weak and neurotic, and urgently wanted to find somewhere to lay the blame. His hatred of authority made him simplistic; he wanted to make people believe that freedom was simply a matter of overthrowing authority and striking off their chains. His philosophy – which now rules half the globe – is fundamentally false in a way that no religious philosophy is fundamentally false. A half-truth can be more poisonous than a downright lie. Rousseau's assertion that freedom is everybody's birthright appeals because none of us feels free, and we are all delighted to have someone to blame. But it is rather like asserting that every lion's birthright is to have an antelope for breakfast. The truth is that a lion can only have an antelope for breakfast if there are antelopes available, and if it will go to the trouble of catching it. There are no rights involved.

This is not to assert that political freedom is unimportant. But it can only be achieved through effort and realistic thinking, not by misdirected resentment. Unfortunately, Rousseau's anti-authoritarianism is now in the very air we breathe. We have come to take it for granted that all right-thinking young people are anti-conservative, and hold strong views about social justice. We expect them to regard protest with favour and authority with disfavour. We even take it for granted that most people hate the police. We have come to accept the notion that 'man is born free' as an unquestionable dogma, just as our ancestors accepted the idea of heaven and hell.

What this means, in effect, is that there is an enormous reservoir of vague resentment in our society, fed by this notion that we ought to be free, and that if we don't feel free, then somebody must be to blame. Of course, where everyday life is concerned, we are all forced to be pragmatists: to earn a living, to struggle for the things we want. But when the going gets too difficult, it is easy to slip into a mood of self-pity; and then we look around for scapegoats, and lay the blame on politicians, or the police, or the establishment.

For the most part, this kind of magical thinking does no harm. We let off steam – by voting against the government, signing a petition, grumbling to a neighbour in the pub – and immediately feel much better. But even reasonable people sometimes feel impelled to go further than that. The philosopher William James was once sitting on a tram when he became irritated by the racket being made by a child; he asked the mother if she realized her child was being a nuisance to the other passengers. A male passenger said: 'How dare you address a lady in that ungentlemanly fashion?' And James lost his temper and threatened to slap his face if he repeated the remark. The man repeated it, and James felt obliged to carry out his threat. All the other passengers jumped to their feet, and offered to testify against James if the man should take him to court. When the commotion died down, James sat there gloomily, aware of being the object of general dislike. He turned to a lady who looked as if she might be sympathetic, and said: 'I hope you understand, madam . . .', but she interrupted him furiously: 'Don't you dare speak to me, you brute!'

If a philosopher can place himself in this position where violence seems the only reaction to annoyance, it is easy to understand how men like Gary Gilmore or Paul Knowles decide that society deserves a slap in the face, and lash out indiscriminately; how a student like Robert Smith, oppressed by a feeling that nobody pays any attention to him, decides to 'make himself known' with an act of pointless violence; how Melvin Rees, Dean Corll, Ted Bundy, decide that they may as well snatch some 'compensation' from life by way of sadistic rape. They have grown up in a society that accepts Rousseau's magical thinking as realistic social philosophy.

It would be pointless to blame Rousseau – or Proudhon or Marx – for this state of affairs, a surrender to the kind of magical thinking we condemn in them. If Rousseau had not existed, someone else would have written *The Social Contract*; it was an inevitable reaction against centuries of Christian dogma. Our purpose here is only to try to grasp how Rousseau's muddled anti-authoritarianism created a reservoir of resentment, and led in turn to the climate of violence that produced so many of the killers in this volume. In the last quarter of the twentieth century, Rousseau's chickens are coming home to roost. Crime in general is an attempt to take short cuts, to take the easy way out, to slide out of responsibilities. It could be defined as the attempt to get something for nothing. In their classic study of American criminals, *The Criminal Personality*, Samuel Yochelson and Stanton Samenow observe that habitual criminals are not, for the most part, poor unfortunates who have been driven to crime by social injustice or hardship; they are fundamentally *responsibility dodgers*, men too unintelligent – or too adept at self-deception – to recognize that in the long run, no one can get something for nothing.

The nature of the problem, then, is clear enough. But what is the solution? One interesting attempt at an answer was made by an American lawyer, Dan MacDougald, who worked with hard-core psychopaths at the Georgia State penitentiary. MacDougald had also reached the conclusion that the criminal is afflicted with magical thinking – a kind of self-chosen blindness and deafness. He stumbled on this when he read of an experiment performed at Harvard, in which a cat's aural nerve was connected to an oscilloscope, so that when a bell was rung in the cat's ear, the needle of the oscilloscope moved. But when a cage with a mouse was placed in front of the cat, the oscilloscope failed to respond to the sound of the bell. The cat was somehow cutting out the vibration at the eardrum itself. It was *refusing to hear*. MacDougald felt that criminals allow resentment to drive them into the same state; they become so fixed in an attitude of rejection and rebellion that they refuse to notice anything good about the world. Using various psychological and religious techniques – but above all, appealing to the criminal's intelligence – MacDougald was able to make his hard-core psychopaths *see* that they were, in effect, wearing earplugs and dark glasses. As soon as they became aware that their mental attitude did most harm to themselves, they stopped behaving in a self-defeating manner, and ceased to be criminals.

MacDougald had discovered one of the most basic and important laws of the human mind. I once formulated this law in the form of a parable. Sherlock Holmes and Dr Watson are sitting on either side of the fire in Baker Street on a foggy November morning. Watson has read all the newspapers, and is yawning with boredom. Lazily – scarcely able to muster the energy to speak – he remarks: 'I see Lord Mancroft is dead, Holmes. Did you ever meet him?' and Holmes replies: 'Yes, I did. As a matter of fact, Watson, that was the beginning of one of the most bizarre cases of my whole career. Would you like to hear about it?' And instantly, Watson is wide awake. What has *caused* it? At first, the answer seems to be Holmes himself. But that is not so. It is true that Watson is responding to Holmes's words; but *he* is summoning the attitude of eager expectancy. It is Watson who pushes a kind of internal button that galvanizes his senses. In theory, he could have done it without Holmes's remark.

If we think about what happened, we can begin to see the mechanism involved. The control-button of the mind is labelled 'expectations'. When I have reason to expect fascinating experiences, I give a little internal sigh of contentment, relax into an attitude of expectancy, and allow my mind to open into a receptive state. When I have decided in advance that something is going to be boring, or that I have exhausted the interest of whatever I am contemplating, I allow my mind to close, like clenching a fist. And once it is in this closed state, it takes a considerable surprise or shock to make it open up. MacDougald's psychopaths had fallen into this closed state; so had the cat in the experiment. At the beginning of *A Christmas Carol* Dickens shows us Scrooge in the same state. The ghost of Marley provides the shock, and after that, the ghosts of Christmas gradually persuade Scrooge to unclench that mental fist and begin to appreciate life. The problem with criminals is that they have taken up certain negative attitudes about the world, so they see no reason to unclench the mental fist. Animals and children are also capable of boredom; but at least their minds remain open, so they instantly become alert and expectant at the least sign of something interesting.

What is involved here is a mental act that could be called 'reprogramming the subconscious'. When we contemplate the day ahead with a feeling of boredom, the subconscious mind reacts negatively and fails to provide us with vital energy. When we *tell ourselves* that life is going to be fascinating, the subconscious floods us with vital energy, and life *becomes* fascinating. Our attitudes, our expectations, reprogramme the subconscious.

All this makes us aware that the problem we are discussing is not simply the problem of criminality; it is the problem of human evolution. Criminality springs out of a cramping of awareness, a narrowing of our faculties that could be compared to tunnel-vision. But this applies to all of us at the present stage of human evolution.

We have to recognize that, in the evolutionary sense, man is little more than a baby. A baby can reach out towards some bright object dangled into its pram, but it cannot coordinate its muscles to grasp it. Man can reach out towards the mental states that he knows to be possible, but he has not yet learned to grasp them. Yet, paradoxically enough, man's problem is that he has become too good at grasping. All animals survive by reaching out for what they want; man has outstripped all the others because he does it better than they do. Most animals can stay focussed on something they want for a fairly long time – a cat will stare at a mouse hole for hours – but man can stay focussed on something he wants for days, weeks, months. He can turn himself into an obsessive, and that is the secret of his success. It is also the secret of his failure. We can see the disadvantages of obsessiveness in misers and criminals: their values have become warped and self-destructive.

Man's most urgent need at this stage of his evolution is to control his obsessiveness. This can only be done if he turns his attention from objects of desire to the mental states they induce. Why does Casanova spend his life pursuing woman after woman? The answer seems obvious: because he enjoys sex. But *what* is it he enjoys about sex? It is that his pursuit of a woman induces that instant glow of satisfaction that comes from a sense of purpose. He has *funnelled* his normally scattered attention, and it is this act of funnelling that induces the satisfaction.

The issue here might be called 'the fallacy of misplaced satisfaction'. In assuming that satisfaction lies in the girl herself, Casanova is failing to grasp the meaning of the sexual experience. He keeps returning to the experience, like a dog going back again and again to a rabbit hole where it has seen a rabbit, but gets no closer to catching the rabbit. This is why each seduction leaves Casanova feeling oddly bored and empty, and he has to start all over again. There is the same self-defeating element about crime. The 'fallacy of misplaced satisfaction' guarantees a failure to achieve its object.

Criminals themselves are aware of this paradox. It is interesting to note, for example, how often they are caught because they seem to have an unconscious desire to be caught. This also explains why MacDougald found it possible to rehabilitate hard-core psychopaths; he simply made them aware that they were pursuing their goals in a way that guaranteed failure.

For more than two thousand years, religious teachers have been attempting to convince mankind that the pursuit of objects is a mistake, and that man should concentrate his efforts upon his own mental states. The Buddha said: 'As the fletcher straightens his arrow, so the wise man straightens his mind.' But the teachings of the great religious thinkers soon hardened into dogmas; that is, man turned religion itself into an object to be pursued instead of recognizing that it is a state of mind. Yet nowadays, for the first time in history, vast numbers of people who are not particularly religious have become concerned with the pursuit of states of mind. Every form of mind control, from transcendental meditation to the martial arts, has an immense following. It seems reasonable to hope that the baby is at last learning to reach out and grasp.

In the meantime, what measures can be taken to try to alleviate the crime problem? In America, an organization called the Thomas

Jefferson Research Foundation in California has been studying the question for several years. The motto of the Foundation is 'The price of freedom is responsibility' and its basic conclusion is that the problem is largely educational. In the nineteenth century, the majority of Americans were brought up under the Protestant ethic, and trained to recognize the value of hard work and responsibility. In modern America this is no longer true, and the result is a generation that associates the word 'responsibility' with authority, and feels that it is something to be evaded. The Foundation believes that the only real solution is for schools and universities once again to teach the religious ethic and the value of responsibility.

There is obviously a great deal of truth in this; but it is easier said than done. The pioneer generation taught responsibility with a stick rather than a carrot; children were made to attend Sunday school, join in church activities, and hoe the cabbages. It seems difficult to imagine an approach like this working today, even if school boards could be persuaded that it is desirable.

Yet the Foundation is clearly correct in its belief that this is a battle of ideas. It was Rousseau who was largely responsible for the problem by giving currency to the idea that freedom can exist without responsibility and discipline. In 1951 Albert Camus aroused the fury of the left with his book *L'Homme Revolté (The Rebel)*, a powerful demonstration that all philosophies of rebellion, from de Sade to Karl Marx and Lenin, have led to tyranny and the destruction of freedom. Since Camus's death, the point has been reinforced: the philosophy of freedom has become the justification for international terrorism. We can see its consequences when we read of Italian terrorists forcing their way into a lecture hall and shooting the professor in the legs, alleging that he is guilty of teaching his students to adapt to a fundamentally immoral society, or when Charles Manson declares in court that his followers committed the murders out of 'love of their brothers'. This is the philosophy of freedom gone mad. As we watch the rising tide of violence, always justified by talk of freedom, it becomes clear that Rousseau was wrong, and Camus was right. And if Rousseau's ideas could gain currency, because at the time there was an urgent need for change, then so can Camus's. Our educational institutions may or may not be capable of teaching 'ethical responsibility'; but they are certainly capable of discrediting the muddled philosophy of freedom that is undermining our society. Changing these attitudes is the key to changing our society.

A

ABBOTT, Jack Henry
Ex-convict and 'killer genius' who murdered again after he had been paroled through the intervention of Norman Mailer.

While writing his book about Gary Gilmore (see page 123), *The Executioner's Song*, Norman Mailer received a letter from a 35-year-old convict named Jack Henry Abbott. Abbott had been sent to jail for the first time when he was twelve (in 1956) and from then on had spent only five and a half months in thirty-three years out of jail – and that included a brief jailbreak during which he committed a bank robbery. In 1966, Abbott had stabbed another prisoner to death and was sentenced to fourteen years. During the trial he threw a pitcher of water at the judge and claimed insanity. The psychiatrist had found him fit to plead. In a maximum security jail, Abbott had read the works of philosophers and social thinkers, and had become a Marxist. Mailer was impressed by the intensity and the natural fluency of his letters, and persuaded Random House to publish a selection of them. Under the title *In the Belly of the Beast*, the book became an immediate best-seller.

Through the intervention of Mailer, who described Abbott to the prison authorities as 'a powerful and important American writer', Abbott was released on parole. He worked for a while as a researcher for Mailer, but apparently found himself totally unequipped to deal with the life of a literary celebrity. His agent reported that Abbott telephoned him to say he had run out of toothpaste and had no idea where to go to for more.

On 18 July 1981, in the early hours of the morning, Abbott went to the Bini Bon all-night diner on 2nd Avenue, New York, with two female companions. He asked the waiter, 22-year-old Richard Adan, an actor and playwright, if he could use the men's lavatory. Adan explained that it was not available for customers. Abbott then asked him to step outside to settle the argument, pulled a knife and stabbed Adan in the heart. He was dead before the ambulance arrived. Abbott told one of the girls, Susan Roxas, a college student, 'Let's get out of here. I just killed a man.' After a two-month hunt, during which time Abbott's book was receiving highly favourable reviews, he was found working as a casual labourer in a Louisiana oil field, and taken back to New York.

Abbott's book is a curious document, full of what one critic called 'the outlaw mystique'. It seems to be based upon the assumption that revolt and physical violence are somehow admirable. 'There is something else ... it is the mantle of pride, integrity, honour. It is the high esteem we naturally have for violence, force. It is what makes us effective, men whose judgment impinges on others, on the world. Dangerous killers who act alone and without emotion, who act with calculation and principles with acts of murder ... that usually evade prosecution by the law: this is the state-raised convict's conception of manhood in the highest sense.' The underlying assumption seems to be that if a man feels a sufficiently violent emotion, he is perfectly justified in letting go. This is what Abbott did with Richard Adan.

The case is reminiscent of the curious affair of Edgar Herbert Smith, accused in 1957 of the murder of fifteen-year-old Victoria Zielinski in New Jersey. The evidence of Smith's blood-covered jeans led to his conviction, although he insisted that he had loaned them to a friend. During fourteen years on Death Row in the Trenton prison, he wrote to author William F. Buckley, who after receiving almost three thousand pages from Smith, became convinced of his innocence and began a campaign to free him. Smith also wrote two books, one of which, *Brief Against Death*, became a best-seller. Smith was released in 1971, but five years later stabbed a woman in a car while attempting to steal her pay cheque. At his trial on the attempted robbery charge, Smith admitted that he had murdered the Zielinski girl with a baseball bat when she refused to have sex with him.

At Abbott's new trial in New York in January 1982, a man in court shouted angrily at Mailer, 'You should hang your head in shame for this. That man should never have been set free.' Mailer commented later, 'What I am going through is nothing to what the family of this poor boy is suffering and to what Abbott is going through. It is such a waste all round.'

APPEL, Hans
German who avenged his wife's incest by killing her brother.

On 7 January 1974 a Mercedes swerved on to the pavement in Frankfurt, West Germany, and the driver rolled out into the street. As he tried to stand up, his passenger shot him twice at short range, then climbed out of the car and walked away up the street.

The dead man was identified as Dieter Poeschke, a 21-year-old garage mechanic. The car belonged to him. The police discovered that he lived with his newly married wife Silvia, his brother Juergen and his sister Renate, in a two-room apartment in Sachsenhausen. All three were shocked to hear of Dieter's murder, but claimed to have no idea of who could have been responsible. A witness had described the killer as tall, husky and clean-shaven.

When the police spoke to Mrs Anna Poeschke, Dieter's mother, they learned that there was one man who had a motive for murder. This was Renate's husband, Hans Appel, the owner of a construction company. When Hans and Renate had married, both had a child from a previous marriage. Subsequently, Renate bore Hans a daughter. Juergen, who was imprisoned in East Germany, had been given amnesty in 1973 to come to West Germany, where he moved in with Hans and Renate. Suddenly, Renate and Juergen had walked out on Hans, and moved in with brother Dieter. Hans Appel's description corresponded to that of the killer.

Appel admitted to the murder of his brother-in-law. He explained that, not long after Juergen had moved into his apartment, he had been tucking one of the children in bed when she offered to tell him a secret. Mummy and Uncle Juergen had spent the afternoon naked in bed, said the child. Appel was shattered by this information. He confronted the brother and sister, who refused to deny it. And when Appel ordered Juergen to leave, Renate had gone with him. Appel was still in love with his wife. He tried hard to persuade her to come back, offering her jewellery and a fur coat, but she refused.

Dieter Poeschke and Hans Appel remained friendly. One afternoon, when Appel's car was being serviced, Dieter offered him a lift from Wiesbaden. Appel confided his suspicions about Juergen and Renate to his brother-in-law, expecting sympathy. Did he, Appel asked, believe that Juergen and Renate could have been engaged in incest? Dieter looked at him in astonishment and said, 'Of course. Juergen and I both fuck Renate all the time.'

It was too much for Appel, who said that something snapped

inside him. He pulled out the pistol he had been carrying ever since Renate left him, and killed Dieter.

In July 1974 Appel was sentenced to twenty-one months' imprisonment, but immediately released on bail – his sentence was set aside on appeal. His wife declined to return to him, and continued to live with her brother Juergen.

D'ARCY, Patrick
Travel-agent whose attempt at a perfect murder was defeated by persistent police work.

On 24 May 1967 a farmer walking along Doolin Strand, in County Clare, on the west coast of Ireland, saw a body wedged between rocks at the foot of the cliffs of Moher. It proved to be the corpse of a young woman, wearing only a pair of black briefs. There were severe head injuries, her ribs were fractured, and a pathologist was able to say that she had been in the water for about three days. A label in the briefs showed they were manufactured in America. But no other clue to the woman's identity was forthcoming.

Fingerprints sent to the FBI eventually revealed that the girl was Maria Virginia Domenech, born in Puerto Rico on 3 February 1939. She had been reported missing by relatives; she had lived with her mother in Washington Heights, New York. She had set out on a tour of Europe on 16 May 1967.

The girl's uncle, the Assistant Attorney General at the Department of Justice in San Juan, Puerto Rico, told the Irish police that they were also looking into the disappearance of Maria's mother, Virginia Domenech. She had not been seen since the end of May – a week after her daughter's body had been found.

Maria had been a beauty queen. At twenty-eight, she was a social worker, and she had left New York to forget a painful love affair with a travel-agent. Maria had discovered too late that he was married. The man had tried to persuade her to come back to him, and asked Maria's mother to help him. Before long, Maria's mother – who at fifty-one was still attractive – had apparently started an affair with the man. At this point, Maria had withdrawn $6,000 from the bank and flown off to Europe. She had sent three postcards from Paris to friends in America, including one to her mother promising a long letter. But the letter was never found in the empty apartment in New York. And Maria's mother had vanished on 30 May. She too had been a social worker – at a children's home in the

Bronx – and when she failed to report for work, her supervisor had notified the Missing Persons Bureau.

What had happened to Maria since she landed at Orly Airport on 17 May? She had stayed in a Paris hotel. And the French police discovered that an American man had arrived at the hotel on 21 May, and Maria had spent the evening with him. She had told the desk clerk that she intended to spend some time in the hotel, yet the next morning she checked out, and drove to Orly Airport with her American friend. She flew on to London with him and cashed all her traveller's cheques there. She had booked a room overnight at the Grosvenor House Hotel in the name of Miss M. Young – the man had been using the name 'A. Young' – but changed her mind, and flew on to Dublin with her companion. There they hired a car, and drove through the night to the west coast. They arrived at the cliffs of Moher at about four in the morning – a local resident saw car headlights on the cliff top – and presumably it was then that her companion struck her with some blunt instrument and battered her to death. He stripped off her blood-stained clothes, but for some reason left her briefs on. It was to be his one mistake. Then he threw her body over the cliff, bundled up her clothes and threw them over too. He decided not to take her jewellery – that could be traced back to him too easily – and so left it concealed on the cliff top, where it was found later. The clothes were later found scattered over inaccessible rocks not far from where the body was found – but by that time Maria Domenech had been buried in the local cemetery in an unmarked grave.

All this the police were able to establish by careful detective work in Paris, London and Dublin. In the hotel at Shannon airport, they discovered that 'A. Young' had checked in at eight in the morning, and checked out again four hours later. Yet his name was not on any airline list for that day. In fact, further investigation showed that he had driven the car back to the hire firm in Dublin, and handed it over at six on the evening after renting it. He flew out of Dublin for Paris that same evening, and arrived back in New York the following Friday – just before the disappearance of Maria's mother.

All the evidence suggested that 'A. Young' was the travel-agent with whom Maria had had the unhappy affair. New York police were soon able to establish that his real name was Patrick J. D'Arcy. He was, in fact, a freelance travel-agent, and his business had recently been doing badly. He was married and had a son and a daughter.

The New York police had, in fact, already interviewed D'Arcy after Maria had been reported missing by her father (who had not received the usual letter or phone call from her on Father's Day). D'Arcy was simply one of several male friends they interviewed, and he had told them that he had not been out of the country for a long time. Now the police went back to D'Arcy, and demanded to see his passport. It revealed that he had been out of the country when Maria Domenech disappeared. His handwriting was pronounced identical with that of 'A. Young' in the hotel registers. But D'Arcy was always travelling around the world for his business, and insisted that he knew nothing about Maria Domenech's disappearance. The Irish applied for extradition. And Patrick D'Arcy suddenly vanished from New York. He realized that his elaborate murder plot had gone wrong.

Police traced him to Miami, to which he had made a number of business trips recently. At the McAllister Hotel, they discovered that he had signed in under the name John J. Quinn. He had not been seen for several days. They opened his room with a pass key, and staggered back as they met a sickening smell of death. D'Arcy had taken a lethal overdose of barbiturates, washed down with whisky. A note addressed to a New York priest was found in the room. The priest later commented that he had been told that D'Arcy 'was engaged in something much bigger than what had happened to that poor girl'. Miami is a centre for drug smuggling, and it is just possible that this could explain D'Arcy's frequent business trips there. A passport in the name of A. Young was also found.

Although certain mysteries remain, the outline of the case seems clear enough. D'Arcy's business was doing badly; he hoped to get money, either from Maria – possibly by bigamy – or her mother. When Maria flew to Paris, D'Arcy contacted her, probably by telephone, and begged her to see him that weekend. He flew to Paris, and he and Maria had some kind of reconciliation. D'Arcy's parents were Irish immigrants who had lived near Galway, not far from the cliffs of Moher. D'Arcy somehow persuaded Maria to change her plans and go with him to Ireland – she told a friend about the intended visit on a postcard. In London he persuaded her to cash the remainder of her traveller's cheques – around $5,000. Then he persuaded her to forget the booking she had made at the Grosvenor House Hotel, and to go on with him to Ireland. Less than thirty-six hours after leaving Paris, he was back again, convinced that no one would ever trace his complicated movements since he left. There was still one problem: Maria might have told her mother about her plan to go with him to Ireland, mentioning him by name. (No doubt he had managed to catch a glimpse of the postcard to the friend, and made sure that she did not mention a companion.) Back in New York, he went to Virginia Domenech's apartment, lured her away somewhere, and killed her (her body was never recovered). Then he made sure that there was nothing left in the apartment that might connect him to the murder – the letter Maria wrote to her mother, for example.

It would have been the perfect murder if he had not left Maria wearing her briefs, and so established the connection with America. As a resident of Puerto Rico, Maria's prints were on file in Washington; moreover, as a city employee, they were on file in New York. If the body had been stripped naked, the identity of the corpse on the rocks would never had been established, and D'Arcy would have been safe.

There are still unanswered questions. How did he explain to Maria that he was travelling under an alias, and how did he persuade her to call herself 'Young'? Above all, why did he kill her? A mere $5,000 seems insufficient motive, although for a man in serious financial trouble it could have meant a breathing space. Was he disgusted at the failure of his 'bigger' plans for Maria, and decided he may as well take what he could get? These are questions to which only one man may know the answer: the priest to whom D'Arcy sent his last letter. And he firmly refused to discuss it.

el ARIDA, Shafik and KADDOURAH, Tallal Khaled
The Athens airport massacre.

On 15 August 1973 two Black September Arab terrorists attacked passengers in the transit lounge of Athens airport, killing three and wounding fifty-five. They opened fire as they awaited a routine search for concealed weapons. Like the Red Army terrorists the previous year at Lod (see Okamoto, Kozo) who killed and wounded the wrong group of people, the Black September terrorists failed to attack their intended targets. They were hoping to kill passengers on a TWA flight to Tel Aviv, but these had already safely embarked.

El Arida, a Palestinian, and Kaddourah, a Lebanese, were both in their early twenties. At their trial the court heard that they had flown to Athens from Benghazi earlier in the month to check security, then returned later via Beirut to carry out the plan. When sentenced to death, they said, 'We are sorry in our hearts that we injured Greeks, but orders are orders and we do not question them. Any plane of any country that flies to Israel . . . is a target for us.'

Three Pakistanis, members of an obscure terrorist group known as Muslim Guerrillas International, seized a Greek vessel at Karachi the following February, and threatened to blow it up with its crew of two unless the Black September terrorists were freed. The sentences were duly commuted on 30 April, and the pair were later granted a full pardon on the orders of the Greek president and released, despite protests from both Israel and the United States.

B

BAADER-MEINHOF GANG
Left-wing terrorists whose revolutionary activities included extortion and murder.

The so-called 'People's War' fought by the Baader-Meinhof gang had its roots in left-wing student protest. It began with scuffles and demonstrations, aimed vaguely at the affluent society basking in post-war Germany's economic miracle, and ended in murder galore. In the minds of the young terrorists who led the violence, such progression was inevitable. They preached the doctrine that the West Germany of the 1960s was tied to the coat-tails of United States imperialism, a situation which could be remedied only by armed revolt.

Berndt Andreas Baader was born in Munich on 6 May 1943, the only son of a middle-class historian who was killed on the Russian Front when his boy was two years old. The infant Andreas was raised by his mother and adoring female relatives and grew up to be a spoiled, handsome, work-shy young man with considerable sex-appeal and a passion for driving fast, flashy cars. When he was twenty he went to Berlin, where he lived with an artist named Ellinor Michel and her husband in a *ménage à trois*. She bore Baader a daughter, Suse, in 1965.

In 1967 he met blonde Gudrun Ensslin at a student demonstration in Berlin. She was three years his senior, the daughter of an Evangelical pastor – and a dedicated communist. When she was eighteen she spent a year in America under a school exchange scheme, but found the US political scene 'naive'. On her return to Germany in 1959 she studied philosophy at Tübingen University, where she met writer Bernward Vesper, an ardent leftist. They lived together and went to Berlin in 1965, where she enrolled at the Free University and herself became a committed leftist. She and Vesper had a child, who was born in 1967. When the boy was still only a few months old, his mother – increasingly the rebel – played a minor role in a pornographic film, *Das Abonnement*. She met Andreas Baader the same year and fell in love with him.

At that time Baader had no deep political convictions. They each left their children and went off to Frankfurt, where she introduced him to left-wing militants of the SDS (Sozialisticher Deutscher Studentbund) as the first stage of his political indoctrination. The 'People's War' began in earnest in April 1968, when Baader, Ensslin and two other militants planted incendiary bombs in two Frankfurt department stores 'to light a torch for Vietnam'. They were arrested and sentenced to three years imprisonment apiece for arson. On 13 June 1969, after serving only fourteen months all four were released to await the outcome of their appeal – and to some kind of fame, as heroes of the left. Only one of the quartet turned up in the appeal court to hear the verdict (it was dismissed): Baader, Ensslin and Thorwald Proll escaped to France. They lived there in style for some time on money brought in by Proll's sister Astrid, but later returned to Berlin. Baader was re-arrested there in 1970 and sent back to jail. It was his subsequent escape from the prison library on 14 May 1970 – engineered by Ulrike Meinhof and friends – which gave the terrorist group its name: but it was the 'Meinhof' half which was then by far the better known.

Ulrike Marie Meinhof was born in Lower Saxony on 7 October 1934. Her father, an art historian, died of cancer in 1940, her mother in 1948: thereafter she was raised by a caring foster-mother. Ulrike Meinhof proved to be an intelligent schoolgirl and a natural leader. She won a Study Foundation scholarship and went first to Marburg University, then on to Münster. In 1959, as a respected bluestocking and outspoken opponent of the atom bomb she was chosen to represent Münster University at an anti-bomb press conference in Bonn. There she met Klaus Rohl, Marxist editor of the student publication *konkret*, who invited her to write for him. They were married in 1961, and when her husband started work for the German Peace Union in preparation for the forthcoming West German elections, Ulrike took over as columnist and editor-in-chief of *konkret*.

In 1962 she gave birth to twins by Caesarean operation. She underwent a trepanning operation shortly afterwards for suspected (but wrongly diagnosed) brain tumour: her husband resumed the editorship of *konkret* and it was several months before she returned, as columnist. Her career prospered however and she established a reputation as an author, a TV and radio playwright, and chat-show personality. She divorced Rohl in 1968 on the ground of his misconduct, but continued her own career as a highly successful journalist. In that capacity she attended the arson trial in Frankfurt, and defended in writing the action of Baader, Ensslin and the others on moral grounds. A year later her apartment in Berlin became a rendezvous for Baader's militant associates while he and Ensslin were on the run. After Baader's recapture in 1970, her apartment became the headquarters where she joined forces with Red Army Faction terrorists to plot his escape. It was her first criminal act and was wholly politically motivated.

The founder of the Red Army Faction was Horst Mahler, an apostle of violence and one of the defence lawyers at Baader's trial. Although it was Meinhof, the glamorous columnist, who was credited with master-minding Baader's daring escape, the staff-work was Mahler's. As the police search spread for the gang, Mahler flew under a false passport to the Middle East, where he, Meinhof, Baader and Gudrun Ensslin all underwent special training at a PFLP (Popular Front for the Liberation of Palestine) terrorist camp in Jordan. The two groups, German and Arab, did not get on over-well together. Peter Homann, Ulrike Meinhof's former lover and fellow journalist who went with them to Jordan, told *Der Spiegel* later what the Palestinians thought of Baader. 'A coward, performing the whole revolt to cover up his cowardice: they wouldn't even take him on a patrol.'

The bank robberies began – under Mahler's leadership – as soon as the Red Army Faction re-formed in Berlin; three in one day on one occasion, and all carried out with clinical efficiency. Mahler was arrested when he walked into a police trap in October 1970, and was sentenced to fourteen years imprisonment. Baader then assumed the leadership, but under police pressure the gang scattered. Two banks in Kassel were robbed at gunpoint on 15 January 1971. The police maintained their pressure until at one stage the gang's strength was reduced to a handful of members. The gang then received reinforcements from an obscure but highly dangerous group calling itself the SPK, which included mental patients undergoing treatment at the Psychiatric Neurological clinic in Heidelberg. In the autumn the killing started in earnest.

On 22 October 1971 a Hamburg policeman named Schmid was shot and fatally wounded as he attempted to arrest a former SPK member, a woman terrorist who was wanted for questioning in connection with the attempted murder of two policemen on the Freiburg-Basle autobahn in south-west Germany. Holger Meins, a leading Baader-Meinhof terrorist, was with her at the time but managed to escape.

On 22 December 1971 Herbert Schoner, another policeman, was shot dead as the gang robbed the Bavarian Mortgage and Exchange bank in Kaiserslautern. Other raids followed and when they reckoned they had sufficient funds to wage the 'People's War', the gang turned its attention to political targets. They had a series of explosive devices made to order, including metal pipe-bombs fitted with a timer that allowed the bomb-layer a delay of up to one hour, and 'baby bombs' – half-spheres slung from shoulder straps and worn under a woman's dress, giving her the appearance of being pregnant.

On 11 May 1972 Baader, Ensslin, Meins and another leading terrorist named Jan-Carl Raspe planted a clutch of home-made pipe – bombs in the American Army's 5 Corps headquarters at Frankfurt, killing Lieutenant Colonel Paul Bloomquist and wounding thirteen others. Structural damage alone was put at more than $1 million. In a telephone call four days later to the German Press Agency offices in Munich an anonymous caller claimed responsibility in the name of the 'Petra Schelm' commando of the Red Army Faction, and said it was in retaliation for American bombing of North Vietnam. (Schelm had joined the gang in 1970; she was shot dead as she tried to crash through a police road-block near Hamburg on 15 July 1971.)

On 12 May 1972 two women terrorists, Irmgard Moller and Angela Luther, walked into police headquarters at Augsburg in Bavaria carrying suitcases packed with time-bombs. Five policemen were injured in the explosion. On the same day, a car bomb went off outside the CID offices in Munich, wrecking sixty vehicles.

On 15 May 1972 Frau Gerta Buddenberg, the wife of Judge Wolfgang Buddenberg, was seriously injured by a car bomb which exploded as she turned the ignition key of her Volkswagen, parked in Karlsruhe. Judge Buddenberg was the legal authority who signed search warrants for police hunting terrorists in the area. On 19 May 1972 two time-bombs were detonated in the right-wing Springer publishing house in Hamburg injuring seventeen people. The motive this time was thought to be personal as well as political, a grudge-bombing planned and led personally by Ulrike Meinhof.

Six days later the gang struck again at the US 'imperialists'. Two cars bearing stolen US number-plates and carrying time-bombs were driven into the army's European headquarters at Heidelberg. One vehicle was parked near the clubhouse, the other close to administrative offices housing a computer. The bombs exploded within seconds of each other, killing three Americans and wounding five more.

The tempo and range of the terrorist bombings evoked an instant response in a badly shaken West Germany. The Ministry of the Interior put up a reward for information leading to the arrest of those responsible. All public buildings in both federal and provincial capitals were placed under reinforced police guard. Senior ministers and public servants were given personal protection, at home as well as at work. NATO forces throughout Germany redoubled security precautions. And there was real alarm, too, among representatives of the legitimate (and non-militant) left. They feared that the so-called 'People's War' would end in a backlash of public opinion which would wreck their electoral chances in Germany for years to come.

Whatever the reason, the gang's betrayal was swift in coming. A caller whose identity is still secret rang police headquarters in Frankfurt shortly after the Heidelberg murders. The information given led the *Terrorismus* squad to the garage of an apartment-building in the northern suburbs of the city, where they discovered a bomb factory. Bomb disposal experts rendered each device harmless and filled it with sand, marksmen were moved into position and the whole area placed under round-the-clock surveillance.

Baader could hardly have made a more conspicuous arrival. Still indulging his passion for flashy cars he roared through deserted streets to reach the bomb factory early on 1 June 1972, at the wheel of a lilac Porsche. With him were Holger Meins and Jan-Carl Raspe. Raspe opened fire and tried to run for it but was quickly overpowered. Baader and Meins shut themselves in the garage, where they were bombarded by tear-gas grenades. The whole dramatic scene was shown live on German television, as an armoured car approached the garage under terrorist fire. Eventually Baader was shot in the thigh. Meins emerged, stripped to his underpants on police orders and with his hands high in the air, to surrender. Security men wearing bulletproof vests then entered the garage and seized the wounded Baader.

On 7 June Gudrun Ensslin was arrested in a Hamburg boutique. She left her leather coat on a chair while she tried on a pullover; the shop assistant who went to hang it up thought it heavy, found a gun in the pocket – and called the police. Another gun was discovered in her handbag. Ensslin was arrested and taken by helicopter to a top-security jail in Essen to await trial.

Ulrike Meinhof, last member of the ruling triumvirate still at large, was arrested in Hanover a week later. A schoolteacher with leftist sympathies (but non-militant views) took in two guests, sight unseen, at the request of a friend. When he discovered who they were – Meinhof and fellow terrorist Gerhard Muller – the teacher rang the police. Muller (later to turn key witness for the prosecution) was overpowered on the evening of 15 June 1972 as he left the flat to make a phone call. Inside, the police seized Meinhof. She weighed less than seven stone and was unrecognizable from the confident, well-proportioned TV personality who had gone to war for the Red Army Faction two years earlier. Police also found a sub-machine-gun, pistols, grenades and a home-made bomb.

When she was arrested Meinhof had a coded letter on her, written by Ensslin and smuggled out of jail. Among other things it said, 'Mac is on holiday, four weeks, to be spent there.' On 25 June police in Stuttgart raided an apartment rented by a Briton, Iain MacLeod. Shots were fired through the door as MacLeod slammed it shut and he was killed. His true role in the overall drama remains unclear. The most widely accepted theory was that he was negotiating an arms deal for the gang; if true, it looked as if the 'People's War' had finally ended.

In fact, worse was to come.

Among the numerous terrorist groups active in West Germany at the time was the anarchist 'Movement June 2'. It took its name from the date in 1967 when a student called Benno Ohnesorg was killed during anti-Shah riots in West Berlin. Some June 2 members had served under Baader, others with the SPK: all fully supported his gang's revolutionary aims. And now, in the three years that it took a nervous West German government to construct a terrorist-proof courtroom at Stammheim to try the gang, the June 2 Movement took over where Baader, Meinhof and Ensslin had been forced to leave off.

On 4 June 1974, a June 2 firing squad executed a fellow terrorist, Ulrich Schmücker, in West Berlin. His body was found next day by American soldiers. Schmücker was accused of informing the police in 1972 of a plot to blow up the Turkish embassy in Bonn, an intended act of reprisal for the execution of three Turkish terrorists.

Five months later Judge Gunther von Drenkmann, president of the West Berlin High Court, was shot dead at his home as he celebrated his sixty-fourth birthday. The assassination squad called at his house carrying bunches of flowers. When the judge – who had tried none of the Baader-Meinhof gang – answered the door he was gunned down at point-blank range. The June 2 Movement claimed responsibility, saying the murder was in retaliation for the recent death in jail of Baader-Meinhof terrorist Holger Meins (he had died following a hunger strike).

Next, on 27 February 1975, a June 2 kidnap squad seized Peter Lorenz as he was being driven to his office in Berlin. Lorenz was leader of the Christian Democrats and candidate for the politically prestigious office of mayor. His chauffeur, who was knocked out in the attack, identified Angela Luther, a former member of the Baader-Meinhof gang, as one of the kidnappers. The price they demanded for Lorenz' freedom was: the release of six imprisoned terrorists (two from June 2, four from the Red Army Faction including Horst Mahler), a jetliner to fly them out of the country with former mayor Heinrich Albertz as hostage, and payment of 20,000 Deutschmarks per terrorist.

The West German government meekly surrendered to all demands, and the getaway plane landed on 3 March in Aden – minus only Horst Mahler, who had refused to leave his cell. Once the South Yemen government granted the kidnappers asylum, Albertz was returned unharmed to Berlin. There he read out a prepared statement on television (thought to contain a hidden codeword) whereupon other terrorists freed Peter Lorenz. He said he had been held captive in a tiny cellar by armed masked guards and could identify none of them.

On 24 April, as the argument over the Bonn government's surrender continued, six terrorists from the 'Holger Meins commando' (the only identification given) seized the West German embassy in Stockholm. Among their prisoners was ambassador Dietrich Stocker and several senior diplomats, including military attaché Lieutenant Colonel Andreas Baron von Mirbach. The terrorists threatened to kill them all unless the Bonn government released twenty-six members of the Baader-Meinhof gang within six hours, and flew them out of the country after payment of over $500,000 as ransom.

As these demands were considered, Swedish police inside the lower part of the embassy were fired on and warned by telephone to quit within fifteen minutes – or von Mirbach would be executed. When the threat was ignored the West German military attaché was marched to the head of the staircase, shot several times and thrown on to the landing below. He died shortly afterwards in hospital. Then, minutes before the deadline expired, the terrorists were telephoned by the Swedish minister of justice who informed them that the Bonn government had rejected all demands. He then offered the gang safe conduct out of Sweden if they freed the remaining hostages unharmed. Their response was to blow up the top floor of the embassy, killing one of their own gang in the process and injuring another. The badly burned body of Heinz Hillegaart, the West German economic attaché, was found later in the wreckage. The injured terrorist died in hospital and the four surviving members of the gang were deported to West Germany. Three were former members of the SPK. The chancellor, Helmut Schmidt, described the Stockholm attack as 'the most serious incident' in the last twenty-six years and promised that any future attacks would be met henceforth with equal firmness.

As the nation held its breath, the trial of the Baader-Meinhof leaders began at Stammheim on 21 May 1975. Defence arguments and political harangues from the prisoners in the dock threatened to reduce proceedings inside the courtroom to a farce. Outside all bore silent testimony to the government's fear of what terrorists still at large might do to halt them altogether. The single-storey steel and concrete building was nothing less than a fortress, constructed on farmland outside Stuttgart and surrounded by a ten-foot steel fence which was floodlit by night and constantly monitored on closed-circuit TV screens. Guards armed with sub-machine-guns patrolled the fence with dogs. Steel-reinforced anti-bomb netting protected the roof, machine-gun squads were sited to ward off any surprise terrorist attack from the air (possibly by helicopter). Holger Meins, who should have been in the dock with the others, was already dead from fasting. The charges against the other four, Baader, Meinhof, Ensslin and Raspe, covered more than 350 pages. No one in West Germany doubted what was ultimately at stake: it was the authority of the Federal government itself.

On 4 May 1976, after almost a year, Gudrun Ensslin claimed responsibility by the gang for three of the four murder-bombings with which they were charged. Although her co-defendants disassociated themselves from her admission, it meant that the trial was now virtually decided. Four nights later Ulrike Meinhof tore her prison towel into strips, made a rope, tied it to the bars of her cell and hanged herself. When she was found next morning she had been dead some hours. Demonstrations followed in a number of German and other European cities, with allegations of 'State murder'. Her funeral in the Church of the Holy Trinity in West Berlin on 15 May

1976 was attended by four thousand sympathisers, some of them masked.

On 7 April 1977 Siegfried Buback, West Germany's Chief Federal Prosecutor, was assassinated in Karlsruhe. Two men on a motorcycle drew level with Buback's Mercedes at the traffic lights, and the pillion rider sprayed the car with sub-machine-gun fire. Buback and his chauffeur died instantly, his bodyguard five days later in hospital.

Three weeks later, on 28 April, the three surviving leaders of the Baader-Meinhof gang were each sentenced to life imprisonment, for the murder of the four US soldiers in Frankfurt and Heidelberg in May 1972. Baader, Ensslin and Raspe were also found guilty of thirty-four charges of attempted murder, and of conspiracy against the State. These convictions added fifteen years to the life sentences already imposed. The five judges, led by Chief Judge Eberhard Foth, rejected their lawyers' submission that the trio should be given POW status.

Few doubted that other terrorists still at large would attempt new kidnappings to bargain against the Baader-Meinhof gang's freedom. As a result the entire West German establishment – ministers, leading politicians, judges and prosecutors, police chiefs, bankers and industrialists, anyone worth holding to ransom – was obliged to live in what was virtually a state of siege. Some had their homes guarded by armoured cars and sentries on watch behind sandbagged emplacements, or by armed police with dogs.

The first kidnap bid came on 30 July 1977, when Dr Jurgen Ponto, head of the Dresdner Bank, was shot and killed at his home near Frankfurt. He was betrayed by his goddaughter Susanne Albrecht: unknown to Ponto she was the former mistress of SPK terrorist Karl-Heinz Dellwo, who had been jailed for life only ten days earlier for his part in the 1975 Stockholm embassy raid. Susanne called on her godfather carrying a bunch of red roses – and accompanied by four other young persons, three women and a man: all terrorists. They shot Ponto five times when he resisted their attempts to kidnap him.

Finally on 5 September 1977 top industrialist Dr Hanns Martin Schleyer was kidnapped in Cologne. Five terrorists armed with sub-machine-guns ambushed his Mercedes as he was driven home from work, escorted by a second car carrying three armed bodyguards. Firing selectively, the gunmen murdered all three bodyguards and Schleyer's chauffeur, then abducted the unharmed industrialist in a waiting van. They then offered his life in exchange for the release of eleven imprisoned West German terrorists (headed by Baader,

Ensslin and Raspe), payment of $43,000 a head and safe transport to the country of their choice.

The Bonn government played for time as a massive search was mounted for Schleyer. Five weeks later the kidnappers released a photograph of their drained, wretched captive, showing him holding a banner bearing the inscription 'Commando Siegfried Hausner' and 'Martyr Halimeh'. Hausner was the SPK terrorist who died of wounds after exploding a bomb in the Stockholm embassy siege of 1975. 'Halimeh' was the Arab name given to the unidentified German woman hijacker shot by Israeli troops during the Entebbe rescue. No one realized its significance at the time, but on 13 October four Arab hijackers from the PFLP (Special Operations) – acting on behalf of the Schleyer kidnap gang – seized a Lufthansa airliner bound from Majorca to Frankfurt. They increased the original ransom demands to a staggering $15 million in cash, and called for the release of two Turkish terrorists in addition to the Germans already named.

In the absence of any positive response they forced the Lufthansa pilot, Jurgen Schumann, to fly from Dubai to Aden shortly before the deadline expired. After landing safely alongside the blocked runway he warned the kidnappers the nosewheel had been damaged. After inspecting it and returning to the aircraft, he was made to kneel in front of his terrified passengers and shot through the head. Schumann's body was then thrown out on to the runway after his co-pilot landed on 17 October at Mogadishu. Passengers and crew had now endured great privation for five days and were nearing exhaustion. Hans-Jurgen Wischnewski, West German minister of state, arrived at Mogadishu soon afterwards and negotiations were begun, ostensibly for their release. A 'final' deadline was set for all demands to be met. Shortly before it expired, on 18 October, a planeload of West German commandos from the Grenzschutz Gruppe 9 landed at Mogadishu, accompanied by two British SAS advisers. With the knowledge and permission of Somali President Barre, the German commandos stormed the hijacked airliner and freed all eighty-six passengers and surviving aircrew. Three of the Arab terrorists were killed outright, the fourth (a woman) wounded. One passenger was injured. There were no German military casualties.

As West Germany rejoiced, the news of the 'second Entebbe' reached the Baader-Meinhof gang leaders imprisoned at Stammheim via Raspe's smuggled transistor radio. Their response was equally dramatic: Baader and Raspe shot themselves in the head (with separate pistols, likewise smuggled into the top-security jail), Ensslin hanged herself from the cell bars with flex. Irmgard Moller, another prisoner, stabbed herself but recovered. Their fellow terrorists still at large, however, refused to admit defeat.

Hanns Martin Schleyer was murdered by his kidnappers a few hours later. His body was found next day in the boot of a car abandoned at Mulhouse in northern France. He had been shot three times in the head and his throat cut. Responsibility was claimed by the Siegfried Hausner commando. The West German police later issued a list of sixteen suspects wanted for questioning in connection with the murder: the fact that half of them were young women from middle-class families told its own story of the influence Ulrike Meinhof exerted in West Germany.

BARBER, Susan
A poisoner who would have gone unconvicted but for the persistence of a pathologist.

Susan Barber had been conducting a passionate affair for eight months with Richard Collins, her husband's best friend and partner in the local darts team, when in May 1981 Michael Barber returned home early from a fishing trip and surprised them naked together in the bedroom. He thrashed his wife, and threw Collins out of the house. Next day she took her revenge. She put a half teaspoonful of weed-killer in his steak-and-kidney pie, causing her husband to die in agony one week later. After his death Mrs Barber set up home with her lover, but when that romance cooled advertised for new admirers on citizen's band radio – under the call-sign 'Nympho'.

The poison she had administered to her husband was Gramoxone, an ultra-deadly variant of paraquat weed-killer. Two teaspoonsful taken together are sufficient to cause instant death; a smaller dose inflicts a lingering one. (Paraquat causes fibrosis of the lungs, thus making breathing progressively more difficult. It also attacks the vital organs and burns the throat.) Mr Barber was first admitted to hospital with suspected pneumonia. Later his illness was diagnosed as Goodpasture's Syndrome, a rare nervous condition. He was thereupon transferred to Hammersmith hospital in West London, where he died. Cause of death was then said to be pneumonia and kidney failure.

Professor David Evans, however, the pathologist who conducted the post-mortem, suspected that the true cause of death might be more sinister. Paraquat tests were ordered but, inexplicably, no samples for analysis were sent to the National Poisons Unit at New Cross Hospital. When the doctors concerned asked for the results, they were told – wrongly – that the tests had been made but ruled out paraquat. Professor Evans remained unconvinced; and at his suggestion the doctors met in conference and examined organs taken from Mr Barber's body and preserved. Blood samples which had been held over were then sent to the National Poisons Unit and also to ICI, manufacturers of the weed-killer. Both confirmed the presence of paraquat, and CID inquiries were begun – seven months after the murder had been committed.

Mrs Barber, who had collected a payment of £15,000 from her husband's pension fund, was arrested with Collins in April 1982. Collins was charged with conspiracy to murder and sentenced to two years' imprisonment, Mrs Barber was jailed for life for the murder of her husband. Det. Chief Inspector John Clarion of the Essex police, who led the murder hunt, was commended by the trial judge who said, 'Bearing in mind the length of time which elapsed in the case, the inquiry . . . presented considerable difficulties.'

BEHESHTI, Ayatollah Muhammad
Iran's ruling-party leader and Chief Justice killed by a terrorist's bomb.

On the night of 28 June 1981 a huge bomb destroyed the headquarters of the ruling Islamic Republican Party in Teheran, killing Ayatollah Khomeini's number two and seventy-three other leading Iranian politicians. Many other people were injured, some seriously. Several cabinet ministers, deputy cabinet ministers and parliamentary deputies were among the dead. It was the worst terrorist incident Iran had known since the Shah was deposed. 'Counter-revolutionary forces', supporters of the recently ousted (and democratically elected) President Bani-Sadr, were blamed for the bombing.

The giant bomb exploded as the Ayatollah Beheshti addressed an audience of the ninety top members of the party on two main problems facing Iran, the Gulf War against Iraq and the measures to be taken against the same 'counter-revolutionaries' who one week earlier had fought openly on the streets of the capital in support of Bani-Sadr. Although all foreign newsmen were excluded from the wrecked building, eye-witnesses said later that Iran's new President,

Muhammad Ali Rajai, was one of the few who survived the blast unhurt.

Ironically, as well as being party leader and unofficial successor-designate to Ayatollah Khomeini, Ayatollah Beheshti was also Iran's Justice Minister. As such he was responsible for ordering the thousands of executions of 'counter-revolutionaries and imperialists' following the overthrow of the Shah.

BELL, Mary Flora
Eleven-year-old killer.

On 11 May 1968 a three-year-old Newcastle boy was playing on top of an air-raid shelter with two older girls, Mary Bell and Norma Bell (no relation to Mary) when he fell and was severely injured. The next day the mothers of three girls, all aged about six, complained to the police that Mary Bell had attacked their children and squeezed their throats. Mary and Norma were interviewed by the police and given a stiff 'talking to'.

Less than a fortnight later two boys poking round a derelict house in a slum area found the body of a four-year-old boy lying in an upstairs room. He was identified as Martin George Brown, and there seemed to be no obvious cause of death. It was assumed that he had swallowed pills from a bottle found nearby. Mary and Norma had followed the two boys into the house and had to be chased out.

The day after Martin Brown's death Norma's father found Mary Bell trying to strangle his eleven-year-old daughter. He slapped her. Later that day, 26 May, a nursery school in the area was broken into and property damaged. Police found a note reading 'Fuch of, we murder, watch out, Fanny and Faggot.' Another said, 'WE did murder Martain brown, fuckof you Bastard [*sic*].'

Mary Bell knocked on the Browns' door four days later, and asked Martin's mother if she could see him. The mother replied, 'No, pet, Martin is dead.' 'Oh, I know he's dead, I wanted to see him in his coffin.'

On 31 May the newly installed alarm at the nursery school went off, and police hurried to the scene, to find Mary and Norma there. The two girls swore that they had not been responsible for the previous break-in, and were released into the custody of their parents.

Mary now began spreading rumours that Norma had killed Martin Brown by putting her hands round his throat. But when Mary heard that Norma's parents were angry, she apologized to them.

39

Two months later three-year-old Brian Howe disappeared from the same area. There was a search, and Mary Bell suggested to Brian's sister that he might be playing among concrete blocks on some waste ground. In fact, Brian's body was found among the blocks that evening. He had been manually strangled, and had puncture marks on his legs, and cuts on his belly. A pathologist noted that not much force had been used, and that the killer could be a child.

Children in the area were asked to fill in questionnaires about what they had done on the day Brian Howe was killed. The police visited several children to get them to clarify their statements; among these were Mary and Norma Bell. After a number of statements, Mary claimed that she had seen Brian Howe in the company of an eight-year-old boy who was hitting him; she also claimed that the boy had been carrying a pair of scissors with one blade broken. In fact, such a pair *had* been found near the body, but this had not been made public. The eight-year-old was interviewed, but proved to have been at Newcastle Airport that day. Norma admitted that she had gone to the waste ground with Mary, and had stumbled over the dead boy. Mary, she claimed, had admitted to killing him.

At the police station, Mary showed an unexpectedly adult attitude, declaring that she wanted to see a solicitor, and that she was being brainwashed.

Now Norma decided to admit that she was present when Brian Howe was killed. She described how Mary had pushed the boy on to the grass, and then 'gone all funny', struggling violently with him. Norma claimed she ran away when Mary asked her to help. Later, they returned to the waste ground, and Mary marked the corpse with the scissors, and made marks like an M on his stomach. The razor with which she did this was found under a stone, where Norma said it would be.

Mary blamed the crime on Norma, describing in detail how Norma had strangled the boy.

At the trial, which began at Newcastle on 5 December 1968, Mary and Norma were allowed to sit with their parents. Mary showed herself to be highly intelligent and lively, and enjoyed parrying questions in the witness box. A psychiatrist described her as 'intelligent, manipulative, dangerous'. She told a policewoman she wanted to be a nurse so she could stick needles in people. 'I like hurting people.'

Norma was acquitted, since it was obvious she was completely under Mary's domination. Mary was found guilty of manslaughter in both cases. She was placed in a special unit of an approved school among boys older than herself. In 1970 a master was brought to trial for indecently assaulting Mary, but the judge decided that the accusations were a fabrication.

In September 1977 Mary Bell and another inmate absconded from Moor Court open prison, met two boys and stayed with them overnight – Mary subsequently described in a Sunday newspaper how she had lost her virginity. They were recaptured after three days. Mary insisted that she wanted to stay at liberty long enough to prove that she was now normal. The authorities obviously felt that the risk would be altogether too great.

Gitta Sereny's book *The Case of Mary Bell* makes it clear that Mary's disturbed personality could be blamed on her upbringing. She was born on 26 May 1957, when her unmarried mother was only seventeen; her mother was a disturbed personality, who often left Mary with relatives; she once gave her to a woman she met outside an adoption agency. Betty Bell, who, after Mary's birth, married the father, was often away from home for long periods, and her husband was frequently out of work. (Mary's father was sent to prison for robbery with force after his daughter's conviction.) The home was dirty and sparsely furnished. At school, Mary was an exhibitionist and an inveterate liar. Her reaction to the lack of affection at home was to develop a desire 'to hurt people'.

BERKOWITZ, David (alias Son of Sam)
Unbalanced killer who kept New York in a state of terror for thirteen months.

On the night of 29 July 1976 two young girls sat talking in the front seats of a car on Buhre Avenue, New York City; they were Donna Lauria, a medical technician, and Jody Valenti, a student nurse. Donna's parents, on their way back from a night out, passed them at about 1 am, and said goodnight. A few moments after they reached their apartment, they heard the sound of shots and screams. A man had walked up to the Oldsmobile, pulled a gun out of a brown paper bag, and fired five shots. Donna was killed, Jody wounded in the thigh.

Total lack of motive for the shooting convinced police they were dealing with a man who killed for pleasure, without knowing his victims.

Four months later, on 26 November, two young girls were sitting talking on the stoop in front of a house in the Floral Park section of Queens, New York; it was half an hour past midnight when a man walked towards them, started to ask if they could direct him, then, before he finished the sentence, pulled out a gun and began shooting. Donna DeMasi and Joanne Lomino were both wounded. A bullet lodged in Joanne's spine, paralysing her. Bullets dug out of a front door and a mail box revealed that the two young women had been shot by the same .44 that had killed Donna Lauria and wounded Jody Valenti.

Although the police were unaware of it at this time, the same gun had already wounded yet another victim. Over a month earlier, on 23 October 1976, Carl Denaro and his girlfriend Rosemary Keenan were sitting in his sports car in front of a tavern in Flushing when there were several loud bangs; then a bullet tore through the rear windscreen, and Denaro fell forward. He was rushed to hospital, and in three weeks, had begun to recover, although his middle finger was permanently damaged. The .44 bullet was found on the floor of the car.

On 30 January 1977 a young couple were kissing goodnight in a car in the Ridgewood area of New York; there was a deafening explosion, the windscreen shattered, and Christine Freund slumped into the arms of her boyfriend John Diel. She died a few hours later in hospital.

On 8 March 1977 Virginia Voskerichian, an Armenian student, was on her way home, and only a few hundred yards from her mother's house in Forest Hills, when a gunman walked up to her, and shot her in the face at a few yards range; the bullet went into her mouth, shattering her front teeth. She died immediately. Christine Freund had been shot only three hundred yards away.

By now police recognized that the bullets that had killed three and wounded four had all come from the same gun. And this indicated a homicidal psychopath who would probably go on until he was caught. The problem was that the police had no clues to his identity, no idea of where to begin searching. Unless he was caught during an attempted murder, the chance of arresting him seemed minimal. Mayor Beame of New York gave a press conference in which he announced: 'We have a savage killer on the loose.' He was able to say that the man was white, about five feet ten inches tall, well groomed, with hair combed straight back.

On the morning of 17 April 1977 there were two more deaths.

Alexander Esau and Valentina Súriani were sitting in a parked car in the Bronx when the killer shot both of them. Valentina died instantly; Esau died later in hospital, three bullets in his head. Only a few blocks away, Donna Lauria and Jody Valenti had been shot.

In the middle of the street, a policeman found an envelope. It contained a letter addressed to Captain Joseph Borrelli, and it was from the killer. 'I am deeply hurt by your calling me a weman-hater. I am not. But I am a monster. I am the Son of Sam. I am a little brat . . .' It claimed that his father, Sam, was a brute who beat his family when he got drunk, and who ordered him to go out and kill. 'I love to hunt. Prowling the streets looking for fair game – tasty meat. The wemen of Queens are prettyist of all . . .' It was reminiscent of the letters that Jack the Ripper and so many other 'thrill killers' have written to the police, revealing an urge to 'be' somebody, to make an impact on society. A further rambling, incoherent note, signed 'Son of Sam', was sent to a New York columnist, James Breslin.

The next attack, on 26 June 1977, was like so many of the others: a young couple sitting in their car in the early hours of Sunday morning, saying goodnight after a date. They were Salvatore Lupo and Judy Placido, and the car was in front of a house on 211 Street, Bayside, Queens. The windscreen shattered, as four shots were fired. The assailant ran away. Fortunately, his aim had been bad; both these victims were only wounded, and recovered.

It was now a year since Son of Sam had killed Donna Lauria; on the anniversary of her death, Queens and the Bronx were swarming with police. But Son of Sam had decided that these areas were dangerous, and that his next shootings would be as far away as possible. On 31 July Robert Violante and Stacy Moskowitz were sitting in a parking lot close to the Brooklyn shore; it was 1.30 am on Sunday morning. The windscreen exploded as four shots were fired. Both were hit in the head. Stacy Moskowitz died hours later in hospital; Robert Violante recovered, but was blinded.

But this shooting brought the break in the case. A woman out walking her dog had noticed two policemen putting a ticket on a car parked near a fire hydrant on Bay 16th Street. Minutes later, a man ran up to the car, leapt in and drove off. Only four parking tickets had been issued in the Coney Island area that Sunday morning, and only one of those was for parking near a hydrant. The carbon of the ticket contained the car's registration number. And the vehicle licensing department was able to identify its owner as David Berkowitz, aged twenty-four, of Pine Street, Yonkers.

On the Wednesday after the last killing, detectives found the Ford Galaxie parked in front of an apartment building in Pine Street. They peered in through its window, and saw the butt of a gun, and a note written in the same block capitals as the other Son of Sam letters. The car was staked out. When David Berkowitz approached it at 10.15 that evening, Deputy Inspector Tim Dowd, who had led the hunt, said, 'Hello, David.' Berkowitz looked at him in surprise, then said, 'Inspector Dowd! You finally got me.'

After the terror he had aroused, Son of Sam was something of an anticlimax, a pudgy little man with a beaming smile, and a tendency to look like a slightly moronic child who has been caught stealing sweets. He was a paranoid schizophrenic, a man who lived alone in a room lit by a naked bulb, sleeping on a bare mattress. The floor was covered with empty milk cartons and bottles. On the walls he had scrawled messages like 'In this hole lives the wicked king', 'Kill for my Master', 'I turn children into killers'. His father, who had run a hardware store in the Bronx, had retired to Florida after being robbed. Nat Berkowitz was not Son of Sam's real father. David Berkowitz, born 1 June 1953, was a bastard, and his mother offered him for adoption. He had felt rejected from the beginning.

He reacted to his poor self-image by boasting and lying – particularly about his sexual prowess. In fact, he was shy of women, and almost certainly a virgin when captured. He told police that demons began telling him to kill in 1974 – although one psychiatrist who interviewed him is convinced that this is untrue, and that Berkowitz's stories of 'voices' was an attempt to establish a defence of insanity. Living alone in apartments that he allowed to become pig-sties, kept awake at night by the sound of trucks or barking dogs, he slipped into paranoia, telling his father in a letter that people hated him, and spat at him as he walked down the street. 'The girls call me ugly, and they bother me the most.' On Christmas Eve 1975, he began his attempt at revenge on women by taking a knife and attacking two of them. The first one screamed so loudly he ran away. The second, a fifteen-year-old schoolgirl, was badly cut, and had one lung punctured, but recovered. Seven months later, Berkowitz went out with a gun and committed his first murder.

The name Sam seems to have been taken from a neighbour called Sam Carr, whose black Labrador sometimes kept Berkowitz awake. He wrote Carr anonymous letters, and on 27 April 1977 shot the dog – which recovered. He also wrote anonymous letters to people he believed to be persecuting him. He had been reported to the police on a number of occasions as a 'nut', but no one suspected that he might be Son of Sam.

Berkowitz was judged sane, and was arraigned on 23 August 1977. He pleaded guilty, saving New York the cost of a trial. He was sentenced to 365 years in prison.

The aftermath is worth describing. His Yonkers apartment block became a place of pilgrimage for sensation-seekers. They stole doorknobs, cut out pieces of carpet, even chipped pieces of paint from Berkowitz's door. In the middle of the night, people shouted 'David, come out' from the street. Berkowitz's apartment remained empty, and a quarter of the building's tenants moved out, even though the landlord changed its number from 25 to 42 Pine Street to try to mislead the souvenir hunters.

BODEN, Wayne
The Canadian who became known as the Vampire Rapist.

On 23 July 1968 Norma Vaillancourt, a 21-year-old teacher, was found in her apartment in Montreal, strangled and raped. Her breasts were covered with bite-marks. Oddly enough, there was no sign that she had made any resistance, and the examining pathologist stated that the expression on her face was serene, amounting to a faint smile. Norma was a popular girl and had many boyfriends, all of whom were eliminated from the investigation.

In 1969 the body of Shirley Audette was found on a patio at the rear of an apartment complex in West Montreal. She was fully clothed, but proved to have been raped and strangled. There were teeth-marks on the breasts. Again, it seemed clear that she had known her killer, for there were no signs of violent resistance – no flesh under the nails or bruises. It appeared that she had felt she was 'getting into something dangerous' with a new boyfriend. Her regular boyfriend said she had telephoned him at 3 am on the day she died and told him, 'I'm scared.' The obvious explanation seemed to be that she had got involved with a man of great charm, but who had peculiar inclinations. Possibly he chose girls he instinctively felt to have masochistic leanings, who would submit to a certain degree of biting and strangling in the course of sex; he then got carried away and had to rape and tear at the breasts with his teeth.

The next case confirmed that the killer was not a rapist who chose his victims at random. On 23 November 1969 Marielle Archambault, a clerk in a Montreal jewellery store, greeted a well-dressed young man as 'Bill'; fellow-workers had the impression she was pleased and excited. He left the store with her at closing time. When she failed to arrive at work the next morning, her employer called her landlady, who went to see if the girl was ill. Marielle's body lay on the living-room floor of her apartment, partly covered with a blanket. There were signs of a fierce struggle, which had ended in her death. The killer had removed her tights to rape her, and torn open her bra to bite her breasts. The police found a crumpled photograph of a young man in the apartment, and fellow-workers at the store identified it as the man who had called for her the previous afternoon. Yet although a sketch was made from the photograph, and published in newspapers, no one was able to identify the 'vampire killer'.

Two months later, he killed again, this time 24-year-old Jean Way. She had a date with her boyfriend on 16 January 1970, but when he knocked on the door of her Montreal apartment at 8.15 pm, there was no reply. Assuming that she had gone out briefly, he went and had a beer, then went back. This time the door was unlocked. She was lying on a sofa, totally nude, and with the usual bite marks on her breasts. It seemed likely that her killer had been with her when her boyfriend was knocking at the door. There was no sign of a struggle and the face looked serene.

In spite of immense publicity and widespread police activity, Canada's most wanted killer remained at large. And the next murder happened 2,500 miles away, in Calgary. Elizabeth Anne Pourteous was a schoolteacher at Browness High School, and when she failed to report for work on 18 May 1971, the apartment manager looked into her apartment and found her on the bedroom floor. Again, there had been a struggle. She had been raped, and her bra had been torn open; there were bites on her breasts. A man's broken cufflink was found beneath the body.

Two fellow-teachers had seen Elizabeth Pourteous in a car with a young man the previous evening. They had pulled up at a traffic-light when a blue Mercedes came alongside them and they could recognize their colleague. The only distinctive thing they could recall about the car was an advertisement sticker for beef – a picture of a steer – in the rear window. Another friend was able to say that the victim had been dating a new boyfriend – named Bill – for the past week or so. The man was described as a flashy dresser with neatly trimmed hair – the description of the Montreal rapist.

The following day, a policeman saw the blue Mercedes not far from the victim's apartment; half an hour later, a young man was arrested as he approached the car. He was Wayne Clifford Boden, formerly of Montreal, who had moved to Calgary a year earlier. He agreed that he had been with Elizabeth Pourteous on the previous evening, and that the cufflink belonged to him, but insisted that she had been alive and well when he left her. He was undoubtedly the man in the crumpled photograph found in Marielle Archambault's apartment.

But the clinching evidence came from an orthodontist, who identified the teeth-marks on Elizabeth Pourteous's breasts as having twenty-nine points of similarity with Boden's teeth-marks. In addition, examination of Boden's underpants had shown seminal stains and pubic hairs from the body of Elizabeth Pourteous.

Boden was sentenced to life imprisonment for the murder of Elizabeth Pourteous. He later stood trial in Montreal, admitting three of the four killings that had taken place there. He denied that he was the killer of the first victim, Norma Vaillancourt. He was sentenced to three more life sentences for the other three rape killings.

In retrospect it seems almost certain that the killings were not premeditated. Wayne Boden was the victim of a sadistic obsession about breasts. It also seems possible that he succeeded in persuading the women that a certain amount of 'strangling' was natural in lovemaking – like the Düsseldorf sadist of the 1920s, Peter Kürten. At a certain point, the desire to bite the breasts overpowered him, and the girls died – in some cases losing consciousness without a struggle.

BONIN, William G.
'Freeway Killer' – homosexual mass murderer found guilty of killing youths for sexual purposes, and dumping them on the freeways of California.

The series of murders which became known as the 'freeway killings' date back to 1972. By 1980, there had been 41 similar killings, most of the victims having been strangled – often with their own tee-shirts – and sodomised. In many cases, it was clear that at least two homosexuals were involved. The boys were literally 'throwaways', used for sexual purposes and then destroyed and tossed on the side of California's motorways. The killers were obviously sadists: in some cases, the bodies were slashed with a knife and emasculated. One of the victims, a 13-year-old boy, had been almost decapitated. Other victims had spikes driven into their skulls and rectums, or ice picks jammed into their ears. Others had been hog-tied and strangled. Some were even dumped in dustbins.

In 1975, three years after the first of the 'freeway murders', a 14-year-old boy was hitching a ride back home after a party when a young man, who had also been at the party, stopped and offered him a ride. As soon as the boy got into the van, the man pulled out a gun, drove him to an isolated spot, forced him to strip, and sodomised him. The boy begged for his life, and the man told him he wouldn't kill him because other people at the party might remember seeing them together.

As he drove the boy back to his own neighbourhood, the rapist told him that he liked to pick up young male hitch-hikers and strangle them with their own tee-shirts. He even told him, 'If you want to kill somebody, you should make a plan and find a place to dump the body before you even pick a victim.' He said that he went out looking for young men to kill on Friday and Saturday, so that he could take his girlfriend roller skating in Anaheim on Sundays.

The boy reported the attack, and the police had little difficulty in picking up a 25-year-old man named William G. Bonin. Bonin was convicted, and sentenced to a period in jail of from one to fifteen years. He was released in October 1978.

By 1980, the police of California realised that the freeway killer was back, although some of the bodies were hidden in remote places in the mountains. By this time, the original victim of the rapist was serving a sentence for car theft in the Los Padrinos Juvenile Detention Center. He read about the 'freeway killer', remembered the boasts of the rapist, and talked about it to his counsellors. They contacted the police, who placed Bonin under surveillance. On 11 June 1980, they saw Bonin pick up a youth and followed him to a dark alleyway in Hollywood. When they broke into the van a few minutes later, they caught Bonin in the act of sodomising a 17-year-old boy. He was arrested and held on a charge of sodomy while they tried to establish whether there was any connection with the freeway murders.

Bonin implicated a 22-year-old youth named Vernon Robert Butts, a labourer with stringy blond hair who had fantasies of being a magician – in his apartment the police found novelty spiders that dropped on callers from the ceiling and two coffins. Under questioning, police established that Butts had been Bonin's accomplice in at least six murders. Two months later, another two men were arrested and charged – 19-year-old James Munro and 19-year-old Gregory Matthews Miley, both regarded as mentally sub-normal. Miley was charged with two of the most recent murders, those of two boys, aged 12 and 14, whose naked bodies had been found in February 1980. Miley alleged that Bonin had actually killed the two boys, strangling them within a few hours of each other in the van. He described how Bonin had sodomised the 14-year-old – who, he said, was a homosexual – and how he had held the boy down while Bonin tied him then strangled him with his tee-shirt. They dumped the body, then drove around and picked up the 12-year-old. The boy entered the van and got in the back with Bonin, but Miley said he heard crying sounds being made by the victim. Miley said he helped Bonin hold the boy down, 'But it didn't seem too hard to hold him because he was so small.' This body was deposited next to a dump truck.

Butts also admitted going on murder forays with Bonin, but claimed that Bonin always committed the murders. It seemed clear that Bonin was sadistic, since in many cases the boys were perfectly willing to have sexual intercourse. In one case, Bonin and Miley picked up a boy who was leaving a cinema in Hollywood, and after Bonin had had sex with the boy in the van, he suddenly began beating him, then tied him up and pressed a tyre lever against his neck until the bones cracked. Miley commented, 'The kid vomited. I jumped down on him the same way, killing the guy.' Butts told a case of a boy who was forced to drink chlorohydrate.

In January 1980, Butts committed suicide in jail by hanging himself with a towel. Butts had declared that Bonin had a 'hypnotic' way with him and stated: 'After the first killing I couldn't do anything about it.'

Bonin's trial began on 5 November 1981, in front of Judge William B. Keene. Miley had agreed to testify against him, which meant that he could not be sentenced to the gas chamber.

The horrifying recital of murder continued for day after day. The prosecutor declared that he would prove that Bonin was the Freeway Killer and that he had bragged to a number of witnesses that he had killed more than 16 people. He carefully planned his operations, lured the victims into the van to sodomise them, then killed them and threw away their bodies 'like garbage along streets and freeways'. 'We will show you that he enjoyed the killings,' said prosecutor

Norris and he mentioned that on one occasion, Bonin had murdered one victim in his van, then he and Munro had gone to eat a hamburger at a fast food stand, leaving the body in the van. After this, Bonin announced: 'I'm horny. I need another one.'

On 8 December 1981, Bonin was in a cell with the man accused of being the Hillside Strangler, Angelo Buono, and a convicted murderer named John W. Stinson, when he was apparently beaten up. He was taken to hospital, where he was treated for cuts and bruises. When the trial resumed, a newsman, David Lopez, declared that Bonin had confessed to him in the County Jail that he had killed 21 young men and boys.

Bonin was finally accused of killing 12 boys, including 13-year-old Thomas Lundgren, who had been emasculated, 14-year-old Sean King, and 19-year-old Daren Kendrick, who had been killed by having an ice pick thrust into his right ear. Bonin told Lopez that the murders began in August 1979 and ended on 11 June 1980, the day of his arrest. He told Lopez, 'I'd still be killing. I couldn't stop killing. It got easier each time.'

The prosecutor told the jury that Bonin had developed an insatiable appetite to torture boys and young men. He used as accomplices people of low mentality like Munro and Miley, who testified that they each took part in three murders.

Munro and Miley were each sentenced to 25 years in prison. William G. Bonin, found guilty of ten counts of first degree murder and ten counts of robbery, was sentenced to death.

BOWDEN, John
The murderer who dismembered his victim alive.

In January 1982 John 'Ginger' Bowden, a 26-year-old Londoner of whose crime his judge said, 'There never was a more horrific case of murder', was jailed for a minimum twenty-five years for his role in the dismemberment of a live victim by machete, saw and electric carving-knife. Bowden's two accomplices – both alcoholics like himself – were each sentenced to fifteen years' imprisonment.

The man they butchered was Donald Ryan, a former amateur boxer. Previously they had preyed on helpless London down-and-outs, none of whom they had killed. Ryan was their first murder victim. Bowden lured him to a flat in South London and then, with Michael Ward, a Camberwell grave-digger and David Begley, a porter from Walworth: knocked Ryan 'semi-conscious' with a machete blow to the head; dropped him into a bath of scalding water, where he fainted; carried him into a bedroom and cut off his arms and legs with an electric carving-knife; beheaded him and scattered his trunk and limbs on waste land and in the streets of South London. Bowden stored the severed head in a refrigerator before finally dumping it in the dustbin, where it was found by dustmen.

After hearing the evidence, Old Bailey judge Mr Justice Mars-Jones commented, 'Bowden is a man who obviously enjoyed inflicting pain and even killing. There never was a more horrific case of murder than this.' When he sentenced him to life imprisonment, with a recommendation that he should serve not less than twenty-five years, Bowden shouted, 'You old bastard, I hope you die screaming of cancer.'

The details of the murder were so gruesome, and the accompanying photographic evidence so horrific, that at one stage the trial had to be adjourned when four members of the jury – one a woman – fell ill. The court was told that Bowden laughed and joked as he held Ryan's head aloft, then placed it on a table. Two teenage boys in an adjoining room had noticed blood seeping under the door of Bowden's flat; after going off for a drink in a local pub Bowden, Ward and Begley had all returned to the flat and slept among the gore.

After the trial Bowden's parents described their son as a 'good boy, gentle and kind' who turned to violence when he was kept in solitary confinement after escaping from arrest. 'He was never the same afterwards,' said his father. By the time he was twenty-four young John Bowden had spent a total of five years in jail for crimes including robbery, blackmail, burglary, assault, wounding and carrying offensive weapons. He had been married but he and his wife separated shortly afterwards.

Bowden was back in the headlines one year after he started to serve his sentence at Parkhurst maximum security prison on the Isle of Wight. Together with another prisoner – James McCaig, serving four years for robbery – Bowden entered the assistant prison governor's office, which was always open to the inmates to discuss grievances, and held him hostage at knife-point. Bowden and McCaig barricaded themselves in and then, while one held a knife to the assistant governor's throat, the other used his telephone to state their grievances to a Fleet Street newspaper. They finally freed the official unharmed when the Home Office promised to look into their case.

BOYLE, Tony .
President of the United Mine Workers Union indicted for arranging the murder of a rival.

Joseph Albert Yablonski and Tony Boyle were senior members of the American United Mine Workers Union. Yablonski was close to the president, John L. Lewis, and expected to replace him, but when the time came for a new president it was Boyle who was selected. Yablonski had suspected Boyle of embezzling union funds, and his disillusionment came to a head in November 1968 when there was a tremendous explosion at a mine in West Virginia. Inspectors of the Bureau of Mines found many violations of safety regulations there, but Boyle declared publicly that the safety record of the company owning the mine was excellent. Yablonski, although near retirement, decided to challenge him for the presidency, and make one last effort to clean up the union.

For the past thirteen years there had been a great deal of intimidation in the coalfields of eastern America. In 1955 a hundred miners visited a coal-owner in Tennessee who had refused to sign a contract with the UMW. They buried him alive in a ditch, but he struggled out. At the trial the jury acquitted them. From then on, the strong-arm gangs terrorized the coalfields, burning coal tips, forcing drivers to dump coal on the roads and shooting the union's 'enemies'. In the long run it did them no good. After a strike involving heavy intimidation in Kentucky in 1959, many mines were forced to close down, and the operators were awarded $1.5 million damages to be paid by the UMW. One of those responsible for the violence was Albert Pass, treasurer of the East Kentucky area branch. In 1968 Pass was plotting the 'elimination' of Ted Q. Wilson, the head of a rival union; then Yablonski declared his candidacy and his murder became the priority.

Pass contacted William Prater, a UMW representative with whom he had previously discussed the murder of Ted Q. Wilson, and told him Yablonski had to be killed. Prater in turn spoke to Silous Huddleston, the elderly president of the local union who had been one of the strong-arm boys. Huddleston talked to his son-in-law, a house-painter named Paul Gilly, a quiet, hard-working man with no criminal record; Gilly wanted to stay out of it but allowed himself to be persuaded into finding a willing assassin. He approached a young burglar and drifter named Claude Vealey, who suggested that Gilly also recruit a burglar named James Phillips. To obtain guns,

Huddleston suggested they burgle Ted Q. Wilson's house. Phillips got drunk on the crucial evening, so Gilly and Vealey took with them another young burglar, Buddy Martin.

In spite of a hard-fought campaign, Yablonski lost the election. He was convinced that Boyle had won dishonestly, and prepared to challenge the result in the courts. Boyle, already nervous about an investigation into the financial dealings of the union, decided he must rid himself of Yablonski.

Phillips had been dropped from the gang for cheating on some burgled goods; Martin replaced him for the murder job. On 30 December 1969 the three men drove from Cleveland, Ohio, to Clarksville, Pennsylvania, and shortly after midnight broke into Yablonski's house. Yablonski was asleep beside his wife Margaret; their daughter Charlotte was in another bedroom. Martin went into Charlotte's bedroom, pointed his .38 at her and fired twice. Nothing happened – the safety catch was on. He tried to pull it off, but released the magazine; cartridges showered on to the floor. Charlotte woke up and screamed. In the next room Yablonski too woke up, jumped out of bed and groped for a shotgun he kept in readiness. Martin, his gun reloaded, ran into Yablonski's bedroom and emptied the magazine into the couple. Gilly meanwhile killed Charlotte with a carbine. Vealey fired two more shots into Yablonski, then all three left the house and drove back through heavy snow to Cleveland, tossing the guns into a river on the way. They had not been expecting to find women in the house.

Six days later, the Yablonskis' son Ken became worried when there was no answer to his repeated telephone calls; he drove to the house and found the bodies.

At first, police were baffled. Yet they had one clue. The would-be killers had actually called at Yablonski's home two weeks before the murders, introducing themselves as miners looking for work. If Yablonski had invited them in they would have killed him; but he talked to them standing at the door, and they decided against it. Yablonski had been suspicious of their nervous manner, and when he saw the car later, noted down its licence number. The car belonged to Annette Gilly. The police found the licence number among Yablonski's papers.

Now police interviewed Paul Gilly, who seemed an unlikely murderer – a mild, stoop-shouldered man. They wanted to know why he had been in Clarksville on 18 December. Gilly replied that he had been there on a 'trip', had met a singer named Jeanne, and dropped her off at a festival in West Virginia where she was due to sing.

Meanwhile Vealey had been drinking away some of the money they had been paid for the murder (a total of $15,000 had been made available), and had been talking loudly about blood money. One of the customers in the bar overheard him, and reported it to the police. Vealey told them that they needed to interview Buddy Martin, who was at present in prison on minor charges of assault, and that Phillips – the burglar who had been dropped from the murder team – knew something about the Yablonski killings. Brought in for questioning, Phillips explained about the murder contract. Gilly and Vealey were arrested. Divers found the murder weapons in the river.

Slowly, the trail led back to the union itself. Huddleston was questioned, and persuaded a local preacher to look after the remaining money for him. Then the police heard about a young miner who had been approached after the abortive murder attempt on 18 December to dynamite Yablonski's house; he identified the men who approached him as Huddleston and Gilly. The name 'Tony' came up again and again in the investigation, but no one yet knew his identity. Huddleston was now arrested, bringing the total up to five – the three killers and Huddleston's daughter Annette were the others.

Vealey decided to tell all and bargain for his life. Tried separately, Martin and Gilly were both sentenced to death. At this point, Annette Gilly decided to talk. She had hidden photographs of her father shaking hands with Tony Boyle, and when she disclosed their whereabouts, the investigators were finally convinced that Boyle was the Tony they were looking for. Annette's confession also led to the arrest of Prater, the go-between. Huddleston, disgusted that the union had not kept its promise to raise a million dollars for his defence, decided to confess, implicating Albert Pass. He also implicated another union official, David Brandenburg, who had cashed the cheque and passed on the blood money to Prater.

Prater and Pass were found guilty of their parts in the murders, and both were sentenced to life imprisonment (the death penalty having been outlawed in 1972 by the US Supreme Court.)

Prater and Pass had implicated another member of the union executive, William Turnblazer. It was Turnblazer's evidence that finally revealed Boyle's part in the conspiracy – Turnblazer admitted overhearing him order Yablonski's murder.

Aware that he was about to be arrested, Boyle attempted suicide with an overdose of a sedative; he was rushed to hospital and the poison was pumped out of his system. For the past three and a half years, since the murders, Boyle had watched his empire slipping away; he had been sentenced to five years for embezzlement of union funds (and was now in the process of appealing) and he had lost the presidency of the union. In April 1974, a jury found Boyle guilty of the murder of the Yablonskis, and he was sentenced to life imprisonment.

BRADY, Ian and HINDLEY, Myra
The Moors Murderers, who assaulted and killed children 'for kicks'.

Ian Brady, the social misfit, and Myra Hindley, dull but outwardly normal, met at work in the early 1960s and founded their deadly partnership on a mutual bewitchment in evil, specifically the Nazi slaughter of the Jews, sadism and obscenity. While it was undoubtedly Brady who led the corruption, Hindley proved a most zealous disciple; by the time they turned to murder she was no longer 'merely clay in the hands of the potter' – as the then Attorney-General, Sir Frederick Elwyn-Jones QC, MP, put it – but an active, and some might even think leading, participant in all that transpired.

Once they joined forces Brady and Hindley showed total disregard for the conventions in everything they did. Soon they were openly living together, and began to indulge their warped sexual appetites first by posing in front of Brady's automatic camera for pornographic pictures complete with hoods, whips, even a pet dog. When that began to pall they talked of armed robbery, but lacked the courage to do it. Instead they turned to murder, choosing the young and unsuspecting as their prey.

Sexual abnormality was the springboard which launched them into this final depravity, bringing in its train the abduction, torture and sexual molestation of two very young children, Lesley Ann Downey and John Kilbride, before putting them to death by means unknown. The 'kicks' included taping the little girl's screams as they subjected her to innumerable indignities, and posing for the camera on the graves of both child victims – so that they could gloat later over the sound and pictures of their iniquity, presumably in order to achieve orgasm.

Sexual perversion aside, the killing of Edward Evans – which led to their arrest – was intended principally as a 'demonstration murder', the ultimate phase in their patient corruption of Myra Hindley's young brother-in-law, David Smith. On the face of it Smith, who was only seventeen at the time, must have seemed ideally cast to play the role they had marked out for him. He was a young man with a record of violence and a fondness for drink: precisely the qualifications Brady had held before he turned to murder. And since Smith's marriage at sixteen to Hindley's sister Maureen (when she became pregnant) Brady had deliberately fed the youth on a regular diet of de Sade and alcohol. Hindley too played her part in his corruption. She drove them all to the Moors in her mini-van, where Brady and Smith discussed armed robbery and practised target-shooting with the hand-guns she had provided. Brady boasted to Smith on more than one occasion that he had already committed multiple murder, that he had buried the bodies on the moors and had photographs to prove it. 'I've killed three or four,' he said, 'and I'll do another one, but I'm not due for another one for three months. But it will be done and it won't count.'

The murder of Edward Evans, to which he referred, was an incredibly crude and bloody affair involving first the use of a hatchet, then strangulation by flex. It was carried out in all its horror in front of Smith, partly to impress upon him that Ian Brady was a man of his word but also to bind him as an accomplice for future crime. It took place in the living-room of the council house in Wardle Brook Avenue, Hattersley, where Brady and Hindley were then living with her grandmother, who awoke to the screams and shouts downstairs but was reassured by Hindley. Smith was deliberately lured to the house by Hindley, who roused him from bed late at night and first asked him to escort her home, then invited him inside saying that Brady had some miniature bottles of wine to give him. Later she tried to involve Smith in the act of murder by calling out, 'Dave, help him!' as Brady turned on his unsuspecting victim. Smith ran into the living-room to see Brady crouched over the screaming youth, hatchet in hand, raining blow after blow on his skull (the pathologist later counted fourteen scalp wounds, measuring from one to five inches in length). After complaining, 'this one's taking a time to go', Brady first tried to smother him with a cushion, then finished him off with a length of flex. Eventually he turned to Hindley and declared, 'That's it. It's the messiest yet.'

No opportunity to try to involve Smith in the killing was lost. Brady handed him the hatchet – 'Feel the weight of it' – and promptly took it back with Smith's fingerprints on the handle. All three of them mopped and scrubbed the room to try to remove the blood-stains: Smith was too frightened to refuse. He even helped Brady truss the dead youth like a chicken, knees to chin, and to wrap the body in polythene before they carried it upstairs to await disposal. Brady cracked a joke as they did so: 'Eddie's a dead weight.' When they all went downstairs again for a cup of tea, Hindley remarked, 'You should have seen the look on his face . . . the blow registered in his eyes.'

She reminisced about the time when a policeman found her parked on the moors in her mini-van. The body of one of their victims lay in the back, covered by a polythene sheet, while Brady was just over the ridge digging the grave. 'Then the police car stopped and the policeman walked up to me and said, "What's the trouble?" and I replied, "My plugs are wet and I'm just drying them out", and the policeman went away.'

David Smith went off in the early hours after promising Hindley to return next day with a pram, to wheel the body out to her car. When he arrived at home he was violently sick and told his wife all that had happened. Fearful of what Brady might do if he suspected treachery, they waited until daylight; then, armed with a knife and a screwdriver they made their way cautiously to a telephone booth and rang the police. Smith warned them that Brady was armed.

At 8.40 that morning an unarmed police superintendent dressed as a baker's roundsman knocked on the door of the house in Wardle Brook Avenue. When Hindley opened it he immediately identified himself, and pushed his way in. There he and another officer found Brady lying on a divan bed, wearing only a vest. A search of the premises revealed a locked bedroom door, and after Hindley handed over the key they found the body of Evans, trussed inside its polythene shroud. Brady was later arrested and charged with murder: Hindley was arrested the following week. As the police widened their search for the unknown 'three or four' others Brady boasted he had murdered, they unearthed the clues which linked both him and Hindley to the Moors Murders.

What kind of people were the Moors Murderers?

Ian Brady was born on 2 January 1938, the bastard son of a Scottish waitress. He never knew his father. Although his mother visited him from time to time he was farmed out, and raised by a foster-mother in the Gorbals – the roughest slum district in Glasgow. When he was twelve his natural mother moved south to Manchester, where she married a man named Patrick Brady. Her son Ian remained in Glasgow, where he gained a reputation as an embryo psychopath with a penchant for torturing other children and maiming dumb animals. He was put on probation a number of times for various offences, including house-breaking and theft. In 1954 the court made it a condition of further probation that he should be sent to Manchester to live with his natural mother. There he became a teenage drunk, and again resorted to petty crime. One week after his eighteenth birthday he was sent to Borstal for two years, for stealing. His last conviction before the murder trial was in 1958, when he was fined £1, under his real name of Ian Duncan Stewart, for being drunk and disorderly.

Somewhere between the Gorbals and Chester Assize Court Brady formed a cult-worship for Hitler and his concentration-camp thugs. By the time he met Hindley he was reading *Mein Kampf* in the original; it was this more than anything else that led her to think of him as an intellectual. In that same period his private library had grown into a revealing collection, including such titles as *The History of Torture Through the Ages, Sex Crimes and Sex Criminals, The Life and Ideas of the Marquis de Sade, Nuremberg Diary, Heinrich Himmler, The Kiss of the Whip, Sexual Anomalies and Perversions*. His views on the human race were every bit as illuminating: he saw other people as insects, morons, maggots, cabbages.

When Myra Hindley first met him she was nineteen, a heavy smoker, a none-too-bright working-class girl – and a virgin. No one would have called her pretty; she was big-hipped and gauche, with heavy features dominated by a large nose which curved down to meet an even more prominent chin pointing up. Although her school reports were cautious ('Personality, not very sociable') neighbours in the Gorton district of Manchester where she was born and brought up knew her as a youngster who loved children and animals, a girl who liked to jive at the local hop, yet never bothered overmuch with boys. In a word, they thought her normal. She was a Catholic convert and (in her youth) a regular worshipper. Ironically it was an inscribed prayer book given her by an uncle and aunt to commemorate her First Communion, *The Garden of the Soul*, which was to link both Brady and herself to the Moors Murders. Police searching through her possessions after the Evans murder found two left-luggage tickets hidden in the spine of the book. They were receipts for the two suitcases she had handed in at Manchester Central station the night before Evans was killed: a precautionary move in case anything went wrong, and their home was searched. Inside the cases the police found wigs, coshes, masks, various notes relating to bank security arrangements – and the damning photographs and tape-recordings relating directly to the murders of Lesley Ann Downey and John Kilbride, already lying buried on Saddleworth Moor.

Hindley held a variety of jobs after leaving school, mostly as an office junior. In January 1961 she joined Millwards, a chemical supply works in West Gorton, as a junior typist. She fell head over heels for the pale invoice clerk who sat in the office across the corridor, read *Mein Kampf* in his lunch hour – and studiously ignored her. Soon she was confiding to her diary, 'Ian looked at me today. I wonder if he'll ever take me out? . . . I almost got a smile out of him today . . . Ian wore a black shirt and looked smashing . . . I love him . . . Eureka! Today we have our first date. We are going to the cinema.'

There was a dreadful inevitability about their first choice of screen entertainment, *Trial at Nuremberg*. On their return to her grandmother's house in Gorton, Ian Brady seduced her. Soon they were inseparable companions and he was driving her about on the pillion of his showy red and silver motorbike. She began to ape Irma Grese (a Nazi concentration camp guard and sadist known to the British army of occupation after World War II as 'the Female Beast of Belsen'), dyeing her hair blonde and wearing leather boots. Well pleased, Brady dubbed her 'Myra Hess'.

Before long they were posing, singly and together, for the pornographic pictures which Brady tried in vain to market. Eventually their talk turned to raising cash by armed hold-up, and it was now that Hindley assumed a more dominant role in the partnership. First she joined Cheadle Rifle Club and took lessons in marksmanship. Next she persuaded people she met there to sell her the ·45 Webley revolver and ·38 Smith and Wesson pistol needed for their proposed joint bank robberies. When Brady made no attempt to pass the driving test which would enable him to drive a getaway car, she herself took lessons and passed the test in November 1963. Thereafter she acted as the team driver until her arrest in 1965, buying three second-hand vehicles in that time as well as hiring self-drive cars on a number of occasions.

How many did they kill?

To this day doubt exists as to who was their first victim, and how many may have followed. The first expression of that doubt was voiced on 13 October 1965, when the police investigating the Moors

Murders case called a press conference. Detective Chief Superintendent Arthur Benfield, head of Cheshire CID, then revealed, 'We have discussed the files of eight people who have disappeared without trace during the past three or four years. We want to find out if there is a common factor in their disappearances.'

Pauline Reade, who was sixteen, vanished on her way to a dance on the evening of 12 July 1963. Pauline lived in Wiles Street, Gorton – two doors away from David Smith, who was later to marry Hindley's sister Maureen. Hindley herself then lived in Bannock Street, Gorton, just round the corner from Pauline, whom she knew. According to some reports her lover, Ian Brady, had already moved in with her. In his carefully documented book, *The Moors Murders*, David Marchbanks writes: 'The Brady-Hindley relationship had been going on for two years, but it was only a month before Pauline disappeared that two significant events took place – Brady moved into Bannock Street with Myra, and Myra acquired her first car, a car being essential equipment in the murders Brady was to commit in the future.'

Pauline was last seen walking across open ground near Bannock Street, on her way to the dance at Gorton Railway Institute. She failed to arrive there, and has not been seen since. Police employing tracker dogs and frogmen failed to uncover any trace of her. Eventually, since there was no hue and cry at the time and the possibility could not be discounted that she had simply run away from home, Pauline was officially listed as 'missing'.

Keith Bennett, a twelve-year-old schoolboy and one of a large family, vanished a year later. On the evening of 16 June 1964 he set off from his home in Eston Street, Chorlton-in-Medlock, to spend the night with his grandmother in Morton Street in the Longsight district of Manchester. At 8 pm his mother saw him safely across the busy Stockport Road, then left him to go to her bingo club. Somewhere on the last short stage of his walk alone to Morton Street, Keith Bennett disappeared. By coincidence Morton Street lies only a short way away from Westmoreland Street in Longsight – where Ian Brady formerly lived with his mother and where he still visited, now driven by Myra Hindley. The off-licence where they bought bottles of wine before setting off on their forays over the Moors is likewise close by: it was a district they knew well.

Nothing else is known to connect Keith Bennett's disappearance, or that of Pauline Reade, with the murders of Downey and Kilbride – save for a quite remarkable similarity of circumstance in each case. All four children vanished in broad daylight from a public place in the same general Manchester area, an area known to and frequented by Brady and Hindley.

Even Edward Evans, who was murdered in Hattersley, was first accosted by Brady in a public place in central Manchester before he was lured to the house in Wardle Brook Avenue. And perhaps significantly, the total of five persons named – all linked in some way, if only coincidentally, with the Moors Murderers – tallies exactly with the maximum estimate of his victims given by Brady himself when he boasted to David Smith, 'I've killed three or four and I'll do another one, but I'm not due for another one for three months ... but it will be done and it won't count.'

To Brady's mind the Evans murder would not count because, it was not committed solely for 'kicks': it was intended primarily as the final lesson in the education of David Smith. Hindley's own gratification from the Evans murder can only have come from her role as voyeur, although her participation in it was both cold-blooded and deliberate. She accompanied Brady in his search for a victim and then drove Evans home knowing what was to become of him. She then enticed Smith to the house in time to see Evans dispatched.

The pathologist who examined Evans's body found it fully clothed except for his shoes, but with the fly buttons undone and with dog hairs on his bare flesh and in his underclothes. Since both the Moors Murderers denied almost every accusation made by the Crown at their trial, it remains open to speculation whether Hindley's perverted pleasure lay in witnessing Brady perform his odd homosexual acts upon Evans before killing him, or in watching the act of murder itself (Smith's evidence revealed that she was present in the room when Brady attacked Evans with the hatchet). This question of their bizarre sexual desires ran like a thread throughout their questioning by the Attorney-General. He asked Brady:

I think you told the court you had met Evans before. I am interested in the club which you claimed ... was frequented by homosexuals. You were a visitor there? – I have been there about three times.

What were you doing in that hive of homosexuals? – Watching the antics of them.

Was the accused Hindley with you? – No.

I thought you always went out together? 'Whatever he did, I did.

Wherever he went, I went.' – That is what Myra said. When I had a motorbike, I used to go all over the place with her.

What I want to come to is this. Some homosexual activity took place between you and Evans in the living-room that night, did it not? – No.

His fly-buttons, when his body was found, were open from top to bottom. That is because you had been interfering with him. – No.

And there were dog hairs on his bare skin and on the inside of his underpants that came from the couch where you and he were engaged in some form of homosexual activity? – No.

What attraction did you hold out to lure – I had better use a neutral phrase – to get Evans to come to Wardle Brook Avenue? – I should think from the conversation that he thought there would be some sort of sexual activity.

Later when he was questioned about the pornographic pictures he had taken of ten-year-old Lesley Ann Downey, Brady claimed that she had agreed to pose on payment of ten shillings but flatly denied murdering her. Again the Attorney-General pressed him:

The tape-recording and the photographs of the naked Lesley Ann Downey would be highly incriminating if anything with a sexual element was contemplated as a crime, would they not? – Yes.

You say that Myra Hindley was a reluctant participant in what happened to that child? – Yes.

That tape-recording is a record of a brutal sexual attack on a little girl of ten, is it not? – No. She was not undressed when the tape was on.

We hear in the recording the child protesting, 'Please don't undress me'? – She isn't protesting, she is asking.

It [the recording] was made on Boxing Day 1964 and we find it in October 1965. Why did you keep it all that time? – Because it was unusual.

Is that the best adjective you can apply to that, Brady? – Yes, that is the best adjective I can find at the moment.

For those interested in perversion and horror it was something of a connoisseur's piece, was it not? – I wouldn't know.

Worth making two copies of, for those that way inclined? – No.

The child asks you at the end, 'What are you going to do with me?' This is the child that had apparently consented to be photographed for ten shillings? – Yes.

Then 'Put it in', you say. Then she said, 'Don't undress me, will you?' and you said 'No, put it in'. – I don't think I said that.

There is not a whisper or a sign of a male voice other than yours throughout the whole of this recording, is there? – There are sounds in the background which they can't read.

There is nothing in this recording to give you any protection at all? – No, Myra wanted me to destroy it.

And you dare not let that child out of the house alive after what you had done to her? – Yes.

Brady also denied he had said all three of them were naked when the recording was made. The Attorney-General reminded him:

You said in evidence on Friday 'After completion, we all got dressed and went downstairs'. – I didn't answer that.

Is that what happened? – I didn't utter those words. I don't know where you got that.

The two junior Crown counsel and a member of the jury confirmed that Brady had indeed said it. With regard to the murder of John Kilbride the Attorney-General asked Brady:

Will you look at this photograph of the body of John Kilbride? Do you see that the trousers are pulled down below the knees, or round the knees? – I can't make anything out on the photograph.

Just try, will you? It is obvious that there is naked skin between the knees and the thigh, save for the earth that covers the flesh? – You can see something which appears to be cloth at the bottom.

It is the prosecution's case from those photographs that that boy was in some way homosexually assaulted. That was something which you were ready and willing to do, was it not? – No.

That is what you did to that boy on that moor, or some other place on 23 November 1963, was it not? – No.

The Attorney-General also referred to Myra Hindley's 'cruel refinement' in forcing Lesley Ann Downey to pose for obscene pictures while the tape-recording was made of her screams and protests, and of Hindley's 'counterfeit shame' when arrested. He asked her:

Were you entertained by the photograph of the naked child in the pornographic attitude in prayer? – No. I didn't see any of these poses when they were being taken.

Where were you? – I was in the room, but I was looking out of the window because I was embarrassed at what was going on.

I suppose the curtains would have been drawn over the window, would they? – Yes.

The taking of the photographs was unpleasant? – Yes.

Unpleasant! Is that the best word you can find for them? – No, you can find much better adjectives and I will agree with you.

They are shameful and disgusting, are they not? – Yes they are.

Who was it got the child to pose? – I don't know. The radio was on.

It is not the Albert Hall, it's a small room and you were there. How was the child made to pose? – I don't know. I didn't want anything to do with it. I was embarrassed and ashamed. The radio was on and I was really listening to the radio.

After admitting that her conduct had been 'cruel and criminal' and saying that she was ashamed, Hindley was asked:

Was this not a carefully taped recording of children's voices singing Christmas carols? – No.

This was a piece of cruel refinement in what you were doing to that child, was it not? – No.

Supposing the child had had the strength to refuse to pose, what would you have done? – I don't know.

We know, do we not, what you said when she was refusing to be gagged? 'Shut up or I'll forget myself and hit you one?' – I don't remember saying that. If it's on the transcript, I must have.

On three of the photographs your fingerprints appear. You examined them from time to time for your delectation and amusement, did you not? – No. I was shown them at the end when the child left and that was the last I saw of them.

You knew a good deal about the sale and distribution of pornographic pictures, did you not? – No.

About the taking of them? – Yes.

How did you know that? – Because Brady took them of me.

She denied that when Lesley Ann screamed and cried out, 'Don't Mum', the child was referring to her. She was then asked:

What woman could it have been, other than you? – Nobody, but it was all in whispers . . . and the 'woman's voice' must have been Brady's.

What was he doing? – I think he was putting a handkerchief in her mouth.

If she had not moved her hand, you would have had no compunction in hitting her? – I wouldn't have hit her much. I never touched her. I never harmed her.

You would have hit her more readily than hitting a dog? – No.

Time and again you were driving into this child's ears your orders, 'Put it in'. – I just wanted her not to make a noise.

Then you say 'Will you stop it? Stop it!' Did you think there was the most terrible threatening note in the second order to stop it, Miss Hindley? – No, it was a desperate tone.

Then one hears the poor little child making a retching noise. This thing was being pushed down her throat, was it not? – No.

Who do you say undressed this child? – Herself.

Can you therefore explain the child's saying 'Don't undress me, will you?' That was precisely what you were trying to do with the child? – No, I was not.

Let us see what else goes on. 'Child: "I've got to go, because I'm going out with my mama. Leave me, please. Help me, will you?"' Did that not strike a chord of pity in you? – I wasn't there then. Shortly afterwards I went downstairs to tell Smith to come up.

A little further on, Brady is saying, 'If you don't keep that hand down, I'll slit your neck.' That is why you do not want to be landed with hearing that, is it not? – No.

Then when the child was whining and you say 'Sh. Hush. Put that in your mouth again and –'. Then there follow the words 'packed more solid'. Why did you want the mouth to be packed more solid? – I wanted her to put the handkerchief in her mouth.

Why more solid? – I don't know.

That was preparatory to suffocating her in due course, was it not? – No.

She denied that both she and Brady, like the girl, were also naked at this point, or that they were indulging in sexual activities. He referred to her earlier confession of 'shame' for what she had done and said '. . . Your shame is a counterfeit shame, Miss Hindley, is it not?' She replied that it was not. Of her role in the Kilbride murder, he asked:

Your sister Maureen has said that you shopped regularly at Ashton Market on Saturdays before you moved to Hattersley? – That is what she said.

Is that true? – No, it is not true.

I suggest to you that you knew that Ashton Market was frequented by little boys who used to run errands? – No, I did not know that.

I suggest to you that you performed the same function in regard to John Kilbride as you did in regard to Evans, in that you took the car there and took the boy to where he was killed? – No.

You hired that car to play your part in a planned murder, did you not? – No.

It was from there that you and Brady picked up this little boy John Kilbride? – No.

It was from there that ultimately, with your assistance, his body ended in that lonely grave on the moors? – No. I was nowhere near Ashton at all.

Like Brady, Hindley lied to the end.

In his closing speech to the jury the Attorney-General spoke of the 'uttermost indignities' to which Downey had been subjected during her ordeal. Of that obscene photographic session, Mr Justice Fenton Atkinson observed in his summing up, 'When the photographing was over, we have that answer (from Brady) . . . "We all got dressed." It possibly casts a flood of light on the nature of the activities that were going on.'

Altogether two tape-recordings found in the suitcases stored by Brady and Hindley at Manchester Central station before murdering Evans were submitted in evidence by the Crown. One was of a conversation they had had with a child named Pat Hodges, the twelve-year-old daughter of a neighbour in Hattersley. To an outsider the conversation would have meant nothing. But thirty-six hours before they abducted Lesley Ann Downey, Brady and Hindley drove Pat Hodges to the site of their moorland cemetery and plied her with wine as they gloated secretly on murders past and yet to come. Then, when the hue and cry for the missing child was at its height, they showed Pat Hodges the story in their local newspaper and tape-recorded her innocent comments.

This was another of the 'kicks' they got out of murder. As luck would have it, it rebounded on them: the Hodges child remembered where they had driven her, and was able later to lead the police to the place where the bodies of Downey and Kilbride were recovered.

It was the other recording, of Lesley Ann's screams and cries as she was forced to strip and pose for her murderers, for which their trial will always be remembered and which aroused such widespread outrage and revulsion. When it was played in court to a shocked audience of judge, jury, press and public gallery the acoustics were such that not every word could be clearly heard, and the jury had to be given a transcript. The voices heard were originally referred to as man, woman and child; later Lesley Ann Downey's voice was identified by her mother, those of Brady and Hindley by a police witness.

On 6 May 1966, Brady and Hindley were jointly found guilty of killing Edward Evans and Lesley Ann Downey. Brady was further found guilty of murdering John Kilbride, Hindley of being an accessory after the fact. Brady was jailed for life on each of the three murder charges; Hindley for life for Evans and Downey, together with a further seven years for her part in Kilbride's death. Sentences were to run concurrently in both cases. Hindley appealed, but the appeal was firmly rejected by the Lord Chief Justice who, with two other judges, found the evidence against her 'overwhelming'.

BROOKS, Charlie
First convicted murderer to be executed by lethal injection.

Forty-year-old negro prisoner Charlie Brooks made legal history on 7 December 1982 at Huntsville Prison, Texas, where he became the first convicted murderer to die by lethal injection. The fatal dose was administered by an unidentified executioner – a medical technician, not a physician – and consisted of a mixture of sodium thipental (more commonly known as sodium pentothal, or the 'truth drug'), pancurionum bromide (or Pavulon, a relaxant drug), and potassium chloride. Brooks had been sentenced to death in 1976 for his part in the killing of second-hand car salesman, David Gregory, of Fort Worth.

Abolitionist issues aside, the execution caused considerable controversy on both legal and ethical grounds. Brooks and another man, Woody Lourdres, were both given the death sentence for shooting Gregory, who had taken them for a trial drive. While it was never established which one fired the actual shot which killed Gregory, Lourdres appealed on the ground that the jury had been wrongly selected. The appeal was upheld and his sentence commuted to one of forty years' imprisonment. As a result, Lourdres will become eligible to apply for release on parole after 1988.

The decision to execute Brooks while his partner in crime was spared aroused considerable controversy in itself; a controversy that reached even greater heights among the medical profession, which condemned the use of doctors for *taking* life. The American Medical Association observed: 'The use of a lethal injection as a means of terminating the life of a convict is not the practice of medicine. A physician who accepts the task of performing an execution on behalf of the State obviously does not enhance the image of the medical profession . . . This is not an appropriate role for a physician.'

Brooks became the first negro and sixth person to be executed in America since the death penalty was reinstituted by the Supreme Court in 1976, and the first to be executed in the state of Texas for eighteen years. (Today Russia, South Africa and the United States are the only developed countries to retain the death penalty for murder.) Minutes before he was given the lethal injection, the US Supreme Court rejected by six votes to three a last-ditch bid by Brooks' lawyers to obtain a stay of execution until his latest appeal could be heard by a Federal Appeals Court.

Following the lead given by the American Medical Association (which decided two years earlier that doctors could not administer a lethal injection, on ethical grounds) a medical technician was chosen to administer the fatal dose – supervised by a qualified practitioner. Brooks was wheeled into the execution chamber, formerly the Gas Chamber, at 11.30 pm, strapped to a rubber-wheeled hospital trolley. At that time his lawyers were still continuing their efforts to save him. Therefore the executioner, who was hidden behind a one-way mirror which allowed him to watch the condemned man yet not to be seen himself, began to administer a non-lethal saline solution. Brooks' arm was bound to a padded board protruding from the trolley, with a hypodermic needle inserted into a vein. The needle in turn was attached to a rubber tube which led across the floor of the chamber to a hole in the wall, leading to the room where the technician worked under supervision.

A few minutes later the news that the bid to win a stay of execution had failed was telephoned to Warden Jack Pursley. He asked the condemned man, 'Do you have any last words?'

Brooks replied, 'Yes, I do.' He turned his head to look at his girlfriend, 27-year-old nurse Vanessa Sapp, who had been permitted to attend as a witness at Brooks' own request. He and Miss Sapp, who were not married, had committed themselves to each other 'for the next life'. 'I love you,' he told her. Then Brooks, who had been converted to Islam while on Death Row, went through a brief Muslim ritual with two Islamic priests which concluded with the blessing, 'May Allah admit you to Paradise.'

Brooks appeared to be calm throughout. Earlier he had been

visited in his cell by an Islamic chaplain, then asked for – and ate – a last meal of steak and chips, peaches and iced tea.

At 12.07 am a dose of sodium thipental was added to the intravenous saline solution to halt his breathing and stop the heart. Witnesses said afterwards that he clenched his fist and raised his head, and appeared to yawn – or gasp for air – as the drug took effect. Then, as he sank into unconsciousness, quantities of Pavulon and potassium chloride were added to the truth drug injection.

At 12.12 am Dr Ralph Gray, medical director of the Texas Department of Corrections, put his stethoscope to Brooks' chest. 'A couple of minutes more,' he ordered. Next a second prison doctor, Dr Bascom Bentley, shone his pen-torch into Brooks' eyes and asked the executioner, 'Is the injection completed?' The answer was, 'Not yet.' Finally, after checking for signs of a heartbeat a second time, Dr Gray declared, 'I pronounce this man dead.'

It was 12.16 am. Earlier Dr Denis Bourke, a Houston anaesthesiologist, described execution by this method as a 'painless, easy, sure and rapid way to go'. Other doctors disagreed. The small crowd of laymen demonstrators waiting outside the jail were equally divided in their reactions. Some carried banners saying 'Lethal injection too easy' and 'Bring back the hangman's noose': abolitionists burned candles and said prayers on hearing that Brooks was dead. Many of them feared that execution by injection, when over 1,100 persons were under sentence of death for murder on the night Brooks died, might soon become standard practice.

BUNDY, Theodore (Ted)
The sex-murderer who killed over twenty girls over two years.

As a killer, Bundy seemed completely atypical. Said one journalist (Jon Nordheimer): 'The moment he stepped into the courtroom in Utah . . . those who saw him for the first time agreed with those who had known him for all of his twenty-eight years: there must have been some terrible mistake.' Yet the evidence indicates that Bundy holds something like a record for mass sex-killings.

Women began to disappear in the Seattle area in the first half of 1974. On 31 January 1974 Lynda Ann Healy, a student at the University of Washington, vanished from her rented room. Her bedsheets were blood-stained, so was her night-dress hanging in the closet. Four weeks earlier, in a house a few blocks away, a young girl named Sharon Clarke had been attacked as she lay in bed, her skull battered with a metal rod; she recovered in spite of skull fractures.

On 12 March 1974 Donna Gail Manson, a student at Evergreen State College in Olympia, Washington, vanished on her way to a concert.

On 17 April 1974 Susan Rancourt, a student at Central Washington State in Ellensburg, disappeared on her way to see a German-language film.

On 6 May 1974 Roberta Kathleen Parks, a student at Oregon State University in Corvallis, went out for a late-night walk and vanished.

On 1 June 1974 Brenda Ball left the Flame Tavern near Seattle airport with a man at 2 am, and vanished.

On 11 June 1974 Georgann Hawkins, a student of the University of Washington, left her boyfriend on her way back to her sorority house, and vanished.

On 14 July 1974 Doris Grayling was sitting at a picnic table by Lake Sammanish, Washington, when a good-looking young man with his arm in a sling asked her if she would give him a hand lifting a boat on to his car. She accompanied him to his Volkswagen in the car-park, but when he said the boat was at a house up the hill, she excused herself and left. He smiled pleasantly and apologized. A few minutes later she saw him walking past with a blonde girl. Her name was Janice Ott, and strangers who happened to overhear the young man introduce himself as 'Ted' later described how he had asked her to help him load a sailboat on to the roof of his car. Janice Ott was never seen alive again. A few hours later, Denise Naslund walked to the lakeside lavatory and vanished. The young man with his arm in a sling had approached other women that day and been politely refused.

On 7 September 1974 two grouse-hunters discovered human bones in the grass on a hillside a few miles from Lake Sammanish. The bodies had decomposed and the bones had been scattered by wild animals; but two fragmentary skeletons were identified as Janice Ott and Denise Naslund. Fragments of a third remained unidentified.

The stories of 'Ted' brought in a number of reports. A woman in Ellensburg recalled seeing a young man with his arm in a sling the night Susan Rancourt disappeared. A girl said a man with his arm in a sling tried to pick her up in downtown Seattle, and when she declined, took his arm out of the sling and drove off. Another said that a brown Volkswagen had driven up on to the pavement close to her and she had run away.

On 12 October 1974 a hunter in Clark County, Washington, found a skull with hair still intact, some 130 miles north of the previous findings. Police subsequently found the remains of two young women. One was identified as Carol Valenzuela, of Vancouver, Washington – near the Oregon border – who had vanished two months earlier. The other body remained unidentified. The police soon had two possible suspects. A man named Warren Forrest had picked up a woman in Portland, Oregon, persuaded her to pose for photographs in the park where he was employed, and then tied her ankles and bound her mouth with tape. He took her to the park, stripped her, and fired darts into her breasts from a pellet gun. Then he assaulted her with a dildo, raped her, and finally strangled her, leaving her for dead. In fact she crawled away, and identified Forrest – known to his friends as a 'quiet, normal type'. And when Vonnie Stuth vanished from her home on 27 November 1974, her sister was able to tell the police that a neighbour had knocked the door while she was speaking to her on the telephone; he apparently asked Vonnie if she would look after his dog while he moved home. The neighbour, Gary Taylor, proved to be an ex-jailbird with a long record of sexual assaults. Taylor, however, had vanished. And in any case, the strange disappearances of women had now shifted from Seattle to Salt Lake City, Utah. By this time, Ted Bundy was also a suspect – a woman had telephoned the police to say he might be the wanted man. But he was only one of more than two thousand suspects.

On 2 October Nancy Wilcox vanished. On 18 October Melissa Smith, daughter of the Midvale police chief, went out for an all-night party, then changed her mind, and walked home in the dark; she also vanished. Her body, raped and strangled, was found in the Wassatch mountains, east of Salt Lake City, nine days later. On 31 October, Laura Aime, a six-foot girl whose passion was horse-riding, set out from a Halloween party in Orem after midnight and never returned home.

On 8 November the Salt Lake City police had their first break in the case. Carol DaRonch was in a shopping mall when she was approached by a well-dressed young man who asked her in an official manner the number of her car. When she told him, he told her he was a police officer and that there had been an attempt to break into her car. She obediently went with him to inspect it – it proved to be still locked – then allowed herself to be persuaded to go with him to 'view a suspect' at police headquarters. Once in his VW, he drove to a quiet street, stopped the car and snapped a handcuff on her wrist. When she screamed he pointed a gun at her head. She managed to lunge out of the car, and grabbed a crowbar he tried to bring down on her head. She ran into the path of an oncoming car, which jerked to a halt, hurled herself into it, and was driven off by a married couple.

That same evening, a good-looking young man tried hard to pick up a young French teacher at the Viewmont High School, but she brushed him off. A young student, Debbie Kent, went off to meet her brother from an ice-rink. She disappeared. In the school grounds the police found a handcuff key.

Meanwhile Utah police had received the name of Ted Bundy as a suspect from their colleagues in Seattle. When Carol DaRonch reported her attempted abduction, they were able to show her a photograph of Bundy as a possible suspect. She said it was not the man.

On 27 November the naked body of Laura Aime was found in tangled undergrowth in a canyon.

On 12 January 1975 a cardiology seminar was beginning in Snowmass Village, a skiing resort in Colorado, and a doctor, Raymond Gadowsky, was there with his fiancée, Caryn Campbell. She vanished from her room in the Wildwood Inn some time during the evening. Her frozen, nude body was found not far away on 17 February; she had been raped and battered to death.

On 15 March Julie Cunningham set out to meet a girlfriend in a bar in Vail, Colorado, and disappeared.

Back in Washington, remains of two more missing girls had been found on Taylor Mountain. From dental evidence, the skulls were identified as those of Brenda Ball and Susan Rancourt, two of the victims from early 1974.

On 15 April Melanie Cooley vanished in Nederland, Colorado; on 23 April her body was found fifteen miles away; she was clothed, unlike the other victims, but her jeans had been pulled down, indicating sex as the motive. She had been battered to death with a rock. On 1 July Shelley Roberton disappeared from Golden, Colorado; her naked body was found in a mine near Berthoud Pass on 23 August. On 4 July a gas-station attendant, Nancy Baird, vanished from her place of work at Bountiful, Colorado.

In the early hours of 16 August, Ted Bundy was arrested in Salt Lake City. A police patrolman, on the lookout for possible burglars, became suspicious of a Volkswagen and followed it. The driver tried to get away. Eventually cornering him in an abandoned gas station, the patrolman found in Bundy's car a ski mask, ice-pick, crowbar and some other tools.

A police check on Bundy revealed that he was a psychology student from Seattle and had worked for the governor's campaign committee; he was in Salt Lake City studying law. A search of Bundy's room revealed nothing suspicious, but maps and brochures of Colorado – including one of Bountiful – reminded the police that there had been a number of unsolved murders of women in Colorado. When hairs taken from Bundy's car were found to be identical with those of Melissa Smith, and a witness reported seeing Bundy at the ski lodge in Snowmass on the night Caryn Campbell had vanished, he was charged with murder. In January 1977 he was extradited to Colorado.

Bundy soon became a popular prisoner. His intelligence and good looks made it somehow unlikely that he was a multiple sex-killer. He had a sense of humour. He acted as his own lawyer, studied law books, and was allowed to eat special health foods. The guards began to allow him to make his court appearances without manacles. The picture witnesses began to build up of Bundy was unflattering: a liar, a smooth talker, a man who always wanted his own way – in short, something of a con-man, yet hardly the type who committed sex murders every week or so. But the evidence against him was strong. Carol DaRonch had – rather hesitantly – identified him as the man who tried to abduct her. And his credit-card receipts showed that at the appropriate time he had been close to the places where Caryn Campbell and Julie Cunningham had vanished.

On the morning of 7 June 1977 Ted Bundy opened a window of the law library in Aspen, Colorado, and dropped thirty feet to the ground. The escape made him something of a hero in the eyes of the local youth. He was caught eight days later, tired and hungry, on Smuggler's Mountain, where he had been hiding in shacks. The pre-trial hearings went forward again, Bundy still conducting his own defence. It was his great good fortune that, in spite of the enormous pile of evidence against him, most of it was circumstantial. It *looked* as if he could be the victim of some incredible chain of coincidence. The court became impatient with the endless motions he used to delay the case. Bundy too became impatient of captivity, and used a hack-saw blade to carve a hole round the light fixture in the ceiling of his cell. On 30 December 1978 he hoisted himself through the foot-wide opening – he had been losing weight – and again walked out of jail. He went to Chicago, then Ann Arbor, then south to Atlanta and Tallahassee, Florida, where he took a room. Two blocks away there were fraternity and sorority houses for Florida State University. On the night of 15 January 1978 a female student glimpsed a man outside the front door, holding a log. While she was wondering whether to call the police, a girl named Karen Chandler staggered out of her room, bleeding heavily. She had been violently beaten about the head. So had her roommate, Kathy Kleiner, whose jaw was broken. In other rooms Lisa Levy and Margaret Bowman were lying still. Margaret Bowman was dead, strangled with pantihose, beaten and sexually abused. Lisa Levy died on her way to the hospital; she had also been badly beaten and abused.

An hour and a half later, another female student awoke in her room a few blocks away from the Chi Omega sorority house, hearing bangs from the room next door, and a girl whimpering. She dialled the girl's telephone number; the bangs stopped as the telephone began to ring, then there was the sound of someone leaving hastily. Police found Cheryl Thomas dazed and bloody, but still alive, her skull fractured.

No one guessed that the young man named Chris Hagen, who lived a few blocks away, was Ted Bundy. He was living on stolen credit cards. On 6 February he stole a white Dodge van and left town. Two days later, the driver of a white van tried to pick up a schoolgirl in Jacksonville, and her brother noted the licence number. That night, Bundy stayed in a Holiday Inn, using a stolen credit card. The following day, a twelve-year-old girl named Kimberley Leach walked out of her classroom to fetch something she had forgotten, and vanished completely. 'Chris Hagen' returned to his lodgings in Tallahassee, took a local girl out to an expensive meal with a stolen credit card, and the following day, left by a fire-escape owing large arrears of rent. He left Tallahassee in a stolen orange Volkswagen. Three days later, in Pensacola, a policeman checked the number-plate of the Volkswagen and realized it was stolen. Bundy tried to escape; there was a fierce but brief struggle, during which the policeman fired a shot. Twenty-four hours later, in police custody, 'Hagen' admitted that he was Theodore Bundy. He was arraigned on charges involving the stolen credit cards and automobiles; but the police were aware that 'Chris Hagen' had been living in Tallahassee at the time of the sorority house attacks.

On 7 April 1978 a highway patrolman looked into an old shed near the Suwannee River State Park, and saw a foot wearing a sneaker. It was the decomposing body of Kimberley Leach; she had injuries to the pelvic region, and had died of 'homicidal violence to the neck region'.

On 27 April law men held the struggling Bundy down and took an impression of his teeth. It was this impression that would finally convict him. Bite-marks had been found on the buttocks of Lisa Levy in the sorority house.

Predictably, Bundy pleaded not guilty in the Tallahassee courtroom, and continued his delaying tactics. The trial was moved to Miami when it became clear that it would be hard to find a dozen totally unprejudiced jurors in Tallahassee. Even in Miami, it proved to be a task that took many days. With television cameras in court, a detective who had interviewed Bundy for three hours soon after his arrest described how Bundy had told him about his sexual problems: how he had become a voyeur in Seattle, how he had experienced a sudden violent impulse to follow a girl on the street and had followed her until she went indoors, how he had admitted, 'Sometimes I feel like a vampire.' His 'problem' had recurred after his escape to Florida. When asked where he had hidden the body of Kimberley Leach, Bundy had replied that 'the sight is too horrible to look at'. But the clinching testimony was given by dental experts, who testified that the teeth-marks on Lisa Levy's buttocks were made by Ted Bundy.

On 23 July 1979 the jury deliberated for seven hours, then found Bundy guilty of a long list of indictments. Asked if he had anything to say, Bundy came close to tears as he insisted: 'I find it somewhat absurd to ask for mercy for something I did not do. The sentence is not a sentence of me. It's a sentence of someone who is not standing here today.' The judge then sentenced him to death. Bundy's mother said afterwards that this was not the end. 'There will be appeal after appeal after appeal.' Judge Cowart showed a certain sympathy for Bundy as he closed the trial. 'Take care of yourself, young man. I say that to you sincerely. It's a tragedy to this court to see such a total waste of humanity. You're a bright young man. You'd have made a good lawyer. I'd have loved to have you practice in front of me. I bear you no animosity, believe me. But you went the wrong way, partner. Take care of yourself.'

Judge Cowart had put his finger on the central mystery of the case. The majority of sex-killers have been 'inadequate personalities', men with a poor self-image, often of low intelligence. Bundy was of high intelligence, attractive, amusing – the friends he had made in Tallahassee found him in every way normal.

Moreover, most sex-killers tend to be schizophrenic – the Yorkshire Ripper said he sobbed in his car after one of the murders. There is often a suicidal impulse which manifests itself in a desire to be caught – in some subconscious act of carelessness which results in leaving a vital clue. Bundy seems to have used his intelligence to justify his crimes to himself. In this respect he resembles Ian Brady, the moors murderer, and another American sex-killer, Melvin Rees, executed in 1961. But Bundy killed more than either – at one point during his questioning he hinted that his actual number of victims far exceeded the eighteen of which he was suspected. (And the picking-up and killing of two separate victims on the same day – at Lake Sammanish – is also some kind of a grisly record.)

The key to Bundy's career of violent sex crime is provided in a book called *The Only Living Witness* by Stephen Michaud and Hugh Aynesworth. Although he refused to confess to any of the murders, Bundy agreed to 'speculate freely' about the killer and his deeds. What emerges is the typical story of a loner, reading violent pornography bought in Seattle paperback stores, and experiencing an increasing desire to commit rape. Bundy became a peeping tom, and his first attack took place in 1973, when he hit a woman on the head with a heavy piece of wood – when she screamed he ran away. It was soon after this that he abducted Lynda Healy, and took her to a remote place where he raped then strangled her. Bundy spoke of the 'entity', a malignant being inside him that gradually dominated his consciousness and made rape a necessity.

C

CHAMBERLAIN, Alice Lynne (Lindy)
The Dingo Baby murder case.

In the Australian winter of August 1980 the Chamberlains, a young family from Mount Isa in western Queensland, set off in their car for a camping holiday at Ayers Rock, a beauty spot near Alice Springs. Michael Chamberlain, a man of thirty-six and minister of the Seventh Day Adventist Church, was at the wheel. Beside him was his wife Lindy, four years his junior. Their two blond sons Aidan, seven, and Reagan, four, rode in the back with their baby sister Azaria ('the Blessed of God') alongside in her carry-cot. There was nothing to suggest that this was the start of a nightmare journey destined to end two years later in the country's 'trial of the century' – with Lindy Chamberlain the central figure in what became known throughout the English-speaking world as the Dingo Baby murder case.

According to Mrs Chamberlain a dingo – a wild dog which normally preys on lambs and rabbits – entered the tent where Azaria lay sleeping on the second night of the holiday, seized the infant in its powerful jaws and vanished with her into the darkness. It happened, she said, after the family had spent a day's carefree climbing round Ayers Rock, a huge redstone pile towering three quarters of a mile high above the outback scrub; a lonely, spooky place which by bizarre coincidence (according to folklore) was once the lair of a giant dingo that preyed on unsuspecting Aborigine families. Lindy Chamberlain told the police she had put the baby to bed soon after they got back to the camp-site, and that the two boys followed later. Then, while she and her husband were preparing an evening meal, they heard a sound from the tent. 'Is that Bubby crying?' asked the pastor: and when she went to investigate, said Lindy, she suddenly saw a dingo race out from the tent apparently carrying something in its mouth. 'It took fright and ran in front of our car,' she claimed. 'But I didn't sort of keep looking at it, I dived straight for the tent to see what had made the baby cry. And when I got in her blankets were scattered from one end of the tent to the other.'

Mrs Judith West, another camper sleeping in a nearby tent, said she heard Lindy cry out, 'My God, the dingo's got my baby!' As soon as Mr Chamberlain discovered what had happened he ran through the camp-site, calling for volunteers to help him search for the missing child. Three hundred men and women using torches clambered over the mist-shrouded slopes of Ayers Rock throughout the night, but found no trace of Azaria. The Chamberlains gave their statements to Northern Territory police, broke off their holiday, and made their way back to Mount Isa. The official search for their baby continued. And although Azaria's body was never found, her blood-stained, torn clothing was recovered one week later – near a dingo's lair, some three miles from the camp-site.

At a televised inquest in February 1981 – televised because of the immense nationwide concern and speculation arising from the baby's disappearance – Alice Springs coroner Denis Barritt found that the child had indeed been taken by a dingo, and that neither parent was responsible.

Northern Territory chief minister Paul Everingham then stepped in, and ordered the police to re-open the investigation. Dr Kenneth Brown, a forensic scientist from Adelaide, was not satisfied that holes found in the baby's clothing had been caused by dingo bites. He therefore called for a second opinion and Professor James Cameron, the eminent London pathologist, flew to Australia to conduct his own examination. He concluded from the blood pattern on the clothing that the baby's throat had been slit. After consultation with another London colleague, Bernard Sims, who had previously dealt with a number of cases involving dog-bites on flesh and clothing, Professor Cameron challenged the theory that an animal had taken the baby. Coroner Barritt's findings were quashed and a second inquest was opened in February 1982. As a result both the Chamberlains were committed for trial at Darwin, beginning on 13 September. Mrs Chamberlain stood charged with her daughter's murder, Mr Chamberlain as an accessory after the fact.

It was a trial which aroused remarkable interest, not only in Australia but also abroad. Four books on the case were being prepared as it began. So many pressmen wanted seats that the overspill had to follow proceedings on closed-circuit television.

Chief Prosecutor Ian Barker, QC, told the jury that Lindy's story of a wild dog snatching her baby was 'a fanciful invention'. The prosecution's case, he said, was that she herself had cut the child's throat some time on the night of 17 August 1980, as she sat with

Azaria in the front seat of the family car on that camping holiday. He said forensic evidence would show that Azaria's throat had been cut – not savaged by a dingo's teeth – and that her blood-stained clothing found lying three miles away had been cut by an implement – possibly a pair of scissors – and not animal teeth. He also claimed that the traces of blood found inside the tent had been left by Mrs Chamberlain, *after* she had murdered her daughter. Tests showed, he said, that the blood in question was that of a child less than six months old, but that the amounts involved were so small they were inconsistent with her story that a dingo had run off with the baby. Furthermore, he told the jury, no traces of saliva had been found on the clothing; something which the scientists would have normally expected to find if a wild dog had carried Azaria in its jaws over those three miles.

'It was murder,' he insisted. 'It was her mother, and there is no room for any other reasonable hypothesis.' Afterwards he said, the body was probably placed in a camera bag, hidden for a time, then dug up and reburied.

Equally eminent forensic experts called by the defence gave totally conflicting evidence in support of the dingo theory; so that the judge warned the jury in his summing-up to treat the evidence given by the differing experts with caution. 'We are not treading in the ground of unequivocal, unchallenged scientific opinion . . . To the contrary, the scientific opinion on these vital issues is divided.' In the event, the jury were out for six and a half hours at the end of a trial which lasted seven weeks, and their verdict was unanimous. Lindy Chamberlain was guilty of murdering her baby daughter, her husband the pastor of being an accessory after the fact.

Lindy Chamberlain was sentenced first. To her Mr Justice Muirhead said, 'There is only one sentence I can pass upon you. That sentence is you will be imprisoned with hard labour for life.'

It was a sentence which shocked many people in Australia and abroad by its severity. Lindy Chamberlain, then thirty-four years old and huge with child, was due to give birth within a matter of days as she was led away to begin that life sentence in Berrimah Jail. Her husband, who had spent the night free on bail, looked pale and drawn as he stood in the dock next day awaiting sentence in his turn. He heard his counsel plead for leniency, saying that he would 'never again be a private person, never again practice as a pastor of the Seventh Day Adventist Church'. Counsel added that it would be intolerable for the family's two sons if their father was sent to jail too. 'They need their father and he needs them.'

Perhaps surprisingly in view of the sentence passed on Mrs Chamberlain, the judge agreed. He gave Mr Chamberlain a suspended sentence of eighteen months' hard labour and placed him on a three-year good behaviour bond of 500 Australian dollars (then worth about US $540 or £300 sterling), and remarked that such a sentence was 'appropriate and in the best interests of justice'. Mr Chamberlain wept openly before he was led away to be reunited with his two boys.

The trial was over, but many questions were unresolved. Lindy Chamberlain never once wavered from her story that she saw a dingo rush out from the tent seconds before she discovered that her baby was missing. The prosecution admitted, 'Precisely *how* she killed the child ... is not clear' – since no body or murder weapon had been found. Even more important, perhaps, was the fact that the prosecution was unable to suggest any motive for the murder, or to assert even that Azaria was anything but a perfectly normal, healthy child. So the doubt lingered in many people's minds: could there have been a miscarriage of justice? Was it possible that a dingo had really run off with the little girl?

Mrs Chamberlain was released on bail three weeks later after the birth in prison hospital of her fourth child, Kablia, pending the result of her appeal against conviction. On 29 April 1983 three federal court judges in Sydney dismissed the appeal, and ordered her to be returned to prison in Queensland to resume her sentence of life imprisonment with hard labour.

CHAPMAN, Mark
Fan who murdered John Lennon, song-writer and founder of the Beatles.

John Lennon's unprovoked and seemingly motiveless murder took place on 8 December 1980 as he and his wife, Yoko, returned to their apartment block in Manhattan after visiting a recording studio. Normally, Lennon was besieged by fans seeking his autograph; he had no known enemies. On that night, Chapman, for whom Lennon had signed a copy of his *Double Fantasy* album only a few hours previously, came up to the couple as they got out of their car, said, 'Mr Lennon?' and then fired five revolver bullets at point-blank range.

John Lennon, who was hit in the chest, managed to reach the

foyer of the apartment block before collapsing. Yoko Ono was unharmed. Chapman waited outside on the pavement, holding his signed album and reading a copy of J. D. Salinger's *The Catcher in the Rye*, until the police arrived and arrested him. Lennon was rushed to hospital and given every available medical aid, but all attempts to save his life failed.

Mark Chapman had been in New York for only a week when he killed John Lennon. Chapman's wife Gloria in Honolulu said he had lived in Hawaii for four years previously, and was unemployed. She said that her husband collected Beatles records and had once played in a group himself.

Following his arrest Chapman was taken to a psychiatric prison for observation. He appeared briefly in court next morning, charged with second-degree murder. At this preliminary hearing the assistant district attorney, Kim Hogrefe, described the murder as a 'deliberate, premeditated execution'. He claimed that Chapman had £1,000 to his name and that he had made the trip to New York solely to kill Lennon. The court was told that Chapman had previous convictions for armed robbery, kidnapping and drugs offences. In 1977 he had undergone mental treatment in Honolulu after an abortive suicide attempt, and he was accordingly remanded in mental hospital pending trial.

On 24 August 1981 Chapman was sentenced by a New York court to serve from twenty years to life for the murder, with a recommendation that he receive psychiatric treatment. Chapman's lawyer, Jonathan Marks, had earlier objected to Chapman withdrawing his original plea of not guilty by reason of insanity, and asked the judge not to impose a minimum sentence. He said Chapman had an 'incurable disease'. He went on, 'All reports came to the conclusion that he is not a sane man. It was not a sane crime. It was . . . a monstrously irrational killing.' The prosecution claimed that Chapman had deliberately stalked John Lennon before murdering him, and showed no regret.

When Chapman was allowed to say a few words in his own defence he simply read out a passage from *The Catcher in the Rye*. He regarded the book as his most prized possession and when he was visited in jail a year later by a *Daily Express* reporter he was still reading or rereading a well-thumbed copy.

COLLINS, Norman John
Sex-killer of seven girls in Michigan.

On 29 July 1969 State Police Corporal David Leik returned from holiday with his family, and was puzzled to find splashes of black paint on the floor in his basement in Ypsilanti, Michigan. He concluded that they had been made in his absence by his wife's nephew, Norman Collins, a student at Eastern Michigan University, who had been coming to the house to feed the dog in their absence.

When Leik called in at the police post later, he was told that his nephew was a prime suspect in the murder of seven girls who had died in the past two years. He fitted the description of a young motorcyclist who had offered a lift to the last of the victims, and waited for her outside a hairdresser's shop.

Back at home, David Leik took a screwdriver and scraped up one of the splashes of spray paint; the brown stain underneath looked like blood. In fact, lab technicians quickly established that it was not blood; it was varnish stain, made by Leik when he had first moved into the house. But underneath a washing-machine, they discovered something that interested them even more: hair-clippings. They came from the heads of Leik's sons; he had barbered them himself before going on holiday. In the vagina of the last victim, Karen Sue Beineman, they had found her briefs; and in the briefs there were hundreds of hair-clippings. They proved to match those on the basement floor. The killer had sprayed paint on harmless old varnish splashes – thinking they were blood – and in so doing, had led the police to the evidence they needed. In fact, other small stains on the basement floor proved to be human blood, of the same type as the dead girl's. She was the last of seven murdered girls in the area.

Two years earlier, on 10 July 1967, Mary Fleszar disappeared; she was a student at Eastern Michigan University. One month later, on 7 August, two teenage boys were standing in a field near Superior Township, two miles north of Ypsilanti, when they heard a car door slam and a car drive away. They went to look behind the ruined farmhouse, and smelt rotting flesh. On a rubbish heap among the weeds, they found a rotting body, minus its hands and feet. Medical examination revealed that she had been stabbed to death, and the hands and feet had been hacked off. Further search revealed clothing under a piece of board – a torn dress and underwear. Two days after the body had been discovered – and identified as Mary Fleszar – a young man driving a bluish-grey Chevrolet went to the funeral home where the remains were lying and asked if he could take a photograph of her, claiming to be a friend of the family; the staff told him it was impossible. A blue-grey Chevrolet had been seen in the vicinity when Mary Fleszar was last seen alive.

Then on 1 July 1968 a second student at the university – Joan Schell, aged twenty – disappeared. She had last been seen on the previous Sunday evening when she had accepted a lift in a red car which had contained three young men. Five days later construction workers in north-east Ann Arbor found her body, the clothes pushed up around the neck. Medical evidence revealed she had been stabbed forty-seven times, and raped. Oddly enough, the lower part of the body was well-preserved, as if it had been in a cool place – perhaps a storm drain – while the upper part was decomposed.

Two male students reported seeing Joan Schell with Norman Collins on the evening she was last seen alive. Questioned by the police, Collins, aged twenty-one, insisted that he had been at home with his mother and family in Center Line that weekend, and had not returned until after midnight on Sunday. The police accepted his alibi.

On 21 March 1969, a child found a shopping bag containing a gift-wrapped present outside the cemetery in Denton Township, four miles east of Ypsilanti. His mother, peering into the cemetery, saw a body covered by a yellow raincoat. It proved to be that of Jane Mixer, again a student at EMU, and she had been shot with a .22 bullet, then strangled with a nylon stocking. She was fully clothed and had not been sexually molested – no doubt because a sanitary pad was still in place. Jane Mixer had put up a notice on the university noticeboard a few days earlier, asking if anyone would be driving in the direction of her home, Muskegon, on Thursday evening; apparently someone had agreed to take her there, because she rang home to say she had found a lift. It seemed that the man who offered her the lift – presumably also a student of EMU – might be her killer.

Only four days later a construction crew, working close to the spot where, Joan Schell's body had been found, came upon a naked corpse covered by wet leaves. A branch of a tree had been forced into the vagina. It was identified as a sixteen-year-old girl named Maralynn Skelton, known to the police as a user of drugs and a small-time pusher. There were marks of straps across her breasts, as though she had been tied up. Then she had been flogged with a belt with a heavy buckle, and beaten with a blunt instrument, which had crushed her skull. A piece of cloth had been stuffed down her throat, obviously to prevent screams. Maralynn Skelton had been on bad terms with her family; but her father had agreed to give her a lift from Flint, where they lived, to a point near Ypsilanti. Evidently she had then accepted a lift from her killer.

On 16 April another body was found in Superior Township. The girl was wearing only a bra and blouse, and had been strangled with black electrical cord and slashed across the torso; her medical report showed she had been raped. She was identified as a thirteen-year-old schoolgirl, Dawn Basom, who had vanished on her way home the previous evening. Her sweater was found in a deserted farmhouse a few miles away. Police theorized that this could have been the place where Joan Schell had been kept for several days; it was also only a mile from the site where Mary Fleszar's body had been found.

A week after the farmhouse had been discovered, a policeman rechecking the place found a gold earring and a piece of a nylon blouse; they had not been there a week earlier, so it looked as if the killer was deliberately taunting the police.

Soon afterwards, an old barn near the farm – in which some black electric cord (like that used to strangle the last victim) had been found – was set on fire. Across the driveway nearby lay five severed lilac blossoms – as if to remind police that they have five unsolved murders on their hands.

On 9 June 1969 three teenage boys taking a short cut across a field near Northfield Township came upon a woman's body sprawled on its back, and covered with blood. Her dress was around her waist, and her briefs and pantihose lay nearby. She had been stabbed all over, as if the attacker was in a frenzy, and her throat had been cut; yet the cause of death was a gunshot wound in the brain.

The police decided that the murderer was the type who liked to revisit the scene of the crime. So they ordered a news blackout, and prepared to wait. Then they learned that a local radio station had broadcast the finding of the body, and they left the field. The dead girl was identified as Alice Elizabeth Kalom, a graduate of the university. She had been raped, and the killer had left no clues.

Peter Hurkos, the psychic, came to Ypsilanti in June, brought by an enterprising journalist. He described the killer as being a young man, under twenty-five, heavily built. He added that there would be one more victim.

This was eighteen-year-old Karen Sue Beineman, who was

reported missing from her dormitory on the EMU campus on 23 July. Her roommates told police that she had gone to a wig shop at lunchtime, and no one had seen her since. At the shop the proprietress said that the girl had come to collect her wig, and had remarked that she had done two foolish things in her life: buy a wig and accept a lift from a stranger. The stranger was waiting outside with his motorcycle, which was new-looking, dark blue and chromium-plated. He was a powerfully built young man of about six foot, with dark hair and wearing a striped shirt. The police made inquiries on the campus and soon learned that the man sounded like Norman Collins.

Three days later a couple walking in the country found the naked body of a girl lying face down in a wooded gulley. She had been throttled and violently beaten about the head, and scratch-marks around the genitals indicated sexual assault. A front tooth had been knocked out in the attack, and her breasts were bruised and covered with what looked like burns. Medical examination revealed that some corrosive fluid, probably ammonia, had been poured on her breasts, and impressions around her wrists and ankles showed that she had been tied. Her briefs had been stuffed deep into her vagina. The body was identified as Karen Sue Beineman.

The police decided to keep the news of her discovery to themselves, and stake out the spot; a mannequin was left in the bracken in place of the body. That evening it rained heavily, and the policemen were soaked and half-blinded. Finally one of them saw a man approaching the 'body'. They jumped up, but the man ran away. They tried to call colleagues on a two-way radio but it failed to work. As they pursued the man they heard a car start up and roar away.

The bad luck of the police continued. They had pinned down Collins as a suspect even before David Leik returned home and found the black paint in his basement. But two investigating policemen – unaware of the delicacy of the situation – picked up Collins and grilled him about the murders on the evening before Leik returned. Collins insisted that he had been with a room-mate at 2.30 on the afternoon Karen Beineman had disappeared; he then went and asked the roommate to support his alibi; in fact, he had returned home about two hours later than that. He took a cardboard box out of the boot of his car and the roommate glimpsed various female items in it – a shoe, rolled-up jeans, and other things. Later that evening he went out with the box, and returned without it – he had probably burnt it in the basement furnace. Told about this later, the police recognized some of the items as being things that were missing from the victims.

David Leik returned from his holiday the following evening. The arrest of Norman Collins followed. When the police went to interview him, he was sullen and withdrawn until he was told about his mistake in spraying black paint on wood stains; then he broke down and cried. Placed in a prison cell, he spent the night overcome by an excess of self-pity.

The evidence began to accumulate. The police had been investigating the theft of a yellow caravan, hired from an Ypsilanti firm in June and never returned. Two men had collected it, and one of them had paid by cheque and offered his identity card. The cheque was returned by the bank, and the hire firm then discovered that the identity card had been stolen from a university student. Now the police in Salinas, California, reported finding the trailer there, where two men had left it. They also reported that a seventeen-year-old girl named Roxie Ann Phillips had been raped and murdered in Salinas on 13 July; she had vanished two weeks earlier – when Norman Collins had been on holiday in California. She had told friends that she had a date with a student from Michigan University. Collins now admitted that he had been the man who used the stolen identity card and the forged cheque to hire the trailer, but flatly denied knowing Roxie Ann. He had gone to California with a friend and roommate, Andrew Manuel. The roommate was picked up and questioned; he was charged with complicity in the theft of the trailer, and with burgling an apartment in Ypsilanti. A lie-detector showed that he was telling the truth when he claimed to know nothing about the murders.

Collins's other roommate was able to tell the police that Collins made a habit of theft and burglary; his motorcycles always looked new because he stole parts from other motorcycles. He had even been expelled from a students' rooming house for persistent stealing. Collins and Manuel committed burglaries together; yet in Collins's case, it was not because he needed money; he had an adequate allowance. It was the thrill of stealing that he enjoyed. Collins had often brought girls back to his room – two or three a week, and on one occasion, had chased a girl, snarling, down the stairs, saying he hated prick-teasers. The description of the girl made police suspect it was Alice Kalom, but it was impossible to establish the date.

The roommate was also able to throw some light on the episode of the three men in a car who had picked up Joan Schell. Collins had been one of them, and he had told the girl that he would drive her home in his own car. Collins and the girl had left together. The next day Collins explained that the girl had refused to 'come across', so he had left her . . .

A number of girls spoke of having been accosted by Collins, who made a habit of trying to pick up anyone with a good figure. (The victims had all been 'well stacked' with the exception of Maralynn Skelton.)

He had certainly not been sex-starved; he had numerous girl-friends. One said that he was oversexed, and that on one occasion when he had tried an intimate caress and found she was wearing a sanitary towel, he had flown into a rage and called her disgusting. At least three of the victims had been menstruating when they were killed. Another girl told how Collins had made mysterious references to killings; he had terrified another by asking her, as they were petting in the countryside, how she would feel if she knew he was the co-ed killer; she had felt he was not joking.

The trial concerned itself mainly with the evidence of the hairs in the briefs, and with the identification of Collins by women who had seen him waiting for Karen Beineman outside the wig shop. The evidence was circumstantial; Collins sat, morose and silent, throughout the trial. But the jury were unanimous in finding him guilty. He was sentenced to serve at least twenty years in prison, with hard labour.

The puzzle of Collins' personality remains. Like another sex-killer, Ted Bundy, he had great charm and good looks, and had no difficulty getting girlfriends. With an average of three 'pick-ups' a week, why did he need to commit sex crimes? We know little about his psychological background except that his mother had married three times, and that one of her husbands was a drunk who beat the children; she had been forced to work long hours supporting the children. (Most delinquents are children who lacked a sense of love and security when small.) A close relationship with an elder sister had soured when she turned 'wild'. She had been pregnant at eighteen and forced to marry; when Collins had found her in a compromising situation with a strange man he had beaten up the man, then his sister. His feeling about her seemed to be one of passionate hatred, obviously with some sexual basis. In beating or stabbing his victims, he may have fantasized that it was his sister. But the rope or strap marks on so many of the victims suggest that Collins was a 'bondage freak', who probably began fantasizing about binding and torturing women years before he killed Mary Fleszar. The petty criminality – thefts and burglaries – is also characteristic of many killers, who slowly become accustomed to the idea of being 'outside society' before they graduate to murder.

Roger Staples, then an assistant professor at Eastern Michigan University, verified that Collins seemed completely normal, but added that he suspected him of some 'pretty ambitious cheating'. In an English paper, Collins had written: 'If a person wants something, he alone is the deciding factor of whether or not to take it – regardless of what society thinks may be right or wrong. . . . It's the same if a person holds a gun on somebody – it's up to him to decide whether to take the other's life or not. The point is: it's not society's judgement that's important but the individual's own choice of will and intellect.' So, like many other contemporary killers Collins believed that the 'superior man' makes up his own mind about what is right and wrong. But the corollary to this is that society too has a right to pass judgement and to demand payment for the crime. Collins's tears after his arrest reveal that the crimes sprang from the self-absorption of a spoilt child rather than a 'superior man'.

COOPER, Ronald Frank
Homosexual child-killer executed in South Africa in 1978.

The chief interest of the case lies in the diaries kept by the 26-year-old killer, in which he outlined his intention to kill thirty boys and six women. On 17 March 1976 Cooper, an unemployed labourer living in the St Kilda Hotel, Berea, Johannesburg, wrote in his diary: 'I have decided that I think I should become a homosexual murderer and shall get hold of young boys and bring them here where I am staying and I shall rape them and then kill them. I shall not kill all the boys in the same way. Some I shall strangle with my hands. Other boys I shall strangle with a piece of cord or rope. Others again I shall stab to death and others I shall cut their throats. I can also suffocate or smother other boys. I shall only take boys between the ages of seven years old to about sixteen years of age. My first few victims shall each be killed in a different way, which shall be as follows. Victim no. 1: Strangled by hands . . .'

He goes on to list nine other methods, including suffocating with a pillow and a piece of plastic, drowning and shooting.

The diary sounds like the fantasies of a lonely sexual misfit. But they were already more than fantasies. A month earlier, Cooper had followed a ten-year-old boy, Tresslin Pohl, into an apartment building in Parktown, Johannesburg, pointed a gun at him, and made him accompany him along the street and to a park. There, suddenly, Cooper either relented or lost his nerve; at all events, he told the boy he could go, and Pohl ran back to his home. Later, the police toured the district with the boy in a car, but they saw no sign of the man.

Four days after the long entry about his projected murders, Cooper followed another ten-year-old boy into a block of flats in Hillbrow, and pushed him against the wall, pressing a knife to his chest and inflicting two superficial wounds. The boy screamed and Cooper ran away. Soon afterwards he followed another ten-year-old boy into a block of flats in Berea, dragged him out of the lift, and tried to strangle him with a rope. The boy screamed. When the lift started coming down, Cooper again hurried away.

The fourth attack had fatal results. On 16 May 1976 Cooper followed twelve-year-old Mark John Garnet into an apartment building in the Parktown area, stepped into the lift with him, and grabbed him from behind by the throat. The boy struggled, and Cooper gradually throttled him into unconsciousness. He then tied a rope round the boy's throat, removed his trousers, and attempted rape. He was unsuccessful, and so left the body on the staircase. He was then struck by remorse, and loosened the rope, hoping the boy was still alive.

Back at home, he described the killing three times in different diaries, adding in one: 'I only wish I can undo what I did. It's a really dreadful thing that I did. I never want to do such a thing again. To strangle an innocent boy is not a good thing to do.' In another he wrote: 'To murder someone is not a nice thing to do, as I have now found out. I really am a monster.' He had realized that there is an abyss of difference between fantasy and actuality.

In fact, Tresslin Pohl, the boy he had allowed to walk away, knew where Cooper lived. Three weeks after his unpleasant experience, he had been sitting in a cinema on a Saturday morning – the children's matinée – when he saw Cooper sitting in front of him. Cooper was evidently on the lookout for more children. The boy followed him when he left, hiding behind parked cars to avoid being seen, and saw Cooper enter the St Kilda Hotel. So when Tresslin Pohl heard of the murder of his schoolfriend Mark, he told his story to a CID officer. The police then waited outside the hotel in a car. Cooper came out, saw them, and ran into the building next door. After a chase, he was arrested. In his room, the police found the diaries, elaborating how, after killing thirty boys (including four who would be killed as 'human sacrifices' so he could drink their blood) he intended to 'start a murder campaign against women . . . I must kill at least six girls and women between about eight and fifty years. . . . Age won't count as long as they look attractive. I can either rape them or not.'

Cooper's mother revealed that he had been a problem child who had hated his father and tried to strangle a girl when he was only eleven. Cooper was hanged on 16 January 1978.

COPPOLINO, Carl
Doctor who murdered his wife and the husband of his mistress.

Carl Coppolino, a lean, good-looking medical student, graduated from Long Island Medical School in 1958, and married a fellow-student, Carmela Musetto, the daughter of a prosperous New Jersey doctor, who had financed Coppolino's studies. Coppolino became the staff anaesthesiologist at Riverview Hospital in Red Bank, New Jersey. In 1961, a nurse anaesthetist began receiving threatening letters ordering her to stop working in the hospital. These were traced to Coppolino, who admitted writing them. The hospital decided not to prosecute, and allowed him to resign. Coppolino had taken out a $20,000 annual disability insurance policy shortly before this, and was now able to claim this on the ground that he had coronary heart disease. With his wife's income as a research physician, he was able to retire.

The Coppolinos had become friendly with Colonel William Farber and his wife, Marjorie, both in their fifties. Marjorie was a compulsive smoker, and Carmela Coppolino suggested that her husband could hypnotize her into giving up smoking. Carl Coppolino and Marjorie Farber, a highly attractive woman, quickly became lovers. When Carl went for a holiday in Florida, and his wife said she could not go with him, it was Marjorie Farber who went to Florida 'to look after him'. They took several more trips together, apparently with the reluctant agreement of William Farber.

A point was reached when William Farber began to display signs of uneasiness about the intimacy between his wife and Coppolino, and Coppolino announced that it was time to get rid of him. Marjorie later claimed that, because of the hypnosis, she was completely in Coppolino's power. He gave her a deadly drug and a syringe, telling her to inject it into her husband when he was asleep. At the last moment, she lost her nerve, but even so, the tiny quantity of drug that went into her husband's leg made him ill. She sent for Coppolino, who placed a plastic bag round Colonel Farber's head, but finally allowed himself to be dissuaded by Marjorie. Later in the day, when he returned to the house, Farber was well enough to order him to leave. Coppolino's reaction was to place a pillow over his face and hold it there until Farber died of suffocation.

During the evening of 30 July 1963 the two Farber children came to Coppolino's house looking for their mother, saying they couldn't wake their father. Coppolino sent his wife, who found Farber dead. Coppolino told her to issue a death certificate saying that he had died of heart failure. Farber was buried without any questions being asked.

Two years later, the Coppolinos decided to move to Florida, borrowing the money for a house from Carmela's father. They moved into Longboat Key, Sarasota County, near Tampa. Soon after this, Marjorie Farber also moved to Florida, buying a house next door to the Coppolinos. She discovered that Coppolino had already found himself a new mistress, Mrs Mary Gibson, a woman in her late thirties whom Carl had met at a bridge club.

Coppolino asked Carmela for a divorce; she refused. At 6 am on 28 August 1965 Coppolino rang the local doctor, Juliette Karow, to say that his wife had died of a heart attack. He claimed that she had suffered from chest pains the night before, and that he'd found her dead the following morning. Dr Karow was surprised; women in their early thirties seldom succumb to heart attacks; but she accepted the diagnosis of the bereaved husband and signed the death certificate. Shortly after this, Coppolino married Mary Gibson.

In November Mrs Farber went to see Dr Karow, and told her that Carmela Coppolino had been murdered. Dr Karow sent her to a priest, who in turn sent her to the sheriff. Eventually, Mrs Farber told the full story of her husband's murder. Both bodies were exhumed. New York Chief Medical Examiner Helpern, examined the body of Carmela Coppolino, and found a puncture-mark on her buttock. It was suspected that Coppolino had used a drug called succinylcholine, an anaesthetic whose effects are similar to those of the poison curare, which paralyses the nervous system. Although this rapidly breaks down into succinic acid and choline, Helpern was able to prove that there were abnormally large amounts of these substances in the body. A colleague, Dr Charles Umberger, who had

91

developed a method for testing the fat of the buttock, also discovered large amounts of succinylcholine in the fat.

Coppolino was represented by the famous lawyer F. Lee Bailey, whose defence centred around the argument that Marjorie Farber was a 'woman scorned', who was trying to get his client into trouble. Two grand juries indicted Dr Carl Coppolino on separate charges of first-degree murder, and his first trial took place in September 1966 in New Jersey. Baffled by medical disagreements, and the complicated nature of the case, the jury acquitted him. But in the subsequent trial in Florida, Dr Umberger's evidence was decisive in convincing the jury that Mrs Coppolino had been killed by an injection of succinylcholine. They brought in the curious verdict of murder in the second degree. Coppolino was sentenced to life imprisonment. There was a great deal of unpleasantness after the trial as F. Lee Bailey lashed out at the prosecution team and the witnesses both in the newspapers and on television. The prosecution retaliated, and Bailey was suspended from practising in New Jersey for one year.

CORLL, Dean Allen
Homosexual mass murderer of Houston, Texas

At 8.24 am on 8 August 1973 the voice of a young man came over the telephone at the Pasadena Police Department: 'I just killed a man . . .' The caller identified himself as Elmer Wayne Henley, and said he was at 2020 Lamar Street. A patrolman who went to the address found three frightened teenagers – two boys and a girl – outside; one of them identified himself as seventeen-year-old Wayne Henley, and produced the .22 calibre pistol with which, he said, he had killed his friend Dean Corll. In the hallway, the body of a heavily built man lay face down, with six bullet holes in the shoulder and back.

Henley's story was that he and the two friends – fifteen-year-old Rhonda Williams and Timothy Kerley, sixteen, had arrived at Corll's house at 3 am for a glue-sniffing party. Corll, a homosexual, had been furious that Henley had brought a girl. 'You spoiled everything.' The teenagers sniffed acrylic paint from a paper bag, and an hour later, all three were unconscious on the floor. When Henley woke up, he was tied and handcuffed, and the angry Corll was threatening to kill him. He had dragged Henley into the kitchen and rammed a revolver into his stomach, screaming: 'I'll teach you a lesson.' Henley had pleaded for his life and tried to 'sweet-talk' Corll into letting him go, promising to help him torture and kill the other two. 'I'm gonna kill you all,' said Corll, 'but first I'm gonna have my fun.' Finally, he agreed to let Henley go; Henley had to promise that he would rape and kill the girl, while Corll did the same to the boy. Back in the other room, Corll stripped the unconscious youth and handcuffed him, face down, to a plywood board; then he stripped himself. Henley removed Rhonda's clothes, lay on top of her and tried to rape her; but he was too upset to succeed. He said: 'Why don't you let me take the chick outa here? She don't want to see that.' Corll ignored him and Henley grabbed the gun shouting, 'Back off! Stop it!' Corll jumped up and taunted Henley, 'Go on, kill me.' Henley fired again and again until Corll collapsed on the floor; then he released the semi-conscious teenagers, who were unaware of what had been going on.

Under interrogation, Henley told the police that he procured boys for Corll. He also reported Corll as telling him that morning that 'he wouldn't be the first one he killed'. 'He said he'd already killed a few boys and buried them in the boat-shed.'

Later that day, Henley took the police to the boat-shed in southwest Houston; it contained twenty boat-stalls. Corll had rented one. Mrs Mayme Meynier, who rented the stalls, provided the key. The stall contained only a half-stripped car. Two detectives began digging. Six inches below the surface, they encountered something strapped in clear plastic, and found themselves looking into the face of a young boy, a rope embedded in his throat. It was the first of seventeen corpses to be uncovered in the shed. One detective described the boat-shed as having 'wall to wall bodies'. Henley led detectives out to a site near Lake Sam Rayburn, and four more bodies were located. Finally, they went to the beach on High Island, and another six bodies were found. The final total of bodies was twenty-seven. Henley insisted there were at least two more buried on High Island, and two more in the boat-shed; if he is correct then Corll committed at least thirty-one murders.

Henley implicated another teenager called David Owen Brooks, who had introduced him to Corll two years previously. Brooks insisted that he had never participated in killings, but said that Henley had. Henley said that Brooks had killed some of the teenagers.

Brooks explained that he had met Corll while he was at school, and that Corll had given him candy. They had become friends, and when his family had moved from Houston, Brooks had returned to see Corll. Corll had paid him $10 a time to allow him to commit 'oral sodomy'. He and Corll had roomed together for various periods. In 1970 he had walked into Corll's apartment in Yorktown unannounced, and found Corll naked, and two naked boys strapped to a board. Corll allowed the boys to leave, and offered Brooks a car if he would keep silent; Brooks accepted the offer.

Brooks had introduced Henley to Corll, and he described how he had one day walked into Corll's apartment and been knocked unconscious by Henley, then tied to a bed and repeatedly sodomized by Corll. In spite of this, he and Corll remained friends.

What gradually began to emerge was that both Henley and Brooks had been actively involved in the murders, as well as in procuring the boys. Brooks admitted: 'Most of the killings that occurred after Wayne came into the picture involved all three of us.' On one occasion, Wayne had shot a boy up the nostril with a revolver; the boy had said: 'Wayne, why did you do that?' and 'Wayne seemed to enjoy causing pain.' Corll had offered to pay $200 each for the boys, but more often than not he failed to pay. Brooks or Henley would take boys along to Corll's house, where they would be invited to join in glue-sniffing and drinking until they were unconscious. Then Corll tied or handcuffed them to specially constructed wooden boards, and committed sodomy. Henley explained that Corll often kept them there for several days, committing various sexual acts – including using a dildo (which was found in the house after his death). One of the bodies in the shed had had the genitals removed – they were found in a plastic bag – and another had teeth marks on the genitals. Asked if Corll had tortured the victims, Henley said, 'It wasn't really what you would call torture.' But he declined to describe it.

A majority of the victims came from a run-down part of the Heights area of Houston; two of them had been neighbours of Wayne Henley and had been taken by him to Corll's house. The first killing, according to Brooks, had taken place in 1970 when Corll was living in Yorktown; it was probably Jeffrey Konen, a University of Texas student who was hitch-hiking. On several occasions Corll killed two at a time, murdering James Glass, fourteen, and Danny Yates, fifteen, in December 1970; two brothers, Donald and Jerry Waldrop (seventeen and thirteen) in January 1971; and Wally Simineaux, fourteen, and Richard Embree, thirteen, in October 1972. He killed two other brothers, Billy and Mike Baulch, at different times in May

1972 and July 1973. The youngest victim was a nine-year-old boy who had lived in a shop opposite Corll's apartment.

Wayne Henley and David Brooks were both sentenced to life imprisonment for their part in the murders.

Dean Allen Corll was born on 24 December 1939, in Indiana. His parents had violent disagreements; his father showed no liking for children and was inclined to think they ought to be punished for every misdemeanour. So Dean Corll grew up a mother's boy. His parents divorced when he was a child, although they remarried after the war. Dean was a sensitive child, who seldom went to play in the houses of other children because his feelings had once been hurt at a birthday party. When his parents separated for a second time, Dean and his brother Stanley were sent to nursery schools and baby-sitters while their mother worked to support them. After rheumatic fever Dean developed a heart problem so he had to be kept home from school for long periods. Mrs Corll married a salesman named West and the family moved to Vidor, Texas, a small town where, as one journalist put it, 'the big event for kids is to pour kerosene on the cat and set it afire'. Mrs West began making extra money manufacturing candy, and Dean took it up with enthusiasm. It became the family business. At nineteen he spent two disagreeable years on the farm where his mother had been brought up, and became engaged; but the girl married someone else. He then saw a great deal of a divorcee named Betty Hawkins, and 'kept company' with her for five years or so, occasionally talking half-heartedly about marriage. His mother left her second husband. Then, in 1964, Corll was inducted into the army – a friend later declared that this was where Corll had 'turned into a fag'. His mother married for a third time, but it turned out as badly as before. On the advice of a psychic, Dean's mother left Houston and went to Dallas. In 1969, when he turned thirty, Corll seemed to suffer a personality change, becoming morose and hypersensitive. Now he worked for the Houston Lighting and Power Company, and spent his time with youthful friends, like David Brooks, organizing glue-sniffing parties. After three years of murder, he had become tense and nervous, and talked of moving out of Houston. Possibly – like most mass killers – he was becoming subject to the law of diminishing returns.

The account of Corll in Jack Olsen's *The Man with the Candy* makes it clear that he was a man who never grew up – one photograph shows him, an adult, holding a teddy bear. His personality seems to have something in common with that of another oversensitive homosexual, Marcel Proust. And in case the comparison seems unflattering to the novelist, it is worth bearing in mind that Proust had a distinctly sadistic streak, and enjoyed watching rats being tortured to death.

CORONA, Juan
Mexican labour contractor who over six weeks in 1971 killed twenty-five vagrants and migrant workers.

On 19 May 1971 a Japanese farmer who owned a few fruit trees near Yuba City, California, was inspecting his orchard when he found himself looking down at a large hole – seven feet long and three and a half feet deep. Not far away, a crew belonging to the labour contractor Juan Corona was working. That evening, the farmer found the hole filled in. His sense of property was outraged by this unauthorized use of his land, and he asked the police to dig into the fresh earth. They quickly uncovered the body of a tramp, later identified as Kenneth Whitacre. He had been stabbed, then his head had been battered with a machete. Whitacre had been picked up that morning, and probably killed after homosexual intercourse; he had homosexual literature in his pockets.

The police began asking questions around Yuba City. On 24 May a tractor-driver on a ranch belonging to a man called Sullivan saw a patch of earth that looked ominously like another grave; it was between two fruit trees. The police dug and found the corpse of an old man. The police searched the ranch, and in an area of heavy brush, found more graves. In one of them, the body was newly buried. In one grave, the police found two meat receipts signed 'Juan V. Corona'. One of the graves was of an elderly negro named John Henry Jackson who had been seen in Juan Corona's pick-up in April 1971.

The motive for the murders seemed to be sexual; some victims had their trousers round their ankles, some no trousers at all. The killings had a sadistic element, too; the knife wounds were enough to kill, but most of the bodies had also been viciously hacked about the head with a machete. One had also been shot. The digging continued until 4 June, when the twenty-fifth – and last known – body was unearthed. In the grave the police found two bank deposit slips signed 'Juan V. Corona'.

Corona was a Mexican who had come to Yuba City as a migrant worker in the 1950s. He had subsequently suffered from a mental illness diagnosed as schizophrenia. Now, at the age of thirty-eight he was a labour contractor who used the Sullivan ranch as a dormitory for his labourers. The police remembered that in 1970 there had been another case involving Mexicans in nearby Marysville. A young Mexican had been left bleeding in the lavatory of the Guadalajara Café, his head wounds resembling those of the dead vagrants. The café was owned by Juan Corona's half-brother Natividad, a homosexual. When the young man recovered and accused the café-owner of the assault, and won a $250,000 suit for damages, Natividad had fled back to Mexico.

The defence had a difficult job at the trial, but emphasized that the case against Corona was far from proven. If the murders were homosexual in nature, then Corona could not be guilty, since he was a married man with children and known as a 'hopeless heterosexual'. The blood in Corona's car was due to a Mexican worker who had been injured. Corona had an alibi for the day Kenneth Whitacre disappeared, which would be supported by his wife.

More interesting was the suggestion at the trial that the killings were carried out by at least two men. In his book *The Road to Yuba City*, Tracey Kidder says: 'The murderer – and many think he had an accomplice – began his spree sometime in February. It grew warmer, the ripening peaches brought more and more men to Marysville and his madness grew with their numbers. Finally he was killing someone almost every day. He raged when his victims resisted. And yet for all of that, he planned his business in advance. He dug at least two of his graves ahead of time . . .'

The jury deliberated for forty-five hours, and Corona was sentenced to twenty-five consecutive life terms. No charge has ever been brought involving another man, although an unsuccessful appeal was based on the plea that the murders were committed by someone else.

The Corona murders aroused less revulsion and excitement than other cases of mass murder – such as Dean Corll or John Gacy – possibly because the victims were mostly alcoholic vagrants. But there remains a disturbing question mark over the whole affair.

CRIMMINS, Alice
Convicted of killing her two children and attempting to make it look like a murder-kidnapping.

Alice Crimmins lived with her two small children, Eddie, five, and Missi, four, in a ground-floor apartment in Queens, New York. A dazzlingly attractive girl of twenty-six, she was in the process of getting divorced from her husband, Eddie, who accused her of constant promiscuity. On the morning of 14 July 1965 the Queens Police Headquarters received a phone call from Eddie Crimmins, who told them that his children had been missing overnight from their mother's apartment on 72nd Drive. Alice Crimmins had gone to the children's bedroom at nine o'clock that morning and discovered they were missing. She had rung up her estranged husband to see if he had taken them.

The police examined the bedroom and saw the beds were rumpled. The window was open. A hook and eye latch outside the bedroom door prevented it from being opened from inside, and Alice Crimmins said that this had been closed during the night. It was, she claimed, to prevent little Eddie from going to raid the refrigerator in the middle of the night – the true explanation seems to have been that she was anxious to avoid him walking in on her when she was entertaining men friends. The police felt that Alice Crimmins was taking the disappearance of the children rather coolly. She said she had put them to bed at nine the previous evening, and that she had finally gone to bed herself at 4 am.

That afternoon, Missi's body was found on a vacant lot on 162nd Street. There were signs of asphyxia and strangulation. Medical examination revealed that the food in her stomach was virtually undigested, which suggested that she had died some time shortly after 9 pm the previous evening, and not after 4 am, which was the last time Alice Crimmins claimed to have seen her alive.

When the boy's body was eventually found, more than a week later, it was lying among vegetation on an area of barren ground by the expressway, and was in an advanced state of decomposition, so that cause of death could not be ascertained.

When Alice Crimmins refused to take a lie-detector test, she was regarded by the police as prime suspect. One of her men friends, Joseph Rorech, a building contractor, admitted that she had confessed to the killings during a night spent with him in a motel. At the trial, he also provided the motive when he revealed that she had said she would prefer to see the children dead rather than let her husband get custody of them. A neighbour, Mrs Earomirski, testified that she had looked out of her window at about 2 am on the morning of the disappearance, and saw a man and a woman carrying a bundle of blankets and leading a small boy by the hand. The man threw the bundle into the back seat, and the woman said, 'My God, don't throw her like that.' As Mrs Earomirski started to close her window, the rusty hinge squeaked and the woman said, 'Somebody's seen us.' She identified the woman as Mrs Crimmins.

As increasing evidence about Alice's lovers came to light, the case attracted widespread attention – although, as the judge cautioned the jury, 'We are not trying Mrs Crimmins's morals.' She was tried only for the murder of Missi, and the verdict of the jury was 'guilty of first-degree manslaughter'. She was sentenced to between five and twenty years' detention at the New York State Prison for Women. She was quickly released on bail and her lawyer appealed. The three judges of the Appellate Court quashed the sentence and ordered a new trial. During this trial, Alice Crimmins frequently screamed hysterical abuse at witnesses (as she had during the first one). This time, she was also tried for the murder of her son Eddie. She was found guilty of first-degree murder of the boy and first-degree manslaughter of the girl. This time, she was sentenced to life imprisonment. Ironically, if she had accepted the sentence of the first trial, she would have been out of prison shortly after the time of her second trial.

There were still more appeals, and after two years, she was released on bail again. Early in 1975, the New York State Court of Appeals upheld the dismissal of the charge that she murdered Eddie but returned her conviction for the manslaughter of her daughter to the Appellate Court. In January 1976 she was transferred to a residential work release facility in Harlem, where she took a secretarial job.

D

DeSALVO, Albert Henry
The maniac who reduced Boston to near-panic in the early 1960s as the Boston Strangler.

Albert H. DeSalvo, a teetotaller and non-smoker with an insatiable sex-drive, was the self-confessed Boston Strangler who raped or sexually abused and killed thirteen women within the space of only eighteen months . . . yet he was never charged with murder.

Instead he was sentenced in 1967 to life imprisonment for a series of lesser sex offences and burglaries committed earlier, at a time when he was known to the police simply as the 'Green Man' (because he wore trousers of that colour when committing the offences). The reason: there was no evidence against him on any of the thirteen murder charges other than his own voluntary confession. But for any mental patient to be judged competent to plead in a court of law – and repeat such a confession without some form of legal safeguard – would have denied him the automatic defence of a plea of insanity. So a compromise was agreed by the authorities and his defence counsel, both of whom accepted that he had to be locked away for life in the interests of public safety.

Albert DeSalvo was born in Chelsea, Massachusetts, in 1931, the third of six children. He hated and feared his father, who regularly beat his wife and children and was twice imprisoned before Mrs DeSalvo divorced him in 1944. As a teenager, Albert DeSalvo had a police record for breaking and entering. He joined the army at seventeen and served in Germany with the occupation forces, where he met and married his wife Irmgard, a Frankfurt girl. Small but strongly built, DeSalvo won the US Army European middleweight boxing championship before returning to the United States to await discharge. It was at Fort Dix, in January 1955, that he was charged with his first sex offence – the molestation of a nine-year-old girl. However the girl's mother refused to press charges because of the publicity involved, and the case was not pursued. The army accordingly took no action, and DeSalvo was honourably discharged in 1956.

There were always problems with his wife over sex, even before his arrest. DeSalvo sought intercourse five or six times a day, and because Irmgard objected he considered her frigid. Although protesting always that he loved her, he felt driven to look elsewhere for sexual satisfaction. The child he had molested in 1955 was the first outward sign of his emergent problem, and that problem grew worse after the birth of his first child in 1958. He was also short of money: in that same year he was given a suspended sentence for breaking and entering. One month later he was arrested again and given another suspended sentence. All the time he was being troubled by his insatiable sex urge: so he became the 'Measuring Man'.

This was the name given by the police to the unknown man who smooth-talked his way into countless apartments and told the women he encountered he was from a modelling agency. If they showed the slightest interest he proceeded to measure their vital statistics with his pocket tape, touching them physically whenever and wherever possible but attacking none. The interview always ended with a promise from DeSalvo that an executive from the agency would be along soon to sign up the woman. None ever came, of course. Some of the women complained, but not all: DeSalvo was to boast later of many easy conquests and much willing cooperation.

Then on 17 March 1960 police in Cambridge, Mass., chased and caught a man they thought was an escaping burglar. They found gloves and the tailor's tape in his possession, and recovered a screwdriver he had thrown away. Under questioning he confessed to being the 'Measuring Man', and said he had taken the idea from a TV programme: but the suspicion that he was 'casing' apartments prior to burglary remained. He was charged with attempted breaking and entering, and various other counts of assault and battery and 'lewd and lascivious' behaviour. He was found guilty only of attempted breaking and entering, for which he was sentenced to two years' imprisonment. And, since he had no conviction for any sexual offence, he was listed thereafter as a 'B & E' criminal, an error which was to cost the State dear when he was eventually released.

With good conduct he served only eleven months in jail, but they were eleven months of increasing sexual frustration. Worse was to follow. When he was released his wife refused to resume marital relations until such time as he proved himself a reformed character: and in desperation he now became the 'Green Man'. This Green Man was a more demanding and violent offender than the Measuring Man, and travelled further afield – into the neighbouring state of

Connecticut, and elsewhere. He tied some of his victims up and raped them, after talking his way or breaking into their homes and finding them alone. Again, not all complained, if DeSalvo was to be believed. He boasted later of six attacks in one morning, and maintained that in other cases many of his victims co-operated with him – including one who offered him $100 'to come back and do it again'. The police put the number of his victims at about three hundred. DeSalvo himself put it at more than a thousand, in his twin roles of Measuring Man and Green Man.

In the autumn of 1964 – by which time the 'Boston Strangler' had murdered thirteen women aged between nineteen and eighty-five, to put the exploits of the Measuring Man and Green Man in the shade – a young married woman student complained to Cambridge police that she had been bound and sexually assaulted by an intruder. The description she gave tallied with that of the Measuring Man, and DeSalvo was arrested. He was then charged with breaking and entering, assault and battery, confining and putting in fear and engaging in unnatural and lascivious acts, and released on bail of $8,000 while further inquiries were made. Police in Connecticut, who were investigating a series of similar crimes committed during the summer and autumn, identified him as the Green Man. As other victims came forward, police in Cambridge built up a picture of widespread sexual assault not only in Massachusetts but also in Connecticut, New Hampshire and Rhode Island.

DeSalvo was held on $100,000 bail and sent to Bridgewater, a mental institution, for the customary thirty-five-day pre-trial period of observation. Incredibly, no one immediately connected him with the search for the Boston Strangler . . . because his record sheet told the computers that he was a 'B & E' felon, and not a sex-offender. At first the psychiatrists found he was 'suffering from a sociopathic personality disorder marked by sexual deviation, with prominent schizoid features and depressive trends'. In layman's terms that meant although he was a borderline case, he was competent to stand trial. He was sent back for further examination, however, after he claimed to hear voices in the night and threatened to kill himself. This time the psychiatrists found him to be 'potentially suicidal and quite clearly overtly schizophrenic' – and not competent to stand trial. On 4 February 1965 Judge Edward A. Pecce sent DeSalvo back to Bridgewater as a mentally ill person, and ordered him to be detained there 'until further order of the court'.

It was that order, plus the perception of another prisoner under observation – himself facing charges of first-degree murder – which finally led to DeSalvo being unmasked as the Boston Strangler.

Four days after DeSalvo was recommitted to Bridgewater, George Nassar, charged with the murder of a garage attendant, shared the same ward while under his own observation period. Nassar realized that this man who was always boasting of his sexual exploits was none other than the Strangler and immediately informed his lawyer, F. Lee Bailey. Bailey, a brilliant young Boston attorney and former Marine fighter pilot, was already making a name for himself nationally. He spoke to DeSalvo, who confessed not only to the eleven murders then firmly attributed to the Strangler, but also to two others; of a 69-year-old woman named Mary Brown and another whose name he could not remember, aged about eighty and who had died of heart failure in his arms after he entered her apartment.

The other victims had presented certain standard Strangler trademarks.

The first was Anna Slesers, a middle-aged seamstress who had been a refugee from Latvia during the war, living in Gainsborough Street, Boston. On 14 June 1962 she was clubbed on the head with a lead weight, raped and strangled. When found she was naked with her legs spreadeagled, as if to announce the reason for her murder. The cord from her housecoat was tied tightly round her neck, the ends in a bow beneath her chin. This positioning of the victim's legs and the big bow were to become gruesomely familiar to the Homicide Squad.

A fortnight later it was the turn of Mary Mullen, aged eighty-five, and she was not known to be a strangler victim until DeSalvo made his confession. When her body was found she was at first presumed to have died by natural causes. DeSalvo had entered her apartment posing as a workman. 'I have a special reason for not liking to talk about this one,' he admitted. Mary Mullen apparently reminded him in looks of his own grandmother. 'All I know is that my arms went round her neck . . . she was so old and weak I wouldn't have had to squeeze her at all, but as it turned out she just went straight down . . .'

The third in three weeks took place on 30 June. A 65-year-old nurse named Helen Blake was found sexually assaulted and strangled in her apartment. She was found face down on her bed with tooth-marks on her naked body, the legs wide apart and a ligature made from her bra and stockings tied tightly round her neck. DeSalvo had again posed as a workman.

His second victim that day was another woman in her sixties, Nina Nicholls. Once again DeSalvo gained entry saying he had been 'sent by the super to check for leaks'. It was a brutally hot afternoon. 'I was all hot, just like my head was going to blow off,' he said. 'I got her from behind . . . she was still alive and I remember grabbing a belt and trying to put it round her throat and strangle her, and it broke. She took her fingernails and dug into the back of my hand . . . she kept doing that until she went.' She was found with her nylon stockings round her neck in the Strangler's Knot. She had been subjected to further abuse with a wine bottle after the rape. Her apartment had been ransacked, but nothing was missing. DeSalvo frequently 'turned over' the homes of his victims, but only once stole something – a $20 note from Anna Slesers' mantelpiece. On his way home on that same day DeSalvo 'felt the urge' again and attempted to pick up a third woman; luckily she would have nothing to do with him.

Ida Irga, aged seventy-five, was the fifth victim, on 19 August. The moment she turned her back on the young workman who called on her, he crooked his arm round her neck and throttled her. She was found strangled, sexually abused, and bitten on her body. The legs were spread wide apart on two chairs, and there was a pillow under her buttocks. A twisted pillowcase was drawn tight round her neck.

The sixth victim, Jane Sullivan, died the following day. Aged sixty-seven, she always kept her front door chained, but eventually let in the young workman. Big-built and Irish, she put up a tremendous fight before she was overpowered. Her body was not found for ten days, when her nephew called. The Strangler had left her kneeling beside the bath, her head dipping into a few inches of water. Her housecoat was dragged up round her shoulders to expose her body, a ligature of nylon stockings twisted tightly round her neck. She had been raped and further outraged with a broomstick.

Boston was seething with rumour and fear of a madman who strangled old women before subjecting them to the most fearful indignities. Then a few months later the Strangler struck again, and when the victim's body was found no woman felt safe. This time it was a girl of twenty.

5 December 1962 was DeSalvo's wedding anniversary and the sex urge was on him again, very strongly. He tried one apartment without success, then knocked on a door at random. Sophie Clark, a Negro girl of twenty-five, was taller than him by nearly three inches. Her

white dress and black stockings proved irresistible bait for DeSalvo, who used his old Measuring Man technique and said he was from a modelling agency. As soon as she turned her back on him he strangled and raped her, leaving behind him all the familiar trademarks of the Strangler. She was his seventh victim.

The eighth, on 30 December 1962, was Patricia Bissette, aged twenty-three. Hers was an apartment DeSalvo knew well; he had called there in his Measuring Man days. Miss Bissette, a pretty – and trusting – secretary, invited him in for a cup of coffee. The moment she turned her back DeSalvo crooked his arm round her neck, then raped and strangled her. The ligature round her neck was formed by blouse and stockings twisted together and tied in the Strangler's Knot. Her body was discovered early next morning when her boss called to drive her to the office.

On 18 February 1963 the woman who should have been victim number nine – 'Gertrude Gruen' (not her real name) – was in bed suffering from a virus infection when 'the workman' called. She admitted him only reluctantly and fought tenaciously, biting his fingers and screaming loudly, until he fled . . .

Victim number nine, on 9 March 1963, was in fact Mary Brown, aged sixty-nine. DeSalvo picked her doorbell from a number of possibles because he thought a card that read '*Mrs* Mary Brown' indicated a widow or a divorcee, living alone. And this time before calling (again as a workman) he picked up a heavy brass pipe, which he used to beat her head to a pulp before assaulting her sexually. He also plunged a kitchen fork into her breast a number of times, leaving it embedded in the flesh. A post-mortem showed that she died from a skull fracture, although she had also been manually strangled. Because of the extreme viciousness of the attack, however, her murder was not thought to be the Strangler's handiwork: that became known only with DeSalvo's confession. There was no familiar ligature tied round the neck, and the body had been covered with a sheet. The police thought she might have died after disturbing a burglar.

The tenth victim was 23-year-old Beverly Samans of University Road, Cambridge. DeSalvo 'felt the urge' at 8.30 in the morning of 6 May as he drove to work and went to Cambridge (a short car journey away) on impulse. Once there he chose his victim's apartment at random. Beverly was an undergraduate. Her body was not discovered until 9 May, when a friend called for her. She was naked, gagged and blindfolded, with her legs spreadeagled and tied to the bed supports. There was a ligature of nylon stockings tied round her neck. The autopsy showed she had been stabbed twenty-two times and sexually assaulted; no fingerprints were found on the jack-knife the killer had left behind, in the kitchen sink. This too was seen at first either as the work of the Strangler, or possibly a copycat killing, until DeSalvo confessed.

Evelyn Corbin, aged fifty-eight and a divorcee, became the eleventh victim on 8 September. Friends became worried when she failed to keep a luncheon appointment, and entered her apartment, only to find that the Strangler had been there before them. Evelyn Corbin lay on the bed with the top half of her body covered by a bed-spread. Two nylon stockings were knotted round her throat. Her legs were spreadeagled to leave her exposed, and a third stocking had been tied in a bow round her left ankle. The post-mortem showed that she had been manually strangled.

This murder coming on top of all the others caused such a public outcry that the state was forced to intervene, and a 'Strangler bureau' was set up. But the murders continued and a feeling of near panic began to grip the citizens of Boston. Husbands rang home a score of times a day to make sure all was well. The police, already working to capacity, were inundated with calls from terrified women. But no one seemed able to prevent the killer from going about his awful business; he just entered apartments at will and left again, without being seen or leaving a clue to his identity.

On 23 November 1963 – the day after President Kennedy was assassinated – Joann Graff, a 23-year-old pattern designer and Sunday-school teacher from Lawrence, was murdered. As always DeSalvo talked his way in as a workman, then threatened Joann with a knife before raping and strangling her. A ligature made from nylon stockings and a black leotard was found tied round her neck. After killing her DeSalvo drove home to help his wife wash up, then played with his two children and watched TV before going to bed. The news of Joann Graff's murder was given in a news flash as he watched. 'I knew it was me who did it, but why I did it and everything else I don't know ... I wasn't excited, I didn't think about it; I sat down to dinner and I didn't think about it at all.'

The last victim, on 4 January 1964, was Mary Sullivan, aged nineteen, of Charles Street, Boston. DeSalvo struck her with his fists, threatened her with a knife, stripped her, tied her up and raped her; then strangled her as he sat on her hands. 'Her eyes was still open, and she was looking like she was surprised and even disappointed with the way I had treated her. She was a good person . . . and yet I did all those things to her.' As always, he left the legs spreadeagled and the stockings knotted tightly round her throat. His final act of madness was to thrust a broom handle into her dead body and to place a greetings card he found in the apartment against her right foot. It read 'Happy New Year.'

F. Lee Bailey played the taped confession back to detectives of the Strangler Squad, after first varying the speed of the playback so that his voice could not be identified. DeSalvo's story included details of the various murder apartments, and of the sexual assaults involved. He also revealed that he had chosen all his victims at random, and that the bow he tied in each ligature – the Strangler's Knot – was the same kind he always tied, even when applying bandages to his daughter Judy's crippled hip.

A tyro might think this would spell the end of the case; but in murder nothing is as simple and straightforward as it may seem on the surface. The Strangler Squad had other likely suspects under review, and it is a fact that a recurring feature in every notorious murder investigation is the number of 'confessions' made by cranks who merely crave to be noticed. What was more, the police knew that DeSalvo had made no such confession when he was questioned as a suspect in the Measuring Man and Green Man investigations. There were even some psychiatrists and police who wondered if Nassar himself might not be the Strangler. Unlike DeSalvo Nassar was facing a charge of first-degree murder. He was regarded as a ruthless, cunning schizophrenic. Was it possible that he might have persuaded the boastful DeSalvo to 'confess' to the Strangler murders, so that he, Nassar, could hope for leniency when the time came for his own case to be heard?

There were other problems facing the Strangler Squad, too. Key witnesses who saw a man believed to be the Strangler in or near the apartments of his last two victims, Joann Graff and Mary Sullivan, were unable to identify Albert DeSalvo as that person. Likewise the one who got away – 'Gertrude Gruen', who fought off the Strangler when he tried to murder her in 1963 – was unable to identify DeSalvo as her assailant; worse, she was inclined to think that George Nassar was the killer. She had suffered from partial memory blackout as a result of her ordeal, which left her unable to recall the most vital clue of all – the Strangler's face.

F. Lee Bailey, who had been asked by DeSalvo to represent him as well as Nassar, tried repeatedly to convince the authorities that his client DeSalvo was indeed the man they sought; not to have him punished, but so that the public could be protected while DeSalvo received the medical treatment he so urgently needed. But there were other problems to overcome, apart from those of identification. DeSalvo's own memory of events was occasionally at odds with the medical evidence – not surprisingly, perhaps, in a man who admitted to more than a thousand sexual assaults as well as the thirteen murders. However, such discrepancies underlined the possibility that there could have been more than one Strangler at work between 1962 and 1964, since no fingerprints were ever found. Finally there was the knowledge that Albert DeSalvo was a mental patient, committed by judge's order to a state institution. As such he had certain legal rights which had to be fully observed, if he was to be brought before a court of law to answer for the Strangler murders.

If for instance he was found to be telling the truth in all thirteen cases (by relating facts which could only be known to the murderer) and ruled competent to stand trial, he would then have to be examined by psychiatrists to determine if he was sane at the time the offences were committed. If he was not, then his defence was assured; he could be committed to prison or an institution. If however the experts should declare him sane at the time then his lawyer would be duty bound to forbid DeSalvo to repeat his confession in open court. To do so would be to deprive him of a defence in law – while paradoxically, without that confession the state would have no case.

Eventually, after much wheeler-dealing between all the interested parties, an acceptable formula was finally agreed. Albert DeSalvo would stand trial only for offences committed as the Green Man. Evidence concerning his mental condition would then be given by state psychiatrists – and if they declared him insane, counsel Lee Bailey would in turn allow his client to confess to the Boston Strangler murders.

The Green Man hearing began on 30 June 1966. A host of lawyers, policemen, doctors, and TV and newspapermen from all over the world, attended. None of DeSalvo's own family was present. Later, after the psychiatrists had had their say, DeSalvo's counsel asked him:

Now, Albert, do you wish further treatment by psychiatrists? – What I always asked for was medical help, and I haven't yet received any.

Are you concerned about going to prison? – No, sir. I am concerned about being helped . . . If not, what is the good of living?

Finally, in 1967 Albert DeSalvo's wish was granted and he was sent to Walpole State Prison for life. It was a life that lasted just six years more, when he was stabbed through the heart by a fellow-inmate who was never identified.

E

EKAI, Paul Wakwaro
African herdsman convicted of murdering Joy Adamson.

On 3 January 1980 Joy Adamson, the famous naturalist and author of *Born Free*, was found murdered in a remote game reserve 170 miles north of Nairobi. She was within a few days of her seventieth birthday and had been in the Shaba Game Reserve for eighteen months studying the behaviour of leopards. She had succeeded in taming a female leopard, and had persuaded her to mate with a wild male. It was Mrs Adamson's habit to walk round the perimeter of the camp each evening before dusk, returning in time to listen to the BBC World Service broadcast.

When she failed to return by 7.30 pm on 3 January, her assistant Pieter Mawson set off with the African cook to look for her. They found her only a hundred yards away, lying beside the dirt road. Mawson saw what appeared to be claw-marks on her arms and shoulders, and assumed she had been mauled by a lion (they had been heard in the vicinity for some nights). However, when they returned to the camp they found there had been a robbery. He drove the body to Isiolo and reported the incident. The autopsy showed that she had died from stabbing by a *simi*, a double-edged, sword-like farm implement. As soon as the findings were confirmed in Nairobi, the Kenyan president ordered an immediate inquiry.

Police rounded up three suspects, all of whom had worked briefly for Mrs Adamson before she fired them. One of them, Paul Wakwaro Ekai, a herdsman of about eighteen, was later charged with the murder. On 28 August 1981 he was found guilty and ordered to be detained 'at the president's pleasure' – indefinitely. If it had been established that he was eighteen at the time of the murder he would have been hanged: he was given the benefit of the doubt. His defence, that he had signed a confession under police torture, was rejected. Mr Justice Matthew Muli said he had no doubt that Ekai murdered Mrs Adamson.

F

FRAZIER, John Linley
Californian drop-out who murdered the Ohta family.

On 19 October 1970 the house of Dr Victor Ohta near Soquel, Santa Cruz, California, was seen to be on fire. When firemen arrived, they discovered five bodies in the swimming-pool: those of Dr Ohta, his wife Virginia, their two children, Taggart and Derrick, eleven and twelve, and Dr Ohta's secretary, Dorothy Cadwallader. Dr Ohta had been shot three times; the others had been shot once in the back of the head, execution-style. The doctor's Rolls Royce was parked across the drive, blocking it; under the windscreen wiper was a note that read:

'Hallowe'en 1970. Today World War III will begin, as brought to you by the people of the Free Universe. From this day forward, anyone and/or company of persons who misuses the natural environment or destroys same will suffer the penalty of death by the people of the Free Universe. I and my comrades from this day forth will fight until death or freedom against anyone who does not support natural life on this planet. Materialism must die or mankind will stop.'

It was signed: 'Knight of Wands – Knight of Pentacles – Knight of Cups – Knight of Swords.' The writer was evidently familiar with the Tarot pack.

Mrs Ohta's station-wagon was found in a railway tunnel near the San Lorenzo river; a goods train ran into it, but fortunately was travelling slowly. It pushed the car out of the tunnel, where it had obviously been left in the hope of causing a serious accident. The car's upholstery had been slashed and set on fire.

The murders caused panic in the area. There were contingents of hippies living in the woods; it looked like another Manson-type killing, a protest against the 'pigs' and the bourgeoisie. As police questioned hippies, it began to emerge that the murders had not been the work of several killers, but of one. The suspect, John Frazier, was a 24-year-old car mechanic in Santa Cruz. For some time before the murders, he had been experimenting with drugs. A 'bad trip' on mescalin had convinced him that he had received a revelation. He left his job, separated from his wife, and went to live in a shack near the village of Felton, where a number of hippies lived. There he studied the Tarot, and read about ecology and the preservation of the environment. He worked up a violent resentment against the 'materialistic society', and one witness describes how Frazier had admitted breaking into the Ohtas' and stealing a pair of binoculars. He had commented that they were 'too materialistic' and should be killed. A check on Frazier revealed that he had a police record – he had been arrested for burglary. A woman had seen someone of Frazier's description – small and bearded – driving Virginia Ohta's station-wagon on the day after the murders. A few days later, Frazier was arrested in a shack near his mother's farm. He made no admissions, and remained silent throughout his subsequent trial. His fingerprints on the door of the Rolls Royce, and on a beer-can found in the burnt house, established his guilt beyond reasonable doubt; he was sentenced to death – joining the queue of murderers awaiting execution in San Quentin since the suspension of the death sentence in 1971.

The evidence indicates that Frazier planned the murders some days before committing them. He had given his wife his driving licence with the comment that he wouldn't be needing it again. He told three hippy acquaintances that 'Big things would be happening Monday' – the day of the murders.

The police reconstructed the crime as follows. Frazier arrived at the Ohta home some time before three o'clock on the afternoon of the murders, and held up Mrs Ohta – who was alone – with a .38 pistol. He tied Mrs Ohta's hands behind her with a scarf, and took her own gun, a .22 pistol. He then 'executed' Mrs Ohta.

Some time after three, one of the teachers called Dr Ohta at his office and told him that Mrs Ohta had failed to turn up and collect the boys from school. Ohta was not alarmed; he sent his secretary, Mrs Cadwallader, to pick up one of the boys; he himself picked up the other, and took him on a visit to his elderly mother in Santa Cruz. Mrs Cadwallader returned to the Ohta home – and was met by the killer, who tied the hands of the new arrivals, and shot them in the back of the head with Mrs Ohta's gun. Not long after five, Dr Ohta arrived with the other boy. He seems to have submitted to being tied but then decided to put up a fight. Frazier shot him three times with the .38, and then shot the boy with the .22. After this he set the house on fire, and left. The Rolls Royce was driven across the drive, and the station-wagon taken away.

The charge of 'destroying the environment' hardly applies to Dr Ohta, who had taken care to leave the natural surroundings of his $300,000 house untouched. Neither was Frazier's assumption that Dr Ohta was 'materialistic' correct. Ohta's life had been difficult. He was the son of Japanese immigrants who had been interned in 1941, when America went to war. In 1943, when he was twenty, Ohta was allowed to join the American army; his elder brother was killed fighting in Europe. After the war, he studied at Montana State College, and also worked as a track-layer on the railway. While studying at medical school he worked as a cab driver. Two years as an air force doctor were followed by a further period of study – to become an eye surgeon – during which he also worked as a doctor to support his family. (There were two elder daughters who were away at college at the time of the murders.) At a fairly late stage he was able to begin work as an eye surgeon, specializing in the removal of cataracts, and became astonishingly successful. He was one of the founders of the Dominican Hospital in the Santa Cruz area, to which he gave considerable financial support; when patients could not afford his fees, he was known to give free treatment. Frazier's 'materialist' was a generous and hard-working man who deserved his success.

As in the case of the Manson family, psychedelic drugs seem to have been largely to blame for Frazier's paranoid tendencies. His wife said that he had once been 'a beautiful person' who had turned resentful and violent. At the same time, the murders showed a lack of planning typical of a disoriented person. He set the house on fire – perhaps to destroy his fingerprints. Although he had a police record he did not take the elementary precaution of wearing gloves, and left prints on the Rolls Royce. As soon as the police checked these prints against their records, they had their man.

GACY, John Wayne
Homosexual killer of at least thirty-three boys.

On 11 December 1978 Elizabeth Piest drove to the Nisson Pharmacy in Des Plaines, Illinois, to pick up her fifteen-year-old son Robert; it was her birthday and she intended to have a party. It was nine in the evening when she arrived, and the boy asked her to wait a few minutes while he went to see a man about a summer job that would pay $5 an hour. By 9.30, Robert had still not returned. She drove home to tell her husband and at 11.30 they rang the police to report his disappearance. The police investigated at the drug store, and noticed that the inside had been renovated recently; they inquired about the contractor, and were told that his name was Gacy, and that he could have been the man who had offered Robert Piest the job.

The police already knew about Gacy. On 21 March, a 27-year-old Chicagoan, Jeffrey Rignall, had got into conversation with a fat man who drove a sleek Oldsmobile, and accepted an invitation to smoke a joint in the car. The man had clapped a chloroform-soaked rag over Rignall's face, driven him to a house, and there spent several hours raping him and flogging him with whips. Rignall woke up in the dawn by the lake in Lincoln Park. In hospital, it was discovered that he was bleeding from the rectum, and that the chloroform that had been repeatedly administered had permanently damaged his liver. The police said they were unable to help, since he knew so little about his molestor, so Rignall hired a car and spent days sitting near motorway entrances looking for the black Oldsmobile. Eventually, his patience paid off; he saw the Oldsmobile, followed it, and noted the number. It proved to belong to John Wayne Gacy. But in spite of issuing a warrant for Gacy's arrest, the police still delayed. It was mid-July before they arrested Gacy on a misdemeanour charge, but the case dragged on; the police felt that if Rignall had been chloroformed so much of the time, he might well be mistaken about Gacy.

Yet a check of Gacy's background showed that he had been

sentenced to ten years in a 'correctional institution' in Waterloo, Iowa, ten years earlier. The charges involved handcuffing an employee and trying to sodomize him, paying a youth to perform fellatio on him, and then hiring someone to beat up the same youth when he gave evidence against Gacy. At that period, Gacy had been married and managing a fried chicken business; he was apparently a model member of the community. He had been paroled after only eighteen months – described as a model prisoner – and placed on probation in Chicago. In 1971 he had been arrested for picking up a teenager and trying to force him to engage in sex. The boy failed to appear in court and the case was dismissed. Another man had accused Gacy of trying to force him to have sex at gunpoint in his house, and had even boasted that he had already killed somebody.

Now the police called at Gacy's house at 8213 West Summerdale Avenue, Des Plaines, and questioned him about Robert Piest. Finally, they raised a trapdoor leading to a crawl space under the house. There was a heavy odour of decaying flesh, and the beam of the torch picked up bodies and human bones.

At the police station, Gacy admitted that he had killed thirty-two teenagers – in the course of forcing them to have sex with him – and said that twenty-seven of these had been buried or disposed of in or around his house; the remaining five – including Robert Piest – had been disposed of in other ways; Piest had been dumped in the Des Plaines River.

Seven bodies were found in the crawl space under the house, and various parts of others. In another crawl space in another part of the house, bodies were found covered with quicklime in trenches that had been dug for them. Eight more were quickly unearthed. Gacy's house was demolished in the search for more corpses; eventually, the remains of twenty-eight were discovered – Gacy had lost count by one. When he had run out of burial space around his house, he had started dumping bodies in the river.

John Gacy had been born on 17 March 1942 in Chicago; his mother was Danish, his father Polish. When he was eleven he was struck on the head by a swing, and had blackouts from then on; at sixteen, the cause was diagnosed as a blood clot on the brain, which was dissolved by medication. He then developed heart trouble. In spite of this he went to business college, became a shoe salesman, and married a co-worker whose parents owned a fried chicken business in Waterloo, Iowa. Gacy was a member of the Junior Chamber of Commerce. He was known as an affable man who badly wanted to be liked, and who tried to buy popularity with generosity. He was also known as a liar and a boaster – in short, a thoroughly weak character. Married life came to an end with his imprisonment, and his wife divorced him. (They had a son and a daughter.) In prison, Gacy worked hard, avoided homosexuals, and obtained parole. In 1972 he married a second time, and started in business as a contractor. But his wife found his violent tempers a strain. His sexual performance was also infrequent. And then there was the peculiar odour that hung about the house ... In 1976 they divorced. Gacy continued indefatigably to try to rise in the world and to impress people – when he became involved with the local Democrats, he had cards printed identifying himself as a precinct captain. In 1978 he was photographed shaking hands with President Carter's wife. He was a 'Billy Liar' personality.

He used the contracting business to contact young males. One of these was John Butkovich, who vanished on 1 August 1975; he may have been the first victim. He had quarrelled with Gacy about pay; Gacy was notoriously mean, and refused to pay his employees for travelling time to the jobs. It was probably John Butkovich's body that caused the unpleasant smell in the house during the last year of Gacy's second marriage. Greg Godzik came to work for Gacy in 1976; on 11 December he vanished. A few weeks later, on 20 January 1977, a friend of Godzik's, John Szyc, vanished; he also knew Gacy. There were many others. Billy Carrol disappeared on 13 June 1976, and in the previous month, three other boys, Randall Reffett, Samuel Stapleton and Michael Bonnin had vanished. Rick Johnston was dropped off by his mother at a rock concert on 6 August, and never seen again. Once Gacy was separated from his wife, there was nothing to stop him inviting young men to his house. Some of these – like a young male prostitute named Jaimie – were handcuffed and violently sodomized, but allowed to go – with payment. The boys who resisted were killed. A nine-year-old boy who was known as a procurer was driven off in the black Oldsmobile, and vanished. The Oldsmobile became familiar in the Newtown district of Chicago, where homosexuals could be picked up in bars or on the pavement. And the disappearances continued, until the killing of the thirty-third victim, Robert Piest, finally brought police with a search warrant to the house.

In 1980 Gacy was sentenced to life imprisonment.

GALLINARI, Prospero
Red Brigades terrorist who killed the Italian ex-premier, Aldo Moro.

Over the last twenty years Italy has suffered increasingly from terrorist activity by extremists of both the right and left. The victims, too numerous to list, include whole groups of innocent people killed indiscriminately by bombs placed in railway stations, banks and other public places, as well as many individual targets stalked by the terrorists because they represent political stability, or simply the forces of law and order. The Red Brigades, an extreme left organization, have perhaps the worst record for these offences.

Carlo Casalegno, deputy editor of *La Stampa*, became one of their victims on 29 November 1977. He died from wounds a fortnight after being shot by Red Brigades terrorists lying in wait outside his house. Unlike most countries, where an unwritten quid pro quo exists between journalists and terrorists – without publicity no organization can achieve the recognition it seeks for its cause – journalists in Italy are at risk for making what the extremists regard as unfavourable comment. Such punishment is normally restricted to knee-capping (standard terrorist punishment for lesser offenders, mainly within their own ranks), and several pressmen had been knee-capped prior to Casalegno. He was the first to be killed. And it was clear that the killing was intended, for he was shot four times in the face and neck.

Another such solitary victim was the internationally known and respected former prime minister, Aldo Moro. As he was being driven through Rome, under escort, to a special session of the Italian parliament on 16 March 1978, he was ambushed by a squad of eleven terrorists from the Red Brigades. The terrorists were dressed in stolen Alitalia airline uniforms, and included one woman. They drove out from a side street, blocked the path of the oncoming Moro cavalcade, and opened fire at point-blank range with automatic weapons.

Ironically, the parliamentary session he hoped to attend was to debate a vote of confidence in the new coalition government; Moro himself, who had already served five times as premier, was expected to become Italy's next president. At the same time fourteen leaders from various Red Brigades terrorist cells were awaiting mass trial in Turin. Their trial had been interrupted three times since it opened in 1976 (the first time over procedure, then through intimidation of jurors, including one murder, and now by the refusal of the defendants

117

to recognize the authority of the court and subsequent withdrawal of counsel). Among those facing trial were Renato Curcio and Maurizio Ferrari, founder members of the Red Brigades: and the government's ability – or lack of it – to proceed was seen throughout Italy as a direct confrontation between the terrorist organization and the central government itself.

A series of telephone calls made after Moro's kidnapping, purporting to come from the Red Brigades and threatening to murder him within two days if the fourteen terrorists in Turin were not freed, were later discounted as hoaxes. However, Moro's kidnapping caused utter consternation throughout Italy, where confidence in the forces of law and order generally had already been shaken by widespread terrorism and a massive increase in kidnapping (criminal rather than political before the Moro incident).

There was fierce criticism in the press for the failure by the authorities to respond quickly enough to the news of the kidnapping by sealing all exits from Rome. The initial search was concentrated in the northern sector of the city, where the kidnapping took place. Later – too late, according to the critics – it spread to the centre of Rome: to embarrass the police still further, some of the cars used in the ambush were driven back into the closely guarded streets.

On 18 March a photograph showing Moro sitting in front of a Red Brigades flag was delivered to a Rome newspaper. In an accompanying message the kidnappers announced that they intended to try the former premier on charges of acting 'against the interests of the people' and of aiding the 'imperialists' of America and West Germany. No mention was made of the fourteen on trial in Turin or any date set for their release. The pressure came eleven days later when a copy of a letter written by Moro to the Minister of the Interior was sent to newspapers in Rome and Genoa. In it he pleaded with the government to submit to the kidnappers' demands, saying that he was afraid he might betray state secrets under interrogation. In a leaflet accompanying the letter, the terrorists said Moro had given them 'complete co-operation' during his trial, including information about Italy's role in 'world imperialism'.

Another turn of the screw came in the release of the copy of a second letter on 4 April. It was addressed to the secretary-general of the Social Democrats. In it Moro called for quick action to help him, including the release of Red Brigades prisoners – and urged the Christian Democrats to go it alone if the other political parties refused. It was all part of a skilfully conducted campaign to try to split the Communist-Christian Democrat coalition, which was anathema to the hard left. Later the government revealed that two other letters had been received from Moro (one addressed to his wife, the other to a former colleague in the government) but refused to disclose the contents. It was a decision which served to heighten rumours that Moro's friends and family were urging the Christian Democrats to make a secret deal with the kidnappers, thus causing further damage to the fragile coalition.

Hoax messages continued to flood in to confuse the searchers. One – thought at the time to be authentic – said that Moro had been executed following his 'trial' and his body dumped in a frozen lake north of Rome. Holes were sawn through the ice and frogmen sent down to search in the icy waters, without result. Then on 20 April the Red Brigades sent a message stating that Aldo Moro was alive – and to prove it, enclosed a photograph of him holding a newspaper dated the day before. Again they offered to exchange him for all Communists held in Italian jails, but this time they added a two-day deadline. This in turn brought renewed pressure by members of his family and friends on the Christian Democrat party to 'cooperate'. The Communists however remained opposed to any such move, since they stood to lose support from all but the ultra-left.

A fifth letter from Moro to his wife was intercepted by the police on 9 April, and again the contents were not revealed. Next day the Red Brigades delivered an open letter from the former premier to the press in which he asked if the decision not to talk to his kidnappers had been taken by the governments of West Germany and America. On 15 April the Red Brigades announced that their captive had been found guilty by a 'people's court' and sentenced to death. A number of dignitaries, including the Pope and the United Nations Secretary-General joined the Italian government in asking that his life be spared.

Nothing was heard for a fortnight and then on 9 May Moro's body, riddled with bullets, was found in a car – parked symbolically near both the Communist Party headquarters and offices of the Christian Democrats in Rome.

It took the police nearly five years to capture and arrest the leaders of the gang.

On 24 January 1983 thirty-two Red Brigades terrorists were each jailed for life for their part in the kidnapping and murder of Aldo Moro, and other major crimes.

Prospero Gallinari, aged thirty-three, was named as the executioner who machine-gunned Signor Moro after his long ordeal, and then dumped the body in central Rome in the boot of an abandoned car. Gallinari joked and smiled with his fellow prisoners – split into groups and shut inside separate cages, like dangerous animals at a zoo – as the long list of sentences was read out. Nine of the accused were women. All had been betrayed by a handful of their erstwhile terrorist comrades, who were rewarded with comparatively light sentences for co-operating with the police. Gallinari did not admit to the role of killer, but read a statement one week earlier saying that the Red Brigades had shot Signor Moro to thwart his plan to form a coalition government.

The thirty-two life sentences were imposed for a series of outrages committed over a four-year period, including seventeen murders and eleven attempted murders. Threats mingled with farewells as police led the manacled prisoners to a waiting convoy of armoured vehicles. Laura Braghetti, named by informers as Moro's co-jailer during his two months in captivity, screamed abuse at repentant terrorist Antonio Savasta in his separate cage. 'You bastard, you would even sell your own mother!' she shouted.

An unsigned document smuggled out later from a prison in Reggio Calabria, in the extreme south-west of Italy, was interpreted by many observers as a tacit admission of defeat by the Red Brigades. The newspaper *La Republica*, which received the document through the post, headlined its story 'The Armed Struggle is over'. The document said, 'The phase of revolutionary struggle which started in the early 1970s on a broad wave of radical student and working class movements . . . is substantially finished.' It added that the armed struggle was 'short-circuited' and advised followers to 'seek new means of revolution'.

GARVIE, Sheila
Eternal triangle in which a rich farmer was murdered by his wife and her lover.

Maxwell Robert Garvie married a pretty secretary, Sheila Watson, in June 1955; they lived at West Cairnbeg farm in Kincardineshire, Scotland, and had three children, two daughters and a son, over the next nine years. Then Max Garvie became interested in nudism, helped found a club near Aberdeen, and founded a local flying club; he used its plane to make trips to London, Hamburg, Amsterdam and Rotterdam. He also founded a local branch of the Scottish

National Party. His life with Sheila was less idyllic than it looked; she complained that his sexual demands were 'abnormal'.

Another member of this branch of the SNP was 22-year-old Brian Tevendale, who began to spend weekends helping around the farm. Tevendale introduced the Garvies to his sister, Trudy Birse, who was married to a policeman in Aberdeen, and soon she was also a regular visitor to the farm. There was a great deal of local gossip about this odd foursome. In March 1968, Sheila Garvie ran away with Brian Tevendale to Bradford. Garvie succeeded in persuading her to come back to him.

On 14 May 1968 Garvie attended an SNP meeting, and left at about ten in the evening. This was the last time he was seen alive by anyone except his killers. Five days later, on 19 May, his sister, Hilda Kerr, reported him missing. Mrs Garvie said she was convinced he would turn up for a flying-club meeting. But when he had not arrived by the following evening, she also conceded that he was missing. Old wells were dredged and woodlands searched; Garvie's car had been found parked across the runway of the flying club at Fordoun. A *Police Gazette* notice said of Garvie that he 'spends freely, is a heavy spirit drinker and often consumes tranquillizers . . . is fond of female company but has strong homosexual tendencies and is often in the company of young men . . . deals in pornographic material and is an active member of nudist camps.'

Sheila Garvie finally admitted to her mother, Mrs Watson, that her husband was dead, and hinted that Brian Tevendale was responsible. It placed Mrs Watson in a dilemma; she disapproved of the affair with Tevendale, and Garvie had once made her promise that if anything happened to him, she would take charge of the children to make sure they did not fall into Tevendale's hands.

Finally, Mrs Watson decided to go to the police. As a result, Sheila Garvie was taken to the police station at Bucksburn, near Aberdeen. Tevendale was arrested and charged with murdering Max Garvie. Another young man, Alan Peters, a close friend of Tevendale's, was also arrested. The three were charged on 17 August 1968 with striking Max Garvie with a butt of a rifle or iron bar and shooting him in the head. The body had been discovered in an underground tunnel at Lauriston Castle, near St Cyrus.

The trial in November was a sensation. It was soon being alleged that the Garvies, together with Tevendale and his sister Mrs Birse, had formed a foursome, mainly on Garvie's insistence. Garvie, it seemed, had been making unnatural sexual demands on his wife;

Sheila Garvie disliked them, but Mrs Birse said she 'could cope'. Garvie insisted on going to bed with his wife and Trudy Birse, while on another occasion, he and Tevendale tossed up to see which should make love to Sheila Garvie first. It seemed that Garvie was perfectly willing for Tevendale to sleep with his wife, and found the idea of sharing her exciting, but objected when they ran away together. He paid to have Tevendale beaten up on two occasions.

Mrs Birse went on to admit that her husband had been to a party where Garvie had provided a girl for him, 'so the foursome turned into a sextet'. In the box, Alfred Birse admitted that he had helped dispose of some of Garvie's clothes.

Tevendale's evidence suggested that Garvie was at least as sexually interested in him as in his wife – in fact, he had said he loved Tevendale more than his wife. Tevendale's story of Garvie's death was that he had been called to the farm by Mrs Garvie when Garvie was already dead. Garvie had been making his 'unusual sexual demands' again, and had told her that if she didn't 'let him put it in up her arse' he would shoot her. There had been a struggle for the gun, and Garvie had been shot. He, Tevendale, had only helped dispose of the body. This story contradicted that of Alan Peters, who said that he and Tevendale had gone to the farm together, and that Tevendale had shot Garvie after Mrs Garvie had gone to bed. This was also the version told in the box by Mrs Garvie, who denied being 'pretty chirpy' during the three months between her husband's death and the finding of his body.

The jury evidently disbelieved this story, for they found Sheila Garvie and Brian Tevendale guilty of murder; both were sentenced to life imprisonment (which, in practice, would mean about nine years.) There was a gasp when the jury announced that it considered the case against Alan Peters 'Not Proven' (a Scottish verdict which does not exist in England).

In his book on the case, *The Garvie Trial*, Paul Harris points out that Mrs Garvie's decision to make her husband's sexual perversions a major item in her defence probably did her no good. It aroused no sympathy, and provided her with a motive to murder Max Garvie. In fact, the sexual aspects of the case caused deep hostility – there is still a strong streak of puritanism in Scotland – and during the trial, Mr and Mrs Birse were pursued by an angry mob and had to take refuge in the office of the *Daily Record*.

GILMORE, Mark Gary
American double murderer who insisted on being executed.

On 17 January 1977 Gary Gilmore, the convicted double murderer who insisted on his right to be executed for his crimes, was shot dead by a firing squad in Utah. After spending eighteen of his last twenty-two years in jail, he spurned the combined efforts of his family to try to help him when released on parole; he murdered two complete strangers without pity, while stealing money he did not need. Yet the publicity focussed on his plea to be allowed to die – as ordered by the court – aroused such a depth of feeling throughout the civilized world that men and women everywhere found themselves caught up in the unique debate; after a ten-year suspension of the death sentence in America, was it now morally right for the state of Utah to take an eye for an eye?

When he was released on parole in April 1976 from the federal penitentiary in Marion, Illinois, Gary Gilmore found himself unable to adjust to the outside world. That fact surprised no one who knew him well. A psychiatrist had observed earlier: 'Gilmore shows himself to be an individual who is very hostile, socially deviant, currently unhappy with his life and insensitive to the feelings of other people. He has a high hostility component towards the establishment.'

At thirty-five years of age he had spent more than half his life in one house of detention or another: reform school, Borstal, state prison, federal prison – much of it under conditions of maximum security, for he was a violent and dangerous man. He admitted to breaking into at least fifty houses by the age of fourteen. His last sentence had brought him over eleven years behind bars, much of it in solitary confinement. While in prison he and a friend had beaten a third convict so badly with iron bars before knifing him, that he had almost died. Most families might have written him off. Instead Gilmore's cousin Brenda, a married woman living in Orem, Utah, and other members of the family offered to sponsor his parole, but it had not worked out.

He drank heavily. As an ex-convict, crime came naturally to him: he deliberately stole from stores when he could have paid. First he stole cans of beer, then it was guns. Everything he did was predictable. Unlike many long-term prisoners, he had always spurned homosexuality as a means of relief. Now, with the natural desires of a physically healthy young man thwarted for so long, he found it impossible to react normally once he was released. He made clumsy advances to

123

every girl he encountered; and when he finally met one who responded to his own urgent needs, he fell in love with her after his fashion.

Gilmore committed the two murders in mid July 1976, three months after his arrival in Utah. The motive was robbery in each case.

Victim number one was Max Jensen, a law student working at the Sinclair service station in Orem during his summer vacation. On the night of the murder he was alone at the garage. Gilmore collected his girlfriend's sister and parked his truck nearby, leaving her in the cab. He held up Jensen and made him empty his pockets. Then he ordered him into the men's room, forced him to lie face down on the floor and shot him twice through the back of the head. Jensen offered no resistance. Gilmore killed him to prevent him raising the alarm. He then took all the cash he could find, about $125.

Next evening he drove (alone) to Provo, a few miles away. First he left the truck at a garage, claiming that it had overheated. When told it would take twenty minutes to fit a new thermostat, Gilmore said, 'Okay, I'll walk around.' He went to the City Centre Motel (next to his uncle's home), forced the young Mormon manager Ben Bushnell to lie face down and shot him through the back of the head. He then made off with the cash box which contained another $125.

He was seen by Mrs Bushnell and a guest at the motel. After finding Mr Bushnell, they called the police. Gilmore left even more clues as he escaped. He dumped the gun but snagged it on a bush as he did so and shot himself in the hand. The garage mechanic who had serviced the truck noticed when Gilmore returned that his hand was bleeding; and when he heard about Bushnell's murder, called the police.

In the meantime Gilmore drove to a friend's home and asked to be driven to the airport. When the friend suggested he should take him to a hospital, Gilmore telephoned his married cousin and asked her to help. She pretended that her husband was on his way over, but rang the police instead. Gilmore tried to escape in the truck but was followed and intercepted by the police. He offered no resistance when he was ordered out of the truck and arrested.

Lawyers who acted for him when he was back in prison (and demanding to be executed for his crimes) questioned him shrewdly as to his likely motive. In his award-winning novel about the Gary Gilmore case, *The Executioner's Song*, Norman Mailer recorded the interview.

When you stopped at the gas station, did you have any intention of either robbing Jensen or killing him? – I had the intention of killing him.

When did the concept form in your mind, to kill somebody? – I can't say. It had been building all week. That night I knew I had to open a valve and let something out, and I didn't know exactly what it would be, and I wasn't thinking I'll do this or I'll do that, or that'll make me feel better. I just knew something was happening in me and that I'd better let some of the steam off, and oh, I guess all this sounds pretty vicious ...

No, no. Did Jensen say anything to annoy you? – No, not at all.

And, later:

Was there any difference in the way you approached the two killings? – No, not really. You could say it was a little more certain that Mr Bushnell was going to die.

Why? – Because it was already a fact that Mr Jensen had died, and so the next one was more certain.

Was the second killing easier than the first? – Neither of 'em were hard or easy.

Had you ever had any dealings of any kind with either of these men? – No.

Well, what led you to the City Centre Motel where Bushnell worked? We're just trying to understand the quality of this rage you speak of ... it wasn't a rage that might have been vented in sex? – I don't want to mess with questions that pertain to sex. I think they're cheap.

If the death sentence had not been suspended in America for ten years, and the law – whatever sentence was handed down – had been allowed to take its normal course, the outside world would have shown little interest in Gary Gilmore. But because of the doubt that existed as to his fate, right up to the morning of the execution, and Gilmore's own apparently unalterable resolve to see that the state performed the duty ordered by its own court, he first became a curiosity, then a celebrity, and finally an immensely valuable commercial property which increased in value with the approach of his death.

Lawrence Schiller, a former photo-journalist and highly successful TV producer, bought the rights to the Gilmore life and death story. He paid him a fair price, and treated Gilmore's relatives and friends with the same scrupulous fairness. He also persuaded Norman Mailer to write the Gary Gilmore book (which won the author a Pulitzer Prize), with the television rights sold for a large sum – all with Gary Gilmore's full co-operation and approval. Soon it became clear that the few brief months which passed between Gilmore's release from maximum security in Illinois and his return to maximum security in Utah had made him a rich man, albeit at the cost of his life and freedom.

The question remained: how badly did he want to die, and why? Significantly, perhaps, right at the end, when the pressures on all concerned were nigh unbearable, Gilmore offered all the money he had to come from the sale of his story (about $50,000) to his lawyer in exchange for a suit of clothes in which he could make a last, desperate break for freedom. The lawyer refused to discuss it seriously, and Gilmore bore him no malice for that: but it was an insight into the man's true thinking. The original reason why he had insisted on being executed may in fact have been pure bravado, a test of will. Norman Mailer reveals that Gilmore told a police informer in jail, 'They're figuring to give me the death penalty, but I have an answer for that. I'm going to make them do it. Then we'll see if they have . . . as much guts as I do.' What was evident in all that he said and did was a horror of long-term imprisonment and the fear of being incarcerated again. When his brother told him he intended to apply for a stay of execution, Gilmore exploded, 'Look, I've spent too much time in jail. I don't have anything left in me.'

His interpretation of 'love' is also open to question. On his own admission he persuaded his girlfriend Nicole to smuggle quantities of drugs into the prison, secreted in her body inside a balloon, so that they could both commit suicide later at a given date. They tried but survived, and she had to endure treatment in a mental hospital as a result. The knowledge did nothing to prevent Gilmore trying again. Before he died he left Nicole a taped message, asking her to commit suicide and join him in the hereafter. On Lawrence Schiller's advice that tape was never delivered, although he honoured every other personal request made by Gilmore.

Gilmore gave a farewell party for relatives and intimate friends on the night before the execution. Nicole, who was in a mental hospital following her abortive suicide attempt, was not among them; nor was she permitted to telephone him. Even so Gilmore showed a droll sense of humour right to the end. When the prison chaplain said mass for him before the bizarre party began, Gilmore handed back the chalice with a gentle wisecrack: 'Padre, I don't think that wine was as strong as it could have been.'

A last-minute stay of execution caused a brief, anti-climactic sense almost of disappointment but Gary Gilmore would not allow the state to cheat him of his 'right to die'. By Utah law the condemned man is given a choice of weapons; Gilmore had elected to die by firing squad, and would not be denied. On his instructions his lawyers appealed, and at 7.35 on the morning he was scheduled to die the judges ruled:

'It is ordered: One, the Writ of Mandamus is granted. The Temporary Restraining Order entered at about 1.05 this morning by the Honourable Willis W. Ritter, Judge of the District Court of the state of Utah, is vacated, set aside and held for nought. The Honourable Willis W. Ritter is ordered to take no further action in any manner, of any kind, involving Gary Gilmore unless such matter is presented by the duly accredited attorney for Gilmore, or by Gilmore himself. Done at 7.35 am, 17 January 1977.'

The ball was now firmly back in Gilmore's court. His belief in reincarnation (he believed he had already been executed, in England in the eighteenth century) was a comfort to him: earlier he had written to the absent Nicole, 'In about thirty hours I shall be dead. That's what they call it – death. It's just a release, a change of form.'

At 7.47 am he was taken in a van to a local cannery. There he was strapped to an old office chair, with a soiled mattress placed behind him to absorb the bullets. Lights shone down on the chair, while the rest of the execution chamber remained in semi-darkness. There were between thirty and forty persons present apart from the principal; the prison warden and officials, doctors and a handful of invited friends and relatives. The four-man firing squad stayed out of sight behind a screen. When Gilmore was hooded, and a white ring (to guide the firing squad) pinned to his black sleeveless sweater above the heart, the chaplain gave him a last sip of water. The warden read notice of execution and then asked Gilmore, 'Do you have anything else you'd like to say?'

Gilmore hesitated and finally said, 'Let's do it.'

GOLDSTEIN, Stuart
Spoilt son of a rich industrialist who committed murder 'for practice'.

On 20 October 1970 the Las Vegas police received a report that a pretty wine waitress from Caesar's Palace had disappeared. Allyce Deeter (known as Jebbie) was a 31-year-old divorcee with three small children. Fellow employees reported that she had been seen getting into a large sedan car at one o'clock the previous morning.

When a Cadillac sedan with no number plates was found abandoned on a desert road, detectives recalled the car that Jebbie Deeter had entered, and examined it closely. They found human blood on the front seat and floor mat, slug-holes in the door, and some .22 cartridge cases inside. It was established that the car had been rented from a Chicago agency by a man named Stuart Goldstein, who had been driving south on a holiday with his newly married wife. Goldstein had also been staying at Caesar's Palace, and had left on the day Jebbie Deeter was reported missing. They had rented a new Cadillac in Las Vegas.

Police work established that the couple had spent two weeks at a dude ranch at Cody, Wyoming. A police officer from Las Vegas went to the ranch, and discovered that Goldstein was negotiating to buy it from its owner. He had plans for turning it into a wife-swapping commune, where wealthy Chicagoans could spend weekends. He had explained that he was not yet able to raise the money, but should be able to do so in the near future. While in Cody, Goldstein had bought a .22 calibre automatic.

Goldstein went voluntarily to the police a month later, explaining that he had heard they wanted to see him.

Under interrogation, Goldstein confessed to the murder. He had been wondering how to raise the money to set up his wife-swapping ranch. His father would not finance it, but he had a rich uncle in California who would leave him a fortune when he died. Goldstein decided to murder his uncle. But he was unsure whether he was capable of murder. So he decided to kill someone 'for practice'. He and his wife had got into conversation with the pretty wine waitress when she served them in Caesar's Palace, and invited her to tour the town with them after finishing her shift at midnight. Jebbie Deeter usually refused all male dates, but this couple seemed safe enough. After an hour touring gambling spots in Las Vegas, Goldstein's twenty-year-old wife had returned to her suite and left her husband to take Jebbie Deeter home. He had, in fact, driven her to Blue Diamond Road, north of Las Vegas, and killed her. He had then stripped the body naked, to give the impression it was a sex crime. Following his instructions, detectives found the body of Jebbie Deeter twelve miles outside Las Vegas. A lie-detector test convinced the police that his wife was telling the truth when she said she knew nothing of the murder.

It seemed to be an open-and-shut case, but the Las Vegas police soon found themselves faced with legal problems. Goldstein's attorney insisted that his confession was inadmissible as evidence because he had not been advised of his legal rights. And since the directions for finding the body had also been part of the confession, then no evidence about the corpse could be produced in court. Eventually, the Nevada Supreme Court ruled against this.

In prison, Goldstein confessed to a fellow inmate that he was the killer of Valerie Percy, daughter of Senator Charles Percy of Illinois, who had been bludgeoned and stabbed to death in her Chicago home four years earlier by an intruder. No motive was ever established. Goldstein's confession to this murder was only one of a dozen investigated by the Chicago police.

In court, a psychiatrist declared that Goldstein was an amoral person 'with the character of a little boy who hits people who do not give him his way'. He said, 'He is a threat to society. He kills people without remorse.' At first, Goldstein pleaded not guilty by reason of insanity, then changed it to a guilty plea. He was sentenced to life imprisonment in 1974 – which meant that he would be eligible for parole in ten years.

GONZALES, Delfina and Maria de Jesus
Mexican sisters who were responsible for the deaths of more than eighty girls.

In 1963 the police of Guadalajara – on Mexico's west coast – noticed a sharp rise in the number of young girls who were disappearing. The evidence pointed to white slavers. The girls were usually looking for employment, and were offered jobs as maids; then they vanished.

Shortly after Christmas 1963, they received a report of the disappearance of sixteen-year-old Maria Hernandez. Her father was ill, and Maria had been looking for work. One day, in the park, she had met a well-dressed woman with a mole on her cheek, who had offered her a job as her personal maid at 250 pesos a week (at that time, £6 or $16). The girl had packed her belongings and caught a bus for San Juan de los Lagos to meet her future employer. She had not been seen since. The description of the woman with the mole convinced the police that it was Josefina Gutierrez, who had been suspected for a long time of luring young girls to brothels where they were virtually held prisoner.

At the town brothel in San Juan de los Lagos, the police were assured that no one of Maria Hernandez's description had been seen there recently. But one local resident, an old woman, confirmed that the woman with a mole on her face was often seen entering the brothel. The police watched the brothel for several days, and finally succeeded in arresting the woman with the mole, Josefina Gutierrez. Under interrogation, she finally admitted that she was the woman who had offered Maria Hernandez a job; she had met her off the bus and handed her over to the brothel-keepers. She was paid 1,000 pesos (£26 or $70) for her. Since Maria was no longer in the local brothel, it was clear that she had been taken elsewhere. Finally, with a promise of police protection, the procuress divulged the names of the owners of the brothel; they were two sisters, Delfina and Maria de Jesus Gonzales. They owned a ranch in Guanajuato State; it was called Rancho El Angel, and was also a brothel. She had no idea where it was situated, but knew that the nearest town was San Francisco del Rincon.

The police chief of Leon, near San Francisco del Rincon, had never heard of the Rancho El Angel. But finally, they discovered it in a remote country area, at the end of a rocky trail. It was surrounded by a high fence, and a man with a gun guarded the entrance. When armed police pointed their guns at him, he allowed them to enter.

The guard was willing to talk, and it was clear that the police had arrived just in time. The Gonzales sisters seemed to have an excellent information network, and had already heard that the authorities in Mexico City had given the State Prosecutor of Jalisco, Dr Paul Aranda Torres, permission to use all available resources to stop the white slave traffic. The sisters had left for the town of Purisma de Bustos to arrange a deal for disposing of their ranch; they intended to leave for the United States with the proceeds.

The woman who had been left in charge of the ranch was also willing to co-operate with the police. Her name was Lucila – she claimed she was unable to remember her last name; she looked middle-aged; in fact, she was only twenty-eight. She had been abducted when she was seventeen, sold to the Gonzales sisters, and forced to become a prostitute. After five years or so she had lost her looks. When that happened, she said, girls were usually killed. But she was a good manager and had been put in charge of the other girls.

In various rooms on the ranch the police found thirteen girls, all locked up. Most of them were young and pretty, and they included Maria Hernandez. Maria had only been in captivity for three weeks, but during that time she had suffered an appalling ordeal. On her first night at the brothel in San Juan de los Lagos, the male customers had been allowed to 'break her in'. They had forced liquor down her throat, torn off her clothes, and then, one after another, raped her. The next day she was too ill to get up; the two men who were now guarding the ranch (and co-operating with the police) had beaten her black and blue; that night she had to submit to various customers. She was then sent to another brothel in San Francisco del Rincon, and finally removed to the ranch. Maria was immediately sent home, a nervous wreck. So was a fourteen-year-old girl who had been abducted in Leon in the previous November.

The girls told appalling stories of ill-treatment. If a girl showed signs of rebellion, she was made to kneel against a wall with a brick in each hand and another on her head while she was flogged. When girls became pregnant they were hung by the hands from a ring in the ceiling and beaten on the stomach until they aborted. Girls who became ill, or lost their looks, were killed. Several of the girls found on the ranch were suffering from venereal disease.

The police began digging, and soon found that the stories of murder were true. Remains of eighty girls, and many newly born babies, were uncovered.

The horror stories shocked the whole of Mexico. Girls were deliberately 'hooked' on heroin and cocaine to make sure they felt no urge to run away. It made no difference that this shortened their lives; they were disposable. A girl named Ernestina had plotted with the guards to escape, and the Gonzales sisters heard about it. Because Ernestina was popular, they had no wish to provoke revolt by ordering them killed. Instead, they provoked a fight between Ernestina and her elder sister Adela, who was a drug addict; Adela had beaten out her sister's brains with a hammer.

The women had been able to operate their vice ring for ten years because they were informed in advance when police intended a raid. Their neighbour, Captain Hermenegildo Zuniga, a wealthy rancher who had been an army officer, had all kinds of influential friends,

131

and was able to buy them protection. Another profitable sideline was the murder of migratory workers who came back from America with their season's wages. When they visited the brothels owned by the sisters, their drinks were spiked with knockout drops, and they disappeared. Eleven male corpses were found.

The sisters got wind of the police raid on their ranch and went into hiding in Purisma de Bustos, but they were found after a few days. They insisted that the corpses being dug up on their ranch were girls who had died naturally through illness, but the police had a powerful case. The two sisters were tried and sentenced to forty years in prison. The police investigation into the corruption that had made their operation possible went on for two more years, and long prison sentences were handed out to many more people. The considerable fortune amassed by the Gonzales sisters was distributed in massive compensation payments to living victims and relatives of those who had died.

GRABOWSKI, Klaus
German child-killer murdered in court by the mother of one of his victims.

By 1970 Klaus Grabowski had a history of child molestation. Compared to most child molesters, his perversion seemed fairly harmless – he liked to remove the child's underclothing and tickle and caress the genitals. In 1970, when the mother of one of his victims complained, Grabowski was given a light sentence and recommended for psychiatric treatment. He was soon released.

In January 1975 he lured a child into his flat, removed her clothes, then panicked when she began to cry. He choked her unconscious, then revived her with cold water and sent her home. The court sent him to an institution for sexual psychopaths, and it looked as if he was going to spend his life in custody. But when he agreed to be castrated, they decided to release him. In ninety-nine cases out of a hundred, a sex offender becomes harmless after castration. Unfortunately, Grabowski was the hundredth case. His interest in little girls was undiminished. He selected them carefully, lured them to his room with offers of candy and toys, and usually persuaded them to say nothing to their parents. In January 1980 Grabowski, now thirty-four, was living in a two-room apartment on the Wahmstrasse.

On the morning of 5 May, Marie Anne Bachmeier went to decorate a café called the Tipasa Tavern that she had just taken over. Her seven-year-old daughter, Anna, stayed at home with the landlady. Some time that morning, Anna went out to play. At 12.30, when she failed to return, the landlady rang Bachmeier, who rushed home and began to search for her daughter. When the police discovered that Klaus Grabowski lived only a block away from the Bachmeiers' home, he was taken in for questioning. The fact that he had been castrated did not allay suspicion. A witness had seen Grabowski talking to a little girl and inviting her to come and play with his cat. When the police learned that Grabowski had been receiving hormone injections, and that he had a girlfriend who vouched for his virility, their suspicions deepened.

Eventually, Grabowski confessed that he had strangled Anna with her tights, and buried her body at the east end of the town. He led the police to her grave.

Grabowski's trial opened on 3 March 1981. The defence made a great deal of the fact that he had allowed himself to be castrated voluntarily, and an expert testified that the murder of Anna Bachmeier was not a sex crime – only a reaction to panic. Grabowski insisted that he had no sexual feelings towards the child, and that he had asked her to his apartment simply because he loved children. Once there he claimed Anna had tried to blackmail him, demanding money. It was because of this that he had strangled her with her tights. Bachmeier's counsel was not allowed to press the question of why Grabowski had removed her tights in the first place. The defence demanded that the charge be reduced from murder to manslaughter. When the court adjourned that day, it was generally expected that Klaus Grabowski would escape with a light prison sentence.

On 6 March Grabowski took his seat in the dock, and turned his back. Marie Anne Bachmeier stood up, crossed the courtroom, and emptied a 5.6 mm Beretta pistol into him. Grabowski collapsed on to the floor, killed instantly. Bachmeier threw down the pistol and waited passively to be arrested.

Public sympathy was understandably overwhelming, particularly when details of Bachmeier's life became known. Daughter of a former Nazi SS officer, she was born in a refugee camp near Hanover, and at nine was sexually assaulted by a man who gave her money and sweets. At sixteen she was thrown out of the family home for being pregnant, and at eighteen was pregnant again by a different man. Before the baby was born she was raped. One of her children was adopted and the other taken into an orphanage. When Anna was born, she swore never to give her away. The father was a local restaurant owner, who persuaded her to marry his Pakistani chef so that the man would not be deported.

A defence fund soon reached many thousands of pounds. But at this point, the press began to criticize Bachmeier. Other women in the prison said that she was arrogant and haughty and behaved like a super star. Others said that she revelled in the role of a sorrowing mother and did not genuinely care for Anna. The defence fund suddenly began to dry up.

In early March 1982 Bachmeier was sentenced to six years for manslaughter. At the time of writing, she is free on bail pending an appeal.

H

HALL, Archibald
Jewel thief and confidence man, guilty of five murders.

Archibald Hall, alias Roy Fontaine, embarked on murder fairly late in his career, and then by accident rather than design. He was born in Glasgow on 17 June 1924, son of a post office clerk. As a child, Hall displayed extreme fastidiousness, washing his hands several times a day; he also enjoyed dressing up his younger adopted sister Violet. He lost his virginity at the age of sixteen with a much older woman, who took him to hotels for meals; his taste for expensive hotels lasted the rest of his life. When the family was living in a large old house, Hall 'adopted' an old lady in one of the other flats, and devoted much time and attention to her. His family noticed that he suddenly seemed to have a great deal of money. When the old lady died, her trunks were found to be stuffed with thousands of pounds in cash – Hall had apparently already made this discovery. It seems conceivable that he regretted not taking the rest of it – since its existence was not suspected – and may have felt that his subesquent life of confidence trickery was a way of making up for the lost opportunity.

In May 1941 Hall's mother gave birth to another son, Donald. Hall believed that Donald was the result of a liaison between his mother and an army officer. Donald, like Archibald (or Roy, as he preferred to be known) became a crook; but he lacked his brother's style and audacity.

Hall seems to have started his career of embezzlement in his teens, when collecting for the Red Cross; he somehow obtained two collection tins. One he reserved for wealthy areas, the other for slums. The tin full of pennies was handed over to the Red Cross, while the tin with notes and silver was opened in the privacy of his bedroom.

In August 1941, at the age of seventeen, Hall went to prison for the first time for theft. He was sentenced again in 1943 for house-breaking. A psychiatrist declared him mentally unstable and he was sent to a mental home. In 1944 he was sent to prison for two years for house-breaking. In London in 1947, he received another two years for forging cheques and house-breaking; he asked for fifty-one other offences to be taken into consideration. But in 1951, he succeeded in obtaining his first job as a butler with a wealthy couple in Stirlingshire. Hall was well-spoken, immaculately dressed, and obviously intelligent; he could have spent a comfortable life as a butler, but he longed for wealth and luxury. While working in Stirlingshire, his employers went on holiday, and Hall noticed in their mail an invitation to a royal garden party at Holyrood Palace. Typically, Hall hired a dress suit, borrowed his employer's Bentley, and attended the party. Afterwards he called at the shop of a wealthy antiques dealer, Mrs Esta Henry, whom he afterwards robbed.

The police found out about Hall's past and informed his employers. Hall told them frankly that he was trying to make a new life, and they decided to keep him on. But local gossip about his criminal past made him decide to give notice.

Hall was a fantasist, a Walter Mitty, and he saw himself as a master crook. In fact, some of his 'jobs' were masterpieces of audacity. On one occasion he darkened his skin with walnut juice, and arrived at a large hotel dressed in Arab garb and driven in a Rolls Royce. In his enormous suite he asked the manager to send jewellers to his hotel room with samples of their wares. Then he hid in the bathroom, his brown hand reaching round the door to take diamond rings and pendants from the jewellers. After a long silence, the jewellers knocked on the bathroom door, to find the Arab clothes on the floor, and the other door to the bathroom standing ajar.

Hall loved confidence tricks in which he posed as a lord. He would run up enormous bills in hotels, cash a large cheque, then vanish. He was a consummate actor, and in Torquay, posed as a wealthy American from the deep south; the Lord Mayor invited him to a civic reception and allowed him to wear his gold chain of office.

In January 1956 Hall received sentences totalling thirty years preventive detention, and went to Parkhurst. Allowed out without escort for his father's funeral, he returned on time, and was congratulated on being a man of his word. He was released on parole after seven years. He again became a butler, formed a close relationship with the cook, and worked at a house in Mayfair. His only criminal activity there was changing diamonds in guests' jewellery for glass cut by underworld accomplices. A job as the butler of Sir Charles Clore, the property tycoon, lasted only five days, until Clore found about his record.

In 1964 he received another ten years for a jewellery theft; this time, he engineered a remarkable escape from Blundeston jail, near Lowestoft, and with two other prisoners, got clean away. More jewel robberies allowed him once more to live in the style he preferred. He became involved with a pretty Irish girl who was pregnant, and became her 'protector' while she had the baby. (Hall was, in fact, bisexual.) In 1966, he was caught, and again sentenced to a long period in jail – another five on top of the ten he still had to serve. He was paroled in 1972 and sent to a hostel in Preston, Lancs; here he met an Irishwoman, Mary Coggle, who became his mistress, and later his accomplice. He also formed a relationship with a widow, then with a divorcee, whom he married. But by September 1973 he was back in prison, this time until 1977.

Hall then found a job with Lady Hudson, widow of an MP, near Waterbeck in Dumfriesshire. And it was here he committed his first murder. He seems to deserve a certain amount of sympathy in this case. Another ex-jailbird named David Wright came to stay with Hall there, and began to do odd jobs about the place. But Wright felt it would be a sin not to steal some of the jewellery and other valuables. Hall liked his new post and wanted a long rest after his years in prison. A silver tray and a valuable ring disappeared. Wright strenuously denied that he was responsible, but Hall checked with a girlfriend of Wright's, found she had the ring, and persuaded her to return it. Wright was infuriated when he found out. That night, Hall was awakened by a loud bang, and saw Wright standing by his bed pointing a rifle at him. Wright was drunk – having consumed four bottles of Lady Hudson's champagne (she was away from home). He jabbed Hall in the face with the rifle, splitting the flesh and causing heavy bleeding. Hall managed to persuade him to put down the rifle by promising to rob the house; then Wright burst into tears, and Hall persuaded him to go to bed. He had some difficulty filling in the bullet hole in the headboard and staining it brown, then cleaning up the blood that covered the bed.

The next day, Hall took Wright rabbit-shooting. When he was sure Wright had emptied his own gun, he shot him three times in the head. Then he dug a grave in a stream, dumped the body in it, and covered it with rocks. He spent much of that summer piling more rocks on the body and making sure it could not be detected by anyone crossing the stream. In September 1977, the police told Lady Hudson that her butler had a criminal record. She was already suspicious about some mysterious telephone calls she had overheard, referring to 'jobs'. She dismissed him, and Hall went to London.

There he had no difficulty in finding a job with a wealthy ex-MP, Walter Travers Scott-Elliott, who was eighty-two, and his wife Dorothy.

Walter Scott-Elliott liked and trusted his new butler. Hall soon realized that the Scott-Elliotts were very rich indeed, and that this was his chance of a haul that would enable him to retire. Their flat in Richmond Court, Sloane Street, was full of priceless antiques. They had several houses, and bank accounts all over the world. Hall became their butler in November 1977. In the same month, he walked into the Lancelot public house in Baker Street, and met Mary Coggle – his inamorata from Preston, now fifty-one, who had engaged in conversation with a man who looked as if he had a full wallet. In fact, Michael Kitto, aged thirty-nine, had recently absconded with £1,000 from a pub at the Oval, where he worked as barman. Soon Hall was proposing that Kitto should become his accomplice in robbing the Scott-Elliotts. It was, he felt, a two-man job. Kitto would break in, so it would look like an ordinary burglary. And the trusted butler could then stay on to await an opportunity to perpetrate a far bigger fraud.

On 8 December 1977 Hall and Kitto went drinking, then went back together to spend the night in Hall's quarters. Mrs Scott-Elliott was away in a nursing home for a few days, and her husband was a heavy sleeper after he had taken his sleeping pills.

Hall showed Kitto over the house, then pushed open the door of Mrs Scott-Elliott's bedroom. To his astonishment, she was in the room. Perhaps because he had been drinking, Hall's usual coolness deserted him; he saw his plans suddenly coming to nothing. Possibly Mrs Scott-Elliott threatened dismissal. At all events, the two men leapt on her, and, when she screamed, pushed a pillow over her face. Suddenly, she stopped struggling. Hall took her pulse and realized with a shock that she was dead. Suddenly sobered, they arranged her in bed to look as if she was sleeping. At this moment, her husband woke up and wanted to know what the noise was about. They told him that his wife had had a nightmare, but was now asleep.

The following day, Scott-Elliott was told that his wife had gone out shopping, and was dispatched to his club for lunch. Then the two men went and found Mary Coggle, and explained their problem. The old man was 'ga-ga', and needed to be kept quiet. With sleeping tablets, he should not be too much trouble. But they needed someone to impersonate Mrs Scott-Elliott. Mrs Coggle returned to the house, and was dressed in Mrs Scott-Elliott's clothes, including a mink coat, and a wig.

That evening, the half-drugged old man was escorted into the back seat of his car, where his 'wife' was waiting; he was so befuddled that he did not seem to realize that the woman was not Dorothy Scott-Elliott. They drove north, stayed overnight at a cottage Hall had rented in Cumberland and finally buried Dorothy Scott-Elliott beside a lonely road in Perthshire, covering her with leaves and bracken.

Their plan was now to kill Scott-Elliott, and then to clean out the flat and drain the couple's bank balance. They stayed overnight at a hotel in Blair Atholl, Perthshire, and on the morning of 14 December 1977 drove off with the old man, who courteously thanked the hotel staff for a 'very nice stay'. That afternoon, on a lonely road in Glen Affric, Scott-Elliott asked to get out of the car to urinate. They went with him into a clump of trees, then tried to strangle him. He fought with unexpected strength, until Kitto went and grabbed the spade with which they had buried Mrs Scott-Elliott, and hit him on the head. Scott-Elliott was also buried in a shallow grave.

Back in Edinburgh the two men quarrelled with Mary Coggle about Dorothy Scott-Elliott's mink coat. Mary was determined to keep it; her fellow criminals could see that this might be their downfall. That night, Mary Coggle tried hard to win Hall over; she lay naked on the mink in front of the fire, and persuaded him to make love to her. But the next morning, 17 December, the argument was renewed in Hall's rented cottage, and when it was suggested that the coat ought to be burnt, Mary had hysterics. Hall picked up a heavy poker and knocked her to the ground. Then, as she gasped, 'I won't give you away,' they placed her on the couch and tied a plastic bag over her head. That night, they drove to a lonely spot on the Glasgow – Carlisle road, and dumped the body in a stream under a bridge.

Over Christmas and the New Year, Hall and Kitto sold off the contents of the Scott-Elliotts' flat, spent some time with Hall's relatives, and were lavish with presents.

Hall's brother Donald was just out of prison. He had served three years for burglary – he had spent earlier terms in prison for sexual assaults on little girls. Hall loathed him, regarding him as a cheap little crook with perverted tastes. Nevertheless, Donald Hall accompanied Kitto and his brother back to the rented cottage at Newton

Arlosh, Cumberland. On the way, they stopped to pick up some car number-plates they had ordered. This was to prove to be their crucial mistake.

Hall hardly knew his younger brother, who had graduated from stealing from his mother's handbag to house-breaking. If he seriously considered taking Donald as a partner in crime, he now changed his mind as it became clear that Donald was both stupid and weak. In the cottage, Donald's curiosity about their money made them nervous. But it was Donald himself who presented them with the opportunity for murder. He began to boast that he could tie someone up with six inches of string, and offered to demonstrate. He lay on the floor, and told them to tie his thumbs behind his back, then place his two feet through his hands. The opportunity was too good to miss; as Donald lay on the floor, bent backwards, Hall grabbed a pad soaked with chloroform and held it over his face. Donald fought his way free, but the two men overpowered him. They carried him into the bathroom, filled the bath, and drowned him.

The next morning they were once more headed for Scotland with a body in the boot, looking for a grave site. But it was snowing heavily and the ground was frozen. That night, 15 January 1978, they drove to the Blenheim House Hotel, North Berwick, and booked two single bedrooms.

The hotelier, Norman Wight, noticed that the two men seemed to be travelling light, and wondered if they might be confidence men who intended to skip without paying their bill. They charged their drinks in the bar to their bill, increasing his suspicion. He had a feeling that, in spite of their apparent respectability, they were not what they seemed. So as they ate dinner, he rang the local police to ask if they knew anything of two con-men in a Ford Granada. The police took the trouble to check the number-plates of the Granada with the computer, and found that it should have been a Ford Escort. The tax disc on the windscreen also proved to be a fake. So as Hall and Kitto were drinking brandy at the end of their meal, they were startled and dismayed when two policemen came in to question them about the false number-plates on their car.

At the police station, Hall was allowed to go to the toilet – the police had no idea that any serious offence was involved – and scrambled out of the window. He was picked up a few hours later, in a taxi on its way to Dunbar – he had told the driver that his wife had been involved in a car accident and was in hospital there. By that time, the police had opened the boot of the Granada and found the body of Donald Hall.

Mary Coggle's body had been found, but not identified. The London police were investigating the disappearance of the Scott-Elliotts. Both Hall and Kitto decided to tell the full story. In November 1978 Kitto was sentenced to fifteen years, and Hall to a life sentence without possibility of parole.

HANRATTY, James
Self-confessed petty crook whose execution for the A6 Murder Case may have been a miscarriage of justice.

On the evening of 22 August 1961 a young couple, Michael John Gregsten and Valerie Storie, had been for a drink at a pub in Taplow, on the Thames near Slough, and then parked their car about two miles away at a spot known as Dorney Reach. Gregsten was married, but living apart from his wife, and he was having an affair with Miss Storie, with whom he worked.

They had been sitting in the car for about half an hour when there was a tap on the window. Gregsten wound it down, and a man pointed a gun at him and demanded the ignition keys. He explained that he was on the run, and climbed into the back of the car. He took their watches and some money. For the next two hours he talked about himself, saying that he had been in remand homes and Borstal. Towards midnight he told Gregsten to climb into the boot of the car, then allowed Miss Storie's pleas to change his mind. Instead he made Gregsten drive towards London Airport and asked him to buy cigarettes from a machine. In the early hours of the morning, he forced Gregsten to pull into a lay-by on the A6 at Deadman's Hill. There was talk of tying them up, and the man asked Gregsten to pass a laundry bag; as Gregsten leaned forward, the gunman shot him twice in the head, killing him instantly. Valerie Storie shouted: 'You bastard, why did you do that?' The gunman replied that Gregsten had frightened him by moving too quickly. Soon afterwards he made her kiss him, then forced her to get into the back seat, where he raped her. Then they dragged Gregsten's body from the car, the man made the girl show him how to work the gears, and, as she returned to Gregsten's body, shot her several times. He kicked her, seemed to be convinced that she was dead, and drove away. She was found by a passer-by at daylight, and taken to hospital. A bullet had passed close to her spine, paralysing her from the waist down.

She was able to describe the gunman – whose face she had seen in the light of a passing car – as having dark hair and deep-set brown eyes.

The car was found abandoned at Ilford, and the gun was found under a seat on a London bus. An Identikit picture of the wanted man was published in newspapers. On 27 August, Superintendent Acott, in charge of the investigation, issued an appeal to landladies who might have a lodger who was 'lying low'. A landlord in Finsbury Park reported that a man named Durrant had booked into his hotel on the day after the murder, and had kept to his room since. The man was questioned by the police, and proved to be Peter Alphon, son of a records clerk at Scotland Yard; he made a living by selling almanacs from door to door. On the night of the murder, said Alphon, he had been staying at the Vienna Hotel, Maida Vale. The police took a statement from him and allowed him to leave.

On 7 September a Mrs Dalal of Richmond answered her door to a brown-haired man who inquired about a room to let; when she showed him into the room, he grabbed her, tied her hands, and forced her on to the bed. He told her, 'I am the A6 killer.' As he was lifting her skirt, obviously intending rape, she screamed and he ran away.

In the Vienna Hotel, the manageress was moving a chair in room 24 when two cartridge cases fell out of a tear in its side. Recalling the inquiry from the police about Alphon, she handed them over; they proved to be from the gun that had killed Michael Gregsten. The man who had stayed in the room on the night before the murder had signed the register 'J. Ryan'. Alphon became a suspect, and newspapers printed descriptions of him, as a man the police wanted to interview. In fact, a Mr Nudds, who had been the manager of the Vienna Hotel on the night Alphon stayed there (but who had since been sacked) told the police that Alphon had been out until well after midnight on the night of the murder – so late that he had still not returned when Nudds went to bed. When Nudds saw him the next morning, Alphon had looked unshaven, dishevelled and nervous. Alphon (who was calling himself Durrant) had told Nudds that he had returned to the hotel at 11 pm, but Nudds knew this was impossible, since Alphon was still not in by 2 am, when Nudds went to bed. Alphon had slept in room 6 – not room 24, where the bullet cases were found.

The police interviewed Alphon's mother, to check his alibi – that he had been visiting her in Streatham; she denied it. On 22 September

Alphon contacted the police and gave himself up. He appeared in an identity parade in front of various witnesses: Mrs Dalal, Mr Nudds, a petrol-station attendant who had served Gregsten with petrol when the killer was in the car, and two men who had seen a man driving the car the following morning. Nudds said that Alphon 'could be' the man. Mrs Dalal failed to point to him, but then collapsed and said Alphon was the man who had tried to rape her. The others failed to identify him. Another identity parade was arranged at Guy's Hospital, where Valerie Storie picked the wrong man. When told that her suspect was innocent, she shouted, 'I've made a mistake, I've made a mistake.' And when Nudds withdrew his own statement implicating Alphon, Alphon was released.

Now the search was on for James Ryan, the occupant of room 24. Police inquiries in London's underworld soon uncovered the information that James Ryan was an alias used by James Hanratty, a 25-year-old petty crook who had spent most of the time since he was eighteen in prison for car-stealing and house-breaking. His father had tried hard to get him to 'go straight', but Hanratty had abandoned an attempt to run a window-cleaning business and left home three months before the murder. In fact, since the murder he had been living by burglary and petty theft. On 5 October, James Hanratty rang Superintendent Acott to say he was innocent of the murder, but that he was not willing to give himself up because he was wanted for house-breaking. He claimed he had spent the night of the murder with three men in Liverpool.

On 11 October, Hanratty was recognized by two policemen in Blackpool and arrested. This time, Valerie Storie picked him out in an identity parade, after asking everyone in the line to say, 'Be quiet, I'm thinking.' (The killer, she said, had pronounced it 'finking'.) Hanratty was charged with the A6 murder.

The strongest piece of evidence against him was undoubtedly Valerie Storie's identification, and it was this that led, in due course, to his conviction and execution the following year. Yet one question mark hangs over this identification. All the early descriptions of the wanted man mentioned his brown hair and brown eyes. These were based on the description Miss Storie gave to the police immediately after being found; it was reported that she was perfectly lucid and calm at the time. Yet eight days later, the description of the wanted man had changed, so that he now had 'saucer-like staring blue eyes' and fair hair. The first description fitted Alphon but not Hanratty, the second, Hanratty but not Alphon.

I (Colin Wilson) became indirectly involved in the case some time after Hanratty's execution. John Justice wrote to me in January 1964; he had noticed that Hanratty was not in the *Encyclopaedia of Murder* and wondered if this was because I doubted Hanratty's guilt? I replied that Hanratty had not been included because the *Encyclopaedia* had been published before the murder, but that I would be interested to hear why he believed Hanratty might be innocent. Not long afterwards, I went with a friend to meet Justice. He was a man of private means with a great deal of time on his hands. He had attended the magistrate hearings at Ampthill in November 1961, and had become convinced that the story of Hanratty's guilt was absurd. Was it really likely that these two men, both suspects in the case, should have been staying in the same hotel in London at the time of the murder? Was it not far more likely that Alphon – who had been the original suspect – had planted the bullet cases in Hanratty's room, so making him the chief suspect?

Justice went out of his way to meet Alphon, who at first declined then, probably driven by curiosity, agreed to see him. They became friendly. Soon Alphon was dropping tantalizing hints that he was the A6 murderer, and showed John Justice a peculiar drawing with the words 'Peter McDougal' (one of Alphon's aliases) and 'Murderer'. But it was after Hanratty's execution that Alphon one day handed Justice a document containing an account of the murder – not a signed confession, but a detailed description of the night of the crime. Later, he said, Alphon had confessed – verbally – to killing Gregsten, and raping Valerie Storie. Alphon subsequently made lengthy telephone calls which Justice had taped. He played us the tapes, and we had to agree that if Alphon was not the murderer he certainly seemed intent on convincing Justice that he was. Alphon never actually confessed, but he described – for example – the problems the murderer must have encountered trying to drive a car through unfamiliar roads back to London, and added precise details that were intended to suggest he was talking about himself.

This drive, said John Justice, was another piece of evidence in Hanratty's favour. Two men who had narrowly avoided a collision with the car on the morning after the murder testified that it was being driven very badly. The murderer had had to ask Valerie Storie to show him the gears before he drove away. Hanratty was an experienced car thief who would not have needed to be told. Alphon was a poor and inexperienced driver.

When we left Justice's house, we agreed that his story left many doubts in our minds. It seemed that Alphon was simply enjoying the attention he was receiving, and was determined to give his money's worth. (He had even added certain lurid details to his 'confession' – for example, that he had forced Gregsten and Valerie Storie to perform the sexual act in front of him in the car.) Justice himself admitted that this 'murder investigation' had given him a purpose in life which he badly needed – he struck us as a man who might easily become bored and depressed when he had nothing to do. The emotional relationship with Alphon struck us both as strange; Justice had showed us a greetings card sent to him by Alphon containing a large stuffed silk heart, and inscribed 'To my little darling'. They were not homosexuals, Justice explained, but he was hoping to give Alphon the confidence and encouragement he needed to reveal the truth. It all suggested that Alphon – also a lonely individual – had been glad to form a close relationship, even though he knew Justice believed him a murderer.

Justice had tried hard to persuade Alphon to make a confession that would save Hanratty. Alphon refused – in spite of his warm affection for Justice. Hanratty was executed in Bedford on 4 April 1962. It was after the execution that Alphon 'confessed'. Eventually it became clear to Alphon that the friendship was one-sided; John Justice only wanted to prove that he was the A6 killer. Naturally, Alphon became embittered, and the interminable calls followed, which Justice taped. In 1963, he prepared a long memorandum on the case, which was submitted to the Home Secretary. The result was that the matter was raised in Parliament by Mr Fenner Brockway in July 1963; he argued strongly in favour of Hanratty's innocence, and read aloud transcripts from the tape-recordings. But the Home Secretary remained unconvinced and declined to take further action. His view – and, at that time, the view of most people – was that Hanratty was guilty.

In view of the case against Hanratty, this is understandable. For although the evidence for Alphon's involvement seems strong, the evidence against Hanratty looks equally convincing. The first person to speak to Valerie Storie as she lay by the roadside near her lover's body was a student named John Kerr; she told him that the killer had 'staring eyes'. She did not reiterate this description until 31 August, eight days later, long before Hanratty was a suspect. From the moment she saw Hanratty in the identity parade, Valerie Storie insisted that he was the man who raped her. She never wavered in her identification. Hanratty torpedoed his own case by first of all insisting that he had spent the night of the murder in Liverpool with three men – criminal acquaintances – then that he had spent it in Rhyl. The police wasted much time trying to track down the three men in Liverpool before Hanratty changed his story. Then a Rhyl landlady *did* agree that a man like Hanratty had stayed on the night of the murder. But the jury found all this chopping and changing suspicious, and remained unconvinced.

In 1965 the journalist Paul Foot became interested in the Alphon tapes, and became finally convinced that Alphon, not Hanratty, was the killer. He published an article to this effect in *Queen* in September 1966. By this time, Alphon had already made more statements to John Justice that seemed to provide a motive for the crime. He had been sent, he told Justice (in an interview quoted in Foot's book *Who Killed Hanratty?*) to break up the affair between Gregsten and Valerie Storie. 'I was there to separate a couple of people ... in a car ... that was the motive ... that is why it took five hours. Five fucking hours it took ... you've got your motive.' He named the sum he was paid as five thousand pounds. 'I killed Gregsten and the Establishment killed Hanratty.' Hanratty had actually been framed for the murder by his friend Charles 'Dixie' France, who had put the incriminating bullet cases in the Vienna Hotel and disposed of the murder weapon on a bus. But France had since committed suicide.

A court order had been made to restrain Alphon from making nuisance calls to various people involved in the case, including Lord Russell of Liverpool, whose book *Deadman's Hill: Was Hanratty Guilty?* was published in 1965. When he broke his undertaking in 1967, he received a summons to appear in court. Faced with the prospect of prison, Alphon went to Paris, and called a press conference in the Hotel du Louvre in which he announced that he was the A6 murderer. Later, he wrote to the Home Secretary – then Roy Jenkins – to repeat his claim. Paul Foot met Alphon at Brighton in November 1968, and Alphon again explained that he had been hired to separate the lovers by an 'interested party', a well-to-do business man, who had met him in the Manor House pub in Finsbury Park, and the money was paid after the murder. Foot, naturally, does not mention in his book the name of the interested party, since it would be libellous, and I am under the same prohibition. Foot saw Alphon's bank statements for the autumn following the murder, and they show that £7,569 was paid into Alphon's account between October 1961 and June 1962.

Paul Foot's book, published in 1971, was written with the active participation of Alphon and argued strongly that he was the A6 murderer, and that Hanratty was deliberately framed and wrongfully convicted. He states his conviction that a senior police officer involved in the case 'had evidence suggesting that Alphon was the murderer'. After declaring: 'I am as sure as it is possible to be that James Hanratty did not commit the A6 murder,' he goes on: 'As for Peter Alphon, either he committed the A6 murder, or he has been leading all of us, and me in particular, a fantastic dance. I tend . . . to the former view.'

HARRIS, Robert Alton
Classic example of a criminal created by early conditioning.

On 5 July 1978 Robert Harris, who had spent seven of the past ten years behind bars, planned to rob a bank with his younger brother Daniel. They drove to the parking lot of the Jack-in-the-Box Fast Food Restaurant, San Diego, California, and tried to steal a car by 'hot wiring'. At that moment, two students, John Mayeski and Michael Baker, drove into the parking lot to eat their hamburgers. They were on their way to a nearby lake for a day of fishing. When Harris could not start the car he was trying to steal, he went over to the two boys in their Ford Galaxy and ordered them to drive east. Daniel followed in the Harris car. At a canyon near Miramar Reservoir, Robert told the youths he was going to use their car in a bank robbery, and assured them they would not be hurt. The boys agreed at gunpoint to report their car stolen. As they walked away, Robert slowly raised his pistol and shot Mayeski in the back. Then he chased Michael Baker down a hill and shot him four times. Mayeski was still alive when Harris came back so Harris put the gun to his head and blew his brains out. They then drove Mayeski's car to the friend's house where they were staying, and Robert ate the hamburgers that the two boys had been about to eat. He laughed when his brother rushed to the bathroom to vomit.

An hour later, they robbed the San Diego Trust and Savings Bank, wearing stocking masks. A passer-by followed them home, and reported them to the police. They were arrested half an hour after the robbery. The $3,000 they took was recovered. Daniel Harris turned state's evidence, and was sentenced to six years in prison. His brother was sentenced to death.

No one was surprised that Robert Harris became a killer. He was born ten weeks early on 15 January 1953, several hours after his mother had been kicked in the stomach by his father, an insanely jealous man who had come home drunk and accused her of infidelity. His father was an alcoholic who frequently beat his children. The mother also became an alcoholic and was arrested several times, once for bank robbery. She blamed Robert for her husband's ill treatment of the family. Their father, a warrant officer in the army, reserved his worst treatment for Robert, who had a learning disability and a speech defect. 'He was the most beautiful of all my mother's children; he was an angel,' said his sister Barbara. 'He would just break your heart. He wanted love so bad he would beg for any kind of physical contact. He'd come up to my mother and just try to rub his little hands on her leg or her arm. He just never got touched at all. She'd just push him away or kick him. One time she blooded his nose when he was trying to get close to her.'

When Robert was nine, his father was convicted of sexually assaulting a daughter, and was sent to Atascadero State Hospital. The family survived on welfare. Several years later, when their father returned home, he was again convicted of the same offence. Robert was a gentle child, who cried when he was taken to the film *Bambi*. Eventually, he began to turn mean. At fourteen, he stole a car and was sentenced to a federal youth detention centre in Kentucky. There he was homosexually raped several times, and slashed his wrists in a suicide attempt. He spent more than four years behind bars as a result of an escape. In prison, he deliberately did exercises to develop his muscles. He began killing cats and dogs, laughing while he tortured them. He once stabbed a prize pig more than a thousand times. Like his father he discovered the only way he could vent his feelings was through violence. Three years after his release, he beat up a nineteen-year-old neighbour so viciously that the man died, and Harris was convicted of manslaughter.

Although his court attorney has appealed against the death sentence for the murder of the two students, Harris is reported as looking forward to it. 'He hates the waiting,' said a fellow prisoner. 'He wants to live, but he'd rather die than be locked up for the rest of his life.' A group of inmates on death row have pledged several dollars for a small celebration on the day he is executed. 'The guy's a misery, a total scumbag – we are going to have a party when he goes,' said the prisoner in the cell next to Harris. 'He doesn't care about life, he doesn't care about others, he doesn't care about himself.'

HILL, John
The wealthy Texan accused of murder but murdered by a contract killer while awaiting trial.

Joan Robinson was the daughter of a Texas oil millionaire. She was a champion horsewoman, and had her own ranch in Houston. In 1958, when she was twenty-six, she married for the third time – a young plastic surgeon called John Hill. With the advantages of a beautiful wife, an expensive home and a wide acquaintance among rich socialites, he soon became highly successful. They had a son, and in spite of a basic difference in their temperaments – he found horses boring, and preferred music and literature – the marriage seemed to be a happy one. Then, some time in the mid 1960s, she discovered that he was having affairs with other women. She became increasingly pre-occupied with her horses.

On 17 March 1969 Joan Hill complained of sickness and vomited after breakfast. She stayed in bed all day although they had house guests. The following morning, she only wanted iced water. On 18 March she was so feeble that Hill drove her to the Sharpstown General Hospital, partly owned by him. She died early the following morning. The medical examiner's office should have been informed of the death, but by the time they heard about it the body had already been embalmed. There was a hasty autopsy in the funeral home, and the medical examiner, Dr Joseph Jachimczyk, had time to give the body only a brief examination before it was buried.

Joan's father, Ash Robinson, was deeply dissatisfied, and accused his son-in-law of allowing his wife to die through neglect. Three months after her funeral, John Hill married a divorcee, Ann Kurth, with whom he had been having an affair for some time. Ash Robinson seems to have become convinced that Joan was murdered. This second marriage lasted only a few months; after a divorce, Hill married again. John Hill's lawyers threatened Ash Robinson with a $5 million lawsuit for slander and libel. In August 1969, Dr Jachimczyk at the request of the District Attorney, carried out an autopsy on Joan Hill's body. The brain had been removed, and there seemed to be some doubt whether the brain that was provided by the Sharpstown Hospital really belonged to Joan Hill. The doctor in charge of the hospital angrily dismissed the notion. Dr Milton Helpern decided that, 'Death resulted from an acute inflammatory ... disease, the origin of which could not be determined.' Ash Robinson continued to press the case, with the result that in April

1970, John Hill was charged with the death of his wife by 'murder by omission' – that is to say that he had killed her by failing to provide proper medical treatment. At the trial, witnesses talked of Joan Hill's despair at his philandering, and guests at the Hill home that weekend told how John Hill had brought home cakes and tarts and personally selected which were to be given to his wife. Ann Kurth, Hill's ex-wife, told how she had found pastries in the refrigerator of the apartment that Hill rented for her, and was about to eat one when Hill stopped her. In the bathroom, she said, she found three Petri dishes, used for growing bacteria. They were under a lamp for warmth.

Ann Kurth's evidence saved John Hill. When she alleged that he had tried to kill her by crashing his car against a bridge, the comment was deemed inadmissible, and the judge declared a mistrial.

The legal wrangling continued, but in September 1972, a gunman burst into John Hill's house in Houston and shot him dead. The killer threw away his gun after the murder, but the Texas Rangers were able to trace it. They arrested a Dallas crook named Vandiver, a contract killer, who had been hired by a former brothel madam in Galveston to shoot him. Vandiver jumped bail and was killed in an encounter with one of the pursuing policemen as they grappled for a gun. The madam and a woman who had procured the gun testified at their trial that Ash Robinson had put out the contract for John Hill's death. Both were convicted of complicity in the murder but Ash Robinson, seventy-nine years old and in poor health, was never indicted. A lie-detector test absolved him. So the Robinson case remains officially 'unsolved'.

HOSEIN, Arthur and Nizamodeen
The murderers in the first British case of kidnap and ransom demand.

When Arthur Hosein, an immigrant tailor born in a wooden shack in Trinidad, landed in England in September 1955 at the age of nineteen his dream was to become a millionaire member of the landed gentry. His brother Nizamodeen (Nizam), youngest in the family of seven, joined him in Hertfordshire in 1969 fired with the same ambition. Arthur Hosein, small and aggressively boastful, was the dominant influence. The taller Nizam, who had a record of petty violence behind him, supplied the brawn. In the evening of 3 October of that year as they debated how to go about making a million, they saw the answer literally staring them in the face ... on television. They watched David Frost interview Rupert Murdoch, the young newspaper tycoon who had earlier thwarted an attempt by Socialist MP and publisher Robert Maxwell to take over the *News of the World*. References were made to Rupert Murdoch's great wealth, and the millions he had put up to defeat the take-over bid: soon the plot suggested itself. The brothers Hosein decided to kidnap Mr Murdoch's wife Anna and then hold her to ransom – for one million pounds.

Arthur Hosein, mockingly called 'King Hosein' in the pubs of Stocking Pelham, had been glad to find a job at £7 a week as a clerk when he first came to Britain. Later he was called up for National Service as a private in the Royal Pioneer Corps, sentenced to six months in military prison for desertion and discharged with ignominy. During his conscript service he met and later married Mrs Else Fischer, a German-born divorcee eight years his senior. After his discharge she ran a hairdressing salon while he tailored men's trousers, and by hard work they saved enough by 1967 to buy Rooks Farm with ten acres of land. Arthur Hosein paid £5,000 down on the sale price of £14,000 and raised the rest on mortgage. He stocked the farm with a few pigs, cows and chickens and saw it as a first step toward realizing his ultimate ambition. He also bought a blue Volvo as a status symbol. The car, the pigs and the farm itself were all to play a part in the police investigation that followed Mrs McKay's disappearance.

Being complete amateurs in crime, Arthur and Nizam Hosein bungled the kidnapping in a manner more suited to comedy than tragedy. To kidnap Mrs Murdoch the brothers first needed to know where to find her. But, since the Murdochs' telephone number was ex-directory this proved beyond them. Next they drove to the offices of the *News of the World* and looked for the blue Rolls Royce used by Mr Murdoch. Armed with its registration number Nizam Hosein then called at the Vehicle Registration Department and demanded the owner's private address, claiming that he had been involved in a minor accident with the Rolls. Again his luck was out: the car was registered as company property. So the Hoseins returned to Fleet Street, waited patiently and followed the Rolls home. Unknown to them, Mr and Mrs Murdoch had left for a holiday in Australia – and the Rolls was being used temporarily by Rupert Murdoch's deputy, Alick McKay, who lived in Arthur Road, Wimbledon.

Having discovered Mrs Murdoch's address – as they thought –

the brothers now awaited an opportunity to kidnap her. On 13 December 1969 Arthur's wife Else, who knew nothing of the plot, left for Christmas holiday in Germany together with their two children Rudeen and Farida, and Arthur's thirteen-year-old sister Haffiza. This meant the Hosein brothers had Rooks Farm to themselves until 3 January. On Monday, 29 December, they returned to the house in Wimbledon, arriving some time between 5.30 pm (when Mrs McKay drove her domestic help home) and 6 pm, when a neighbour walked by and saw 'a dark coloured car' in the drive. She also noticed that the outside light was on, as were other lights in the downstairs rooms: everything seemed normal.

When Mr McKay arrived home in the chauffeur-driven Rolls at 7.45, he found the page of a Sunday newspaper (the *People*) blowing about in the drive – of which he thought nothing at the time – and the front door unchained. This was most unusual: since their house had been burgled three months previously Mrs McKay had insisted on chaining the outer door at all times when she was on her own. Mr McKay himself rang the doorbell 'in code' on arrival and used his key only as a last resort. What he found then told him immediately that something was wrong. The contents of his wife's handbag lay scattered on the stairs. A rusty billhook, an opened tin of adhesive bandage and a bale of twine lay on the hall table. The hall telephone had been disconnected and the disc listing their telephone number removed. He entered every room calling his wife's name. There was no sign of her, although the television was switched on, the open fire burning unguarded, his dinner prepared but uncooked in the kitchen; all the outward signs of a hurried and unpremeditated departure. Oddly, his wife had left him no note: more ominously he found money and items of jewellery missing from her handbag.

He did then what most husbands would probably have done in similar circumstances. He called next door, to ask if perchance his wife had left a message there: and when he was told she had not, rang the police from the neighbour's house. So the long investigation into Britain's first kidnapping began.

From the outset the police seemed to have no more luck with their inquiries than had the Hoseins in plotting the crime. In spite of the obvious signs of entry and Mrs McKay's disappearance it was some time before the police became convinced she had been kidnapped. There were a number of reasons for that. Mr McKay was by nature an undemonstrative person, so much so that when he was first questioned the police found it remarkable that any man who believed his wife might have been forcibly abducted should be so calm. Then again, he was a newspaperman who felt, not unnaturally, that the quickest way to find out what had become of her lay in maximum publicity. That is not the police way, and it led to inevitable differences with the family on how best to find Mrs McKay. But the main reason why the police were reluctant to accept the obvious was quite simply because Britain had never known a kidnapping before; to police and public alike it was a crime which happened only in America, or the movies. And finally the Hosein brothers, being complete tyros, committed such elementary, incredible blunders in their greed to lay their hands on the ransom that the British police just could not equate such behaviour with a serious kidnap attempt.

Instead, the police were most influenced at the outset by the fact, still unexplained, that Mr McKay found the front door unchained. The chain had been fitted at Mrs McKay's own insistence after the burglary. And since she was so nervous of intruders, the assumption had to be that on this dark winter night she would unchain the door only to admit someone she knew. This compelled the police to examine seriously the possibility – not uncommon in missing wife cases – that she might have left voluntarily, perhaps even have been involved with another man. To anyone who thought along those lines, Mr McKay himself was therefore a possible suspect in any disappearance. Other officers half-suspected some kind of dubious publicity stunt. The first person Mr McKay telephoned (after reporting his wife's disappearance) was Larry Lamb, the editor of the *Sun*. The *Sun*, which headlined the disappearance next day and is a sister paper of the *News of the World*, was then engaged in a bitter circulation battle with its tabloid rivals.

Both theories were wholly without foundation, as events later proved, but they were typical of the distrust between police and media which soured the entire investigation, to the point where in the end each felt the other was in part to blame for the delay in rescuing Mrs McKay. In their definitive book on the case, *Murder in the Fourth Estate* Peter Deeley and Christopher Walker comment, 'It was one of the less wholesome features of the case that at times the kidnapping itself was almost over-shadowed by the press-police infighting. The case has shown that it is certainly time the relationships between the two bodies were thoroughly re-examined. The police must be prepared to put more trust in press, television and radio; the media must be prepared not to exploit that increased trust for its own ends.'

First word from the kidnappers came at 1.15 am on 30 December from a phone booth in Epping. The caller had to ask the operator to connect him – so that his whereabouts were instantly known. The operator himself listened to part of the call, and was able to describe the caller's voice most accurately as 'an American, or coloured [man's] voice'. Mr McKay and his family were in no doubt that the message was genuine, since they were adamant that Mrs McKay would never have left home voluntarily. Possibly the most noticeable thing to emerge from a transcript of the conversation is Mr McKay's obvious shock and bewilderment.

This is Mafia Group 3. We are from America. Mafia M3, we have your wife. – You have my wife?
You will need a million pounds by Wednesday. – What are you talking about? I don't understand.
Mafia. Do you understand? – Yes, I've heard of them.
We have your wife. It will cost you one million pounds. – That's ridiculous, I haven't got anything like a million.
You'd better get it. You have friends, get it from them. We tried to get Rupert Murdoch's wife. We couldn't get her so we took yours instead. – Rupert Murdoch?
You have a million by Wednesday night or we will kill her. Understand? – What do I do?
All you have to do is wait for the contact, that is for the money. You will get instructions. Have the money or you won't have a wife. We will contact you again.

The police reacted cautiously. For the kidnappers of any suburban housewife to demand a million pounds in ransom money sounds preposterous, even today when such an amount is no longer unusual. And for them to make such a demand via a GPO operator over an open telephone line, from a known call-box where they could have been intercepted at any moment by a cruising police patrol car, seemed frankly unbelievable. None the less it happened and it presented an opportunity never to be repeated: all subsequent calls from 'M3' came via the STD system, which is untraceable.

Although the police opened their Crime Index File promptly enough (in which every meaningful report and incident is listed and cross-referenced) the importance of another clue which emerged early on did not become apparent until much later. A Wimbledon resident reported seeing a Volvo carrying two men, one of 'a tanned, Arab colour' – first at 4.40 pm on the day of the kidnapping, and later turning into a street which led directly to Arthur Road. Perhaps taken in conjunction with the telephone operator's statement that an American or coloured man made the ransom call from a phone booth at Epping, which lies some thirty miles from Rooks Farm where the Volvo was garaged, it might have led to an early breakthrough. However, inquiries remained centred on the McKays' home for some time.

On New Year's Eve, Mr McKay received the first letter from his wife. It was postmarked in North London, and contained no information to say how the ransom was to be paid. Mrs McKay wrote (to dictation), 'Please do something to get me home. I am blindfolded and cold. Please co-operate for I cannot keep going. I think of you constantly and the family and friends. What have I done to deserve this treatment? Love Muriel.' It was a form of mental torture, and it was deliberate. In a subsequent ransom demand 'M3' told the McKays, 'You see we don't make our customer happy, we like to keep them in suspense. In that way it is a gamble. We give the order and you *must* obey.'

The police made several attempts to try to persuade the kidnappers to make fresh contact. The McKays' daughter Diane appeared on television, Mr McKay issued an appeal through the press. 'Will you please inform me what I have to do to get my wife back? What do you want from me? I am willing to do anything in reason to get her back. Please give me your instructions and what guarantee I have that she will be safely returned to me. I have had . . . so many cranks communicate with me that I must be sure I am dealing with the right person.'

When there was no immediate response the family, in their desperation, sought help from a medium in England as well as the famous clairvoyant, Gerard Croiset of Holland. Images 'seen' by Mr Croiset led searchers to a deserted farmhouse building on the Essex-Hertfordshire border, but the trail petered out. Later Sheffield police, who interviewed a billhook manufacturer, reported that the implement found in the McKays' house on the night of the kidnap was of a type sold and used around Bishop's Stortford. Subsequent inquiries showed that such billhooks were so numerous it was impossible to trace any single one, and the lead was not pursued.

Next Mr McKay gave an interview in which he read from a prepared statement – drawn up by the police – and said that his wife needed urgent medical treatment. 'I ask . . . whoever is holding Muriel to get in touch with me immediately and let me know exactly what they want. If it is money then I must know how and where it can be exchanged for my wife. In order to be certain I am dealing with the person who is holding Muriel I must have positive proof that she is safe. To whoever is holding her: do you realize, whoever you are, how dangerous will be the state of my wife's health if she doesn't get the drugs she needs quickly?'

In fact Mrs McKay had been taking cortisone for arthritis, but the kidnappers had no way of knowing that: and alarmed by the prospect of losing the million pounds ransom they responded immediately. Next morning a letter was delivered to the editor of the *News of the World*, saying that instructions would be passed to Mr McKay as soon as the police left his house and he was free to talk. Four days later the editor received a phone call from 'M3': 'Tell McKay to get a million. I have proof of Mrs McKay's existence.'

However after almost three weeks of fruitless investigation the officers in charge felt duty bound to warn the family that they feared Mrs McKay might be already dead. Mr McKay was naturally reluctant to accept that, and when 'M3' rang him next day he offered £20,000 for the safe return of his wife. 'M3' turned it down flat. 'That's not enough pounds. It's up to you to get the money. It's an order, it must be half a million first delivery.'

More letters written by Mrs McKay began to arrive, together with a ransom note containing fragments of her clothing and a demand for payment of the million by 1 February. If anything, they served only to increase police fears that she was already dead. They believed she had been forced to write several letters in the early days of the kidnap, and that they were now being released – but in the wrong order (one referred to a television appeal made three weeks beforehand). The final ransom demand said, 'I am now sending you final letter for your wife reprieve [*sic*] she will be executed on 2 February 1970 unless you keep our business date on the 1 February without any error. We demand the full million pound in two occasion when you deliver the first half million your wife life will be saved and I shall personally allow her to speak to you on telephone.'

In the note 'M3' ordered Mr McKay to drive to a telephone booth on a road leading north out of London to await further instructions. It was the moment the police had been waiting for and a Scotland Yard conference was called to finalize plans. Two armed policemen were to travel in the Rolls, one posing as Mr McKay, the other as his chauffeur. A task force of nearly two hundred men in unmarked cars was brought in to give back-up support. 'Ransom money' consisting of £300 in genuine £5 notes (loaned by Mr McKay) together with counterfeit notes, printed on police instructions and sufficiently realistic only to deceive someone making a hurried check, was prepared. The suitcases in which it was packed were fitted with electronic homing 'bugs', so that the kidnappers could still be followed even if they eluded the trap.

It sounded foolproof in theory. In practice it went hopelessly wrong. The Rolls was shadowed by police outriders whose Hell's Angels gear fooled no one. So many unmarked cars and motorcycles and plain-clothes men passed and re-passed the pick-up point – located in a quiet country lane – that not even the bungling Hoseins could fail to smell a rat. Thoroughly alarmed, they drove home without attempting to touch the ransom money.

Their car was seen in the area and identified as a Volvo, although it was too dark to read the number. Next day detectives posing as insurance salesmen learned that the Hosein family of Stocking Pelham owned a Volvo, registered in Mrs Hosein's name. When they checked back with local police they were told, correctly, that apart from minor motoring offences nothing was known against the Hoseins. The facts were reported, making this the third time a Volvo had been identified during the kidnap investigation: near the McKay house on the night of the kidnapping, near the ransom collection point overnight, and now in a village only a few miles away. Why was no immediate action taken? Answer: the police had received reports on the movement of thousands of cars since 29 December and its significance was not realized at the time.

Following the failure of the first attempt to arrest the kidnappers few of the principals involved – the McKay family or the police – imagined they would came back for more. Incredibly they did, and within hours. 'M3' called again on 2 February. He told Mr McKay's son Ian he knew the Rolls had been followed by the police, but promised to meet 'his bosses' and plead for Mrs McKay's life. 'I am fond of her – your mum – you know. She reminds me of my mum.' On 5 February he rang again and said Mr McKay and his daughter Diane were to drive next day in the Rolls to the same telephone booth as before, and await new instructions. They were to have the first down-payment of £500,000 with them.

Warned by previous mistakes, the police made none this time. No overt attempt was made to shadow the Rolls. The number of men in the back-up team was greatly reduced. Instead, three armed policemen travelled in the car; two posing as Mr McKay and the chauffeur and a third hidden in the boot, with a woman PC dressed as Diane. They were given complicated instructions ordering them to leave the Rolls in London, take an Underground train to Epping, then hire a taxi and drop the suitcases containing the ransom money at a garage forecourt in Bishop's Stortford. All went smoothly – until the closing stages, when the Hoseins were frightened off by members of the public who knew nothing about the police operation. First a garage hand told Nizam Hosein not to hang around in the Volvo. Then two passers-by saw the unattended suitcases, and thought they must have fallen from a passing car; so one stood guard over them while the other reported their find to the local police!

Once again the Hoseins drove off without attempting to touch the money. But this time the Volvo was seen by police keeping surveillance and the number related to Scotland Yard – where it was instantly identified as the Hoseins'. Forty days after Mrs McKay had been kidnapped, the end was in sight.

Although her body was never found in a most intensive search of Rooks Farm and its surrounds, overwhelming evidence was discovered to link the two brothers with the kidnapping. Arthur Hosein's palm-print matched one found on the newspaper blowing about in Mr McKay's drive on the night of the kidnapping: he had wrapped the paper round the billhook. A police inspector identified Nizam as the driver of the Volvo at Bishop's Stortford. Mrs McKay's letters were written on leaves of paper taken from a notebook found in Nizam's room. An Old Bailey jury found them guilty of murder, kidnapping and blackmail, but added a recommendation for leniency for Nizam. The judge sentenced them both to life for murder, plus twenty-five years for Arthur and fifteen for Nizam on the other charges. But what became of the body?

The most widely held theory was that Muriel McKay was shot dead at Rooks Farm on or about New Year's Day, and her body cut up and fed to the pigs. There was some evidence to support this: a neighbour said she heard the sound of a shot coming from the farm around New Year's Day, while a sawn-off shotgun belonging to Arthur Hosein – and found to have been fired, although the barrels had been cleaned – was discovered on the premises. Most of the pigs had been sold and butchered, however, and it was too late to examine the carcases for possible traces of cortisone. The only ones who knew for sure what became of Mrs McKay were the brothers Hosein, neither of whom confessed.

I

IRISH REPUBLICAN ARMY
The world's oldest terrorist organization.

The IRA is the world's senior terrorist organization. Irish nationalists have resisted British authority for eight hundred years, since the Norman king Henry II set up his capital in Dublin. Its leaders, the men who plan and direct the organization's shifting strategies, do not see themselves as terrorists, far less as criminals. Although outlawed by their own government they regard themselves as patriots, fighting against an occupying power.

Today's IRA is directly descended from the Fenians, a secret society formed in Ireland in the mid-nineteenth century which spread to America, where there was a vast Irish immigrant population. Its members organized armed rebellion in Ireland, as well as fighting an underground war in mainland Britain with crude gunpowder bombs. Those in New York formed the Irish Republican Brotherhood, whose supporters, then as now, sent money and arms to help the cause. Members of the Brotherhood took an oath, which began with the words: 'I . . . do most solemnly swear in the presence of Almighty God that I will do my utmost, at every risk, while life lasts, to make Ireland an independent democratic republic . . .' In 1866 a force of several hundred Irish-American volunteers, most of whom had fought in the American Civil War, crossed the border into Canada, defeated a company of militia and captured Fort Erie. They held the post briefly, raised a symbolic republican flag, and withdrew.

The modern IRA was created after the sitting of the first Irish Parliament in 1919. It was intended to be what the name implies, an armed force raised to fight for a republican Ireland, then under the British Crown. Its name was changed from the original 'Irish Volunteers' to protect its members from summary court-martial – and possible execution by firing squad – as irregulars in the war that followed. It fought against British regular troops until the truce of 1921, when an Irish Free State was proclaimed in a peace treaty with Britain. Britain suffered 600 dead, 1,200 wounded in the campaign, the IRA 750 dead and 850 wounded.

It went into action again almost immediately, this time in the Irish civil war of 1921–2. This time it fought the 'Free Staters', Irishmen like themselves – many recent comrades-in-arms. Their 'crime' was that they had settled for a *divided* Ireland, accepted that the 'Six Counties' of the predominantly Protestant north should remain an integral part of Great Britain (as the vast majority of its people still demand). Although it lost in the civil war, the IRA refused to accept partition as lasting. Its rallying call, sixty years on, is still 'unity with independence'.

In pursuit of that dream it went to war again from 1938–45, and continued to fight on even though it was proscribed in June 1939. Not only did its members fight in Ulster, they also waged a terrorist campaign on the mainland – mostly with suitcase bombs in crowded English cities. During World War II the IRA carried out minor acts of sabotage, using supplies parachuted by the Luftwaffe. It fought yet another campaign, the 'border war' of 1956–62, but failed to win public support and achieved nothing.

Official casualty figures for its latest campaign, inclusive from 1969 to 1982, are as follows.

All terrorist-type murders	3,155
Army deaths	526
Royal Ulster Constabulary	147
RUC Reservists	65
Ulster Defence Regiment	160

The IRA of the 1980s is split into three main factions: the Official IRA, Provisional IRA, and the Irish National Liberation Army. All three maintain they have no quarrel with each other, but Officials and 'Provos' have fired on each other in the past. On 27 July 1977, for example, four men were killed and eighteen injured in one incident in Belfast.

The name 'Official IRA', meaning 'original' IRA, dates from January 1970 when the old Movement divided because of growing fears of Marxist infiltration. Cathal Goulding, leader of the Official IRA – a Dublin builder and decorator with a lifelong republican involvement – was imprisoned by the British in 1953 for his part in an arms raid in Essex, and interned by the Dublin government, for his beliefs. After his release he put forward the Marxist views which later became associated with Official Sinn Fein policy, but he denied to the author, in a rare interview in 1970, that he was a Communist. ('I am a Socialist,' he said.) Goulding, physically tough and highly intelligent, advocated a change in direction of IRA policy from militant to political activity after the border campaign of the 1950s collapsed through lack of popular support. He and his associates sought to win seats in the parliaments of Westminster, Dublin and Stormont and promote their cause via the ballot box. This was strongly opposed in the IRA Supreme Council by those who believed, equally passionately, that the only message Britain would heed was one backed by force of arms. Came the split, and the Provisional IRA was formed. The Officials have been largely inactive since 1972, when they declared a ceasefire.

The Provisionals set up their headquarters in Kevin Street, Dublin. Like the Officials, they had their own Sinn Fein (political wing: sometimes referred to as the 'Kevin Street Sinn Fein' as distinct from the Officials' 'Gardiner Place Sinn Fein'). They quickly won support in the Catholic ghettos of Northern Ireland during the violence of 1969. Provisional 'brigades' (each brigade consists of three fighting battalions, plus an HQ unit) were established in Belfast and Derry, with an estimated total strength of 1,500.

The Provisionals announced their own ceasefire from 22 December 1974 to 2 January 1975, to give the British government 'time to consider' various peace proposals. A number of unofficial meetings were held and the ceasefire was extended. On 10 February an open-ended ceasefire was announced, although some violence continued. (The official casualty figures for the year of the ceasefire, were: 30 members of the security forces killed, 1,803 shooting incidents, 399 explosions.) The ceasefire ended altogether in February 1976 with the death of hunger striker Frank Stagg. On 30 November 1978 the group warned that it was preparing for a long war. In October 1979 it declared that it could not 'in all conscience' respond to the plea by Pope John Paul in Drogheda for an end to violence. The Provisional IRA is now the biggest terrorist group in Northern Ireland, and is held responsible for the deaths of many soldiers, policemen and civilians over the years. Leadership has changed since the opening of the present campaign in 1969. In 1972 a three-man council was reported to have taken over direction of terrorist operations.

The INLA, the smallest but perhaps most ruthless of the three main groups, took its original membership from each of the other two. It is held responsible by the security forces for many murders and acts of violence since its formation in 1976. Its most notorious achievement was the car-bomb assassination of Airey Neave, MP, in March 1979. The group said he had been killed 'because of his rabid militarist calls for more repression against the Irish people'. The INLA was later outlawed, after the Northern Ireland Secretary told the Commons it was engaged in violence and had contacts with terrorist groups overseas. No details of its leadership have emerged.

The first major bombing outrage of the current terrorist campaign in Ulster was carried out by Loyalists. On 4 December 1971 a bomb exploded in McGurk's Bar in North Belfast, killing fifteen Catholics, including two children. Among the thousands of terrorist incidents spread over the past fourteen years, too numerous to record in detail, were:

On 22 February 1972 an IRA bomb wrecked the officers' mess of 16 Parachute Regiment HQ in Aldershot, killing three waitresses, a gardener and the regimental RC chaplain and wounding seventeen others. The Official IRA claimed responsibility, saying that the attack was in retaliation for the 'Bloody Sunday' shooting of thirteen civilians in Londonderry by paratroopers during street disturbances on 30 January.

On 4 March 1972 two women were killed and 186 other persons wounded – mostly shoppers taking an afternoon tea-break – when a bomb exploded in the packed Abercorn Restaurant in central Belfast. Among the wounded were two sisters. Each lost both legs. One, who was buying her wedding dress, also lost an arm and an eye. No group claimed responsibility.

On 20 March 1972 six people, including two policemen on duty, were killed and 147 injured when a 100 lb car bomb exploded in a central Belfast street. Almost all the casualties were civilian shoppers.

On 21 July 1972 eleven died and 130 more were injured when the Provisional IRA set off twenty-six explosions in Belfast. Two soldiers were among those killed. Most of the casualties were civilian, out shopping or waiting for buses to take them home. Public outrage was so great that the date is permanently remembered as 'Bloody Friday'.

The official death toll in Northern Ireland for 1972 was 467. Among them were 343 civilians, of whom 121 died by sectarian assassination (81 Catholics, 40 Protestants). More than 3,400 persons were injured.

In 1973 the IRA extended the terrorist campaign to the British mainland, concentrating mainly on London, Manchester and Birmingham. All three cities suffered considerably. The bombing in

London began on 8 March with attacks on the army's recruiting office near Trafalgar Square, and the Central Criminal Court at the Old Bailey. The gang responsible was caught. On 15 November 1973 eight of the bomb squad, said to be responsible for killing one person and wounding two hundred more on the one day, were each sentenced to life imprisonment. The ring-leaders were two sisters, Dolours and Marian Price, attractive young student teachers from St Mary's, one of Belfast's premier Catholic training colleges. The elder, Dolours, aged twenty-two, was described in newspaper reports after the trial as head of the gang and a former IRA brigade courier. It was said that army intelligence believed she helped to plan the Bloody Friday bombings in Belfast. Her sister was nicknamed 'the Armalite Widow' by troops serving in Northern Ireland, because of her reputed skill as a marksman. The two sisters had spent their entire lives in the shadow of Irish terrorism. Their father, Albert Price, spent more than ten years in internment for IRA activities: their aunt was said to have been blinded by a British army rubber bullet in 1971.

The two sisters staged a hunger strike to win the right to serve their sentences on Irish soil, and were transferred to Armagh (the only women's prison in Ulster) in March 1975. Seven years afterwards Marian Price, then aged twenty-six, was freed on licence to return to the family home in Andersonstown, Belfast. A Northern Ireland spokesman said she was suffering from severe physical illness with psychological complications, and stood to die within months if not released.

The three bombs the gang had set off in London were intended as a protest against the British government's decision to hold a referendum in Northern Ireland concerning the future of the Province. The result was entirely predictable: Protestants voted overwhelmingly to remain part of the United Kingdom, Roman Catholics boycotted the referendum.

On 4 February 1974 eleven were killed and fourteen others injured when an IRA bomb exploded aboard a coach carrying British servicemen and their families along the M62 motorway in Yorkshire. One family – soldier, wife and two children – died in the blast.

On 17 May 1974 a Loyalist bomb squad from Northern Ireland carried out a series of co-ordinated reprisal bomb attacks in Dublin and the border town of Monaghan. In Dublin, where car bombs exploded without warning at the height of the evening rush-hour, twenty-three died instantly. Altogether the Ulstermen killed thirty-four people and injured two hundred. A new terrorist group calling itself the Young Militants Association – a Protestant organization – claimed responsibility, and warned of further retaliatory action to come if the IRA attacks in Ulster continued.

In October 1974 two IRA bombs were planted in pubs in Guildford, Surrey, which were often used by Guardsmen on leave from Pirbright and Aldershot. Six people were killed and thirty-five injured. The Provisional IRA was thought to be responsible.

Following the 'year of the truce' in 1975 in Northern Ireland a further 296 murders were committed in Northern Ireland in 1976. Many of them were sectarian; there were fifty sectarian murders in North Belfast alone. Among the victims was Marie Drumm, former vice-president of Provisional Sinn Fein (the group's political wing). She was assassinated by three gunmen who forced their way into the Belfast hospital ward where she was undergoing treatment for a cataract and nervous exhaustion. The Ulster Volunteer Force (UVF), a paramilitary group sometimes known as 'the Protestant Secret Army' claimed responsibility.

The worst single incident of sectarian violence occurred at the beginning of the year, on 5 January 1976, when ten Protestant textile workers were lined up against a bus in South Armagh and machine-gunned in cold blood. A little-known Catholic organization calling itself the South Armagh Republican Action Force claimed responsibility in a telephone call to a Belfast newspaper. It said the assassinations were a reprisal for a previous multiple killing of five Roman Catholics in the same area.

On 21 July 1976 Mr Christopher Ewart-Biggs, British ambassador to the Irish republic, was murdered by terrorists as he drove to a meeting with Foreign Minister Garret FitzGerald. His car was blown up by a land-mine soon after he left his residence at Glencairn. Both the ambassador and his personal secretary Miss Judith Cooke were killed instantly. The two others in the car, civil servant Brian Cubbon and chauffeur Brian O'Driscoll, were injured. Three men, two of them armed with rifles, were seen running away. No IRA group claimed responsibility, but the police said later the assassination was thought to be the work of the Provisionals.

On 1 September both Houses of the Irish Parliament approved a request by Prime Minister Liam Cosgrave to declare a State of Emergency (the first in Eire since the outbreak of World War II). Legislation which followed gave the police powers to hold IRA suspects for seven days without preferring charges, and increased the maximum possible prison sentences for terrorism.

Ulster casualty figures for 1976 were: British army, 14 dead, Royal Ulster Constabulary 24, Ulster Defence Regiment 15, civilians 243.

The number killed by terrorist activity in 1977 fell to 111 (68 of them civilians) but the undeclared war went on.

On 17 February 1978 terrorists from the Provisional IRA firebombed the Le Mon restaurant in the Protestant Castlereagh district of Belfast, burning twelve people to death and injuring another thirty. A high-explosive charge was fired into jerrycans filled with petrol to blast a fireball through the restaurant, which was packed with people, many of them children. The motive was said to be to refute government claims that the security forces were 'winning the war'.

Among the worst terrorist outrages in the years of renewed violence was a dual bomb explosion in the heart of London on 20 July 1982, killing eleven soldiers and wounding fifty-one other persons, both military and civilian. In addition seven cavalry horses were either killed outright or so badly injured by nails and bomb splinters that they had to be put down. It is a measure of the anger and revulsion aroused in animal-loving Britain that the bombings are recalled by a single name – that of Sefton, a grievously injured horse which recovered and was eventually returned to ceremonial duty.

The first bomb exploded in Hyde Park as a troop of Blues and Royals from the Household Cavalry trotted along South Carriage Drive on their way to relieve the guard at Horseguards Parade. Troop commander Lieutenant Anthony Daly, aged twenty-three, just returned from his honeymoon, was killed with Trooper Simon Tipper, nineteen. Two others died later of wounds. The bomb which killed them held 25 lbs of gelignite and was packed tight round with another 30 lbs of six-inch and four-inch nails to cause maximum wound effect. It had been placed in a parked car and was detonated by remote control as the troop rode by. All such ceremonial duties are carried out with great regularity, so the IRA was able to plan the attack in advance at little risk to themselves.

The second bomb went off nearby in Regent's Park as the band of the Royal Greenjackets staged an open air concert. Bandmaster David Little learned of the first bombing only an hour before the concert was due to start. He went to the Regent's Park bandstand and carried out a full check of the area, but nothing suspicious was discovered. After warning his men to keep watch – particularly for parcels left behind by members of the audience – the concert went ahead. Shortly afterwards the bomb, which was hidden beneath the grandstand, exploded, killing seven bandsmen and injuring several other persons, including members of the public. The injuries sustained by the seven murdered soldiers were so horrific that Coroner Dr Paul Knapman asked reporters attending the inquest not to attribute them to individual victims, to avoid causing further distress to their families.

A briefcase containing traces of nitroglycerine was later recovered from Regent's Park lake, along with a saw, plastic explosive and large nails. Commander William Hucklesby, head of Scotland Yard's Anti-Terrorist Branch, said if the nails had been used they would have 'decimated' the audience. (After sawing through the floorboards, the bombers found there was insufficient room to include the nails, and dumped them in the lake along with anything which could have betrayed the presence of the bomb.)

On 7 December 1982 terrorists from the INLA planted a 15 lb gelignite time-bomb in the Droppin Well Inn at Ballykelly, near Londonderry in Northern Ireland. The device was deliberately placed against a main roof-support, so that the blast would bring down the ceiling to crush survivors of the explosion. Sixteen persons were killed, including eleven soldiers of the Cheshire Regiment and four young women. Sixty-six others were injured, some seriously. Several lost limbs and two were said to be paralysed for life. About 150 people, mostly soldiers with their wives or girlfriends, had been attending a pre-Christmas disco at the pub.

A heavy lifting crane was transported eighty miles from the Harland and Wolff shipyard at Belfast to move the jagged concrete boulders that were hampering the search for survivors. The scene was described as 'beyond belief', with cries from victims still trapped beneath the debris mingling with the screams of the wounded above.

Ironically, Ballykelly – with a mixed Protestant-Catholic population – has long been regarded as a model community where members of the two religious denominations live in harmony. Catholics and Protestants alike joined in the rescue work after the explosion. Northern Ireland Secretary James Prior denounced the attack as 'a massacre without mercy, ranking among the worst acts of savagery ever carried out in Northern Ireland'.

The following day the *Daily Telegraph* reported: 'The Provisional IRA said it was prepared for another twenty years of campaigning, and would continue attacks both in Britain and Northern Ireland.'

On 16 January 1983, as shocked worshippers looked on in horror, gunmen from the Provisional IRA shot Judge William Doyle as he left St Bridget's Church, Belfast, after attending mass. Two young men armed with hand-guns blazed away at close range as the judge unlocked the door of his car to offer an elderly woman friend a lift. She was hit in the stomach and seriously wounded. The judge was hit a number of times. Three doctors from the congregation fought to save him, using the first-aid equipment and respiratory stimulants all doctors carry with them in Belfast for emergency use. Finally the priest who had earlier celebrated mass administered the last rites. The Provisional IRA claimed responsibility for the judge's 'execution', claiming that he was 'a key figure in Britain's oppressive occupation machine'. They added that the fact that he was a Catholic was 'irrelevant'.

A percentage of Catholic judges are by tradition appointed in predominantly-Protestant Northern Ireland as a legal safeguard. Judge Doyle's murder was one of a number among the judiciary, who were declared 'legitimate' targets earlier by both the Provisional IRA and the INLA. Earlier victims included Judge Roger Conaghan and magistrate Martin McBirney, both shot dead in front of their families on 16 September 1974. Both were said to be part of 'the British war machine'. Mr William Staunton, another magistrate, was murdered as he took his children to school.

el ISLAMBOULI, Khaled Ahmed Shawki
Ringleader of the group which assassinated President Sadat.

On 6 October 1981 President Anwar as-Sadat of Egypt was assassinated by Muslim extremists as he reviewed a huge military parade in Cairo to commemorate the re-crossing of the Israeli-held Suez Canal by Egyptian forces in the Yom Kippur war of 1973.

Theoretically speaking it was the murder that could not happen. The flower of the Egyptian army was marching by at the time. Jet fighters patrolled overhead. Armed plain-clothes men and soldiers stood within yards of the President. Security appeared to be absolute: no one dreamed that danger might lie in the parade itself.

As a flight of F-4 Phantoms and Mirage trainer aircraft flew in formation above, a camouflaged Russian-built army truck carrying eight soldiers and towing a field-gun halted opposite the VIP stand. Four men, led by a lieutenant, jumped out and ran towards the podium. The officer was armed with a sub-machine-gun, the three gunners with AK47 assault rifles. For several seconds no one in the stand realized what was afoot: most of the attention was focussed on the fly-past. According to one eye-witness, President Sadat stood up briefly as if to salute the approaching soldiers.

Suddenly, one threw a grenade. It fell short and exploded harmlessly. A second grenade was thrown but failed to explode. By this time the two leading men had reached the stand. They raised their automatic weapons on to the parapet, and fired a hail of bullets from unmissable range at the dignitaries assembled there. Eleven of them, including President Sadat, fell fatally wounded. Thirty more were injured.

President Sadat was hit four times, twice in the chest, and in the neck and thigh. Vice-President Mubarak, on his immediate right (who succeeded him) sustained a slight hand wound. Defence Minister Abu Ghazala, on the President's left, was wounded in the head – again, not seriously. Sadat's personal secretary and head of security, Fawzi Abdul Hafez, seated immediately behind the President, tried in vain to protect him with an upturned chair but fell seriously injured in the leg. Senior presidential adviser Said Marei was among those wounded: so were Belgian ambassador Claude Ruelle and Australian first secretary John Woods. Omani Prince Shabeb bin Teymour died of wounds. Egypt's Islamic leader Sheikh Al-Azhar, together with President of the Assembly Sobhl el Hakim – both sitting alongside Sadat – escaped unhurt.

The President – still alive – was flown by helicopter to Maadi hospital for emergency treatment. Hospital chief Major General Karim headed a team of eleven specialists who fought to save him, but two hours later Sadat was pronounced dead. News of his assassination was withheld until 8 pm. It was the first the Egyptian people knew of the attack: TV coverage of the military parade had been cancelled earlier without explanation.

More than eight hundred people were rounded up following the President's assassination, of whom twenty-four men were eventually indicted on charges of premeditated murder and conspiracy. They appeared before a military court which opened in public session in Cairo on 21 November 1981. The indictment divided the accused into groups – assassins, accomplices, and conspirators. Five, including Lieutenant Khaled el Islambouli, named as the ringleader, were sentenced to death. Seventeen others received prison sentences ranging from hard labour for life to five years. The remaining two were acquitted. Among those in the dock was a blind Muslim preacher who was described as a leader of 'renegade groups' and said to have foreknowledge of the plot.

The five assassins were executed at dawn on 15 April 1982. The two army men among them – el Islambouli and reservist Hussein Abbas Muhammad – were shot by firing squad. The other three, civilians who posed as soldiers to take part in the parade, were hanged. All five were self-proclaimed 'Muslim fundamentalists', Islamic extremists who seek to replace Egypt's secular government by a religious administration to rid the country of 'permissive' Western influence. Lieutenant el Islambouli was said to be 'calm and controlled' as he met his death. During the trial he proudly admitted to leading the attack on Sadat but denied that it was part of a wider coup. 'Get Abu Ghazala [Egypt's Defence Minister] here to testify,' he demanded. 'Ask him. During the shooting I looked him in the eye and said, "I don't want you, I want your dog [Sadat]."'

Correspondents in Cairo, however, reported that Egyptian intelligence services had heard of a plot to murder the President, but did not know the full extent of the conspiracy or how the attempt was to be made. Fears of a possible *coup* were heightened by the bloody but abortive uprising in Asyut, upper Egypt, two days after Sadat's assassination. President Mubarak was later reported to have said that a 'limited net' of fanatics attempted to wipe out the whole of the leadership when they opened fire on the presidential stand on 6 October, so that an Iranian-style Islamic republic could be established. He named an extremist sect known as Takfir Wal-Hajira ('Repentance of the Holy Flight') as the organization behind the conspiracy.

JACK THE STRIPPER
An unsolved series of murders that took place near the Thames in London.

On 2 February 1964 boatmen on the Thames at Hammersmith found a naked corpse in the water. It was a prostitute, Hannah Tailford, and she had died of drowning. Her stockings were around her ankles, and her briefs had been stuffed into her mouth. It was just conceivable that she was a suicide, and an open verdict was returned. Her clothes were never found.

Two months later, on 9 April, another nude body was found floating in the river, only three hundred yards from where Hannah Tailford had been found; she was identified as Irene Lockwood, another prostitute, who specialized in snatching the wallets of her clients and vanishing while they were removing their trousers. She had also been involved in blackmailing clients who were trustful enough to allow themselves to be photographed with her in compromising states. She was four months pregnant, and had died of drowning.

The deaths caused widespread alarm among London's prostitutes, who recollected two more mysterious deaths among their ranks in earlier years: Elizabeth Figg who had been found strangled by the Thames on 17 June 1959, wearing only an underslip; and on 8 November 1963, another prostitute, Gwynneth Rees whose skeleton was uncovered by a mechanical digger clearing a Thames-side rubbish dump.

Later in April it looked as if the police had solved the case of Irene Lockwood; a caretaker named Kenneth Archibald walked into Notting Hill police station and confessed to murdering her. However, he later retracted his confession, saying he had made it because he was depressed, and a jury found him not guilty.

The first body to be found away from the river was that of Helene Barthelemy, another prostitute, who had been convicted in 1962 of luring a man on to Blackpool sands to be robbed. She had been a prostitute in the Notting Hill area, where most of the previous victims had been known. She was naked, and a dark ring around her waist indicated that her briefs had been removed after death. Four of her teeth were missing, and a piece of one was found lodged in her throat. They had obviously been forced out. The body was lying near a sports ground in Brentford, about a mile from the Thames. Her room in the Portobello area of Notting Hill was found unlocked, the record-player on, and two coffee cups on the table. There were traces of spray paint on her body, of various colours; it looked as if she had been strangled in a car, taken to a spray-paint shop somewhere, kept for twenty-four hours, then dumped at night. Sperm in her throat indicated that she had either performed fellatio on her last customer, or that he had raped her orally as she lay in the paint shop; the missing teeth made this hypothesis more likely.

During the night of 14 July 1964 painters working all night near Chiswick High Road heard a car door being slammed, and saw a man standing near a van in a dead end. When he became aware of the painters, he drove hurriedly away. The van drove so fast out of the dead end that it had almost collided with a car, and the driver had been so angry that he contacted the police. Unfortunately he had not noted the van's number. The following morning, the nude body of a woman was found in a sitting position against a garage door. She was identified as Mary Fleming, a prostitute who lived in a room in Notting Hill with her two young children. Her false teeth were missing, there was sperm in her throat, and traces of spray paint on her body. She had been missing for three days.

Now it was clear that a kind of Jack the Ripper was operating in the Notting Hill area, the police launched one of their biggest operations to try to catch him before he killed again. Numbers of cars and vans that were seen more than once in red light areas were noted. The killer may have been frightened by his near-miss, for there were no more murders for four months. Yet it was obvious that a man who had a violent need to have oral sex with prostitutes, and to choke them in the process, would feel a compulsion to find more victims. On 25 November 1964 a naked body was found in a carpark in Hornton Street, Kensington. She was another prostitute, Margaret McGowan, who had vanished a month earlier. Again, there were traces of paint on her body, and sperm in the throat. A tooth had been forced out.

On 16 February of the following year another prostitute, Bridie O'Hara, was found in the undergrowth on the Heron Trading Estate, Acton; she had last been seen on 11 January in a Shepherd's Bush hotel. Her body was partly mummified, indicating that it had been kept somewhere cool. Fingerprints on the back of her neck indicated that she had died in a kneeling position; there was sperm in her throat and some of her teeth were missing.

Now certain things were becoming clear. The killer would pick up a prostitute, usually in the Notting Hill area, and take her somewhere in his van, requesting her to perform fellatio. While they were doing this he would force her head down on his penis, so that the glans lodged in her throat and choked her. After this, he presumably took her to the hiding place near the paint spray shop, and then performed more acts of oral rape after forcing out some teeth. Finally, the body was taken away and dumped.

And it was on the Heron Trading Estate that the police finally located the place where the women had been kept – a disused warehouse near a paint spray shop. Analysis of the paint revealed that this was the place they were looking for.

This discovery should have taken the police several steps closer to the killer; but thousands of people were employed on the Heron Estate. John du Rose, in charge of the case, threw a police cordon around the trading estate, and noted all vans that were seen in the area more than once. He deliberately waged a war of nerves against the unknown killer, dropping hints on television that the police were now very close to catching him. A list of twenty suspects had been reduced to three when one of the three committed suicide, leaving a note saying he could not bear the strain any longer. He was a security guard who had access to the estate, who worked at nights, and whose rounds included the spray shop. He was unmarried.

In his book *Murder is My Business* du Rose has suggested that the death of the first victim – possibly Elizabeth Figg – in the act of performing oral sex triggered a need in the killer to repeat the experience of orgasm at the moment his victim choked. The size of the victims – all were small women – suggested that the killer himself was of less than average height. It seems just possible that a survey of prostitutes in the Notting Hill area, to find out whether any of them had a client who, before 1964, used to pay for oral sex, might have pinpointed the killer before he took more lives. As it is, Jack the Stripper has joined Jack the Ripper as one of the most puzzling and elusive of killers in British criminal history.

JONES, James Warren
Paranoid messiah who ordered the mass suicide of members of his People's Temple in Guyana.

James Warren Jones was born on 13 May 1931, the only child of a poor family in Indiana, in the bible belt. At the age of twelve, he gave his first hell-fire sermon to an audience of young children. In 1947 he married Marceline Baldwin, a nurse, and started a mission for local Methodists, directing his attentions mainly at the poor blacks. In 1954 he was evicted from the Methodist Church. In 1957 he set up a People's Temple in Indianapolis. He was a charismatic personality, and faith healer, but segregationalists called him a 'nigger-lover' and broke his windows and threw explosives into his yard. In 1963, he told his congregation that he had experienced a vision of a coming nuclear holocaust that would poison the world and announced that two places would remain unaffected, Ukiah, California, and Belo Horizante, Brazil. In 1965, he moved to California, with large numbers of his followers in minibuses.

His success in Ukiah was immediate, and by 1970 he had moved his church from Redwood Valley to San Francisco. Here again, most of his followers were poor blacks, although there were whites among them. The congregation provided money, and Jones opened a church in Los Angeles, and began flying around the country with a retinue of bodyguards and aides. He bought a fleet of Greyhound buses. He expected his followers to be sexually abstinent, but he himself used his congregation as a harem. He seems to have been bisexual. He became the father of at least three children by members of his congregation. One woman chose to have an abortion rather than bear Jones's child. Jones became increasingly obsessed by the idea of persecution, and made his cult members rehearse what he called 'revolutionary suicide' – mass suicide of the entire Temple. He called these rehearsals 'White Nights'.

Increasing notoriety and press hostility made him decide to move to Guyana, where a million dollars contributed by followers enabled the Temple to build Jonestown. In 1977 a thousand followers moved there, and the San Francisco *Chronicle* published a report the following year that stated: 'The People's Temple jungle outpost in South America was portrayed yesterday as a remote realm where the Church Leader, the Rev. Jim Jones, orders public beatings, maintains a squad of fifty armed guards, and has involved his 1,100 followers in a threat of mass suicide.'

When Californian congressman Leo Ryan heard these stories, he asked the federal authorities to intervene. His study of the Patty Hearst case had made him familiar with the concept of brain-washing. On 14 November 1978 Ryan and a team of journalists went to Jonestown. Jones seems to have treated them well, and when Ryan made a speech at dinner, saying he believed that 'there are many people here who believe this is the best thing that has ever happened to them' there were frenzied cheers and clapping for three minutes. Jones, said a member of the delegation, seemed 'both frightened and fascinated by the press'. He denied that any beatings had taken place but spoke frankly about his mistresses. He dismissed allegations that his followers were not allowed sexual intercourse with the comment, 'Bullshit. Thirty babies have been born since the summer of 1977.'

As the delegation left – taking with them two defectors – Jones arrived with several followers, and opened fire. Ryan, three journalists and the two defectors were killed. Jones then hurried back to Jonestown and ordered mass suicide. The babies had cyanide squirted into their mouths with syringes, then the older children lined up and accepted cups of Kool-ade laced with cyanide. After this, the adults all drank poison. Finally, Jones killed himself with a single bullet in the right temple. A few followers succeeded in escaping.

After the suicides, a white American professor who with his common-law wife and child had been members of Jones's Ukiah community in its early days, explained that it had been similar to the Oneida Community led by John Humphrey Noyes in its indulgence in multiple marriages. He also said that for many weeks after the mass suicide members who had remained in California were terrified that Jones was still alive and might come back and kill them.

Jones's nineteen-year-old son Stephan, who was not in Jonestown at the time of the suicides because he was away with the Guyanan basketball team, said of his father: 'I can almost say I hate the man. He has destroyed almost everything I have lived for.'

JUDY, Steven
A dropout who insisted on being executed for a rape murder.

On 28 April 1979 men looking for mushrooms on the north bank of White Lick Creek, Indiana, found the body of a woman, almost naked, lying face down in the water. Further down stream, the bodies of three young children – two boys and a girl – were found. Medical examination showed that the woman, in her early twenties, had been raped and strangled. The three children had apparently drowned when they had fallen – or been thrown – into the creek. A bankbook found near the body helped to identify it as that of Terry Chasteen. The boyfriend with whom she lived was able to tell police that she had set out at seven o'clock that morning to take the children to a baby-sitter before she went on to work in a big store. She had been divorced from the father of her children.

An appeal to the public brought the information that a red and silver pick-up truck had been seen close to the site of the murder at eight o'clock that morning. And by an odd coincidence, the same man's child had seen the truck parked at a building site. The police were soon able to identify it as belonging to a bricklayer named Steve Judy. On the day after the murder, Judy was arrested at the home of his foster parents in Indianapolis.

Judy, aged twenty-two, was the child of a broken home, and remembered his natural parents fighting violently. Although he had been given love and affection by his foster parents, it was apparently too late. At the age of twelve, he had knocked at a door in the neighbourhood and asked the young woman who answered it if she wanted to buy boy scout cookies. When he found she was alone in the house, he had forced her into a bedroom, raped her at knifepoint, and stabbed her forty-one times. He had then tried to kill her with a hatchet. She recovered after brain surgery and testified against him. Judy was sent to a mental home, but only spent nine months there. When he was eighteen, he was convicted of badly beating a woman in Chicago. He spent twenty months in jail for this crime. In Indianapolis, he forced a young woman to drive to a spot not far from the site where he would murder Terry Chasteen, but she managed to jump out of the vehicle and run away. He was sentenced to a year in prison.

In court Judy confessed how, on the morning of 28 April, he had dropped off a girlfriend, and then noticed Terry Chasteen driving along with her three children. He had pulled alongside and pointed at her tyres. She stopped to see what was wrong, and he managed to raise the bonnet of her car and rip out the ignition coil. He then offered to drive her to a filling station. She trusted him, but as soon as they were on the highway, he turned to her and said, 'I guess you know what's going to happen now?' They drove to the bridge at White Lick Creek, and the children were sent for a walk while Judy made her undress and then raped her. When she began screaming, he strangled her. The children came running at the sound of their mother's screams, and Judy picked them up one after the other and threw them into the creek.

In court, Judy told the jury, 'You had better put me to death because next time it might be one of you or your daughter.' The woman he had attacked when he was twelve was called into court, and showed jurors the stub of her index finger which had been cut off in the struggle.

Judy was sentenced to death on 16 February 1980. He thwarted every attempt to appeal the death sentence. On 8 March 1981 he had his last meal and took a sedative tablet provided by the doctor, and was then electrocuted. His foster mother said later that he had told her he had raped and killed more women than he could remember. He said there was a 'string of bodies' across Texas, Florida, Louisiana, Illinois and Indiana. She said she was giving this information in case other men might be executed for murders that Steven Judy had committed.

K

KEENAN, Brian Paschal
Mastermind behind the IRA bomb attack on London in 1975 and the Balcombe Street gang.

Ross McWhirter, co-editor of the *Guinness Book of Records*, was a campaigning journalist with political ambitions and an outspoken opponent of the IRA. In November 1975 he launched his 'Beat the Bombers' campaign after the chance murder of cancer specialist Gordon Hamilton Fairley by a car bomb intended for his neighbour, Hugh Fraser MP. McWhirter put up a £50,000 reward for the capture of the IRA death squad who had been responsible for murdering eight civilians and wounding two hundred others in a series of bomb incidents. He was also head of Self-Help, an organization which sought the reintroduction of the death penalty (by making terrorism a treasonable offence) and the registration of all southern Irish nationals living in England. He had no illusions about what might befall him as a result of these activities. 'I live . . . in constant fear of my life,' he admitted. 'I know the IRA have got me on their death list.'

They had. Two gunmen lay in ambush in his garden in Village Lane, Enfield, and shot him as he stood silhouetted against the light, opening his front door to greet his wife, who was walking up the drive towards the house. He was hit in the head and body and died minutes after reaching hospital. Mrs McWhirter was not harmed. The killers made off in a car which was later abandoned in Tottenham, seven miles away. The Chicago-style assassination profoundly shocked the public by the apparent ease and callous deliberation with which it was carried out; there were renewed demands in Parliament for the death penalty for capital crimes.

Four members of the IRA gang were captured shortly afterwards. On 6 December they drove past Scott's restaurant in Mayfair, firing sub-machine-guns. This time however Scotland Yard had mobilized a powerful stand-by force, and they chased the men to a flat in Balcombe Street, in Marylebone, where the gang took a middle-aged couple, Mr and Mrs John Matthews, hostage. The area was promptly sealed off by police, and after a classic six-day siege the four terrorists surrendered on 12 December, releasing Mr and Mrs Matthews unharmed. Metropolitan Police Commissioner Sir Robert Mark wrote later in his autobiography: 'During the siege we managed to obtain ... the vital fingerprints we wanted. We then knew with certainty that we had "Z", who had been formally "buried" in Eire long before the bombing started, so that he could come over to England as a "sleeper".' Information gleaned from the four terrorists – Martin O'Connell, Harry Duggan, Edward Butler and Hugh Doherty, all in their mid twenties – led police to two bomb factories in London and a third in Liverpool. Fingerprints found there on an unfinished crossword puzzle implicated 'Z' – unit commander Brian Keenan of Belfast, aged thirty-nine, the mastermind behind the London bombing campaign.

At their trial on 10 February 1977 the Balcombe Street gang faced charges of murdering nine people and wounding two hundred others. Their victims included Gordon Hamilton Fairley, Captain Roger Goad (a police bomb-disposal officer), two people at the London Hilton, where sixty-three others were injured, and other people killed by bombs in West End restaurants. O'Connell, Duggan and Butler were each given massive prison sentences, including life, all to run concurrently, and Doherty received eleven life sentences for murder, twenty-one years for manslaughter, five terms of twenty years and one of eighteen for terrorist offences. Mr Justice Cantley, who had himself been threatened by the IRA, recommended that all four should serve at least thirty years in jail.

After they left the dock, one shouting 'Up the Provos' and another giving him the V-sign, the judge said: 'I have been dealing so far with criminals who called themselves soldiers and shot unarmed men, murdered unprotected and unsuspecting women, sneaking up and throwing a bomb through a restaurant window before running away. I want now to commend men of true worth – unarmed policemen who faced and chased these criminals, and the bomb disposal officers like Major Biddle, Mr Henderson, Captain Cole and others who staked their lives against the chance of being able to make the bombs safe for others.'

Keenan, the father of six children, was not arrested until March 1979. He was caught in County Down after a combined anti-terrorist drive by police on both sides of the Irish border and taken to England. He knew the evidence against him was thin, but did not know that Scotland Yard had found the tell-tale fingerprints in the Liverpool bomb factory three years earlier. While awaiting trial he was obligingly provided with more crossword puzzles to solve (he was a crossword fanatic); the two sets of handwriting were matched by graphologists, and the police were thus able to link him positively with the 1975 bombing campaign. A senior anti-terrorist detective was quoted as saying, 'I cannot think of a bigger fish we could have caught. The Provos could never find a good enough replacement.'

On 25 June 1980, by a majority verdict of ten to two, an Old Bailey jury found Keenan guilty of conspiring to cause explosions to endanger life, and plotting to possess firearms. He was jailed for eighteen years.

KEMPER, Edmund Emil
Necrophiliac mass murderer.

Ed Kemper, born on 18 December 1948, began to show signs of severe psychological disturbance as a child. His mother and father separated when he was seven; he was one of those children who badly needed a man to admire and imitate, and became an ardent fan of John Wayne. He had been a boy scout, and was taught to shoot and handle a knife at summer camp. He claimed that his mother ridiculed him, and grew up with a highly ambivalent attitude towards her. As a child, he played games with his sister in which she led him to die in the gas chamber, and he once cut the hands and feet off her doll. At thirteen he cut the family cat into pieces. He had sadistic fantasies which included killing his mother, and often went into her bedroom at night with a gun, toying with the idea. He grew up to be six feet nine inches tall and weighing twenty stone (280 pounds). He also had fantasies of sexual relation with corpses. In spite of his powerful sexual interest in women from an early age, he was pathologically shy; when his sister once joked with him about wanting to kiss his teacher he replied, 'If I kissed her I'd have to kill her first.' Which is precisely what he did to his victims in manhood. Like the English sex murderer Christie, he killed women because he would have been impotent with a living woman.

At thirteen Ed ran away to his father, who promptly returned him to his mother. He was then sent to live with his father's parents on a ranch in California. His mother rang her ex-husband to warn him that he was taking a risk in sending Ed to live with them; she said, 'You might wake up one day and find they've been killed.' Which is exactly what happened. When he lost his temper with his domineering

179

grandmother one day in August 1963, he pointed a rifle at the back of her head, and killed her. He then stabbed her repeatedly. When his grandfather came home, he shot him before he could enter the house. Then he telephoned his mother, and waited for the police to arrive. Donald Lunde, a psychiatrist who examined him later, remarked: 'In his way, he had avenged the rejection of both his mother and father.'

After five years in mental hospitals, he was sent back to his mother. She moved to Santa Cruz, where she became administrative assistant in a college of the University of California. She and Ed had violent, screaming quarrels, usually about trivial subjects. Kemper loathed her. He bought a motorcycle and wrecked it, suing the motorist involved, then did the same with a second motorcycle; using the insurance money he bought himself a car, and began driving around, picking up hitch-hikers, preferably female. And on 7 May 1972, he committed his first sex murders, picking up Anita Luchese and Mary Anne Pesce, both students of Fresno State College, in Berkeley. He produced his gun, drove to a quiet spot, and made Anita climb into the boot while he handcuffed Mary Ann and put a plastic bag over her head. She seemed unafraid of him, and tried to talk to him reasonably. He stabbed her several times in the back, then in the abdomen; finally he cut her throat. After this he went to the boot, and stabbed the other girl repeatedly. He then drove home – his mother was out – carried the bodies up to his apartment, and decapitated and dissected them. Later, he buried the pieces in the mountains.

On 14 September 1972 he picked up fifteen-year-old Aiko Koo, a Eurasian girl hitch-hiking to a dance class in San Francisco. He produced his gun, drove her to the mountains, and then taped her mouth. When he tried to suffocate her by placing his fingers up her nostrils she fought fiercely. When she was dead, he laid her on the ground, and raped her, achieving orgasm within seconds. He took her back to his apartment, cut off the head and hands, and dissected the body, becoming sexually excited as he cut off the head. He took the remains out to the mountains above Boulder Creek and buried them.

On 8 January 1973 he picked up Cynthia Schall who usually hitched a lift to Cabrillo College. He produced the gun, drove her to the little town of Freedom, and stopped on a quiet road. For a while he played a cat and mouse game with her, telling her he had no intention of harming her, enjoying the sensation of power. Then he shot her, dumped the body in the boot, and drove home. She was a heavy girl, and he staggered with her into his bedroom, placing her in his closet. His mother came home, and Kemper talked to her and behaved normally. As soon as she was gone the next morning, he took out the body and engaged in various sex acts. Then he dissected it with an axe in the shower, and drove out to Carmel, with the body in plastic sacks, and threw them off cliffs. This time, parts of the body were discovered only a day later, and identified as Cynthia Schall.

After a violent quarrel with his mother on 5 February, he drove to the local campus, and picked up Rosalind Thorpe, who was just coming out of a lecture. Shortly after, he picked up 21-year-old Alice Lui. As they drove along in the dark, he shot Rosalind in the head. Alice Lui covered her face with her hands; he shot her several times in the head. He put both bodies in the boot, and drove home. His mother was at home, so he could not carry them in. Unable to wait, he took his big hunting knife (which he called the General) and hacked off both their heads in the boot. The next morning, when his mother had gone to work, he carried Alice Lui into the bathroom, cleaned off the blood, and had sexual intercourse with the headless corpse. He also cleaned up Rosalind Thorpe, although it is not clear whether he again performed necrophilia. He placed both bodies back in the boot, cut off Alice Lui's hands, then drove to the coast highway south of Pacifia and disposed of the heads; the bodies were dumped in Eden Canyon, Alameda. They were found nine days later.

Shortly after this, a policeman checking through gun licences realized that Ed Kemper had a criminal record, and had not declared this. He drove to Kemper's house, and found him in his car with a young blonde girl. Kemper handed over the gun, and the policeman drove off. His call probably saved the life of the blonde hitch-hiker.

Kemper felt that he was going to 'blow up' soon, commit a crime so obvious that he would be caught. He decided to kill his mother. On the morning of Easter Sunday 1973, Kemper walked into his mother's bedroom and hit her on the head with a hammer. Then he cut off her head with the General, and dumped the body in a closet. He felt sick, and went out for a drive. He saw an acquaintance who owed him $10 and they went for a drive in his friend's car; his friend offered him the $10, which, said Kemper later, 'saved his life'. But he needed to kill somebody else at that point so he rang a friend of his mother's, Sara Hallett, and invited her for dinner with himself and his mother. When she arrived, she was breathless, and said,

'Let's sit down. I'm dead.' Kemper took this as a cue, and hit her, then strangled her. Later, in removing her head, he discovered he had broken her neck.

That night he slept in his mother's bed. The next day he drove west in Mrs Hallett's car. Then, using money he had taken from the dead woman, he rented a Hertz car. At one point he was stopped by a policeman for speeding, and fined $25 on the spot. The policeman did not notice the gun on the back seat.

He was expecting a manhunt, but when, after three days, there was still no news on the radio of the finding of the bodies, he stopped in Pueblo, Colorado, and telephoned the Santa Cruz police to confess to being 'the co-ed killer'. They asked him to call back later. He did, several times, before he finally convinced them that he was serious. They sent a local policeman to arrest him. And in custody in Pueblo, he showed himself eager to talk loquaciously about the killings, describing them all in detail – even how he had buried the head of one victim in the garden, facing towards the house, so he could imagine her looking at him, and how he had cut out his mother's larynx and dropped it in the ash can 'because it seemed appropriate after she had bitched me so much'. He explained that he had driven to Pueblo before turning himself in because he was afraid that if he went straight to the local police they might shoot first and ask questions later, and he was 'terrified of violence'.

Kemper was adjudged legally sane, and sentenced to life imprisonment for his eight murders.

KIM, Jae-Kyu
Chief of intelligence who murdered the President of South Korea.

On 26 October 1979 President Park Chung-Hee, an anti-Communist hardliner who had already survived one assassination attempt (in 1974, when the bullet hit his wife) was shot dead at dinner in Seoul by the man responsible for his personal safety – Kim Jae-Kyu, head of the Korean Central Intelligence Agency. Five presidential bodyguards were murdered at the same time.

Kim feared that he was about to be dismissed from office, following violent student riots in Pusan and other cities earlier in the month. He was also resentful because the President was increasingly turning to his chief bodyguard, Cha Ji-Chul, for advice. He therefore planned to murder them both on the night of 26 October, and to seize power himself.

Before they arrived he hid a loaded revolver in an ante-room, and told his agents to fire on the President's other bodyguards as soon as they heard him shoot Park and chief bodyguard Cha. Two women hostesses waited on the four principals as they sat down to dinner at KCIA headquarters – President Park, bodyguard Cha, head of the KCIA Kim and a collaborator, Kim Kae-Won. Kim excused himself soon after the President asked him, 'Do you think that trouble erupted at Pusan because of lack of information from your agency?' He collected the revolver and returned to the dining-room. He baited the President by pointing to Cha and asking, 'How can you do a good job when you use an insect like that?' and opened fire on them both.

Cha, who was unarmed, was only slightly wounded and hid in a nearby toilet. Kim's second bullet struck President Park in the chest. Kim's agents in the ante-room opened fire on the other bodyguards with revolvers and MI6 rifles, killing four and wounding a fifth. When Kim found Cha hiding behind some furniture he shot him in the stomach, and President Park in the head, killing them both.

He tried to get Army Chief of Staff General Chung (who had no part in the plot) to join him in the coup. Chung refused and the conspirators were all rounded up and arrested. Prime minister Choi Kyu-Hah was named as the new president. America placed her 38,000 troops in South Korea on full alert and warned North Korea not to intervene, and the crisis passed.

At their trial by court-martial in Seoul on 20 December 1979 Kim, aged fifty-three, was sentenced to death. Sentenced with him were his chief collaborator Kim Kae-Won (President Park's secretary-general) and Colonel Park Heung-Joo, Kim's senior KCIA aide. Colonel Park was refused the right of appeal since he was in active military service. Four other agents who had taken part in the mass murder of the bodyguards were also sentenced to death.

Kim thanked the court-martial and told them, 'As I leave this world I will keep within me this deep gratitude to you all.'

KINNE, Sharon
A young mother who briefly succeeded in blaming her husband's murder on their baby daughter.

Nineteen-year-old Sharon Kinne had been married for almost four years to James Kinne, an electronics worker. They lived between Kansas City and Independence. On 19 March 1960 she rang the police in hysterics to say that her husband needed help. She had found him lying on a bed, a bullet-hole in the back of his head. When the police came to the scene, Mrs Kinne explained that she had been in another room when she heard a loud bang and had rushed into the bedroom to find her 2½-year-old daughter had apparently shot her father with his pistol. The child often played with the gun, she said, and her husband had left it on a low shelf; the child had presumably taken it and gone into the bedroom to play some kind of game . . .

A detective who talked to the child left the gun on a nearby table, and observed that she seemed to handle it as if she had done so before – she even released the safety catch. The coroner ruled that James Kinne's death was an accident, and his young widow received the insurance money. She bought a new car, a Thunderbird, from a good-looking young salesman named Jones, and he and Sharon became friendly.

A mere two months later, on 27 May, Sharon Kinne reported that she had discovered the body of a young woman in a heavily wooded lovers' lane in Jackson County. The dead woman, who had been shot four times, was Patricia Jones, wife of the car salesman. Sharon explained that she and her boyfriend had been out looking for Patricia that evening, because she was convinced that the salesman's wife was having an affair with another man. They had looked in a number of bars, and were cruising down the lovers' lane when she had seen the body in the headlights . . .

The police were inclined to believe that she had seen it because she knew it was there. The woman had been shot with a .22 pistol, and in Sharon Kinne's home they found a box that had held a .22 pistol – she explained that she thought she had left it behind on a visit to Washington, but it could not be located. It was discovered that Patricia Jones had been seen with Sharon Kinne earlier on the evening she had been murdered – getting into her car. Sharon Kinne admitted this, and said that she had wanted to test the woman's

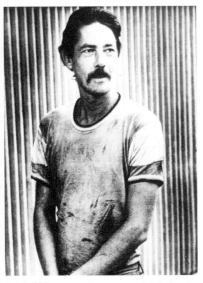

Jack Abbott on the way to the federal
court in New Orleans

Mary Bell, photographed shortly
before she absconded from Moor
Court in 1977

Ulrike Meinhof

Andreas Baader

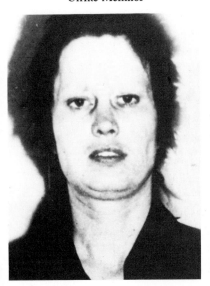

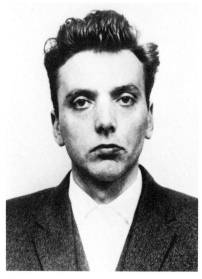

Police photographs of Ian Brady and Myra Hindley on the day they began
their sentences

Lindy Chamberlain outside the Alice
Springs court house

David Berkowitz after being formally
booked by Brooklyn police

Mark Chapman in 1975, giving a Vietnamese refugee a ride at Fort Chafee

Alice Crimmins outside the court house at her second trial

Albert DeSalvo after his arrest in Lynn, Massachusetts

James Hanratty, convicted and executed for the murder of Michael Gregsten

Steven Judy, who refused to appeal against his death sentence

The Kray twins as teenage professional boxers

Joachim Kroll at his court hearing in Duisberg

The first permitted photograph of Charles Manson during the long trial of his 'family'

Donald Neilson, beaten up by members of the public just after his arrest

Lee Harvey Oswald at the police station in Dallas, denying that he had assassinated President Kennedy

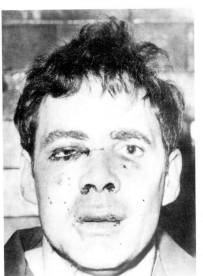

James Earl Ray at the announcement
of his sentence in Washington

Sirhan in a relaxed mood in Soledad Prison, California

Richard Speck laughing for pressmen
during the hearing in Chicago

Charles Sobhraj, escorted by an armed Indian policeman, entering the court
at Varanasi in March 1982

Top left: A University of Texas regulation photograph of Charles Whitman

Top right: Michael X with his girlfriend Trixie Warner after being released on bail in England in August 1967

Left: Graham Young took this sinister picture of himself in a do-it-yourself photo kiosk

reaction to a suggestion that her husband might be seeing other women.

When a fellow employee from the camera store where Sharon worked told the police he had bought a.22 gun for her, and that she had urged him not to register it in her name, they decided they had enough circumstantial evidence to charge her with the murder of Patricia Jones – the motive, presumably, being a desire to rid herself of an obstacle that stood between herself and the car salesman.

In September 1960 she was indicted for the murder of Patricia Jones. There was excitement in court when the previous owner of the missing gun – which had been bought second-hand – revealed that he had fired some shots from it into a tree. The tree was now being chopped up to recover the bullets and see if they matched those that killed Mrs Jones. Unfortunately, they did not, and the owner now admitted that he had owned several guns, and could have been mistaken about which one had fired the shots. The jury nevertheless returned a verdict of not guilty. She was immediately re-arrested and charged with the murder of her husband – police experts testified that a 2½-year-old was not strong enough to pull the trigger. In January 1962 she was found guilty of murder and sentenced to life imprisonment. Her defence challenged the verdict on a legal technicality, and a retrial was ordered. Another legal technicality led the judge to declare a mistrial. At a fourth trial, a woman who had been in the same cell as Sharon testified that she had admitted to shooting her husband after an argument about divorce. The jury nevertheless found it impossible to agree and were dismissed.

On 14 September 1964 Sharon Kinne drove to Mexico City with a man and they booked in at the Hotel Gin. Four days later she went out alone, met a middle-aged Mexican named Francisco Paredes Ordonez, a radio announcer, and accompanied him to his motel room after being introduced to the motel proprietor. Not long afterwards the proprietor heard shots and rushed to the room. Ordonez lay dead, and Sharon Kinne was about to leave with a gun in her hand. As he turned to retreat she shot him in the back. He grabbed her and they were still wrestling when the police arrived.

Her story was that she had been ill when Ordonez had picked her up, that she had accompanied him to the motel room on a misunderstanding, and that when she had lain down on the bed, he had tried to rape her. A Mexican judge found the story frankly incredible, and sentenced her to ten years in prison. Meanwhile the prosecutor in Kansas City asked if he might see the .22 pistol with which she had killed Ordonez; it turned out to be the gun that had killed Patricia Jones.

Sharon Kinne appealed against her conviction, but the appeal judge decided that her sentence was too short, and added three years.

KNOWLES, Paul John

Multiple killer and rapist shot by a police officer shortly after his arrest.

Knowles was a petty crook – car thefts and burglaries – who spent an average of six months of every year in jail from 1965 (when he was nineteen) to 1972. He was serving a slightly longer term in Raiford Penitentiary, Florida, when he began to study astrology, and started corresponding with a divorcee named Angela Covic whom he contacted through the magazine *American Astrology*. After a while she flew to Florida to meet him, agreed to marry him, and hired a lawyer to work on his parole. This took some time; it came through on 14 May 1974. The tall, red-headed man with the gaunt face flew to San Francisco to embrace his future wife and take a job she had located for him. But a psychic had told Angela Covic that she had a very dangerous man in her life, and when Knowles turned up at her apartment, she experienced a deep, instinctive uneasiness that made her change her mind about marrying him. She made him sleep at her mother's – who liked him – but after four days, told him she had decided against marriage, and put him on a plane back to Florida. Knowles later told his lawyer that on the night she had thrown him over, he had gone out on the streets of San Francisco and killed three people. This was never verified. Angela Covic became reconciled with her husband, and when Knowles rang her, told him that she did not want to see him.

Back in Florida Knowles got into a fight in a bar and was locked up in Jacksonville police station. He picked the lock and escaped. Later that evening – 26 July 1974 – Knowles broke into the home of a 65-year-old teacher, Alice Curtis, bound and gagged her, and stole her money and her car. But he rammed the gag too deep into her mouth, and she died.

He hung around Jacksonville for a few more days. By this time, the police had linked him to the Curtis murder, and his description was announced on radio and television. As he parked the stolen car on a quiet street, he saw two girls staring at him. Their mother was a friend of his family, and they looked as if they recognized him. Knowles forced them into the car and drove away. The bodies of Mylette Anderson, aged seven, and her sister Lillian, eleven, were later found in a swamp.

The following day he drove to Atlantic Beach, Florida, broke into the house of Marjorie Howe, and strangled her with a nylon stocking. He stole her television set.

Some days later – the date is not known – he picked up a teenage hitchhiker; the girl told him she was a runaway. Knowles later claimed that he took her into the woods, raped her, then strangled her with his hands. Her body remained unidentified.

On 23 August he broke into the home of Kathie Pierce in Musella, and strangled her with a telephone cord while her three-year-old son looked on. He left the boy unharmed and left. For the next three days he stayed around Musella until someone reported seeing the stolen white car near the house of the murdered woman; once again he left.

On 3 September near Lima, Ohio, he struck up a conversation with an accounts executive, William Bates, and the two had several drinks together in Scott's Inn. They left at midnight, and Bates was not seen again until a month later, when a strangled, nude body was found in woods not far from the abandoned stolen car. Knowles had driven off in the dead man's white Impala.

Using Bates's money and credit cards, Knowles went to Sacramento, California, then to Seattle, then back east into Utah. In Ely, Nevada, he saw a camping trailer, and forced his way in. The elderly couple who were on vacation from San Pedro were later found shot behind the ear; they were Emmett and Lois Johnson. Knowles took their credit cards. It was September 18.

Three days later, he saw a woman in a car beside the road near Sequin. He pulled in, ordered her to move over, then strangled and raped her. He dragged the body through a barbed wire fence.

Two days later, in Birmingham, Alabama, Knowles met an attractive woman, Ann Dawson, who owned a beauty shop in Fairfield. The two seem to have taken a liking to one another and for the next six days, they travelled around together, living on her money. He killed her on 29 September and her body has never been found.

For over a fortnight Knowles drove around through Oklahoma, Missouri, Iowa and Minnesota without, apparently, committing more crimes. But on 16 October he parked outside a house in Marlborough, Connecticut, and rang the doorbell. A pretty teenager, Dawn Wine, broke off her homework to hurry to the door, thinking it was a girlfriend. Knowles forced his way in at gunpoint, made the girl go up to the bedroom, and spent the next hour raping her. Her mother, Mrs Karen Wine, then returned, and Knowles made her cook him a meal. Then he ordered mother and daughter into the bedroom, made them both strip, and tied their hands. After raping Mrs Wine, he strangled them both with a nylon stocking. He left with a tape-recorder and Dawn's collection of rock records. The bodies were found later that evening by Mrs Wine's other daughter.

Knowles headed south; on 19 October he was in Virginia. He approached a house in Woodford, south of Fredericksburg, and knocked on the door. 53-year-old Doris Hovey answered. He told her he needed a gun and would not harm her. She unlocked her husband's gun cabinet and gave him a .22 rifle. Knowles loaded it and shot her through the head. He then wiped the rifle clean of prints, left it beside the body, and left the house without taking anything. That one had been purely for pleasure.

Knowles drove to Key West, Florida, still driving the white Impala stolen from Bates. He picked up two hitch-hikers, intending to kill them, but was stopped by a policeman for pulling up on a curve. Knowles expected to be arrested; but the policeman only glanced at the documents, and allowed him to drive on with a warning. The policeman's inefficiency was to cost more lives.

In Miami, Knowles dropped his hitch-hikers, and called his lawyer. When the attorney met him, Knowles told him he wanted to confess to fourteen murders. The lawyer suggested he give himself up. Knowles refused, but agreed to tape a confession, using the recorder he had stolen from the Wine household. He delivered the tape to the lawyer, Sheldon Yavitz, declined again to turn himself in, and left. Yavitz notified the Miami police, but Knowles had already escaped.

On 6 November in a gay bar in Macon, Georgia, Knowles met a man named Carswell Carr; they had a few drinks, and Carr invited Knowles to spend the night at his home. Later that evening, an argument developed, and Carr's daughter was awakened by the shouting. She went downstairs, to find Knowles standing over the body of her father, whom he had stabbed to death. He then strangled the fifteen-year-old girl, tried unsuccessfully to rape her, and left. There were almost certainly more victims between the time Knowles left Miami and the time he killed Carr. In woods near Macon, police found the body of a hitch-hiker, Edward Hilliard, and there were also items belonging to Debbie Griffin, who had been hitchhiking with him. Her body was never found. A medical examination determined that Hilliard had been killed about four days before Knowles killed the Carrs.

In Atlanta on 8 November Knowles met an English journalist called Sandy Fawkes. Attracted by his 'gaunt good looks', she agreed to dance with him, then went for a meal; they ended in the same bed. But Knowles proved to be sexually incapable. She sensed he was inexperienced. However, the two got on well enough to spend the next day together – he had introduced himself as Daryl Golden – and to leave Atlanta in the stolen Impala. He hinted at being a mass murderer. In a motel, they succeeded in having a slightly more satisfying sexual experience, with Knowles masturbating as he performed cunnilingus on her, and entering her as he achieved orgasm. But on the only other occasion they achieved coitus, he had no orgasm. This might explain why some of the rapes were not fully consummated.

In her book *Killing Time* Sandy Fawkes describes the few days she spent with Knowles. He often behaved like a tender, protective husband. After they had parted, Knowles spent an evening sitting in a bar waiting for her; she went out with someone else, and Knowles spent the evening talking to three of her newspaper colleagues, including Jim and Susan MacKenzie, who had only just arrived from England. The following morning, 11 November, Knowles went to see the MacKenzies; Susan was in alone, and mentioned she had to go to the hairdresser. Knowles offered to drive her there. On the way, she noticed they had taken the wrong turn. He told her that he wanted to have sex with her, and wouldn't hurt her if she complied. He stopped the car and pointed a gun at her; she managed to get out and run away, waving at a passing car. Knowles drove off, and Susan MacKenzie rang the police. Later, a patrol car spotted Knowles's car, and flagged it down. Knowles pointed a sawn-off shotgun out of the window, and the policeman quickly dropped back.

Knowles's next stop was in West Palm Beach. He knew now that he needed to get rid of the stolen Impala. He stopped at random and knocked on a door in Locust Street; it was answered by a woman in a wheelchair, Beverly Mabee. He told her that he was from the Internal Revenue Service and she let him in. Once inside, he told her he needed a car; she explained that her twin sister, Barbara Tucker, was out with the Volkswagen. In that case, said Knowles, he'd wait. When Barbara Tucker came home, with her six-year-old son, Knowles tied up the boy and Miss Mabee and took Barbara as a hostage.

That night, Knowles took his captive with him into a motel in Fort Pierce, Florida, and kept her there with him until the following night. Finally, he left her tied up, and drove off in her car.

The next morning, Patrolman Campbell saw the Volkswagen though he was not sure it was the wanted vehicle, because Knowles had changed the licence-plates. He flagged it down and found himself looking at a sawn-off shotgun. Knowles handcuffed Campbell and made him sit in the rear of the patrol car. Then he drove off. But the brakes of the patrol car were poor; Knowles disliked its performance. Using the police siren he forced another car into the side of the road. It was driven by a businessman, James Meyer. Meyer was handcuffed and made to get into the back of his car, together with the policeman. Once again Knowles drove off. In Pulaski County he stopped the car at a wood, made his victims get out and handcuffed them to a tree. Then he shot both in the back of the head.

Still in Georgia, Knowles spotted a police road-block ahead. He accelerated through it, but skidded and lost control. The car crashed into a tree; Knowles leapt out and ran into the woods. Two hundred police with tracker dogs and helicopters searched for him. Knowles was seen from the window of a house by a young man, Terry Clark, who was courageous enough to grab his shotgun and go out to meet the fugitive. Knowles, who had left his own weapon in the car, gave himself up quietly. It was 17 November 1974; his murder spree had lasted almost four months and cost at least eighteen lives. Knowles once said he had killed thirty-five people.

Knowles made a preliminary appearance in court and gave newspaper interviews. Sandy Fawkes noted that he looked pleased with himself and smiled at everyone. 'He was having his hour of glory. The daily stories of the women in his life had turned him into a Casanova killer, a folk villain, Dillinger and Jesse James rolled into one. The long years of failure, rejection and loneliness were over. He had an identity now. He was already being referred to as the most heinous killer in history.' Knowles was quoted in a newspaper as saying that he was 'the only successful member of his family'.

The day after his capture, Knowles was being transferred to a maximum security jail when, according to the police, he picked the lock of his handcuff and made a grab for the sheriff's gun. FBI agent Ron Angel shot him dead.

KÖHLER, Gundolf
Right-wing German terrorist.

On 26 September 1980 Gundolf Köhler, a young member of the Bavarian-based extreme right terrorist organization calling itself the Wehrsportgruppe Hoffmann, planted a bomb which exploded prematurely among crowds thronging the streets for the traditional Munich Oktoberfest, killing thirteen and injuring some two hundred others. Köhler's body was discovered among the dead, and he was thought to have killed himself in the blast. It was clear that he must have had accomplices, but they were assumed to have escaped in the confusion which followed the bombing.

The neo-Nazi organization to which they all belonged was led by Karl-Heinz Hoffmann, and claimed a membership of several hundreds. Although they sported military uniforms and carried guns at their meetings, the 'Military Sportsmen' had been in existence for almost a decade and were generally regarded as an odious but relatively harmless group of cranks. However, the organization was proscribed in January 1980 on the orders of Federal Minister of the Interior Gerhardt Baum; and the Oktoberfest outrage followed seven months later. If it was a protest bombing, it was deemed to be an unofficial one. Although Hoffmann and five others in the Wehrsportgruppe were arrested after the bombing, they were later released and cleared of complicity.

Right-wing terrorism was on the increase in West Germany in 1980, partly because of nationalist agitation, partly as a reaction to the long years of left-wing Baader-Meinhof terrorism. The neo-Nazis fed on public concern about the vast number of foreign workers in Western Germany and the ever-growing list of applications for political asylum (150,000 in 1980 compared with less than 15,000 three years earlier). As always, the Jews were a target, even the Vietnamese 'boat-people' came under attack (two were killed in a bomb explosion at Hamburg).

KRAY, Reginald and Ronald
Celebrated London gangster twins each sentenced to thirty years for murder.

Ronald and Reginald Kray were born in the East End of London in October 1933. At school they acquired a reputation as fighters. In their teens, both became professional boxers; then, after a period in the army – much of it spent in detention – they worked at a night-club in Covent Garden as bouncers. They moved into the protection racket and 'cut themselves in' on a billiard hall in the Mile End Road at the club called the Green Dragon. With their reputation for violence, they were soon known and feared from Woolwich to the City of London. Then in 1956 Ronald Kray strode with two companions into the Britannia pub in Stepney, approached a man named Terence Martin and shouted, 'Come on outside or we will kill you in here.' In front of a crowd of witnesses, they attacked Martin, and one of Kray's companions, Robert Ramsey, stabbed him with a bayonet. They were quickly arrested. Robert Ramsey received seven years in jail; the other two three years.

In Winchester Jail it became clear that Ronald Kray was mentally unstable and he was transferred to a mental home in Epsom. One day, his twin Reggie came to visit him, and it was Ronnie who walked out with the other visitors. Reggie then established his own identity and had to be allowed to go. A journalist eventually persuaded Ronnie to give himself up, and he was sent back to the mental hospital.

Freed in the spring of 1959, he went back into partnership with his brother, and they opened the Double R Club – with the initials intertwined like those of a Rolls Royce – in Bow. They also opened a West End night-club and restaurant called Esmeralda's Barn, off Knightsbridge, and began to acquire a certain celebrity as they mixed with show-business people and politicians. Their hospitality eventually cost them too much, and the restaurant collapsed. A venture called the Kentucky Club in the East End was more successful.

To their friends, and to the celebrities they cultivated, they seemed charming, civilized and incapable of violence. Those who crossed them knew better. One man who placed a hand on Ronald's shoulder and said jokingly that he was getting fat, had his face slashed so that it needed seventy stitches. A man who was suspected of cheating the twins was shot in the leg; their cousin, Ronald Hart, who worked for them commented, 'I saw beatings that were unnecessary even by underworld standards and witnessed people slashed with a razor just for the hell of it.' Reginald Kray told Hart after shooting someone, 'You want to try it some time. It's a nice feeling.'

In 1965, Reggie Kray married his childhood sweetheart Frances Shea, seven years his junior. The marriage was a disaster from the beginning; on their honeymoon in Athens, he locked her in the bridal suite and went to get drunk. She claimed that the marriage was never consummated. Two years later she left him and soon after killed herself with an overdose.

It was also in 1965 that the Krays were arrested and charged with demanding money with menaces; they were refused bail on the ground that they might 'seek to interfere with prosecution witnesses'. Lord Boothby – who had twice met Ronald Kray – caused something of a sensation by asking in the House of Lords how much longer they were to be held without trial. After ninety days and two trials, the twins were acquitted. Chief rivals of the Kray brothers were the Richardson brothers, Eddie and Charles, who organized crime on the south side of the river. The rival gang leaders had nothing but contempt for one another. The chief lieutenant of the Richardsons, a man named George Cornell, was also hated by Ronald Kray because he had openly taunted him with being a homosexual, and warned the father of Kray's boyfriend of the nature of the relationship. By March 1965, most of the Richardson gang had been arrested. Cornell was the only prominent member who had escaped arrest. On the evening of 6 March, he walked into a pub called the Blind Beggar in Bethnal Green – the heart of the Krays' territory. Ronald Kray was told about it at a pub half a mile away, the Lion in Tapp Street. He left immediately, with a henchman named John Barrie. At 8.30, they walked into the bar of the Blind Beggar and Barrie fired warning shots into the ceiling. Ronald Kray drew a pistol, and shot Cornell above the right eye. Then the two gunmen walked out. When Reggie was told that Ronald had just shot George Cornell, he remarked, 'Ronnie does some funny things.' Questioned at the Commercial Road police station Ronald Kray denied all knowledge of the shooting; he repeated his denial soon afterwards to a crowd of reporters specially called together for a briefing. Everybody in the East End knew that 'the Colonel' (as Ronald was known) had killed George Cornell, but apparently no one in the pub had actually seen the shooting.

The shooting of George Cornell was designed to impress London's underworld that Ronald Kray was above the law, and completely ruthless with anyone who crossed him. As the months went by without an attempt to arrest him, it began to look as though he was, indeed, above the law. At this point, Ronald Kray urged his brother to commit a murder. Hart told reporter Norman Lucas, 'He was very proud that he had murdered, and was constantly getting at Reggie and asking him when he was going to do his murder. He used to goad him.'

The Krays selected a victim almost at random. A small-time crook called Jack McVitie, known as 'the Hat' because he always wore one to cover his baldness, had allegedly made a number of satirical remarks about the Kray brothers. On 28 October 1967 the Krays and several henchmen arrived at the Regency Jazz Club in Hackney – one of the establishments they 'protected' – and informed the proprietor that they intended to kill Jack 'the Hat' on his premises; he begged them to do nothing of the sort, and they finally agreed to do it elsewhere. They borrowed a basement in nearby Stoke Newington from a girl, and left two brothers named Lambrianou at the club to escort McVitie to the 'party'.

As soon as McVitie entered the basement, Reggie Kray pushed him against the wall, pressed the revolver against his head and pulled the trigger. It misfired. As McVitie fought and struggled, the others punched him. Reggie pressed the gun to his head and fired again; nothing happened. He threw away the gun in disgust and another gang member handed him a carving knife which he jabbed into McVitie's face then into his stomach. As Ronald Kray shouted, 'Don't stop, Reg, kill him!' he stood astride McVitie, held the knife with both hands, and plunged it into his throat; the blade came out of the back and went into the floorboards.

The body was wrapped in an eiderdown and driven away in a car. The twins' elder brother Charles was aroused from his bed, and told to get rid of it. He took it along to a man called Fred Foreman. Neither the body nor the car has ever been found.

Fred Foreman was later alleged to have already committed one murder for the twins. In 1966 a simple-minded giant named Frank Mitchell, also known as the Mad Axe Man, had walked out of Dartmoor shortly before Christmas, and apparently vanished into thin air. He had been a 'trusty' who was allowed out with working parties, and apparently used to stroll into pubs on the moor and take bottles of beer back into the prison. It emerged at his trial that the

Krays had arranged his escape, and a hideout for him in East London. They also provided a pretty night-club hostess named Liza Prescott to share his bed. But when it became clear to the Krays that Mitchell was going to be an embarrassment and had no intention of surrendering in exchange for parole investigations, he was lured out to a van where, the prosecution later alleged, he was shot in the head by Fred Foreman. His body also disappeared.

After the killing of Jack the Hat, the twins decided it would be discreet to move to the country. They bought themselves a large house close to Hadleigh in Suffolk, where they had been evacuated during the war, and there lived the life of country squires – they were popular in the village because they bought the children a donkey, and generally behaved with courtesy and good humour.

Back in London a special team had been formed under Commander John du Rose of Scotland Yard to try and smash the Kray gang. They used spies and informers, and even policewomen disguised as charladies. Houses were kept under constant surveillance, and members of the gang were shadowed.

At dawn on 8 May 1968 a squad of sixty-eight men made surprise raids in the East End. They found Reginald Kray in bed with a blonde girl and Ronald in bed with a youth. John Barrie, the Lambrianou brothers, Frederick Foreman and Charles Kray were also arrested. In January 1969 eleven men stood in the dock. With the Krays in custody, many witnesses came forward, including the barmaid who had been present when George Cornell was shot. After a forty-day trial, ten of the men were found guilty, and the Kray twins received thirty years each; their brother Charles received ten.

KROLL, Joachim
The cannibal killer.

Between July 1959 and July 1976 the police of the Ruhr area of West Germany hunted a sex-killer with a uniquely unpleasant trade mark: he removed portions of his victims' bodies. And the nature of the cuts – taken from such areas as the buttocks and thighs – suggested that he was taking them home to eat them.

The first body was that of a sixteen-year-old girl, Manuela Knodt, found near the village of Bredeney, south of Essen. Medical evidence revealed that she had been a virgin before her killer strangled her into unconsciousness, then raped her. Lack of scratches or bruises in the genital area suggested that she had made no resistance to the rape. The killer had then taken slices from her buttocks and thighs.

On 23 April 1962 thirteen-year-old Petra Giese went to a carnival at the village of Rees, near Walsum. She and a friend became separated, and the friend went home without her. The following day, her body was found in a forest a mile away from the scene of the carnival. Her red dress had been ripped from her body – the killer was apparently in a frenzy. After raping her, he had removed both buttocks, as well as the left forearm and hand, and taken them away.

Two months later, on 4 June, another thirteen-year-old, Monika Tafel, was on her way to school in Walsum when she met a similar fate, and was dragged into a rye field. Again the killer had cut steaks from her buttocks and the backs of her thighs.

The police had meanwhile arrested a steel-worker for the murder of Petra Giese, but were finally obliged to admit there was no evidence against him. The man's neighbours remained convinced he was the killer, his wife divorced him and the man committed suicide. Fourteen years later, a confession would reveal that he had been innocent.

On 22 December 1966 the killer – whom police had nicknamed the Ruhr Hunter – strangled five-year-old Ilona Harke in a park in Wuppertal, close to a playground, raped her, then removed steaks from buttocks and shoulders.

Almost ten years later, four-year-old Marion Ketter was playing with friends in a playground in the Duisburg suburb of Laar; it was a hot day and she was dressed only in knickers. A balding, mild-looking man spoke to her and persuaded her to go off with him. She called him 'uncle'. When her mother went to look for her a little later, she rushed to the police to report the abduction. The police moved into the area in force, and began making door-to-door inquiries. An elderly tenant told the police that his neighbour, a lavatory attendant named Joachim Kroll, had just told him not to use the lavatory on the top floor of their apartment building because it was stopped up. When the man asked, 'With what?' Kroll had replied, 'Guts.' Of course, he could have been joking. . . .

A plumber was soon investigating the toilet. Kroll had not been joking. It was blocked with the internal organs of a small child, including the lungs. And when the lavatory attendant admitted them to his flat, they quickly found more parcels of flesh, in plastic bags, in his deep freeze. In a bubbling saucepan on the stove they found a child's hand among the carrots and potatoes.

Kroll, a mild, brown-eyed little man, looked anything but a monster, and he was obviously mentally subnormal – as his admission to the other tenant suggested. At the police station, he said he was looking forward to being allowed home again – convinced that, after an 'operation' to make him harmless to women, he could be released.

As the police questioned Kroll, they discovered that he had committed far more than the five 'cannibal' murders. As far as he could recall (and his memory was poor) he had committed his first rape-murder in February 1955 near the village of Walstedde. Nineteen-year-old Irmgard Strehl, a pretty blonde girl, had been dragged into a barn, stripped naked, and raped. Lack of bruising of the genitals suggested that she had been unconscious when raped. On 17 June 1959 Klara Tesmer was found in woods near Rheinhausen, a long way from Walstedde. Again, she had been stripped naked and raped when unconscious.

Kroll talked freely about his career of sex-murder. He lived alone in a flat full of electrical gadgets and rubber sex dolls. He often strangled these with one hand while masturbating with the other. Kroll – like the English sex murderer Christie – was too nervous and self-conscious to be capable of sex with a conscious woman. So at twenty-two he began satisfying his sexual appetite with rape. Most of his life was devoted to this occupation. He had plenty of time on his hands. He would wander round, looking for a girl walking alone, and often follow her home, then study her movements for days, waiting for the chance to catch her alone. He had killed so often that he had lost count of the number of victims – he was able to recall a dozen, but there had undoubtedly been many others.

On 22 August 1965 Kroll had been hiding near Grossenbaum, watching a couple engaged in sex in the front seat of a Volkswagen, and finally became so sexually excited that he decided he had to rape the girl. He drove his knife into the car's front tyre, causing it to explode. But the driver, instead of getting out to see what was the matter, started the engine and drove off. Unfortunately, he made a wrong turn, saw it was a dead end, and reversed the car. As he was driving away, Kroll leapt out, waving his arms. The driver, Hermann Schmitz, thought it was someone in trouble, and stopped the car and got out. His girl-friend saw the man's arm rise and fall, and Schmitz staggered to the car, groaning and bleeding from the stomach. His girlfriend started the car and tried to run the man down. Other cars suddenly appeared on the scene, and the man ran away. Schmitz died shortly afterwards.

Over a year later, on 13 September 1966, Ursula Roling, who shared an apartment with her boyfriend, set out to meet her parents in the little town of Marl. She never arrived. Two days later, her body was found among bushes in a park, naked from the waist down, the legs spread in the typical rape position. Her boyfriend was arrested and questioned for three weeks, although, as he pointed out, he had no reason to rape and murder a woman with whom he was sharing a flat. What made the police suspicious was that there were no signs that she had resisted the rape; they suspected that her boyfriend had killed her in a quarrel, then arranged her in a rape position to mislead the police. He was finally released, and Kroll's confession ten years later exonerated him.

One of the secrets of Kroll's success was that he killed over such a wide area that the police had no cause to link the murders together. Germany has always had a high rate of sex murders; Kroll was only one among many. In 1967 he came very close to being caught. He was living in the little town of Grafenhausen, and he was known to the local children as 'uncle'; they all loved the friendly little man. One afternoon he invited a ten-year-old girl named Gabriele into a meadow to 'show her a rabbit'. Instead, he took out a book of pornographic photographs. Gabriele clapped her hands over her eyes in horror, and felt a light touch on the throat. Instinctively, she leapt to her feet and bolted. Kroll assumed that she would report the experience to her parents; but for some reason, she kept silent. It was not until nine years later that police interviewed her to check on Kroll's confessions, and she realised for the first time that she had been close to death. Kroll left Grafenhausen the same day.

On 12 July 1969 a 61-year-old widow, Maria Hettgen, opened the door of her flat in Hueckeswagen, and was throttled. Kroll stripped and raped her in the front hall, and walked out; again, no one connected the murder with the crimes of the Ruhr Hunter.

On 21 May 1970, thirteen-year-old Jutta Rahn walked from her home in Breitscheid to catch a train for her school in Essen; because part of her journey lay through woods, her mother and brother usually accompanied her. It was raining heavily, and she urged them not to bother to meet her that afternoon. Instead, it was Joachim Kroll who followed her from the railway station that afternoon, and strangled and raped her. A twenty-year-old local man was arrested and interrogated – the only evidence being that his blood type was the same as that of the killer. He was released, but neighbours continued to regard him as a sex-killer until Kroll finally confessed.

In 1976, ten-year-old Karin Toepfer was strangled and raped on her way to school in Dinslaken Voerde; again, the police had no reason to associate the crime with the Ruhr Hunter.

In fact, Kroll was to tell the police that his cannibalism had no sexual origin – unlike the urge that had made the American sex-killer Albert Fish in 1928 eat parts of his ten-year-old victim after strangling her. He merely felt he might as well save money on meat, and he only took steaks from the victims if their flesh struck him as suitably tender.

It was clear to the police that there must have been other murders. For example, it seemed unlikely that Kroll had waited from 1955 until 1959 before committing his second sex-murder. Careful questioning finally made him recall murdering and raping twelve-year-old Erika Schuleter in the town of Kirchhellen in 1956. Then he recalled another twelve-year-old, Barbara Bruder, whom he had killed in Burscheid in 1962. This brought the known victims up to fourteen. Kroll never attempted to deny any of his murders, once his memory had been jogged; he had simply lost count. He was a mental defective – John Dunning points out, in his account of the case, that Kroll showed the child Gabriele pornographic pictures because he assumed that they would excite her as they excited him. It was this combination of stupidity and animal cunning that allowed one of Germany's worst mass murderers to operate unhindered for more than twenty years.

KU KLUX KLAN
A conspiracy to murder three civil rights workers.

Three young civil rights workers, Michael H. Schwerner, Andrew Goodman and James E. Chaney, were murdered near Philadelphia, Mississippi in 1964 by a Ku Klux Klan lynch mob. Schwerner was employed by the Congress of Racial Equality. He and Goodman were both white, Chaney was a Negro.

At the trial in 1964 at Meridian, nineteen whites arrested by the FBI in connection with the murders were freed by the Federal Commissioner hearing the case, Esther Carter, on the ground that a confession by one of them was inadmissible as evidence. Because murder is a state offence, not a federal crime, in the United States – and as such beyond the jurisdiction of the FBI – the nineteen were charged with 'conspiring to deprive' the three murdered men of their civil rights. When they were freed, Prosecutor Robert Owen declared,

'This is not the end of the case as far as the government is concerned ... we shall go direct to a Grand Jury and seek a fresh hearing. If the Grand Jury agrees, this would mean rearresting all or some of the defendants to face new charges.'

Three years later, in October 1967, charges were brought against eighteen of the defendants that they 'conspired to deny the three young Civil Rights workers life or liberty without due process'. At this second trial evidence was given that the three men had been arrested and jailed by a deputy sheriff, held in custody until a mob assembled, then set free and recaptured after a chase down the highway. After they were shot, their bodies were taken to a dam site and buried by bulldozer. One witness testified that the Imperial Wizard of the White Knights of the Ku Klux Klan had approved of the killings, saying that Schwerner was 'a thorn in the side of everyone living, especially the white people – and should be taken care of.'

The all-white jury at Meridian found seven of the defendants guilty of the new conspiracy charges on 20 October. By 23 October all were freed on bond of $5,000 apiece. Eight more were acquitted, and mistrials were declared in the case of the remaining three on whom the jury failed to reach a verdict.

L

LANHAM, Harry and KNOPPA, Antony Michael
Multiple sex-killer and his willing accomplice.

On 3 November 1971 the body of a girl was found near Conroe, Texas. She was fully clothed, and had been killed by three shotgun blasts. She was identified as sixteen-year-old Adele Crabtree, who had been living in a rooming house for hippies in Houston.

On 8 November a woman out riding near Pearland, Brazoria County, saw the body of a woman lying under a bridge in a gully. It proved to be a girl who had been killed with a shotgun. She was fully clothed but her dress was around her waist. Nylon pantihose had been knotted around her neck. She was identified as Linda Faye Sutherlin, who five days earlier had been reported missing from the apartment in Houston she shared with a friend. She had failed to return home after working an evening shift. Her car was found in Houston, and there was dried blood in it.

Police investigation revealed that Miss Sutherlin had stopped at a bar near her home after midnight on the day she disappeared. Another witness had seen her talking to a tow-truck driver at half-past midnight. The man's description – very big, with dark curly hair – reminded the police of a man who had been reported by his girlfriend for beating her and a five-year-old girl. His name was Harry Lanham. When the police discovered that he was a tow-truck driver, they decided to question him. He was arrested on 8 December. Lanham refused to talk to the police, but another prisoner reported that he had boasted he had 'his own private graveyard'.

In April 1972 Lanham decided to talk. He told them that the killer of Linda Sutherlin was a man called Tony Knoppa. Antony Michael Knoppa, aged twenty-four, had already been arrested on a charge of raping a girl, but she had changed her story before he came to trial. Nevertheless, he had received seven months in jail.

When re-arrested, and told of Lanham's accusation, Knoppa said angrily, 'That's a lie. We killed her together. And Harry killed Adele Crabtree too.' He went on to suggest that Lanham had killed several women in the course of rape. After spending some time in prison for an earlier rape, Lanham had apparently declared that in future, he would kill any girl he raped so that she could not testify against him. 'He said I should stick with him, then I'd see a lot of women killed.' Knoppa said that he and Lanham had picked up Adele Crabtree, taken her to an old house, and both had sex with her. Afterwards they asked her to help them with a robbery, though their aim was to lure her to a lonely spot where they could kill her. This they did.

Two days later, Lanham and Knoppa had seen Linda Sutherlin having trouble with her car, but she had refused to go with them. Her car had started, and they followed her. When she came out of the bar, they forced her into Lanham's tow-truck, then took her to an empty house, and both raped her. After this, they took her to the lonely spot where she, like Adele Crabtree, was killed.

Lanham was also linked to the murders of Collette Wilson, aged thirteen, of Alvin, Texas, whose bones were found mixed with those of Gloria Gonzales, who had disappeared from Houston in October 1971.

Lanham and Knoppa were sentenced to life imprisonment.

LEE, Bruce
British arsonist whose fires claimed twenty-six victims.

Lee was born Peter George Dinsdale in 1960, and later changed his name to that of the Japanese film star who specialized in Kung Fu. His mother was a prostitute, and he was born with a partly paralysed and deformed right arm as well as being an epileptic. A police officer later described him as the classic product of a broken home. His mother left her mother to bring him up; at the age of three Lee went to live with her, but was put into a home when her common-law marriage broke up. Until he was sixteen, he attended a school for the physically handicapped. It was there that he was introduced to homosexual practices which, according to the prosecution, 'eventually led to his downfall and discovery'.

Lee seems to be a classic case of a pyromaniac – he later described how, when his fingers began to tingle, he knew that meant he had to start another fire. His first fire was in a shopping arcade when he was only nine, causing £17,000 worth of damage. His usual method was to pour paraffin through a letter box, and toss a match after it. The first fire in which anyone died was in June 1973; then in a fire at an old men's home on 5 January 1977, eleven old men died in the blaze, and six rescuers were injured. When an elderly man 'clipped him across the ear' for disturbing his pigeons, Lee shouted 'I'll kill you'; a few days later, the old man's pigeons were found with their necks wrung, and the man himself was found burned to death in his armchair. The inquest decided he had slipped against the fire while drying clothes. In fact, Lee had crept into his home, found him asleep and set him alight with paraffin.

In 1980 there was a fire at the home of Mrs Edith Hastie, in Selby Street, Hull, and her three sons all died. The eldest could have escaped through the bedroom window, but died trying to rescue his brothers. When police found paper soaked in paraffin near the front door, they began an intensive investigation in which some eighteen thousand people from the area were interviewed. The Hastie family was greatly disliked in the area, the neighbours alleging that the boys were uncontrollable, and at first it was believed that some resentful neighbour had started the fire. When it was learned that Charles Hastie had been acquainted with homosexuals, the police watched a block of lavatories in Anlaby Road, near his home, and forty suspects were rounded up. Among these was Bruce Lee, who had changed his name from Peter Dinsdale in the previous year. All the suspects denied knowing anything about the fire, except for Bruce Lee who said, 'I did not mean it.' He went on to describe all the fires he had started in the past eleven years. A total of twenty-six people had died.

Lee was charged with the manslaughter of twenty-six people, and with arson. He was ordered to be detained in a special hospital with no time limit. Because the trial only occupied a few hours full details of his crimes have not become available. The prosecution remarked, 'The sad fact is that this is his only real accomplishment in life, and something he had expressed himself as being proud of.' Lee commented, 'I am devoted to fire. Fire is my master, and that is why I cause these fires.' He was described as being of low intelligence but with a high degree of animal cunning.

LITTLE, Russell Jack and REMIRO, Michael
Symbionese Liberation Army murderers.

Marcus A. Foster, a highly respected black superintendent of schools at Oakland, California, was ambushed and murdered by gunmen as he left a local education committee meeting on 6 November 1973. His deputy, Robert Blackburn, was wounded. An obscure terrorist organization calling itself the Symbionese Liberation Army claimed responsibility in a letter sent to the local radio station. In it the SLA stated that Mr Foster and his deputy had been found guilty by a court of the people of 'crimes against the children and life of the people'. Their 'crimes' included the proposal to form a schools police unit, the introduction of identity cards for pupils, and co-operation among teachers, police and probation officers generally to help reduce juvenile crime. The post-mortem on Mr Foster revealed that his killers had used bullets filled with cyanide crystals as double indemnity.

Russell Jack Little, aged twenty-four, and Michael Remiro, twenty-seven, were arrested near Concord, California on 10 January 1974. A ballistics report showed that the gun in Remiro's possession was the one used to kill Marcus Foster, and both he and Little were charged with the murder. Shortly afterwards a house in Concord (later found to be owned by another SLA member, Nancy Ling Perry) was set ablaze. Police called to the scene found guns, ammunition, explosives, cyanide and SLA pamphlets inside. There was also a list of officials marked out for kidnapping and execution.

The founder of the SLA was a thirty-year-old escaped Negro convict, Donald DeFreeze. Its roots ('Symbiosis' or 'Team Spirit') sprang from the black prison population in California, and its aims were wholly revolutionary. DeFreeze styled himself 'Field Marshal Cinque', taking the name from the leader of a slave-ship revolt in the 1830s.

At its peak, membership of the SLA was no higher than thirty and this soon dropped to about twelve, white as well as black. Some came from good middle-class families, the most famous being Patricia (Patti) Hearst, the daughter of millionaire newspaper publisher Randolph Hearst. At the age of twenty Patti was kidnapped at gunpoint from her apartment in Berkeley, California, on 5 February 1974 by four members of the gang. The SLA ordered her father to pay a ransom of millions of dollars in the shape of food handouts to the poor and under-privileged.

The letter to her father telling him she was in the SLA's 'protective custody' carried a letterhead in the shape of a seven-headed cobra, representing its seven aims: self-determination, cooperative production, creativity, unity, faith, purpose, and collective responsibility. Its motto: 'Death to the Fascist insect that preys upon the life of the people.' Accompanying the letter was a tape-recording in which Miss Hearst said she was unharmed and asked him to comply with the demands.

The distraught Mr Hearst began a $2 million food distribution operation, putting up half a million dollars personally, with the balance coming from the William Randolph Hearst Foundation. This was scornfully described by the SLA as 'throwing a few crumbs' to the people, and it demanded that a further $4 million be spent on food distribution. In a further tape-recording 'Field Marshal Cinque' warned that Miss Hearst would remain a prisoner 'until such time as the status of our captured soldiers (Little and Remiro) is changed. Should any attempt be made to rescue the subject prisoner . . . the subject is to be executed immediately.'

Ten days after the distribution scheme began, to her parents' – and America's – consternation, Miss Hearst joined the ranks of the SLA herself. In another tape-recording she denounced the food distribution scheme as a sham, accused her parents of deceit – and enclosed a colour photograph of herself armed with a sub-machine-gun and standing before the SLA flag. Twelve days later the FBI said that pictures taken by hidden camera during the armed robbery of a San Francisco bank showed Patti Hearst to be one of the gang involved, and a warrant for her arrest was sworn out the same day. Four other members of the SLA were also identified in the pictures, including 'Field Marshal Cinque'. On 17 May, as America debated whether Patti Hearst had joined the SLA voluntarily or been coerced, 150 armed police surrounded the gang's Los Angeles hideout following a tipoff. Those inside chose to fight rather than surrender, and newspapers said that in the fierce gun-battle which erupted some six thousand shots were exchanged. In the end the building caught fire and burned down. Among the six bodies found inside were those of 'Field Marshal Cinque', his senior lieutenant, William Wolfe – with whom Miss Hearst was said by other members of the gang to be in love – and four women. Miss Hearst was not among them. Instead of returning home, however, she remained on the run for a further sixteen months. She was eventually arrested by the FBI on

18 September 1975 in San Francisco with other members of the gang.

On 20 March 1976 she was found guilty of bank robbery, and use of a firearm in the commission of a felony. She was sentenced to seven years for armed robbery, plus two years (to run concurrently) on the firearms charge. On 19 November she was released on bail of $1.5 million, put up by her parents, and on 9 May 1977 she was sentenced to five years' probation by Superior Court Judge E. Talbot Callister, who remarked that he did not think there was 'a heart in America that was not full of compassion' for her parents.

In the meantime, Little and Remiro, who both admitted to membership of the SLA, were sentenced on 27 June to life imprisonment for the murder of Marcus Foster, and from six months to twenty years for the attempted murder of his deputy Robert Blackburn, the sentences to run concurrently.

LONGHI, Luigi
Shampoo-and-strangle murderer.

On 11 March 1983 Luigi Longhi, an unemployed lorry-driver with a mania for shampooing women's hair, was sentenced at Sonderberg, Jutland, to indefinite psychiatric confinement for the murder of Heike Freiheit, a young West German girl hitch-hiker.

Longhi, aged twenty-nine and born of Italian parentage in Switzerland, strangled Miss Freiheit in May 1981 after inviting her to his room, tying her up and washing her hair four times in a row. Longhi, who pleaded not guilty, insisted that the strangling was accidental. He said he put the noose round her neck solely to restrain her when she objected, 'just like you do with a dog on a leash'.

The Danish court was told that Longhi had been deported from Switzerland in 1977 after spending several years in confinement as a mental patient. According to institution records he began stealing bottles of shampoo and wigs from hairdressers when he was ten years old. As he grew up he formed an obsession for washing women's hair, and succeeded either by persuasion or force – but without abusing his victims sexually. Evidence showed that he had never had sexual intercourse with a woman.

Longhi said that before he picked up Heike Freiheit on the Danish – German border on 30 May 1981, 'at least' twelve women in the Padborg area had allowed him to shampoo their hair and claimed he had harmed none of them. Miss Freiheit agreed to go to his room to be shampooed after he agreed to pay her train fare to Copenhagen. After washing her hair the first time they both fell asleep. Later he woke up with an uncontrollable urge to shampoo her again, and said he bound and gagged her while she slept in case she objected. He then dragged her to a chair in front of the hand basin and began to wash her hair a second time, but ran out of shampoo. So he used whatever else he could find – honey, cottage cheese and salad dressing – to wash it again and again. Finally he ripped off or cut off the girl's clothes 'because I wanted to see how she looked naked'.

When she tried to summon help by drumming her feet on the floorboards, he said he tried to restrain her by slipping the noose round her neck and tugging on it. 'I never intended to kill her,' he maintained. 'But suddenly she went limp and I realized she was dead.' He panicked and hid the body behind the wall of his room. When he abandoned plans to get rid of the body he covered it with lime, and left it where it was. 'I was a prisoner of my own acts,' he said. 'I had to go on living with her because I knew as soon as I moved out, the new tenant would immediately discover the body.'

Heike Freiheit's body was eventually found by a workman who came to insulate the roof more than nine months later. He told the police and Longhi was arrested the same evening. Doctors who examined him said although he had never made love to any woman he had a sexual obsession about women's hair. They said that in their opinion he was dangerous and should be confined indefinitely. When their plea for a normal prison term was dismissed Longhi's lawyers served notice of appeal.

M

MacARTHUR, Malcolm
Murderer whose arrest precipitated the Irish governmental crisis of 1983.

On 12 January 1983 Malcolm MacArthur, aged thirty-six, scion of a well-to-do County Neath family and arts graduate of the University of California, was jailed for life for the murder of Nurse Bridie Gargan. His killing of the 25-year-old girl, whom he had not met before, was unprovoked and brutal. In terms of Ireland's domestic politics it had all the damaging effect of a remote-controlled bomb.

For Malcolm MacArthur was a friend and house guest of the then Irish Attorney-General, Patrick Connolly, and his arrest in the senior law officer's flat on a murder charge sparked off a political crisis of major proportions for the already hard-pressed administration of Prime Minister Charles Haughey. Mr Connolly himself added fuel to the fire by going ahead with a planned holiday in the United States – a blunder of the first magnitude. (He said at the time he had no knowledge that the police were looking for MacArthur. The two men had become friends through Miss Brenda Lyttle, MacArthur's common-law wife and the mother of his nine-year-old son.)

Mr Connolly was recalled from America by Mr Haughey personally. He sent a private jet to bring him back, and immediately accepted the Attorney-General's offer of resignation on his arrival in Dublin. Mr Haughey's Fianna Fail party was later defeated in a general election.

MacArthur pleaded guilty to Bridie Gargan's murder when he was brought before the Dublin Central Criminal Court. According to newspaper reports he was a spendthrift who had dissipated his £70,000 share of his father's farm, plus a further £10,000 from the sale of property in Dublin. When funds ran low during a holiday in Tenerife in 1982, he flew back to Dublin to raise more by 'armed' robbery. To do so he first had to steal a getaway car. As he walked through Phoenix Park on a warm July day he came across Bridie Gargan, sunbathing beside her Renault. He threatened her with a replica hand-gun, and as she screamed when he forced her into the car, struck her over the head with a hammer.

He used the replica gun again to frighten off a gardener from the American ambassador's residence nearby, and drove off with Miss Gargan in the back, unconscious and bleeding from her head wound. An ambulance driver who saw the hospital sticker on the car when it was held up in the traffic assumed that MacArthur must be a doctor, and Miss Gargan his patient in urgent need of treatment. He therefore sounded his siren and led MacArthur through the mass of traffic to St James's Hospital. Instead of stopping, MacArthur drove out by another exit and abandoned the car two miles away with Miss Gargan inside. She died in hospital four days later.

He was sentenced to penal servitude for life by Mr Justice McMahon for her murder. Other charges, including a second murder (of a farmer) and illegal possession of a shotgun, were not proceeded with.

McCRARY, Sherman
Head of a family that left a trail of murdered women across the United States.

On 16 June 1972 Jordan's Supermarket in Santa Barbara, California, was held up by an armed man. As he fled he fired at and wounded a policeman.

A passerby with a photographic memory was able to describe a vehicle parked in a nearby street at the time of the robbery, and recalled some of the licence numerals. The car was traced to an address in nearby Goleta, the home of Sherman McCrary, his wife Carolyn, and their nineteen-year-old son Danny. The man who had robbed the supermarket was believed to be McCrary's son-in-law, Raymond Carl Taylor, aged thirty-eight, who was married to McCrary's daughter Ginger. They had three small boys. Taylor was later arrested at his mother's home in Athens, Texas. Taylor and McCrary were accused of two other supermarket robberies in the area, and pleaded guilty to both. Taylor also admitted shooting the policeman. Both were sentenced to terms of five years to life imprisonment. The remaining three members of the family were given nine-month sentences for harbouring felons.

As the police began to investigate the background of the McCrary family, they saw that they had been involved in far more serious crimes than supermarket robbery. The family were virtually nomads, and both Taylor and McCrary had spent time in various jails for robberies, burglaries and forgeries. Bald, tired-looking Sherman McCrary, who was a heavy drinker, explained that he became a hold-up man in Texas because he had a bad back and was out of work. He was forty-seven.

Detectives investigating the case found themselves looking into no less than twenty-two murders that had taken place between Florida and California between August 1971 and February 1972.

On 12 August 1971 seventeen-year-old Sheri Martin was abducted from the bakery where she worked in Salt Lake City by two men who took $200 from the till. A month later, the girl's body was found near Wendover, Nevada, naked from the waist down. She had been raped and shot with a .32 weapon. On 20 August twenty-year-old Leeora Rose Looney was abducted by two men from a shop in a suburb of Denver, Colorado, late in the evening. Money had been taken from the cash register. Her naked body was found three days later, two hundred miles away. She also had been raped and shot. On 28 September a 26-year-old waitress, Elizabeth Perryman, vanished from the Toddle House restaurant in Lubbock, Texas. She had been alone in the restaurant just before closing time. Money was missing from the cash register. On 19 December a farmer near Amarillo, Texas, discovered a human skeleton scattered around a pasture. A pile of women's clothing was found nearby, and the dental work of the skull identified it as Elizabeth Perryman. It seemed clear that she had been abducted for the purpose of rape.

On 17 October the police of Mesquite, Texas, were called to the drive-in grocery owned by Forrest and Jena Covey. The grocery had been locked up, but money was missing from the till, and cartons of cigarettes had been taken. Three days later, while police were still searching for the Coveys, a sixteen-year-old schoolgirl, Susan Shaw, vanished from the cake shop where she worked, only two blocks from the Coveys' grocery. When her mother came to pick her up at 10.15 pm, the shop was empty, and the till had been robbed. A customer had noticed two men entering the store.

On 24 October young men walking near Lake Ray Hubbard noticed the body of a young girl in the water. It was identified as Susan Shaw. She had been shot and raped. The bodies of Forrest and Jena Covey were found the same evening in a barn near Quinlan, Texas. Both had had their hands tied, and were shot several times. Jena Covey had not been raped. The police put out the description of the two men – one about forty with a flat nose and heavy build, the other about ten years younger, with long sideboards.

On 30 November a customer arriving for an appointment at a hairdresser's in Melrose, Florida, found the bodies of Bobbie Turner and Patricia Marr lying in a storeroom at the back of the shop, almost naked. They had been shot several times. Also in the shop were school books belonging to Mrs Turner's daughter Valerie, who was sixteen. She had vanished. A small amount of money was missing from the cash register, but the women had apparently not been raped. A truck driver had seen Valerie Turner being led out of the shop by two men, one of whom had his hand in his pocket. Valerie Turner's body was found by two teenage boys in a wood near Jacksonville, Florida on 25 June 1972. Little more than a skeleton remained, but a blouse lying nearby was identified as hers. Lack of other clothing suggested to the police that she had been raped.

The FBI laboratory in Washington established that Sheri Martin, Leeora Looney, Elizabeth Perryman, the Coveys and Susan Shaw had all been killed with .32 calibre slugs, and that as far as could be determined, these were from the same pistol.

Investigation revealed that the McCrary family had lived in Athens, Texas, for several years, and had arrived in California in April 1972. Three supermarket robberies there had gained them respectively $23,000, $12,000 and $11,000, and with this money they were able to take two adjoining homes in a respectable middle-class district.

Danny McCrary gave statements to the police to the effect that he, his father and brother-in-law had abducted the Coveys, taken them to the barn near Quinlan, and that the two men had shot them. Taylor's wife Ginger was indicted in Denver, Colorado, on a dud cheque charge and the three men were charged with being involved in the rape-murder of Leeora Looney. Charges of murder were also filed against McCrary and Taylor in the case of Sheri Martin. An FBI spokesman was quoted as saying that the family had been linked to twelve killings, and was suspect in six others. A probation officer from Santa Barbara commented: 'Basically, these people just wandered the American South-West. They went around trying to get jobs as ranch hands, in carnivals, in honky-tonks and as fry cooks and waitresses.' Ginger Taylor told interviewers: 'I love my husband very much and it never occurred to me to do anything other than to stay with him. I guess that staying with him and doing what my husband told me to do was born and raised into me because I never really

211

thought there was really anything else for me to do.' Carolyn McCrary wrote: 'I am guilty of staying with my husband while he cometed roberys [*sic*] because I don't have anywhere else to go ... It may sound crazy, but I love him very much.'

MACDONALD, William
Australian homosexual and sadistic killer.

On 4 June 1961 the body of a man was found under the dressing sheds of the Sydney Domain Baths. His body was naked; he had been stabbed thirty times, and the genitals hacked off. He was identified as Alfred Greenfield, but nothing could be discovered about his final hours. The location – at a public baths – suggested a homosexual pick-up.

This seemed to be confirmed by the discovery of another victim in a public lavatory at Moore Park, William Cobbin. Again, he had been stabbed repeatedly and the genitals mutilated. It looked as if he and his killer had retired into the lavatory for homosexual intercourse, and then the man had been stabbed.

Squads of police began patrolling areas of the city where tramps and derelicts congregated at night, and homosexuals who hung around public lavatories became more cautious.

Late on Saturday night, 31 March 1962, a man was found lying in Darlinghurst, a Sydney suburb, with the typical stabs and mutilations. Frank McLean was still alive when found but too badly injured to describe his attacker; he died soon after.

In another suburb, Concord, the Municipal Council received complaints about a smell from 71 Burwood Road. It was a shop that had been bought by a man called William MacDonald only two weeks earlier. MacDonald had not been seen by neighbours after 4 November. Now the local Inspector of Health looked through the shop, finding nothing to account for the smell until he looked under the house, and saw a body. It was the naked corpse of a man. A shirt found under the body had forty-one knife-stabs. It looked as if William MacDonald was the latest victim of the homosexual mutilator. A police check revealed that a man named Allan Brennan, missing from his work for the postal authorities at Alexandria, South Sydney, had given his address as 71 Burwood Road. So it seemed that Brennan and MacDonald were the same person.

Further search of the murder scene revealed broken linoleum, stained with blood, under the shop. In the shop were a number of paperback books on murder, including one on Jack the Ripper, and *Ritual in the Dark* by Colin Wilson, a study of a homosexual sadistic killer.

A number written in indelible pencil on the victim's coat was finally traced to a dry-cleaning establishment, whose records showed that the coat had belonged to an Irishman named Patrick Hackett. It now became possible that the dead man was not MacDonald, as they had formerly assumed. And on 22 April 1963 this was confirmed when a former workmate of the 'dead' man passed him in George Street, Sydney. He reported his sighting to the police, and an Identikit picture of MacDonald was circulated throughout Australia. In May two junior clerks at Spencer Street Railway Station, Melbourne, thought they recognized the picture as that of a station assistant. Detectives from Sydney flew to Melbourne, and interviewed the man, who called himself David Allan. When they asked him if he was Allan Brennan, of 71 Burwood Road, Sydney, he replied that his correct name was William MacDonald. And when questioned about the corpse found underneath the house, he admitted that he had killed the Irishman, whom he knew as McNulty. He explained that he had been drinking when he felt a compulsive urge to kill. He approached a drunken man outside the People's Palace Hotel and invited him home for drinks; the man agreed. They went back to Burwood Road, and McNulty drank until he stretched out on the floor and said he wanted to sleep. MacDonald waited for him to fall asleep, then began to stab him with a knife. He then tried to remove the genitals, but the knife was not sharp enough. MacDonald later went to a hospital to have his own hand bandaged – he had cut it in the frenzy of his stabbing. He dragged the corpse under the house, packed his belongings, and left. He threw the knife off Sydney Harbour Bridge, determined not to kill again. But the compulsion returned, so he bought another knife. Fortunately, he was unable to find a suitable victim.

In his lodging in Melbourne police found more paperbacks, including the first volume of this *Encyclopaedia of Murder*. Asked by the detective why he read such rubbish, he replied, 'I have been reading this sort of stuff for the past four years. It's the only thing I can get any pleasure from.'

Sentenced to life imprisonment, MacDonald was later transferred to the Morriset Home for the Criminally Insane.

MACKAY, Patrick David
Young English psychopath charged with three murders and questioned about eight others.

Mackay was born on 25 September 1952, the son of a mild-looking clerk, at the Royal Park Hospital, Middlesex. Every Friday Patrick's father would come home extremely drunk and violent – he kicked his wife in the stomach when she was carrying Patrick. Patrick was a backward child who loved to bully smaller children, a liar and a thief. He was ten when his father died, and soon afterwards he began to develop sadistic tendencies, torturing a cat and a rabbit and roasting his pet tortoise alive. He loved playing with dead birds and seemed obsessed by death. He began to steal regularly. When he set a Catholic church on fire with a candle he appeared before Dartford juvenile court, where he was put on probation – to the fury of neighbours who had hoped to see him put away.

At thirteen he smashed the furniture and attacked his mother and sisters, and for the first time was admitted to a psychiatric hospital. He was turning into a very large boy – over six feet tall in his mid teens – yet he insisted in taking a doll to bed with him in hospital. Mackay later claimed he was bullied there and brutally treated. By the age of fifteen his police record showed a string of violent offences, including an attempt to strangle his mother and an attack on a younger boy in the street which would have been fatal had he not been interrupted. A psychiatrist then described Mackay as a 'cold, psychopathic killer'. Released from another mental home, against the advice of the staff, he went to stay with two aunts, one of whom he tried to strangle. He began to drink heavily and to take drugs; he became an admirer of the Nazi regime, decorating his bedroom with photographs, making himself a kind of Nazi uniform and calling himself 'Franklin Bollvolt the First', a world dictator.

In 1973 Mackay was befriended by a Catholic priest, Father Anthony Crean, aged sixty-three. Shortly after meeting him Mackay broke into his cottage and stole a cheque for £30, changing the figure to £80. He was caught, but released with a £20 fine.

By early 1974 police believed that Mackay had killed six people. These suspected cases were Heidi Mnilk, an au pair girl pushed from a train near New Cross in July 1973 (Mackay was staying nearby); Mary Hynes, battered to death in her flat in Kentish Town, also in July 1973; Stephanie Britton and her four-year-old grandson, stabbed at their home in Hadley Green, Hertfordshire, in January 1974; an old tramp thrown from Hungerford Bridge in the same month (to which Mackay subsequently confessed). In February he called on 84-year-old Isabella Griffiths in Chelsea, and asked if he could do any shopping for her. She refused to let him in, so Mackay lost his temper, snapped her door chain, strangled her and stuck a kitchen knife into her stomach. None of the murders showed any form of sexual assault. Mackay was never charged with any of them.

At the time he killed Isabella Griffiths he was staying with a friend in Finchley, north London. He seemed to think he was possessed by evil spirits, and would end up in hell; he made models of Frankenstein monsters and burned out their eyes. He was thrown out of his friend's house and, after attempting to burgle it, was caught and received six months in prison.

In the autumn of 1974 Mackay took up a career of mugging old women and stealing their handbags. The police map was soon clustered with red dots where the mugger had struck. They later suspected him of three more murders which took place during that period: a 62-year-old tobacconist in Finsbury Park, battered to death with a piece of lead piping; 92-year-old Sarah Rodwell, beaten to death on her doorstep in Hackney (her £5 Christmas bonus was stolen) and Ivy Davies, a café proprietress in Southend, killed with an axe.

Then, on 10 March 1975, Mackay followed an elderly widow, Adele Price, as she entered a block of flats in Lowndes Square. He jangled his keys as if to let himself in, and she was deceived into allowing him in. He pretended to feel faint, and when she brought him some water he strangled her. Soon afterwards, on 21 March, Mackay went to visit his mother in Gravesend, and while there went to call on Father Crean. The house had been left open. When the priest returned to find Mackay in his house, he was nervous and tried to rush out; Mackay intercepted him and began to batter him. The priest ran to the bathroom for shelter, and was pursued by Mackay who attacked him with an axe. The blows were so violent that the priest's brains were exposed. Mackay also stabbed him with a knife. Then he sat on the bath and watched for several minutes while the priest died. He filled the bath with water and sat trailing his fingers in it, the old obsession with death keeping him there for almost an hour before he recollected that his mother was expecting him.

Mackay was an obvious suspect for the murder of Father Crean, and police caught up with him two days later. During that time

Mackay had robbed another old lady, but left her unharmed, presumably because she did not 'annoy' him. He confessed to the priest's murder, and his thumbprint was found on a teaspoon belonging to one of the mugging victims. He was sentenced for life. In their book about the case, *Psychopath*, Tim Clark and John Penycate raise the question of how a youth with such a history of violence was ever allowed to run loose.

McMAHON, Thomas
Specially chosen IRA assassin of Lord Mountbatten.

Earl Mountbatten of Burma, national war hero and statesman, and the last Viceroy of India, used to spend part of every summer at Cassiebawn Castle at Mullaghmore in County Sligo, Eire. Still very much a sailor, one of his main pleasures there was to drop lobster pots and fish from his yacht, *Shadow V*. He refused to adopt maximum security precautions after the IRA resumed its terrorist campaign in 1969, and in 1976 he asked the Sligo police to withdraw the discreet watch they maintained on Cassiebawn Castle, saying that it was a waste of time and manpower. 'What would they want with an old man like me?' he said.

On 27 August 1979 the IRA planted a radio-controlled bomb weighing five pounds in *Shadow V*'s engine-room. As Lord Mountbatten and various members of his family headed for Donegal Bay for a day's fishing, holiday-makers on the beach heard and saw the yacht explode into matchwood. The bomb had been activated by a home-made pocket transmitter from the cliffs above Mullaghmore at 11.45 am. Lord Mountbatten, his fourteen-year-old grandson Nicholas Knatchbull and the Irish boat-boy, Paul Maxwell, were all killed outright. Four others aboard were injured, including Lord Mountbatten's daughter, son-in-law and another grandson. The Queen was immediately informed, and her horrified reaction to the outrage was shared by both Britain and India, where seven days of official mourning were proclaimed.

In a separate terrorist attack on the same day, the IRA exploded a land-mine at Warren Point in County Down, killing eighteen British soldiers and wounding many more. Even the news of this death toll, the largest loss suffered in a single incident by British troops for ten years, was overshadowed by the assassination of Lord Mountbatten.

A vigilant Irish policeman at Granard stopped a car on a routine check and observed that both driver and passenger seemed very nervous. It was only a few hours after the Mountbatten bombing. He arrested them both, and they were charged on suspicion of being members of the IRA. The driver, Francis McGirl, a farmer aged twenty-four, was found not guilty by the Special Criminal Court; the three judges said they were unable to convict on suspicion alone. But the passenger, Thomas McMahon, a member of the Provisional IRA from Carrickmacross in County Monaghan, was convicted of the murder of Lord Mountbatten by forensic evidence. Traces of nitroglycerine were found on his clothes; sand on his boots had come from the slipway at Mullaghmore; flakes of green paint also found on his boots exactly matched the hull of *Shadow V*. 'Bomber' McMahon was thought to be one of a hand-picked assassination squad who chose Mountbatten in order to go one better than the rival INLA, whose sophisticated car-bomb murder of Airey Neave MP had received extensive publicity. McMahon was jailed for life on 23 November 1979. His appeal against the sentence was thrown out by the Dublin Appeals Court.

MANSON, Charles
The hippie leader whose organized multiple murders horrified the world.

Charles Manson began life in 1934 simply as 'No Name Maddox' after his mother, a young prostitute named Kathleen Maddox. Mystery still surrounds the identity of his father. In 1936 Ms Maddox sued a Colonel Scott – first name unknown – for maintenance, and the court in Boyd County, Kentucky, awarded her a lump sum of $25 plus a further $5 a month for the upkeep of her infant son 'Charles Milles Manson'.

Manson later denied that his mother was a prostitute, as the press alleged; he preferred to describe her as a 'Flower Child'. Whatever the truth, she was sentenced to five years' imprisonment for armed robbery when her son was only a toddler, and from then on he was shuttled from one home to another. When he was nine he was sent to reform school. At twelve, he ran away from another institution back to his mother – only to be told that she did not want him. At thirteen he committed his first armed robbery. While on parole at seventeen he committed homosexual rape on a younger boy. By the time he was eighteen Manson was listed as 'dangerous, with homosexual and assaultive tendencies'.

In 1954 he was sent to live with an uncle and aunt at McMechen, West Virginia, as a condition of further parole. There he met and married a seventeen-year-old waitress named Rosalie, who bore him a son after they moved to California and then divorced him, in 1958. Manson became a pimp; and after a brief period out of jail was sent back in 1960 to serve out the remainder of a ten-year sentence – for transporting girls over the state line for immoral purposes, plus cheque fraud, credit card offences and car stealing. During this period in jail he became a protégé of Alvin 'Creepy' Karpis, a notorious gangster and former member of the Ma Barker gang which committed fourteen murders. Karpis taught Manson to play the guitar, well enough for him to boast later that he 'could be bigger than the Beatles'. In 1966 Manson was transferred from the state penitentiary on McNeil Island, Washington, to San Pedro, California to prepare him for release. His conduct sheet warned prophetically, 'He has a pattern of criminal behaviour and confinement that dates to his teen years. This pattern is one of instability, whether in free society or a structured institutional community. Little can be expected in the way of change in his attitude, behaviour or mode of conduct.'

When he was eventually released in 1967 after spending more than half his life behind bars, Manson admitted he was afraid to face the outside world. 'I didn't want to leave jail but they insisted ... and gave me back my $35 and a suitcase filled with old clothes.' He drifted into San Francisco, where he spent the first few days riding round on the buses – and sleeping on them – as he emerged from his institutionalized shell. The metamorphosis proved quicker and easier than he expected. These were the days of Flower Power; battalions of long-haired young men and women, the males bent on dodging the Vietnam draft and all on avoiding work, cocked a snook at the conventions by practising free love and 'freaking out' on LSD and cocaine in the Haight-Ashbury district. To Charles Manson it was like entering the gates of some amoral Paradise.

First he met Mary Brunner and 'shacked up' with her. Later they were joined by Lynette 'Squeaky' Fromme who came from a good middle-class family only to be picked up by Manson the day she left home after a domestic row. That threesome soon became a group – always dominated by Manson – who moved en bloc into the Haight district for a 'summer of love' in 1967.

Among other early arrivals who later became members of the Family inner council were Susan Atkins and Patricia Krenwinkel.

Atkins was only twenty-one when she first met Manson but unlike Mary Brunner, Fromme and Krenwinkel had already served three-month sentences for armed robbery. Krenwinkel, also twenty-one and an ugly girl who craved admiration, simply walked out of her job as secretary to join the hippie band; her father (like many others that summer) assumed that Manson must have hypnotized her. What is unarguable is that Manson's hold over all members of the Family was complete and wholly evil.

Manson did it by styling his hair and beard in the image of Jesus, and then corrupting all the young people attracted to him with hallucinogenic drugs and sexual perversion. Members of the Family would be ordered to strip when they were high on LSD and encouraged to take part in group sex – some of them as young as thirteen and fourteen. Manson's orders were that each of his disciples must rid himself or herself of their particular sexual aversion (or 'hang-up'), be it sodomy, rape, fellatio, flagellation or whatever – by performing the act in front of the entire Family. None ever refused. Susan Atkins explained their compliance: 'He is the king and I am his queen. The queen does what the king says. The king? Look at his name, Manson. "Man's son." Now I have visible proof of God, proof the Church never gave me.' Another Family ceremony was to strap Manson to a Cross and follow the mock crucifixion with a sexual orgy. Probably because they were drug-addicted – and very young – Manson was able to exploit this crude sex and drugs hocus-pocus to a point where his followers committed murder on his orders, without hesitation. The progression from Flower Power to ritual killing took only two years to bring about.

By the autumn of 1967 Manson decided that he wanted to become 'bigger than the Beatles' in his role as guitarist and singer. Accordingly he traded a grand piano for a Volkswagen bus and drove his followers around California. When their numbers grew too big for the Volkswagen they exchanged it for an old school bus, and headed south. Now they drove through Nevada, Arizona and New Mexico into Arkansas and the Bible belt of the Deep South, before returning to California – this time to Los Angeles. After a number of moves they then set up camp in the grounds of a house-cum-club known as the Spiral Staircase, where Manson played the guitar and sang.

He was able enough to attract the attention of other musicians and agents, and made a record and a film (neither of which brought the hoped-for fame and money). It was at this time that the seeds of murder were first planted. Manson befriended a young musician called Bobby Beausoleil, a student of black magic and admirer of Aleister Crowley. Beausoleil in turn introduced Manson to another musician, Gary Hinman – who was later killed on Manson's orders, for the large sum of money he was reputed to keep in his house.

It was also at this time that Mary Brunner (Manson's 'favourite wife') bore him a son: the entire Family, then numbering about twenty, took part in the delivery and Manson bit through the umbilical cord. Later another member of the Family named Sandra Good, the daughter of a wealthy stockbroker, told Manson about the Spahn movie ranch. This was an isolated property in the Simi Hills above Chatsworth, thirty miles from Los Angeles, big enough to accommodate the growing hippie band. Formerly the home of silent movie cowboy star William S. Hart, it was owned by George Spahn who rented the location out for westerns. After moving in briefly in the autumn of 1967, the Family made it their murder h.q. eighteen months later after persuading near-blind octogenarian Mr Spahn (who was enamoured of 'Squeaky' Fromme, sixty years his junior) to allow them to live in the 'outlaw' shacks at the rear of the ranch.

Meantime Manson dreamed of establishing a fallout-free hideaway in Death Valley, on the far side of the Mojave Desert from the movie ranch, ready for the day – which he was convinced was at hand – when Russian nuclear missiles began to fall on American soil. With this in mind he ordered his disciples to arm themselves with guns and knives and to build up a fleet of 'dune buggies' ready to transport them through the desert. At the same time he still envied the rich and successful in American society, just as he had when he left prison with only $35 in his pocket. So he drew up a private death list of enemies ('pigs') who would have to perish anyway, for slights real or imagined, when doomsday finally arrived. It included film stars Warren Beatty and Julie Christie, as well as Doris Day's son Terry Melcher (with whom Manson had hoped to sign a recording contract) plus a handful of his former disciples, who had tired of his drug-induced schemes and returned to lead a normal life. Manson's code-name for this general day of reckoning was 'Helter Skelter', taken from a Beatles' record and seemingly in ignorance of the fact that it means a fairground ride.

Until Helter Skelter came about, however, Manson continued to use the Spahn movie ranch as headquarters for the Family, not only to live in but also as a disposal centre for stolen property ranging from credit cards to vehicles (and including a truck stolen from the NBC television company, loaded with expensive equipment). He also began to cultivate the friendship of roving motorcycle gangs, California's 'Easy Riders', apparently with the idea of enlisting them as allies in his war on the 'pigs'. His approach was crude as always, but effective; he offered them the services of the female members of the Family. One such gang was known as Satan's Slaves, a name which was wrongly attributed to the Family later.

But all the time, no matter where he was living or with whom he was trying to form an alliance, Manson went on picking up the young social dropouts he called his 'disciples', as easily as a stray dog picks up fleas. At its peak the Family numbered more than forty.

In the summer of 1969 Manson and his followers, now increasingly under the spell of hallucinogenic drugs, began to talk openly of murder. In July Manson shot – and was thought to have killed – a Negro drugs dealer named Bernard Crowe. Crowe's offence had been to threaten reprisals after Tex Watson of the Family appropriated $2,400 handed to him to buy marijuana for Crowe to peddle. Manson, who hated Negroes, shot him in the stomach. Although Crowe recovered, his failure to press charges served only to heighten Manson's prestige in the commune.

On 25 July he sent Bobby Beausoleil, Susan Atkins and Mary Brunner to Gary Hinman's house, ostensibly to invite Hinman to join their Death Valley exodus but in reality to rob him of the $20,000 he was said to keep there. When Beusoleil telephoned the movie ranch to say Hinman insisted there was no $20,000, Manson drove to the house wearing his 'magic sword' (a home-made weapon with a two-foot blade, given to him by one of the Satan gang). He used it on Hinman, almost severing his ear: Mary Brunner stitched it on again while Beausoleil continued to search for the money. Before he left the house, Manson gave orders for Hinman to be killed. Under torture, he was made to sign over his Fiat sports car and another Volkswagen bus to Beausoleil before he was stabbed and left to die from loss of blood. Beausoleil wrote 'Political Piggy' in blood on the wall, together with a sign that was intended to resemble a panther's paw (to mislead the police into thinking that the Black Panthers, the Negro terrorist organization, was responsible for the crime).

One week after Hinman's body was found Beausoleil was stopped while driving the Fiat, and asked to prove ownership. When he produced the transfer document – signed by Hinman – he was held for further inquiries. Two days later Mary Brunner and Sandra Good were also arrested, for possessing stolen credit cards. When Manson was told what had happened, he ordered his disciples, 'Now is the time . . . for Helter Skelter.' Whether it was a panic reaction, or simply another wild, drug-inspired plan to secure the release of the three Family members under arrest, is not certain. Susan Atkins claimed later that the Tate murders were committed as a copycat version of the Hinman killing to try to get Beausoleil freed.

The Polanski house on Cielo Drive, Benedict Canyon (Sharon Tate was married to film producer Roman Polanski, then in Europe) was chosen only because Terry Melcher – one of the names on Manson's death list – had lived there earlier. On the evening of 8 August 1969 Miss Tate, aged twenty-six, the star of *Valley of the Dolls* and now eight and a half months pregnant, was entertaining three guests. They were her former lover Jay Sebring, a hair-stylist whose clients included Frank Sinatra, Paul Newman, Steve McQueen and Peter Lawford; coffee heiress Abigail Folger and her lover Wojiciech Frykowski, a writer and friend of Polanski's. Folger and Frykowski were both drug-takers and quantitites of MDA (a hallucinatory drug) were found in their bodies after they were murdered.

Tex Watson climbed a telegraph pole outside the Polanski house and cut the phone wires. Then he, Susan Atkins and Patricia Krenwinkel scrambled over the fence into the garden. Watson carried a .22 revolver. All three were armed with knives and in addition carried with them a long length of nylon rope. As they walked up the drive a car approached from the house, and caught them in its headlights. At the wheel was delivery boy Steven Earl Parent, who had been visiting his friend William Garretson, the Polanskis' houseboy. Parent slowed down and asked who they were, and what they wanted. Watson's response was to place the barrel of the .22 against the youth's head and blast off four rounds. He then broke in to the house via the nursery being prepared for the baby, and admitted the others by the front door. A fourth member of the Family – Linda Kasabian, who was to lose her nerve after the killings that night and later turn witness for the prosecution – remained outside as lookout.

Frykowski, who was asleep on a settee in the living-room, woke up to find Watson standing over him gun in hand. When he demanded to know who he was, Watson replied, 'I am the Devil, and I'm here on the Devil's business.' None of the gang knew how many others

222

there were in the house, so Susan Atkins was sent upstairs to reconnoitre and fetch a towel to bind Frykowski. She looked into Abigail Folger's bedroom, and waved casually as the coffee heiress gazed back and smiled; both had taken enough drugs to see nothing unusual in the incident. Atkins also peered round the door of Sharon Tate's room. Jay Sebring and the actress, who were inside talking together, failed to notice her. When Atkins reported to Watson that there were three more people upstairs he ordered her to bring them down, which she did at knife-point. Then, when Sebring was told to lie face down on the floor, he tried to grab Watson's gun; whereupon the trigger-happy Watson shot him through the lung.

Next the intruders demanded money. Susan Atkins marched Abigail Folger upstairs and rifled her handbag, taking all the cash she had with her ($72) plus the inevitable credit cards. When they returned to the living-room Watson looped one end of the nylon rope round the prostrate Jay Sebring's neck, threw the free end over a beam and tied it round the necks of the two women prisoners, who had to stand upright to avoid being choked. Then the killing began.

Watson ordered Susan Atkins to stab Frykowski, who got to his feet and tried to run for it. Atkins pursued him into the garden, and knifed him in the back. As he screamed, lookout Linda Kasabian called on Atkins to stop. 'It's too late,' she said: no one now could be allowed to leave the house alive. Watson then shot Frykowski twice and, when his gun jammed, continued to beat him over the head with the butt. Back in the living-room the two women panicked, and struggled desperately to free themselves from their dual noose. Like her lover Frykowski, Abigail Folger got as far as the garden. She too was pursued by Susan Atkins, who stabbed her a number of times. Watson joined in too, after first knifing Jay Sebring. Now both turned on the heavily pregnant Miss Tate.

Watson told Atkins to stab her. When the actress begged to be spared for the sake of her unborn child, Atkins sneered, 'Look, bitch, I don't care. . . I have no mercy for you.' She hesitated, none the less – so Watson showed the way. Within moments both Atkins and Patricia Krenwinkel joined in. Between them the three stabbed her sixteen times, inflicting several wounds after she was dead. Finally Susan Atkins dipped a towel in Sharon Tate's blood and daubed 'Pig' on the living-room door.

The three killers changed in their car, where Linda Kasabian waited for them and tried to hide their blood-stained clothing in an embankment (it was found later by reporters). They then drove to a house with a hose on the lawn and attempted to wash the car down; the noise disturbed the owners, who took their number as they drove off. When they got back to the movie ranch Manson asked them why they were back so soon, but seemed relieved when he learned that the occupants of the house were all dead. It was not until later, when they watched television, that any of them knew who they had murdered. Susan Atkins was delighted to hear that their victims included someone so well known as Sharon Tate. 'It really blew my mind,' she said.

Not surprisingly the brutality of the killings caused some panic in Hollywood, which produced extra police patrols, bodyguards and guard dogs. Well pleased, Manson told his disciples to strike even more terror into the hearts of the 'pigs'. He led the next raid himself, taking with him Watson, Atkins, Krenwinkel and Kasabian – the four involved in the Tate murders – plus Clem Grogan and Leslie van Houten. Again all were 'high' on hallucinogenic drugs. This time their victims were supermarket boss Leno LaBianca, aged forty-four and his wife Rosemary. Neither was known to or had the remotest connection with Manson or the Family; their misfortune was to live next door to a house which Manson and Atkins had once visited and apparently taken a dislike to their host.

Manson walked into the LaBiancas' bedroom shortly after 1 am, armed with a gun. 'You won't be harmed,' he promised them as he tied them up. He then went back to the car and ordered Watson, Krenwinkel and van Houten to go into the house and kill them. 'They're very calm', he declared. When they were done, he said, Watson and the others were to make their own way back to the movie ranch – while he, Grogan and Kasabian moved on to another house and murdered the 'pigs' there.

Mrs LaBianca was taken to her bedroom and made to lie down with a pillowcase over her head. Downstairs Tex Watson slashed her husband's throat and began to stab him, to hurt not to kill. When Mrs LaBianca heard his screams and asked, 'What are you doing to my husband?' she, too, was attacked. Krenwinkel stabbed her in the back, severing her spine. Watson joined in, then van Houten – who plunged her knife sixteen times into the prisoner's buttocks. Altogether Mrs LaBianca was stabbed forty-one times. Her husband sustained twelve knife-wounds, plus fourteen punctures from a big double-pronged fork. He also had the word 'war' scored in his abdomen. The words 'Death to Pigs', 'Rise' and 'Healter Skelter' [sic] were found daubed in blood on the walls. The murderers took a shower, ate a meal – and fed the three dogs before leaving. (The dogs watched the murder without barking, and licked the trio's hands afterwards; although they barked loudly enough some hours earlier, when a neighbour called.)

Manson was arrested less than a week later, together with twenty members of the Family, when police raided the movie ranch, not for murder, but on suspicion of car theft. All were eventually released for lack of evidence. Then in October 1969, their luck ran out. Another member of the Family named Kitty Lutesinger, Bobby Beausoleil's girlfriend – who had already quit the group once but returned voluntarily – was arrested as a suspect in the Hinman murder case. She denied taking part, but named Susan Atkins and Mary Brunner. Atkins (already in custody on a minor charge) also denied involvement, but admitted to a cellmate that she had taken part in the Sharon Tate killings. The news filtered back to the police, and on 1 December 1969 the chief of police in Los Angeles announced that three members of the Family, Watson, Krenwinkel and Kasabian, had been charged with the murders. Later Manson himself, Susan Atkins and Leslie van Houten were similarly charged, and their trial – the first of many involving members of the Family – began in 1970. Together with Patricia Krenwinkel they were all sentenced to death, as were several other members of the group at their subsequent trials. In each case, however, that sentence was commuted to one of life imprisonment, after the California Supreme Court voted in February 1972 to abolish the death penalty for murder. The major sentences are listed below.

Manson, Atkins, Krenwinkel and van Houten were all sentenced to death on 19 April 1971 for the Tate – LaBianca murders.

Manson, Bruce Davis and Clem Grogan were later found guilty of the murders of Gary Hinman and Donald 'Shorty' Shea, a bit-part cowboy actor and movie ranch employee, and sentenced to life imprisonment. Shea's body was never found.

Charles 'Tex' Watson was found guilty of seven counts of first-degree murder, and of conspiracy, at a separate trial in 1971. He too was sentenced to death, and had his sentence commuted to life imprisonment. Bobby Beausoleil was also found guilty of murder and sentenced to life imprisonment. Susan Atkins pleaded guilty to Hinman's murder, for which she was sentenced to life imprisonment with a recommendation by the judge that 'she should spend her entire life in custody'.

No charges were brought against Mary Brunner or Linda Kasabian, both of whom gave evidence for the prosecution.

The total of murders committed by Manson's Family has never been established. In his book *Helter Skelter* Vincent Bugliosi, the prosecutor at the Tate – LaBianca trials, wrote: 'Manson bragged to Juan Flynn [another member of the Family] that he had committed thirty-five murders. When Juan first told me this, I was inclined to doubt that it was anything more than sick boasting on Charlie's part. There is now evidence, however, that even if it wasn't true *then* the total to date may be very close to, and may even exceed, Manson's estimate.' He also said: 'The average incarceration in California for first-degree murder is ten and a half to eleven years. Because of the hideous nature of their crimes and the total absence of mitigating circumstances, my guess is that all will serve longer periods; the girls fifteen to twenty years, the men – with the exception of Manson himself – a like number. As for the leader of the Family, my guess is that he will remain in prison for at least twenty-five years, and quite possibly the rest of his life.'

In November 1982 Charles Manson, by then aged forty-seven and with applications for parole already turned down, was put into a maximum security cell at Vacaville Prison in California after reports that he was planning an escape by balloon. The reports arose after a catalogue for hot-air balloons, a hacksaw and other contraband items including tin-cutters, rope and a container of flammable liquid were discovered in the jail.

MARKOV, Georgi
Bulgarian defector assassinated by umbrella-gun.

Georgi Markov angered the Bulgarian president in the late 1960s by writing a play about a plot to murder a general. He left Bulgaria to work in Italy, and moved on to England where he was granted political asylum in 1969. He was murdered in broad daylight by a man with a foreign accent; the method might have come straight from the pages of James Bond.

On the morning of 7 September 1978 Markov drove from his house in Clapham to work at the Bulgarian unit of the BBC at Bush House in the Aldwych. Because of the heavy traffic in central London he parked his car near Waterloo Bridge and walked the rest of the way. He went back to the car soon after 6 pm and moved it near to the office, and walking along the Strand he felt a brief stinging sensation in the back of his right thigh. He thought it came from an accidental prod from an umbrella held by a man standing in a bus queue. When he turned, the man apologized for the 'accident' in a pronounced foreign accent, hailed a taxi and vanished. When his leg began to stiffen up, Markov told a BBC colleague what had happened and showed the wound – a small but bright red spot, not unlike a pimple. Mr Markov stayed on to read the evening news bulletin but felt increasingly feverish and finally went home at 11 pm.

He was too ill to work next day. His wife Annabella took him to St James's Hospital, Balham, for examination. He was found to have a high temperature and there seemed to be no rational explanation for the puncture in his thigh, which was too big to have come from an insect bite or hypodermic injection. His condition worsened the following day, when he was given massive antibiotic injections to try to counter an alarming rise in the white corpuscle count in his bloodstream. Markov failed to respond and died two days later.

At the inquest on 2 January 1979 – which was attended by Commander James Neville of Scotland Yard, the head of the Anti-Terrorist Squad – the coroner found that Markov had been murdered by ricin poison 'administered in a metal pellet'. Evidence was given by a number of specialists, including Dr David Gaul from the top-secret Chemical Defence Establishment at Porton Down (which supplies MI5 with antidotes to all poisons known to be used by KGB assassins). Dr Gaul said tests ruled out the possibility that Mr Markov's death was caused by poison from snakes, spiders, scorpions or marine life. Ricin tests were then carried out on a live pig. The symptoms it developed, he said, were almost identical with those exhibited by Mr Markov. (Ricin comes from the seeds of the castor oil plant, which grows in abundance in Bulgaria. Research into the effects of the poison – for which there is no known antidote – has mostly been carried out in Czechoslovakia and Hungary.) 'There is no legitimate use for ricin,' he told the coroner.

The doctor who treated Mr Markov at the Balham hospital said that the patient's white cell blood count had soared from 10,600 on entry to an 'astonishingly high' 26,300 one day after admission.

Forensic scientist Dr Robert Keeley described the tiny metal ball which had been found in Markov's right thigh after X-rays. It measured 1.52 millimetres in diameter, and was made from an alloy of platinum and iridium – a compound noted for its resistance to corrosion and one which could only be worked in a high-temperature furnace. The minute sphere was drilled through with two holes that measured only .35 mm in diameter, and met in the middle to form a reservoir which held the poison. The technical knowledge and equipment needed to make such a pellet were beyond the range of an ordinary jeweller, he said. Dr Keeley had examined a similar metal ball sent from Paris. It had been recovered from the back of another Bulgarian defector named Vladimir Kostov, who had survived a previous umbrella-gun attack. Tests showed that the pellets were identical to within 0.02 mm. (Kostov had been attacked on 24 August 1978. He had heard a muffled report which sounded like an airgun being fired, and felt a stinging sensation in his back, just above the kidneys. Subsequent examination revealed the presence of tiny fragments of metal, and the pellet was recovered. In his case the poison content was not fatal.)

Mrs Markov said at the inquest that her husband had always feared death at the hands of the Bulgarian secret police. But there was no direct evidence of their involvement and the West London coroner, Gavin Thurston, found only that Markov had been 'killed unlawfully'.

MESRINE, Jacques
'Public enemy number one' in France who was shot in a police ambush.

Mesrine was born in Clichy, Paris, in 1937. In 1940, his mother moved her family to Château-Merle, near Poitiers, where she had been brought up, while her husband was in the army. Mesrine was an attractive child, and his biographer Carey Schofield reports that he was usually able to get what he wanted from adults by smiling at them. But he was also solitary. Once, when asked to go and play with other children, he replied; 'No, I always have a nicer time on my own.'

After the war, the Mesrines returned to Clichy. Mesrine later claimed that he never had enough affection from his father, who worked hard in a textile designing business. He was a poor student at school, but made a strong impression on his schoolmates with his charm, his prowess at fighting, and his love of argument. His constant absenteeism led to his expulsion from two schools. He began joining other teenagers stealing cars for joyrides. At the age of eighteen, he married a beautiful black girl from Martinique, and they moved into a small flat. But he soon found marriage boring and when his wife had a baby, decided that his mother could bring it up.

At nineteen, Mesrine was conscripted into the army, and asked to be sent to Algeria, where the French were trying to put down a Muslim revolt. There was much brutality on both sides. Mesrine thoroughly enjoyed being in action, and received the Military Cross for valour. While in the army, he was divorced from his wife.

His return to civilian life was an anticlimax. He soon committed his first burglary. With two other men, he broke into the flat of a wealthy financier. When a drill broke off in the lock of the safe, he went out to a hardware shop, broke in and got more drills. They escaped with 25 million francs.

When de Gaulle came to power in 1958, he began seeking a political solution to the Algerian problem. Mesrine, like many Frenchmen, regarded this as a betrayal. The right-wing General Salan set up a secret organization, the Organisation Armée Secréte. Mesrine became involved, and it reinforced Mesrine's attitude to law and order – the typical criminal attitude that it is a question of individual choice and that men who can think for themselves should make up their own minds whether to obey the law.

In the spring of 1962, Mesrine was arrested when on his way to rob a bank, and sentenced to three years in prison. He was released on parole a year later. For a while he decided to 'go straight'. He married a second time, had a young daughter, and now with his father's help, began to study to become an architect. There is evidence that he was a good architect. But when, in late 1964, he was made redundant, he went back to crime. His cool nerve served him remarkably well. Once, in the course of holding up a jewellery shop, the police arrived. Mesrine ran into the back yard, unlatched the gate to make it look as if he had run through, then hid in a dustbin until the coast was clear. On another occasion, he escaped from a flat he was burgling through a lavatory window, and escaped across the roof-tops, walking out of a building further down the street, and asking the police what all the commotion was about.

In 1967 another attempt to 'go straight' as an innkeeper – financed by his father – again proved to be a failure as he found respectability too unexciting. He went off with a woman, Jeanne Schneider, and together they carried out a daring robbery at a hotel in Switzerland. In 1968, as one of the most wanted robbers in France, he decided to move to Canada.

He and Schneider went to work for a Montreal millionaire, Georges Deslauriers, as chauffeur and housekeeper, but the gardener took a dislike to Jeanne, and Deslauriers dismissed them. Mesrine's response was to kidnap Deslauriers, and hold him for a $200,000 ransom. Deslauriers managed to escape before the ransom was paid, and Mesrine and Schneider moved to a small town, Percé, where they made the acquaintance of a wealthy widow called Evelyne le Bouthillier. After an evening spent with the pair, Mme le Bouthillier was found strangled. Mesrine always claimed that he knew nothing about the murder.

They slipped over the border into the United States, but were arrested by a border patrol and taken back to Canada. There they were charged with the murder of Mme le Bouthillier. Mesrine was furious at being accused of the murder of an old woman. He claimed that he *had* committed several murders, and tortured people who had insulted him, but that he would have been incapable of this particular crime. Held in the Percé prison pending trial, Mesrine succeeded in escaping by attacking a guard and stealing his keys. He also released Jeanne. They were recaptured only two miles away. Mesrine was given ten years for the kidnapping of Georges Deslauriers; Schneider was given five. But they were acquitted of the murder of Evelyne le Bouthillier.

A year later, Mesrine led a number of other prisoners in a spectacular escape from the 'escape-proof' prison of St Vincent de Paul at Laval. He became a celebrity in Canada and it gave him the idea of a still more daring exploit. After robbing a bank in Montreal, he and another escaped convict drove back to the St Vincent de Paul prison with the intention of freeing the remaining prisoners in the top security wing. But when a police car approached them on the way to the prison, Mesrine opened fire. With bullets whistling past them, they escaped back to Montreal. A week later, Mesrine and two accomplices were in the forests near Montreal where they were stopped by two forest rangers. One of the rangers recognized Mesrine, and made the mistake of showing it. Both were shot down, and their bodies dumped in a nearby ditch and covered with branches.

There were more bank robberies – on one occasion, Mesrine robbed the same bank twice because a cashier had scowled at him as he walked out after the first robbery. Then Mesrine met a beautiful nineteen-year-old, Jocelyne Deraiche, who became his mistress. With two accomplices, they crossed the border again into America, continuing south to Venezuela where they were able to live comfortably on the profits of their bank robberies, aided by ex-OAS men living there. When a police official told them that Interpol was on their trail, Mesrine and Deraiche flew to Madrid.

All the publicity he had received in Canada had given Mesrine a taste for fame. He decided to become the best known criminal in the world. In the remaining seven years of his life, he achieved that ambition.

Back in France, in 1973 Mesrine committed a dozen armed robberies, netting millions of francs. He gathered around him a gang he could trust. As the hunt for him intensified, he made preparations for the future by examining the courthouse at Compiègne. The precaution proved useful. When police finally caught up with him on 8 March, Mesrine staged a spectacular escape from the Palais de Justice in Compiègne, getting hold of a gun that an accomplice had left in a lavatory, then holding up the court, and escaping with the judge as a human shield. He was shot in the arm in the course of his escape, but had the bullet removed when he was safe in a hideout.

Once again at his old occupation of robbing banks and factories, he carefully nurtured the image of the gentleman crook, the modern Robin Hood. When a female bank clerk accidentally pushed the alarm button, Mesrine commented courteously, 'Don't worry, I like to work to music,' and went on collecting the money. When he heard his father was dying of cancer in hospital, he made a daring visit to see him dressed as a doctor in a white coat with a stethoscope round his neck. Not long after this, a bank robbery went wrong, and the accomplice waiting in the getaway car was arrested. As a result, the police tracked down Mesrine to his flat in the rue Vergniaud and placed him under arrest.

La Santé prison proved to be escape-proof, and Mesrine passed the time by writing a book, *L'Instinct de Mort* (*The Killer Instinct*), which was smuggled out and appeared in February 1977. In it Mesrine admitted that a previous claim to have killed thirty-nine people was a lie, but it contained detailed descriptions of other murders – for none of which a body had been found. After three and a half years, the prosecution finally opened in May 1977. Mesrine astounded the court by telling his audience that it was easy enough to buy the keys that could open any pair of handcuffs, then extracted a matchbox from the knot of his tie and within seconds had removed his handcuffs. The gesture brought him the kind of publicity that he had now come to crave. He was nevertheless sentenced to twenty years.

A year later Mesrine staged another of his spectacular escapes. An accomplice named François Besse squirted soapy water into the eyes of a guard, and Mesrine, who was in the interview room with his lawyer, grabbed some guns from a ventilation shaft. Two warders were made to undress, and the convicts dressed in their uniforms. They let another prisoner, Carman Rives, out of his cell, and then all three rushed across the prison yard. Mesrine and Besse escaped over the wall with a ladder, but Rives was shot.

The police commissioner, Serge Devos, was placed in charge of the squad whose business was to recapture Mesrine. Mesrine moved to Deauville, a seaside resort in Normandy. He was unable to resist the temptation of walking into the local police station, announcing that he was a police inspector from the Gaming Squad, and asking to see the duty inspector. They were told he was not there. As they walked out, one of the policemen said, 'That's Mesrine', and the other told him that was impossible. Mesrine then robbed a casino in Deauville, and in the desperate chase that followed, was almost caught. After this, he invaded the home of a bank employee who had given evidence against him at his trial, and forced him to go to the bank and hand over nearly half a million francs.

A Paris department store was the scene of another one of Mesrine's typically quixotic gestures in the summer of 1978. He saw the floor-walker seizing a shoplifter – a boy of fifteen. Mesrine announced himself as a police inspector with special responsibility for juvenile affairs, flashing a fake identity card, then grabbed the boy by the scruff of the neck and led him out of the store. There he let him go. In August, he gave an interview to a journalist from *Paris Match*, which caused a sensation. Then Mesrine came to London where he spent several weeks undisturbed by police. There he planned another astonishing crime – to kidnap the judge who had sentenced him to twenty years in prison. On 10 November 1978 Mesrine and an accomplice returned to France, went to the judge's flat and held up his wife, daughter and son-in-law. But the accomplice was inexperienced, and the daughter succeeded in getting word to the judge's son when he came to the door. Mesrine saw the arrival of the police, ran down the stairs, and as he came face to face with several policemen, pointed behind him. 'Quick, Mesrine's up there.' And they went rushing past. A young policeman who recognized Mesrine outside was handcuffed to a drainpipe.

In hiding, Mesrine wrote an open letter to the French police denouncing conditions in French prisons and claiming that this had 'evoked a fanatical passion for human rights'. During his last year there was an obvious deterioration in Mesrine's character. 'Mesrine believed in his lies more than anyone else did,' said his biographer. 'Any suggestion, even from his closest friends, that perhaps he was exaggerating a little, could send him into an uncontrollable fury. He had always been subject to fits of rage, and these were becoming more and more frequent. .... He would smash everything that was in his way, and it is extraordinary that he never killed anyone while in a rage.' Mesrine explained to journalists – whom he still allowed to interview him – that he now 'identified ideologically with the extreme left'.

When the police finally located his hideout, in a flat in the rue Belliard, they decided to take no chances. Mesrine had sworn never to be taken alive. On 2 November 1979 Mesrine came out of the building with his girlfriend, Sylvie Jean-Jacquot, and walked towards his BMW, parked nearby. At a road junction, a blue lorry signalled that he wanted to cut across him and turn right. Mesrine waved him on. The lorry stopped in front of the car, and another lorry drew up behind. Four policemen climbed out, and within seconds, twenty-one bullets had shattered the windscreen. Mesrine was killed immediately. Sylvie Jean-Jacquot was shot in the arm, and her dog was also hit. The police flung their arms around one another and danced for joy.

MORRIS, Raymond Leslie
The Cannock Chase child-murderer.

On 8 September 1965 six-year-old Margaret Reynolds vanished on her way to school in the Birmingham suburb of Aston. A massive search failed to provide any clues. On 30 December, in nearby Bromwich, five-year-old Diane Tift set out to walk home from her grandmother's and never arrived.

The police suspected that a rapist who had a year earlier lured an eight-year-old girl into a car, taken her to a lover's lane and raped her, might now have graduated to murder. The first victim had been half-strangled and badly beaten, then left for dead at the side of the road, but she had recovered and was able to give the police a description of the man.

On 12 January 1966 a colliery worker on a bicycle ride found the body of a girl in a field near Cannock Chase, only a few miles north of the homes of the two missing girls. When it was moved another body was found beneath it, sunk into the silt of the ditch. The lower body was Margaret Reynolds, and it had been there a great deal longer than the upper one, Diane Tift.

Ten-year-old Jane Taylor went for a bicycle ride on 14 August 1966 and vanished. She lived in Mobberley, near Altrincham, Cheshire, close to the A34 which runs north to the Cannock Chase area. Her body was never found.

On 19 August 1967 seven-year-old Christine Darby was playing with friends in Walsall, when a car stopped and a man asked the way to Caldmore Green. When the children pointed out the road, the driver asked Christine if she would get in and show him the way; he pushed open the front door of the car and the child got in. The driver then reversed out of the street and, to the astonishment of the children, turned in the opposite direction to Caldmore Green. The children were able to say that the man had a local accent, and had pronounced Caldmore Green in the local way – as Karmer Green. Like the other children, Christine vanished. One of her shoes was found two days later by the A34, and her briefs not far away. Five days after her disappearance, her body was found by one of five thousand volunteers who were searching the area around Cannock. The child's vagina had been badly torn. She had died of suffocation, probably by hands held across her nose and mouth.

The car had been described as large and grey, and the owners of all large grey cars in the area were questioned, including Raymond Morris, a foreman in an engineering factory who lived close to the Walsall police station. He declared that he had gone shopping with his wife on the Saturday afternoon when Christine Darby vanished: his wife confirmed this.

Ten-year-old Margaret Aulton was helping her brother make a Guy Fawkes bonfire on 4 November 1967 near their home in Walsall. At 7.45 pm a man got out of a car and asked them if they wanted fireworks; Margaret said yes, and followed the man to his car. The man opened the driver's door and pointed, saying the fireworks were 'over there'. Then he grabbed her arm and tried to pull her into the car. She resisted, and the man tried persuasion, saying, 'I'll open the other door for you.' He walked round the car, and Margaret hurried away.

A neighbour had been watching this, Mrs Wendy Jones. She asked the child if she knew the man, who was now sitting slumped over the wheel of the car; she said no, and Mrs Jones made a mental note of the registration number. That evening, she rang the police and told them what had happened. She described the car as green with a white roof – not the car the police had so far been searching for. Unfortunately, she had transposed two of the digits of the registration number, telling the police it was 429 LOP when it was, in fact, 492 LOP. Undiscouraged by the negative result of their check – 429 LOP proved to be a grey Anglia that had not left Yorkshire – they tried all possible permutations of the number. Two were motorcycles. Only one car fitted the description: a green Corsair owned by Raymond Morris.

The next day police called on Morris at his work in Oldbury. Later that day he appeared in an identity parade, but neither Margaret Aulton nor Wendy Jones recognized him. He walked out a free man.

But the more the police looked into Morris's background, the more likely it seemed that he was the man they wanted. He had admitted that his previous car was a grey Austin Cambridge, which fitted the description of the car they had been looking for. In October 1966 he had been the subject of a complaint about child assault; it was alleged that he had taken two young girls up to his flat at 20 Regent House, Green Lane, Walsall, and undressed them in different rooms. But since the girls were in different rooms and so could not corroborate one another's testimony, the case was dropped. After being interviewed about Christine Darby – and given an alibi by his wife – he had been interviewed a second time because police felt he was a likely suspect, resembling the Identikit picture of the wanted man (compiled from the description of the first victim, who had lived). They had asked him to specify which shops he had visited that Saturday afternoon with his wife, and he had claimed to remember only one of them. Later, two detectives doing a routine check on all males in the block of flats had questioned him again – to his intense annoyance – and agreed that his nervous manner, and his resemblance to the Identikit picture, made him a likely suspect.

It was decided that there was enough evidence to justify taking Morris into custody, and he was arrested the next day. His reply to the policeman who arrested him was, 'Oh my God, was it my wife?' He obviously felt his alibi had been cracked.

Morris's wife, told of the arrest, now decided to admit that the alibi had been false. When Morris was told, he buried his face in his hands and said: 'My God, my God, she wouldn't.' A man who had seen a grey car – and its driver – close to the spot where Christine Darby's body had been found told the police that he felt he recognized Morris. Morris was then charged with murder.

A search of Morris's flat revealed some snaps showing a five-year-old girl lying almost naked with her legs open. On one of the photographs, a pair of hands could be seen touching the child – presumably taken by a timing device; there was a Timex watch on one of the wrists. Morris had tried to hide a Timex watch round his right ankle when the police were searching him; now they knew why. The little girl was a relative, who had stayed twice in the Morris's flat with her elder sister. On both occasions, she had returned home with a sore vagina. Oddly enough, she didn't explain how this happened.

After seeing these photographs, Morris's wife Carol decided to give evidence against him. She explained that she had supported his alibi because she was totally convinced of his innocence, and wanted to save him trouble; now she wanted to see him convicted. (She had earlier insisted that she had been genuinely mistaken, but admitted in the witness box that this was untrue.)

At the trial, Morris stonewalled every inch of the way, refusing to make any admissions. The evidence against him was basically circumstantial, but was so strong that the jury had no hesitation in finding him guilty; he was sentenced to life imprisonment.

Raymond Leslie Morris was born in Walsall on 13 August 1929, and had married his first wife Muriel when he was nineteen. He was good looking and above average intelligence. His hobby was photography, and his work was up to professional standards. He wrote poetry, was fond of reading aloud, and was a good mimic. He loved to impersonate Humphrey Bogart or Leslie Charteris's Saint (his favourite fictional character). He was never known to lose his temper, and most people found him cold and emotionless. His first wife described him as a man who could turn on enormous charm, then change in a moment. 'Often when we were together watching television he'd suddenly say, "Strip!" And if I didn't obey at once, his eyes would go cold . . . and his cheeks very white.' When they separated, after nine years, he refused to support her unless she allowed him to call on her once or twice a week for sex; she describes him making her bend over a table so he could have her in the 'animal position'. His second wife, Carol, never seems to have brought out this sadistic side of his character, and described him as a tender and thoughtful husband.

The picture that emerges is of a kind of Walter Mitty, living a rich fantasy life, talented and artistic, with a slightly feminine streak (he was building a doll's house at the time of his arrest). Yet he had

236

lived in the same small area of the Midlands ever since he was born, with no real attempt to find a wider field for his talents. The dominance, the need for self-assertion, the violent rages when his wife showed any tendency to disobey, all indicate that Morris was one of Van Vogt's 'violent men', the type of man who will never, under any circumstances, admit he might be in the wrong. His first wife, Muriel, was slightly built and small, definitely childlike. His second wife was built on more buxom lines, but was fourteen years his junior, and apparently very much under his domination. Morris's obsession with young children was the expression of an urge to be the completely dominant male, the combination of the Saint, James Bond and the Marquis de Sade that he had never had a chance to become in real life.

A sum of more than £2,000 reward money was divided between Wendy Jones and three other witnesses, one of them being a child who had been with Christine Darby when she was abducted. Morris's grey Austin Cambridge was later bought at auction and ritually burnt.

MOUSSAN, Jeanne and PICHON, Pierette
Young French sensation-seekers.

In July 1981 a forestry supervisor driving through a forest track in the Beaujolais region of France saw a parked Fiat and a man's body lying beside it. The man was identified as Raoul Duplessis, an iron-worker from Lyon. He had been killed with multiple stab wounds. The only clue was a woman's hair pin found on the grass nearby. Forensic examination showed that the man had been stabbed with two separate knives, probably kitchen knives. They assumed that he had picked up two hitch-hikers who had killed him in order to rob him.

A number of hitch-hikers had been on the road on the morning when Duplessis vanished. The police interviewed many of these, and eliminated them from the investigation. But they had more difficulty tracing two young girls in miniskirts who had been seen by several drivers. Drivers who had picked up the girls said that they were from Macon. Eventually, the Macon police were able to identify them as eighteen-year-old Pierette Pichon and sixteen-year-old Jeanne Moussan, both from respectable middle-class families. They had met in a hospital in Macon when they were both suffering from a stomach ailment. On 14 July, Bastille Day, they had discharged themselves, and set out to hitch-hike to Lyon. A check of all the hardware shops in Macon revealed that the girls had bought two carving knives that same morning.

The girls were picked up when they returned to Macon. The carving knives were found on Jeanne Moussan when she was arrested. They still had caked blood near the handles. The girls confessed to the murder; they said they had deliberately set out to murder and rob anyone who came along. Raoul Duplessis had been happy to accept their suggestion of going into the woods with them. One of the girls had dropped her hair pin. As he bent over to pick it up, Jeanne Moussan stabbed him in the back. The girls stabbed him twice more, then stood and watched him for an hour and a half as he slowly bled to death. They robbed the corpse of four francs. A psychiatrist reported that both girls were so jaded that they could achieve sexual satisfaction only in sadism and various other perversions.

Being under age, neither girl is eligible for more than a short term of imprisonment.

MULLIN, Herbert
Paranoid mass murderer operating in Santa Cruz at the same time as another mass murderer, Ed Kemper.

Herbert Mullin was born on 18 April 1947, in Salinas, California; his mother was a devout Catholic, and Mullin's upbringing was – according to his later confession – oppressively religious. But he seems to have been a completely normal boy, voted by his class 'most likely to succeed'. By the age of seventeen he had a girlfriend, to whom he was engaged, and a close male friend named Dean; both were members of a group of school athletes who called themselves the Zeros. Dean's death in a motor accident in July 1965 seems to have marked the beginning of the schizophrenia that led Mullin to commit thirteen murders. He arranged his bedroom as a kind of shrine round his friend's picture, and told his girlfriend that he was afraid he was homosexual. When he became eligible for call-up in the army, he decided to become a conscientious objector; his girlfriend – whose father was a military man – broke off the engagement. In February 1969, when he was twenty-one, he announced that he was going to India to study religion, and his family noted that he seemed to be becoming 'more and more unrealistic'. A month later, at a family dinner, he began repeating everything his brother-in-law said and did. His family persuaded him to commit himself to a mental hospital. He remained there for six weeks, but was unco-operative, and continued to talk about yoga and his odd religious ideas.

By October 1969 Mullin was suffering from full-blown paranoid schizophrenia, hearing voices that told him to shave his head and burn his penis with a lighted cigarette. He had been smoking pot and taking LSD for a number of years, and this undoubtedly contributed to his mental derangement. Back in a mental home that autumn, he wrote dozens of letters to people he had never met, signing himself 'a human sacrifice, Herb Mullin'. He was given anti-psychotic drugs, and after a month was discharged. In June 1970 he went to Hawaii, against his parents' advice, and was soon in a mental hospital. His parents had to provide money for his return and he was escorted on to the plane by a policeman. Back in Santa Cruz he behaved strangely and got in trouble with the police. In June 1971 he moved to San Francisco and lived in cheap hotels; when evicted from his hotel in September 1972, he returned home – still highly disturbed. He began receiving telepathic messages ordering him to kill.

On 13 October 1972 he was driving along a deserted stretch of highway in the Santa Cruz mountains when he saw an old man walking along. He stopped the car and asked the man to take a look at the engine; as the tramp bent obligingly over the car, Mullin hit him with a baseball bat, killing him. He left the body – later identified as Lawrence White – by the roadside and drove off.

On 24 October he picked up a Cabrillo College student, Mary Guilfoyle. As they drove towards downtown Santa Cruz, he stabbed her in the heart with a hunting knife, killing her instantly. Then he took her to a deserted road, and began cutting open the body with the knife, pulling out the internal organs. He left her there to the vultures, and drove off – her skeleton was found four months later. A week later, on 2 November, he entered the confessional of St Mary's Church, Los Gatos, and stabbed to death Father Henri Tomei.

Now Mullin was hearing voices from potential victims, begging him to kill them. In December 1972 he bought a gun. On 25 January 1973 he drove out to Branciforte Drive, looking for Jim Gianera, the man who, years before, had introduced him to pot; he now believed Gianera had deliberately set out to destroy his mind. The door of the primitive cabin in which Gianera had lived was opened by 29-year-old Kathy Francis, who told him that Gianera no longer lived there. She gave him Gianera's address in Santa Cruz. Mullin drove there, and shot down Gianera; then, as the dying man's wife bent over him, he stabbed her in the back, then shot her. Then he went back to the cabin, and killed Kathy Francis and her two small sons, sleeping in the same bed. Kathy Francis's husband had been out of town at the time.

On 30 January, Mullin went to discuss his problems with a Lutheran minister in Santa Cruz, explaining mysteriously that 'Satan gets into people and makes them do things they don't want to'. He did not elaborate.

On 6 February Mullin was hiking aimlessly in the state park in Santa Cruz when he saw a makeshift tent. He told the four teenage boys inside that they were camping illegally and that he would have to report them. The boys, all in their teens, tried to talk him out of it. Suddenly, Mullin pulled out his revolver and shot them in rapid succession. They brought the number of his victims up to twelve.

A few days later, Mullin was preparing to deliver firewood to his parents' house when the mental voices told him he had to kill someone. It was 13 February. He stopped his station-wagon, went up to an old man, Fred Perez, who was working in the garden, and shot him. A neighbour looking out of her window saw the station-wagon driving away, and Fred Perez lying face down. She called the police, and within minutes Mullin was under arrest.

At his trial Mullin explained his reasons for killing. He was convinced that he was averting natural disasters – like another San Francisco earthquake – and had saved thousands of lives. Murder, he said, decreases natural disasters. He was found sane by legal standards, and guilty of ten murders – he was not charged with all thirteen. He will become eligible for parole in the year 2020.

In his book on the killings, *The Die Song*, psychiatrist Donald T. Lunde argues that Governor Reagan's economy measures that forced the closing of many mental hospitals in California, and deprived Mullin of treatment, was a false economy that cost both money and lives.

N

NEAVE, Airey Middleton Sheffield, MP
Shadow Northern Ireland Secretary killed by an INLA bomb.

Airey Neave MP, shadow Northern Ireland Secretary, was a wartime hero who escaped from Colditz, and close friend and adviser of Margaret Thatcher (then Opposition Leader). A highly sophisticated dual-trigger car bomb, which had been clamped to the underside of his vehicle, exploded beneath him as he drove from the House of Commons underground car-park in mid afternoon on 30 March 1979. His car had just cleared a short incline at the start of the exit ramp, and investigators concluded that the angle of tilt together with the acceleration required had been sufficient to detonate the device.

Mr Neave, who was sixty-three, lay trapped in the wreckage for half an hour while rescue and first-aid teams fought to save him. However he died within minutes of his arrival at Westminster Hospital, before his wife Diana could reach his bedside. At first his killers were thought to have penetrated House of Commons security (the underground car-park is guarded by officers of a special police unit, and monitored on closed-circuit TV screens). Later it became known that the magnetized device had been clamped to the chassis of Mr Neave's car while it was parked near his house in Westminster, before he left for the Commons. With the initial movement of the car, a globule of mercury then armed the bomb (the first trigger). When he left just before 3 pm Mr Neave – a most careful driver – successfully negotiated the first five floors of the underground car-park before he came to the exit ramp. The tilt and acceleration then combined to move the mercury globule again, to complete the circuit and explode the device.

A review of security measures at Westminster, including personal protection for leading politicians of all parties, was carried out following Mr Neave's assassination. Commander Peter Duffy, head of Scotland Yard's Anti-Terrorist Branch, was recalled from the United States to head the investigation into the murder. Mr Neave's personal courage was legendary, and some observers felt he may have under-estimated the threat posed by the IRA (as did Earl

Mountbatten; see McMahon, Thomas). Gilbert Kelland, Scotland Yard's Assistant Commissioner (Crime), revealed after the House of Commons explosion that he had previously discussed the question of personal security with Mr Neave. 'He was aware of the need to take precautions,' said Mr Kelland, but added, 'We do have to take into account the wishes of the person concerned when supplying special security measures.'

Mr Neave had been MP for Abingdon, Berkshire, for more than a quarter of a century. He acted as campaign manager for Margaret Thatcher when she took over the leadership of the Tory party in 1975, and became shadow Northern Ireland Secretary as well as one of her most trusted political advisers. Most observers – including terrorists both from Protestant organizations as well as the IRA – assumed that if the Conservatives won the forthcoming general election, his appointment as Northern Ireland Secretary would herald the introduction of tougher security measures in the Province. As such he was an obvious target for assassination. What his murderers achieved by his death, however, remains problematical. Mrs Thatcher pledged that, 'They must never, never, never be allowed to triumph, they must never prevail.'

NEILSON, Donald
The Black Panther killer of three sub-postmasters and an heiress.

In the early hours of 16 February 1972 sub-postmaster Leslie Richardson of Heywood, Lancashire, was awakened by sounds of an intruder, and went to grapple with a hooded raider who carried a gun; it went off, blasting a hole in the ceiling. The sub-postmaster managed to snatch off the man's hood, and was surprised to see he was white, for he had spoken with a West Indian accent. The intruder escaped through the back door.

It was two more years before the hooded burglar killed. On 15 February 1974 he entered another sub-post office by drilling three holes in a window and releasing the safety catch. He entered the bedroom of the youngest son, Richard Skepper, and demanded the keys to the safe. When he failed to find them in the place indicated by the boy, the man entered the parents' bedroom, waking them up. Donald Skepper shouted, 'Let's get him', and was instantly shot. He died in the arms of his wife, and the gunman fled.

There had been fifteen other robberies of post offices that fitted the same pattern, netting the burglar over £20,000. And on 6

September 1974 the police had another murder on their file. Sub-postmaster Derek Astin, of Higher Baxenden, near Accrington, woke up to find a man in the bedroom. He jumped out of bed to tackle him, and was shot. His wife and two children all saw the killing, and described the man as short, slim and wiry.

Because the Yorkshire police were so active, the Black Panther committed his next burglary in Langley, Worcestershire, where Sidney and Margaret Grayland, a middle-aged couple, ran the post office. In mid November the Graylands were stocktaking at about seven in the evening when Mr Grayland went to the storeroom; his wife heard a shot and rushed in to find him on the floor. As she leaned over him, she was struck on the head and blacked out; she woke up in hospital, her skull fractured. Two policemen had passed by several hours later and noticed the light; Mrs Grayland would have died of loss of blood if she had been left any longer. Her husband was dead. The burglar had taken about £800 from the cash box.

On the morning of 14 January 1975, Dorothy Whittle, who lived in the village of Highley, Shropshire, wondered why her seventeen-year-old daughter Lesley had not come down to breakfast; her brother Ronald was due to come and drive her to college. Lesley's bedroom was empty. Then, on a piece of tape with embossed lettering, they discovered a ransom demand for £50,000. It ordered the family not to call the police, and said that the kidnapper would telephone a message to a shopping centre in Kidderminster that evening. But no message came. In fact, Ronald Whittle telephoned the police. That evening, the television carried a news item about the kidnapping – and, as a result, Ronald Whittle waited in vain for the telephone call.

On the following night, the kidnapper parked a stolen car at Dudley, in Worcestershire, and made his way to a transport depot nearby where he meant to leave another kidnap message for Ronald Whittle to find. A security guard saw the shabby little man hanging around and asked him what he wanted. The answer was unsatisfactory, and the guard made the mistake of saying he intended to call the police, then turning away from the man. He was shot six times in the back. He was able to tell the police about the 'tramp' before he lapsed into unconsciousness – fortunately, he recovered later.

The following evening Ronald Whittle's telephone rang at 11.45. A voice told him that he was to take the money to a telephone kiosk in Kidsgrove, near Stoke-on-Trent, where he would find a message.

243

The police, listening on an extension, had taped the message. In the early hours of the morning, Ronald Whittle found the message on a piece of Dynotape. It told him to drive to nearby Bathpool Park and flash the lights of his car; the kidnapper would make contact by flashing a torch. But it was a waste of time, and Ronald Whittle drove back to Highley in a state of grim discouragement. In the meantime police officers drove round the park in a police car, taking the numbers of all parked cars in the area.

The cartridge cases at the freight depot were studied microscopically, and found to come from the same gun that had killed the sub-postmasters; this argued that the kidnapper of Lesley Whittle was the Black Panther.

The stolen car was now found, containing Lesley's slippers, more messages designed to lead Ronald Whittle to Dudley Zoo, and a tape-recording made by Lesley asking them to co-operate with the kidnapper.

A further call from the kidnapper led to no result – Ronald Whittle asked for evidence of his identity, and the man agreed to ask Lesley a certain question and ring back. He never did.

Ronald Whittle and Chief Superintendent Booth, in charge of the case, appeared on television together, seemingly hostile to one another. They had agreed to put out a story that Ronald Whittle was refusing to co-operate with the police in his anxiety to get his sister back, and that the police were furious. This, they hoped, would lead the kidnapper to contact Whittle again.

The day after the television broadcast, 6 March, the police received an important clue. Weeks before, a schoolboy in Bathpool Park had found a torch with an orange piece of Dynotape stuck to it, reading 'Drop suitcase into hole'. He handed it to his headmaster, who failed to see the connection with the kidnapping until he heard the broadcast. He contacted the police, who now decided that perhaps the kidnapper had left other clues. Police and tracker dogs searched the park. The following day, a policeman climbed down a drainage shaft, and saw the naked body of a girl – Lesley Whittle. It was suspended by the neck by a wire rope. On the narrow ledge above the body there was a maroon sleeping-bag. Bathpool Park proved to have a network of sewage tunnels underneath it, and evidence showed that the Black Panther had explored these and decided they would make an ideal hideout. The investigation dragged on for the rest of the year. The police followed many leads, but none led them to the killer. On 11 December 1975 the Panther was caught by accident.

Two policemen, Tony White and Stuart Mackenzie, were driving through Mansfield Woodhouse, Nottinghamshire, at 11.45 pm, when they noticed a suspicious-looking man carrying a black holdall loitering near the post office. As a matter of routine they stopped to question him. The man said he was on his way home from work – and then produced a sawn-off shotgun from a parcel he was holding. He ordered White into the back of the car, then sat in the passenger seat with his gun jammed into Mackenzie's ribs. He ordered them to drive to Blidworth, six miles away. As they were cruising along Southwell Road, the gunman asked if there was any rope, and as White pretended to look for rope, he saw that the gun was no longer pointing at his companion; he pushed up the gun as Mackenzie stamped on the brake. They were outside a fish and chip shop, and they called for help. The gun went off, grazing White's hand. Two men ran from the queue outside the fish and chip shop and helped to grab the man and subdue him – photographs taken immediately after his arrest show his badly battered face. The man was handcuffed to iron railings. When the police found two Panther hoods on him, they realized that they had probably caught the most wanted man in Britain.

At the police station, the man finally broke silence and identified himself as Donald Neilson, aged thirty-nine, and that he lived in Grangefield Avenue, Thornaby, Bradford, with his wife and daughter. In the attic there, police found more Panther hoods, guns and burgling equipment.

Neilson – who had changed his name from Nappey (perhaps because in England babies' diapers are called nappies) – had lived in the street for fifteen years, hardly known to his neighbours, who regarded him as a loner. He worked on and off as a taxidriver and a joiner. He was a keep-fit fanatic who insisted on his daughter joining him in 'war games' that were rigorous training exercises. He was an embittered man with a grudge against society.

Neilson was first tried for the murder of Lesley Whittle. His defence was that she had accidentally fallen from the ledge where he had tied her, on the night Ronald Whittle had visited Bathpool Park. He admitted he had been alarmed by the activity of the police car and suspected a trap. This seemed unlikely, in view of the wire round the girl's neck. The jury found Neilson guilty of murdering Lesley Whittle. A second trial, on a charge of killing the three sub-postmasters, followed immediately, and he was found guilty – in spite of his defence that each of the shootings had been an accident.

The death of the security guard, Gerald Smith, which came fourteen months after he was shot, took place too long after the shooting to form the basis of a murder charge. Donald Neilson was sentenced to life imprisonment for the murders, and to sixty-one years for the kidnapping.

NESSET, Arnfinn
Scandinavia's worst mass murderer.

After a trial lasting five months – the longest in the country's legal history – Arnfinn Nesset, manager of a nursing home for the elderly in central Norway, was found guilty on 11 March 1983 of the murder of twenty-two patients in his care by injecting curacit poison into their veins. Curacit is a derivative of curare, used by primitive South American Indians in the tips of their arrows. It paralyses the respiratory system to bring swift, agonizing death by suffocation. Nesset was sentenced to twenty-one years' imprisonment, the maximum for murder under Norwegian law, and up to ten years of preventive detention.

The patients were murdered in the space of three and a half years, between May 1977 and November 1980. The total alone was sufficient to make Nesset, a balding, bespectacled man of forty-six, the biggest mass murderer of modern times in the whole of Scandinavia. The true number of old folk he killed in this way may have been even higher, however. According to State Attorney Olaf Jakhelln, Nesset confessed during preliminary police interrogation, 'I've killed so many I'm unable to remember them all.' He then asked for a list of all the patients who had died at the three institutions where he had worked since 1962, to help him refresh his memory. As a result, investigations were made into a grand total of sixty-two suspicious deaths spread over the twenty years before his trial opened in October 1982. No post-mortems were held because curacit is difficult to trace in the human body after any lapse of time: the last victim died in November 1980, but the police were not called in until March the following year. When the trial began Nesset retracted all his alleged confessions and was charged with 'only' the twenty-five murders the prosecution felt it could prove. Nesset pleaded Not Guilty to all of them.

The patients concerned, fourteen women and eleven men, were aged between sixty-seven and ninety-four. More than 150 witnesses were called to give evidence. A feature of the case was that none had actually seen Nesset administer the lethal injections, although several testified that they had seen him alone with various patients shortly before they were found dead in their beds – with signs of a hypodermic injection showing on their arms. It took fifteen minutes to read the full indictment, and three days for the jury to arrive at its multiple verdict. As well as being found guilty on twenty-two counts, he was also found guilty on one count of attempted murder. Nesset was acquitted on the remaining two murder charges, but found guilty of five charges of forgery and embezzlement of patients' money equivalent to about £1,200 or $1,800. The money was intended for the Salvation Army and for missionary work.

A woman reporter on a local newspaper first became suspicious about the deaths of the Orkdal Valley Nursing Home after she was tipped off that Nesset had ordered large quantities of curacit. She notified the police who began investigations and arrested Nesset on 9 March 1981. No clear motive for the murders was established despite lengthy police interrogation. According to the prosecution Nesset first claimed he had ordered the curacit to use on a dog, but later confessed to killing twenty-seven patients at Orkdal Valley Nursing Home after it opened under his management in 1977. He was said to have given a variety of reasons for doing so, including mercy killing, pleasure sensation, schizophrenia coupled with self-assertion, and a morbid need for killing.

Four psychiatrists who examined him found Nesset sane and accountable for his actions when administering the curacit, but added that his 'emotional development' had been disturbed. He grew up as an illegitimate child in a small, tightly-knit rural community on the west coast of Norway and felt both unwanted and emotionally isolated. This left him with a pronounced inferiority complex combined with pent-up aggressive tendencies which were liable to erupt in certain given situations. He seemed remarkably unaffected by what he had done, showing no sign of remorse or guilt.

Defence counsel Alf Nordhus argued that the confessions had been made under police pressure, while Nesset was mentally depressed. He submitted that the patients' deaths in fact were mercy killings, and said that Nesset saw himself as a kind of demigod who believed he possessed power of life or death over the elderly patients in his charge. Nesset admitted only to the embezzlement of 3,000 kroner (£320 or $480). Judge Karl Solberg, who sat with two brother judges, heard submissions from both defence and prosecution on the plea of euthanasia before passing sentence.

NILSEN, Dennis ('Des')

Homosexual mass killer who holds Britain's record for multiple murder at the time of writing.

On the evening of 8 February 1983, a drains maintenance engineer named Michael Cattran was asked to call at 23 Cranley Gardens, in Muswell Hill, north London, to find out why tenants had been unable to flush their toilets since the previous Saturday. Although Muswell Hill is known as a highly respectable area of London – it was once too expensive for anyone but the upper middle classes – No. 23 proved to be a rather shabby house, divided into flats. A tenant showed Cattran the manhole cover that led to the drainage system. When he removed it, he staggered back and came close to vomiting; the smell was unmistakably decaying flesh. And when he had climbed down the rungs into the cistern, Cattran discovered what was blocking the drain: masses of rotting meat, much of it white, like chicken flesh. Convinced this was human flesh, Cattran rang his supervisor, who decided to come and inspect it in the morning. When they arrived the following day, the drain had been cleared. And a female tenant told them she had heard footsteps going up and down the stairs for much of the night. The footsteps seemed to go up to the top flat, which was rented by a 37-year-old civil servant named Dennis Nilsen.

Closer search revealed that the drain was still not quite clear; there was a piece of flesh, six inches square, and some bones that resembled fingers. Detective Chief Inspector Peter Jay, of Hornsey CID, was waiting in the hallway of the house that evening when Dennis Nilsen walked in from his day at the office – a Jobcentre in Kentish Town. He told Nilsen he wanted to talk to him about the drains. Nilsen invited the policeman into his flat, and Jay's face wrinkled as he smelt the odour of decaying flesh. He told Nilsen that they had found human remains in the drain, and asked what had happened to the rest of the body. 'It's in there, in two plastic bags,' said Nilsen, pointing to a wardrobe.

In the police car, the Chief Inspector asked Nilsen whether the remains came from one body or two. Calmly, without emotion, Nilsen said: 'There have been fifteen or sixteen altogether.'

At the police station, Nilsen – a tall man with metal rimmed glasses – seemed eager to talk. (In fact, he proved to be something of a compulsive talker, and his talk overflowed into a series of school exercise books in which he later wrote his story for the use of Brian

Masters, a young writer who contacted him in prison.) He told police that he had murdered three men in the Cranley Gardens house – into which he moved in the autumn of 1981 – and twelve or thirteen at his previous address, 195 Melrose Avenue, Cricklewood.

The plastic bags from the Muswell Hill flat contained two severed heads, and a skull from which the flesh had been stripped – forensic examination revealed that it had been boiled. The bathroom contained the whole lower half of a torso, from the waist down, intact. The rest was in bags in the wardrobe and in the tea chest. At Melrose Avenue, thirteen days and nights of digging revealed many human bones, as well as a cheque book and pieces of clothing.

The self-confessed mass murderer – he seemed to take a certain pride in being 'Britain's biggest mass murderer' – was a Scot, born at Fraserburgh on 23 November 1945. His mother, born Betty Whyte, married a Norwegian soldier named Olav Nilsen in 1942. It was not a happy marriage; Olav was seldom at home, and was drunk a great deal; they were divorced seven years after their marriage. In 1954, Mrs Nilsen married again and became Betty Scott. Dennis grew up in the house of his grandmother and grandfather, and was immensely attached to his grandfather, Andrew Whyte, who became a father substitute. When Nilsen was seven, his grandfather died, and his mother took Dennis in to see the corpse. This seems to have been a traumatic experience; in his prison notes he declares 'My troubles started there.' The death of his grandfather was such a blow that it caused his own emotional death, according to Nilsen. Not long after this, someone killed the two pigeons he kept in an air raid shelter, another severe shock. His mother's remarriage when he was nine had the effect of making him even more of a loner.

With his mother's second marriage, the family moved to Strichen, not far from Fraserburgh, and Nilsen lived there until August 1961, when he enlisted in the army. As a child, he was quiet and withdrawn, and read a great deal; he also developed some artistic skill. He and his elder brother Olav – two years his senior – never got on together, but he seems to have been fond of his younger sister, Sylvia, and to have been on good terms with the daughters of his mother's second marriage. There was more than a touch of Scots puritanism in the home – for example, his mother insisted that the children should change their clothes in the privacy of the bedroom or bathroom; for the boys and girls to glimpse one another in a state of undress would have been thought indecent. Nilsen loved birds and animals, using them as an outlet for an emotional warmth that would otherwise have remained unexpressed. At school, he was well behaved and shy. Discipline seems to have appealed to him, and as soon as he was old enough, he joined the local army cadets, and was delighted with the uniform. He was still a few months under sixteen when he joined the army. Three years later, he became a cook. He was in Aden, then at Sharjah, on the Persian Gulf, then in Cyprus, then Berlin. He remained a loner, befriending animals, reading and writing poetry, avoiding close relationships. Photographs of the time show him as a good-looking young man with a sensitive mouth and an almost feminine lower lip, full and sensuous. He even considered marriage at one point, but was too shy to propose.

He spent twelve years in the army, until 1972. Then he went to London, and became a policeman. But it was not the kind of life he enjoyed. As an army cook he had been able to come and go much as he pleased, get drunk when he liked – which was fairly frequently – and feel part of an organisation. Being a policeman was altogether more restrictive. He was older than most of the other probationers, and inclined to talk down to them – Nilsen seems to have been an obsessive talker. There was an attitude of intolerance about homosexuals—although his colleagues were unaware of his leanings – which made him irritable. He enjoyed the uniform and the authority, but otherwise felt like a fish out of water. After only eleven months, he resigned from the force. The station at which he had spent much of his time – Kilburn – later became a search headquarters when the Cricklewood house was being investigated.

His next job was as a security guard, working for the Department of the Environment, mainly patrolling government buildings. That was also unsatisfactory. He became a clerical officer for the Manpower Services Commission, and his duties included interviewing job applicants. He was always immaculately dressed, and was regarded as an efficient officer. The Jobcentre was in Denmark Street, in Soho, close to Leicester Square, and he became aware of the immense number of down-and-outs and homosexuals who sleep rough in central London. It seems possible that this job was the disastrous turning point in Nilsen's life, the point at which temptation was placed under his nose.

In 1975, Nilsen was living in Teignmouth Road, Willesden, and there was a curious episode when a young man went to the police and alleged that Nilsen had attacked him in the flat there; Nilsen denied it, and no further action seems to have been taken.

It was while living in Teignmouth Road that Nilsen met a young man – ten years his junior – named David Gallichan, and when Gallichan said he was looking for a flat, suggested that they should share. Because Teignmouth Road was too small, the two of them looked for a larger place, and found the flat in Melrose Avenue, into which they moved in November 1975. Gallichan insists that there was no homosexual relation with Nilsen, and this is believable; many heterosexual young men were later to accept Nilsen's offer of a bed for the night, and he would make no advances, or accept a simple 'No' without resentment. Nilsen was certainly not a 'sex maniac' in the sense of a Dean Corll or John Gacy. The drive behind the later killings appears to have been a combination of loneliness and a morbid obsession with death.

The loneliness seems to have been assuaged by the relationship with Gallichan. It was, in many ways, a domestic situation. They shared the cooking; Gallichan did some gardening. They acquired a dog – a bitch called Bleep – and took her for walks on Sundays. They also took in a stray cat. Nilsen had a strong protective streak about stray animals, as well as about human waifs and strays. He was far more dominant than Gallichan, and was inclined to hold forth at length, usually on political subjects – his views were strongly left wing, and Mrs Thatcher seems to have been one of his detestations. Gallichan found a job as a railway porter. For Nilsen, Christmas 1976 was unusual in that he celebrated the festivity like any normal householder, with a Christmas tree, a turkey and seasonal booze. If they had continued to live together, it seems fairly certain that Nilsen would never have become a killer. It seems clear that, whatever Gallichan's feelings, Nilsen was strongly attached to him, and the relationship provided him with a kind of emotional stability that he had always wanted.

So it came as a severe shock when, in May 1977, Gallichan announced that he was leaving. He had a craving to live in the country, and had been offered a job by an antique dealer. Nilsen was furious but, as usual, his fury showed itself as a cold and highly controlled rage. 'It was as though I had insulted him, and he wanted me to go immediately,' said Gallichan. Nilsen felt rejected, and it may have aroused neuroses that had been latent since childhood. For Nilsen, self-assertion and self-esteem, were immensely important. To be 'deserted' by someone he had always dominated seemed the ultimate insult. He became cold and dismissive. When he and Gallichan met for a drink six months after the separation, Gallichan offered his address, and Nilsen said he didn't want it.

It was after this that the killings began. Nilsen was drinking heavily – he had always spent much of his spare time in pubs. Towards the end of December 1978, he picked up a young Irish labourer in the Cricklewood Arms, and they went back to his flat and continued drinking. Nilsen wanted the young man to stay with him over the New Year, but apparently the Irishman had other plans. In the notes he later wrote for Brian Masters, Nilsen gives as his motive for this first killing that he was lonely and wanted to spare himself the pain of separation. In another 'confession', he also implies that he has no memory of the actual killing – that he woke in the morning 'and found I had a corpse on my hands'. Nilsen strangled him in his sleep with a tie. Then he undressed the body, and carefully washed it, a ritual he observed after all his killings.

What happened then? This may be something we shall never know. As incredible as it sounds, Nilsen kept the corpse in his flat from late December 1978 until August 1979. He placed it under the floorboards, now once more fully clothed. He denied that there were any acts of necrophily with the corpses, and in view of his frankness about other details of the murders, this could well be true. Eight months later, on 11 August 1979, he removed the body, which had been encased in two plastic bags, and noted that there was little decomposition. He built a large bonfire at the bottom of the garden (of which he now had exclusive use), took his unnamed victim down to it, and burned the corpse together with a quantity of rubber, to cover the smell.

Nilsen's first reaction to his discovery that he had committed murder was – according to his own account – panic; he was convinced that he would be arrested the same day. When no one called him to account, he found it almost unbelievable.

Three months after burning his first victim, Nilsen picked up a young Chinaman in the Salisbury pub, and took him back to his flat. Nilsen claims the Chinaman offered sex, but that he did not want it. The Chinaman offered to tie him up; Nilsen made a counter-offer, and was allowed to tie the Chinaman's legs with a tie. Then he placed another tie around the man's neck and tried to strangle him. The man broke free and threw a brass candlestick at his attacker. Then he rushed off and told the police what had happened. When the police arrived, Nilsen told them that the Chinaman was trying to 'rip him off', and, to his astonishment, they accepted his explanation. He had expected to be arrested.

The next murder victim was a 23-year-old Canadian called Kenneth James Ockenden, who had completed a technical training course and was taking a holiday before starting his career. He had been staying with an uncle and aunt in Carshalton after touring the Lake District. He was not a homosexual, and it was pure bad luck that he got into conversation with Nilsen in the Princess Louise in High Holborn around 3 December 1979. They went back to Nilsen's flat, ate ham, eggs and chips, and bought £20 worth of alcohol. Ockendon watched television, then listened to rock music on Nilsen's hi-fi system. Then he sat listening to music wearing earphones, watching television at the same time. This may have been what cost him his life; Nilsen liked to talk, and probably felt 'rejected'. 'I thought bloody good guest this . . .' And sometime after midnight, while Ockendon was still wearing the headphones, he strangled him with a flex. Ockendon was so drunk that he put up no struggle. And Nilsen was also so drunk that after the murder, he sat down, put on the headphones, and went on playing music for hours. When he tried to put the body under the floorboards the next days, rigor mortis had set in and it was impossible. He had to wait until the rigor had passed. Later, he dissected the body. Ockendon had large quantities of Canadian money in his moneybelt, but Nilsen tore this up. The rigorous Scottish upbringing would not have allowed him to steal.

The murder made Ockendon's family frantic; his parents came to England to search for him. It was only much later that Nilsen became aware of the misery his casual murders had caused.

In May 1980, Nilsen picked up a 16-year-old butcher named Martyn Duffey, and they went 'on the piss'. The next morning, says Nilsen, Duffey was dead on his floor. He put the body under the floorboards, besides Kenneth Ockendon. By now, he says, he was resigned to the notion that the killings would happen again. There are moments in the confessions when it sounds as if, like so many killers, Nilsen felt he was being taken over by a kind of Mr Hyde personality.

Sometime between July and September 1980 – Nilsen is not sure of the date – a 26-year-old Scot named Billy Sutherland spent an evening drinking with Nilsen around West End pubs, and went back with him to Melrose Avenue. Sometime that night, he strangled Sutherland with his tie. After leaving the body around for two days, he placed it under the floorboards. Sutherland was in many ways typical of Nilsen's victims. He had been in trouble with the police in Scotland, and served time in jail. His girlfriend had given birth to a baby in 1977 and came to live with him in London. He was unable to find work, and she returned to Scotland. When Billy found work, he asked her to return to London and marry him, but she disliked the metropolis. When he stopped writing to her, she experienced a sad conviction that she would never see him again.

The next victim was a Mexican or Filipino, who was picked up in the Salisbury a few months after the last murder. Says Nilsen, 'I can't remember the details. It's academic. I must have put his body under the floorboards.' Nilsen kept chunks of the bodies in a wooden garden shed, enclosing them in a kind of makeshift tomb of bricks; he sprayed the inside of the shed daily with disinfectant.

Nilsen's accounts of the murders are repetitive, and make them sound almost mechancial. The next victim – soon after number five – was another Irishman, a building worker. 'My impression was that I strangled him.' Number seven was an undernourished down-and-out he picked up in a shop doorway on the corner of Charing Cross Road and Oxford Street. Nilsen took him home, gave him a meal, then watched him fall asleep. Nilsen then got drunk on Bacardi and 'experienced some kind of a high'. He got out a tie, went up behind the sleeping man, who was in an armchair, and strangled him; the man did not struggle. This man 'was so thin that I didn't want to look at him', so he was wrapped in plastic and burned on a bonfire in one piece. Nilsen burned many other decomposing fragments from the brick shed at the same time.

Nilsen could remember almost nothing of number eight, killed soon after the previous one ('this was a period of intense activity'). He later took the body from under the floorboards and cut it into three pieces, then put it back again; it was burned one year later.

Victim nine was picked up in the Golden Lion in Dean Street, a Scot of about 18 years of age, with short fair hair. 'I remember sitting on top of him and strangling him.'

Victim ten Nilsen refers to simply as 'this guy', a 'Billy Sutherland type.' He found him dead in the morning, and placed the corpse under the floorboards, to join two intact bodies and one dismembered body.

Victim eleven was a skinhead with a London accent, who boasted how tough he was. When he was in a drunken sleep in Nilsen's armchair, a substance like vomit dribbling from his mouth, Nilsen strangled him, then went to bed. The youth had many tattoos, including a line of dots around his neck with the inscription: 'Cut here.' Nilsen did just that when dismembering him. In May 1981, Nilsen had to have yet another body-burning session in the garden.

Victim twelve was picked up in September 1981. He was sitting with his back against the garden wall, and complained that he could not use his legs. Nilsen took him indoors and sent for an ambulance, which took the man to hospital. The next day, the man made the mistake of coming back. Nilsen cooked him a meal, and the man drank Bacardi, together with his pills. He became unconscious, and Nilsen strangled him. He claims that his motive was to save trouble: 'I didn't want to deal with ambulance men asking silly questions.' The man's name was Malcolm Barlow, and he was the last victim to die at Melrose Avenue. Nilsen was a sitting tenant, and when offered an 'incentive payment' of £1,000 to leave the flat, he accepted, and had one final large bonfire to cover his tracks.

In October 1981, Nilsen moved into the upstairs flat in Cranley Gardens. Seven weeks later, on 25 November he met a homosexual student, Paul Nobbs, in the Golden Lion in Soho, and took him back to his flat. Nobbs remembers nothing until he woke up the next morning with a hangover. He went into University College Hospital for a check-up, and was told that the bruises on his throat indicated that someone had tried to strangle him. Nobbs decided not to take any action. Nilsen's own account is that as he was strangling Nobbs with a tie, he became aware of what he was doing, and tried to revive him by throwing a glass of water in his face.

The first victim to be killed in Muswell Hill was a man named John Howlett, and he gave Nilsen the hardest struggle of his murderous career. As Nilsen tried to strangle him, Howlett fought back hard; Nilsen had to strike his head against the headrest of the bed. He strangled him, then went to pacify the dog, which was barking; when he returned, Howlett was breathing again. Nilsen then drowned him in the bath. Then he placed the body in a cupboard, and went to work. Howlett had to be disposed of 'because a friend was coming to stay for a few days', so Nilsen hacked up the body in the bath and boiled chunks of it in a large pot (which has subsequently become an exhibit at Scotland Yard's Black Museum).

In May 1982, Nilsen picked up a homosexual revue artist named Carl Stottor, whose stage name was Khara Le Fox. Stottor was another 'one that got away'. Stottor met Nilsen in a pub called the Black Cap in Camden High Street, and returned to his flat. Nilsen offered him a number of very large whiskies, then gave him a sleeping bag, warning him that the zip was dangerous. In the early hours of the morning, Stottor woke up with the zip tightening around his throat. He asked, 'What are you doing?' and passed out. When he woke up he was in a bath of cold water, and Nilsen was pushing his head under. Then he woke again on the settee with the dog licking his face. Nilsen told him that he had almost choked on the 'dangerous zip', and that he had placed him in the cold bath to revive him. It seems clear that the killing urge had vanished before the murder was completed; Nilsen may well have anticipated something of the sort when he warned Stottor about the zip – providing himself with a kind of alibi. The next morning, Stottor went for a walk with Nilsen in the woods, and was suddenly struck a violent blow in the neck that knocked him to the ground. But Nilsen only jerked him to his feet and continued the walk. They parted with an agreement to meet again, but Stottor decided not to keep the appointment. He went to the police only after he read of Nilsen's arrest a year later.

Victim fourteen was a drunk Nilsen picked up in Shaftesbury Avenue. In the Cranley Gardens flat, the drunk fell asleep while he was eating an omelette. Nilsen claims to be unable to remember the actual killing. He removed the man's clothes and washed him in the bath; he left him there for two days. Then he dissected him, and boiled parts of the body, placing some of the bits in a tea chest, and others in a plastic sack. Other pieces he flushed down the toilet.

Victim fifteen – the last – was a drug addict whom Nilsen picked up in the George in Goslett Yard on 1 February 1983, eight days before his arrest. They sat in front of the television, while Nilsen drank whisky and lager and the man injected himself with drugs. Nilsen listened to the whole of the rock opera *Tommy*, then killed his guest – he claims to have no recollection of the murder, but later admitted to Brian Masters that he had.

For a few days, the body lay in the bedroom, with a blanket over it. Then Nilsen cut off the head and boiled it in the pot; while it was boiling, he went out with his dog to a pub. The next day, Saturday, tenants complained that the drains were blocked. Nilsen could easily have removed the blockage himself, and so avoided arrest; instead, he simply dismembered the body.

Mike Cattran, the Dyna-rod man, discovered the drain blocked with human flesh the following Tuesday. That night, Nilsen went out and tried to buy chicken to put down the drain, but could not get enough; so he simply removed the human flesh. Then, knowing that his arrest was imminent, he went and spent a perfectly normal day at work; no one noticed that he seemed in any way tense or distressed.

His trial began on 24 October 1983, in the same court where Peter

Sutcliffe, the Yorkshire Ripper, had been tried two years earlier. Nilsen was charged with six murders and two attempted murders, although he had confessed to fifteen murders and seven attempted ones. Nilsen gave the impression that he was thoroughly enjoying his 'moment of glory'. The defence pleaded diminished responsibility, and that the charge should be reduced to manslaughter. There was considerable discussion around the question: Mad or bad? Nilsen insisted that he was not mad, and this is the view that was eventually taken by the court. Nilsen's own theory was that he was a 'creative psychopath' who became a destructive psychopath under the influence of alcohol. At the root of his crimes, he said, was 'a sense of total social isolation and a desperate search for sexual identity'. Paul Nobbs and Carl Stottor both gave evidence against him, as did another 'one that got away', a Scots barman named Douglas Stewart, whom Nilsen had tried to kill at Melrose Avenue on 12 November 1980. After trying to strangle Stewart, and then threatening him with a carving knife, Nilsen had finally allowed him to go. Stewart went to the police, but Nilsen managed to convince them that he and Stewart had had a 'lovers' quarrel', and they decided not to pursue the matter.

The defence psychiatrist, Dr James MacKeith, argued that Nilsen suffered from a severe personality disorder, due to lack of a father, the death of his grandfather, and loneliness. He also recounted how, at the age of ten, Nilsen had lost his footing when paddling in the sea and almost drowned. When he recovered consciousness, he was lying naked in the dunes with his wet clothes beside him and a sticky substance on his chest. He believed that he had been rescued by a nearby 16-year-old boy, who had then masturbated on him.

Later, according to Nilsen, he had acquired the habit of masturbating in front of a mirror with his body covered with talcum powder, to look like a corpse. He said that he powdered the bodies of his victims, and then looked at them – and himself – in the mirror. Another psychiatrist, Dr Patrick Gallwey, said that Nilsen was suffering from the 'false self syndrome'.

On Friday 4 November 1983, Nilsen was found guilty of all murder charges by a jury vote of 10–2, and was sentenced to life imprisonment.

In prison, Nilsen met the gunman David Martin, for whom there had been a nationwide manhunt after the shooting of a policeman; Martin was a bisexual transvestite, and Nilsen formed a powerful emotional attachment to him, although it is not clear how far Martin reciprocated. A girl who had sheltered Martin was charged with aiding and abetting him, and Nilsen is reported to have made an offer to reveal details of yet more murders if the police would stop their 'persecution' of the girl (who was subsequently sentenced to six months in jail). But it seems unlikely that the offer was genuine; Nilsen's painstakingly detailed confessions make it clear that he was not the kind of person to 'forget' several murders.

What general conclusions can be reached about Nilsen? The most obvious thing that emerges from accounts of those who knew him is his dominance; there can be no doubt that he belongs to the 'dominant five per cent'. Said one acquaintance: 'The only off-putting thing about him was his eyes. They can stare you out, and not many people can stare me out.' From his writings, it is also clear that he is a man with a fairly high IQ. Dominant and intelligent people urgently require some means by which they can express their dominance; they have an urge to be 'recognised', to be admired, to be accepted among equals. In this sense, Nilsen never seems to have met any equals. He undoubtedly put his finger on the root of his problem when he spoke of his 'total social isolation'. One of the notebooks he wrote for Brian Masters begins: 'I was always a loner.' A similar temperament seems to have led to the crimes of Ian Brady, the Moors murderer. And the loneliness leads to a sense of alienation and of contempt for other people – the kind that made Brady refer to them as 'insects'.

A powerful sex drive is also characteristic of most highly dominant individuals. When such a person lives in isolation, the result is likely to be a morbid build-up of sensuality that can explode into violence – like the Wisconsin necrophile Ed Gein who, in the late 1950s, dug up female corpses from graves, had sex with the bodies, and even made waistcoats from their skin. Nilsen's morbid obsession with corpses and death, combined with the sense of unreality that develops from isolation, would have been seen as a danger signal by any psychiatrist who could have interviewed him in the late 1970s.

An important determining factor was, of course, his homosexuality, and the fact that he was brought up in a small Scottish community where he had to conceal it. This is what may have caused him to enter the army at sixteen; it is certainly what made him leave his home to go to London when he came out of the army. Nilsen does not seems to have been exclusively homosexual; he told psychiatrists that he was excited by homosexual and 'normal' pornography, and that he had had sex with women as well as men. The early desire to marry shows that he recognised that one of his major problems was to find close contact with at least one other human being. He achieved this to some degree when living with Gallichan – only to experience an embittered sense of isolation and rejection when Gallichan left him to live with another man.

But the chief determining factor in the murders was undoubtedly the heavy drinking. It seems clear that drink acted as the catalyst that finally removed all inhibitions and allowed all his negative emotions – self-pity, resentment, irritation, contempt – to build up into an orgasm of violence.

The increasing casualness of the murders, and his increasing carelessness, suggest that his originally robust self-esteem was being undermined by self-contempt and a desire to 'make an end of it' by being caught. The same point emerges, in a less direct way, from an incident reported during his early days in custody. The prison chaplain is said to have suggested that Nilsen might like to come to chapel and ask forgiveness for his sins; Nilsen retorted: 'I'm a mass murderer, not a bloody hypocrite.' It is as if he had finally established some perverse sense of identity through this notion of being Britain's 'highest scoring' mass killer.

The final impression of Nilsen's life is of a man whose basic craving was to find himself, and who somehow drifted further and further away from this objective.

O

OHERN, Michael and **BRADEN**, Howard
Multiple rapists operating in Houston in 1973.

For several months the women of Houston suffered a wave of violent rapes. They were committed by two men, and the method was always the same. The girl was accosted as she was climbing into her car late at night and forced to drive to a remote area. There she was beaten into submission, raped, and sometimes forced to perform fellatio on her kidnappers. Finally she was left naked – a final act of humiliation – as the men drove off in her car.

On 3 June 1973, Cathy Dworin, a graduate of the University of Texas, offered to drive her boyfriend, a young executive, to the airport for a midnight flight. She went to the apartment she shared with a girlfriend to collect her car, but failed to arrive at her boyfriend's home. Her disappearance was reported in the early hours of the morning; the police suspected she might be a victim of the two 'sex terrorists'. But all previous victims – more than thirty – had usually returned by dawn. Two days after her disappearance, police found Cathy Dworin's Fiat five miles from her apartment; her body was in the boot. The left window had been shattered and the car's soft top ripped open. The girl had been bludgeoned to death. Her body was still fully clothed. It was clear that the attackers had tried to force their way into the car; she had locked the doors, and they had smashed their way in. They had killed her in their attempts to subdue her, and dumped the body in the boot. Her wallet and jewellery were untouched.

Three teenage boys had seen the car being parked; the man who got out – a white man, about twenty-five – ran past them. But attempts to identify the man by showing the boys photographs of sex offenders were a failure. The investigation led nowhere.

Later in the month there was another rape; the girl was left naked in the woods. In September, there were two. Both girls said that one of the men boasted of killing Cathy Dworin, and that he had killed a girl in Pasadena, by 'cutting her up'. The previous October, fifteen-year-old Mildred Knighten had been found stabbed sixty times in a ditch in Pasadena.

In November, two more young women were raped on consecutive nights; one, an airline stewardess returning from a late flight, described how they had threatened to kill her with a lead pipe. The second victim also mentioned the lead pipe.

The police were now desperate. There had been forty rapes. They decided to 'stake out' every car-park in Houston, an operation demanding vast numbers of men, and many civilian volunteers. On 13 November, nothing happened. But on the following night, as two patrolmen sat in a car-park near Cathy Dworin's apartment, a man ran towards them saying that he had heard a woman scream. Moments later a red sports car screeched to a halt, and a girl behind the wheel gasped with relief as she saw the police. Behind her came a blue Chevrolet Malibu, but when the driver saw the police, he tried to turn. As the girl shouted, 'They were following me', one driver of the police car blocked the Malibu's path, while the other policeman ran up to it with a shotgun. The two occupants of the car were ordered out – both unkempt and long-haired. They were Michael Ohern, twenty, a mechanic, and Howard Braden, nineteen, a carpenter. On the floor of their car there was a length of lead pipe. There were also car keys belonging to one of the victims.

The men denied everything, but as victim after victim identified them as the sadistic rapists, their determination wavered. When Ohern was shown photographs of Cathy Dworin's body, he burst into sobs. Ohern was tried on one count of murder and twenty-two of rape; Braden was tried on nineteen counts of rape. Ohern was sentenced to life imprisonment for the rape of the airline stewardess, Braden to life for the rape of a young company executive. Neither can be paroled.

OKAMOTO, Kozo
Red Army terrorist who carried out the PFLP massacre at Lod Airport.

On 30 May 1972 three Japanese Red Army terrorists on voluntary contract to the PLO lobbed hand grenades and fired sub-machine-guns into an unsuspecting crowd of passengers waiting to pass through customs at Lod airport, Tel Aviv. They slaughtered twenty-four and wounded a further seventy-six, many seriously. (Four of the wounded later died in hospital, bringing the total to twenty-eight dead.) The carnage they caused between them added up to one of the worst terrorist incidents Israel had known.

The three Japanese, all men in their early twenties, had joined a normal Air France flight from Rome to Tel Aviv. They passed the routine airport screening (for personal weapons) easily enough before boarding; by then their guns and grenades were all neatly packed in suitcases – which were loaded aboard without being checked. After reclaiming the baggage at Lod the Japanese simply opened the cases, took out their weapons and blasted away from point-blank range. For several minutes screams mingled with the sound of explosions and gunfire in the hall as panic-stricken travellers sought to escape. When the first terrorist fell dead from the blast of one of his own grenades, another opened fire through the door of the loading bay at aircraft parked on the runway. Then when he was shot the third man, Kozo Okamoto, made his way on to the runway, firing indiscriminately at passengers and ground crews he encountered. He was eventually overpowered and captured by an El Al mechanic.

When he was first questioned Okamoto gave his name to Japanese embassy officials as Daisuke Namba. Two days later he was identified by police in Tokyo under his real name of Okamoto, brother of another Red Army terrorist who had taken part two years earlier in hijacking a JAL aeroplane to North Korea. His accomplices were named as Rakeshi Okudeira and Yoshuyiki Yasuda. The three of them formed part of a bigger group of Red Army volunteers sent over a period of months to Arab terrorist camps near Baalbeck in the Lebanon for specialist training with the PLO, proof positive of the growing co-operation among international terrorist groups. (Subsequent Red Army – PLO combined operations included the hijacking of a JAL plane in 1973, an attempt to blow up oil storage tanks at Singapore in January 1974, and the take-over of the Japanese embassy in Kuwait shortly afterwards.)

The PFLP (Popular Front for the Liberation of Palestine) claimed responsibility for the Lod airport attack, describing it as a 'brave operation . . . launched by one of our special groups in our occupied land'. Calling the three Japanese by their Arab names, it said they were all members of a group called 'the squad of the martyr Patrick Uguello' (a Nicaraguan revolutionary, shot dead during the attempted hijacking of an Israeli airliner over London in 1970). The statement added that the attack was in reprisal for the killing of two of their guerrillas during another hijack bid earlier in the year. A PLO spokesman claimed that the Japanese had orders not to fire on the Air France passengers, only on El Al passengers due to land ten minutes later and on friends and relatives waiting to greet them. 'We were sure that 90–95 per cent of the people in the airport would be Israelis or people of direct loyalty to Israel,' he said.

At his trial later Okamoto declared, 'I shot not only at tourists and visitors but at policemen as well. I do not know how many I killed . . . We did all this in cooperation with that organization [the PLO]; we did it in partnership with them.' The prosecution did not seek the death sentence. He was jailed for life.

The United Red Army, or Japanese Red Army as it is known in the West, was formed in 1969, drawing its membership mainly from extreme left student groups. It lost much public support among the younger Japanese first after the murder of twelve of its members in 1971–2, for opposing plans to assassinate leading politicians, and then by the indiscriminate killings at Lod. Tsuneo Mori, leader of the organization, hanged himself in prison on 1 January 1973. The Red Army's partnership with the PLO was seen by some as an attempt to revive its flagging fortunes.

OSWALD, Lee Harvey
The man who killed the President of the United States.

On 22 November 1963 John Fitzgerald Kennedy, President of the United States and standard-bearer for the free world, was assassinated as he drove through the streets of Dallas. He was forty-five, the youngest man and first Catholic to assume the office of president. His killer was a former US Marine, aged twenty-four. Because John F. Kennedy was who he was, and because the man who murdered him had lived in Russia, the sound of the shots that struck the President echoed round the world. Even today, twenty years on, not all the ghosts surrounding the assassination have been laid to rest.

The most recent official inquiry, conducted by a Select Committee of the House of Representatives in 1979, overturned previous findings in one major respect. The committee, having studied all the evidence, both scientific and human, stated that there was a 'high probability' that *two* gunmen fired at the President that day – but that identification of the second gunman or the extent of the conspiracy was not possible. The committee cleared the Russian and Cuban governments. It exonerated the anti-Castro groups gathered in America, although it did not rule out the possibility that certain individuals from those groups may have taken the law into their own hands. It also provided a possible answer to the most fascinating riddle of all: if the second, unidentified gunman was *not* politically motivated, what might have inspired him to try to murder John F. Kennedy? 'The committee believes, on the basis of the evidence available to it, that the national syndicate of organized crime [the Mafia] as a group was not involved in the assassination of President Kennedy, but that the available evidence does not preclude the possibility that individual members may have been involved.'

Jack Ruby, the night-club owner who entered Dallas police headquarters and shot Lee Harvey Oswald dead two days after the Kennedy assassination, had numerous underworld contacts. The apparent ease with which Ruby was able to fire on the captive Oswald also worried the Select Committee. 'The committee was troubled by the apparently unlocked doors along the stairway route, and the removal of security guards from the area of the garage nearest the stairway shortly before the shooting; by a Saturday night telephone call from Ruby to his closest friend Ralph Paul, in which Paul responded to something Ruby said by asking him if he was crazy; and by the actions of several Dallas police officers, particularly those present when Ruby was initially interrogated about the shooting of Oswald.'

No federal government had ever taken a tougher line against the Mafia than the Kennedy administration. 'During this period the FBI had comprehensive electronic coverage of the major underworld figures . . . the committee had access to and analysed the product of this electronic coverage . . . An analysis of the work of the Justice Department before and after the tenure of Robert Kennedy as Attorney General also led to the conclusion that organized crime directly benefited substantially from the changes in government policy that occurred after the assassination. That organized crime had the motive, opportunity and means to kill the President cannot be questioned . . .'

Like every American president, Kennedy accepted the possibility of an attempted assassination as an occupational hazard. Three of his predecessors were shot and killed (Abraham Lincoln, 1865, James A. Garfield, 1881 William McKinley, 1901) and three others suffered assassination attempts (Andrew Jackson, 1835, Franklin D. Roosevelt, 1933, Harry Truman, 1950). Kennedy himself was a man who liked to travel, and he made the onerous task of guarding him more difficult by his refusal to adopt various protective measures suggested by the Secret Service. He would not allow blaring sirens in his motorcades; only once (in Chicago) did he permit police out-riders to travel alongside the presidential limousine; he told the Secret Service agent in charge of the White House detail he did not want bodyguards riding on the rear of his car.

Yet the Kennedy administration faced formidable problems at home as well as abroad in the autumn of 1963, and each one presented a potential source of danger of attack on the President's life. The Communists feared him: one year earlier he had gone to the brink of war over Cuba and forced Kruschev to back down. America was committed in Laos and Vietnam. The 'black protest' was growing at home, while his own liberal civil rights policies had brought resentment and hostility from whites in the South. The defeat of the Bay of Pigs invasion – and in particular the failure of the US Air Force to give it support – had aroused intense bitterness among anti-Castro Cubans gathered in exile. And, last but not least, the Kennedy government was bearing down hard on the world's best organized and most powerful crime syndicate, the Mafia. There was no lack of enemies to recruit to kill the President.

Lee Harvey Oswald was born in New Orleans, on 18 October 1939, two months after the death of his father. His mother remarried, but her second marriage ended in divorce when Oswald was nine. His school record showed him to be a chronic truant; a psychiatrist thought him 'emotionally disturbed'. He dropped out of school at sixteen and enlisted in the Marines a year later. He sought and obtained his discharge in 1959 on compassionate grounds (his mother's poverty and failing health), but spent only a short time with her and went to Russia a few months later. He lived there until June 1962, and married nineteen-year-old Marina Nikolalaevna Prusakova. He was granted a residence visa, but when he was later told he could not stay in the Soviet Union he attempted suicide. Later he and Marina were granted an exit visa and went to America with their baby daughter, arriving on 14 June 1962.

In March 1963 while living in Dallas Oswald bought a 6.5 mm Mannlicher-Carcano rifle and telescopic sight from a Chicago mail-order firm, using a false name, 'A. Hidell'. He also bought a ·38 Smith and Wesson hand-gun from a Los Angeles firm. According to Mrs Oswald he 'probably' used the rifle first in April of that year, in an abortive attempt to assassinate a retired army general, Edwin A. Walker.

A few months later Oswald made another bid to return to Russia. In September 1963 he flew to Mexico City and called at both the Russian embassy and the Cuban consulate, but failed to obtain a visa to either country. He returned instead to Dallas, and got a job at the Texas School Book Depository. At that time his wife and two children (the Oswald's second daughter was born on 20 October 1963) were staying with a woman friend in Irving, Texas. Lee Harvey Oswald last visited his family on 21 November, the day before the Kennedy murder.

President and Mrs Kennedy flew into Dallas at 11.20 on the morning of 22 November, a balmy day with bright sunshine. The reason for the visit was strictly political; Lyndon Johnson had won Texas for the Democrats only by a narrow majority. As a result the President's visit had been publicized well in advance, and some – including Governor John B. Connally – remained apprehensive at the possibility of anti-Kennedy demonstrations (but not violence). A hostile advertisement had appeared that morning in the *Dallas Morning News*, accusing the President of being 'soft on Communists, fellow travellers and ultra-Leftists in America'. The presidential limousine travelled third in the long motorcade. The first two cars carried Dallas police and Secret Service agents. Press and more officials, including other security men, followed behind.

Two Secret Servicemen sat in the front of the President's car, one acting as chauffeur. The President and First Lady sat in the back of the open car, Governor and Mrs Connally facing front on jump seats, between the Kennedys and their bodyguards. Instead of demonstrating against the President the Dallas crowds were warm and friendly, and far bigger than anyone had foreseen. As the motorcade neared Elm Street and the Dealey Plaza, Mrs Connally said, 'Mr President, you can't say Dallas doesn't love you.' 'That's obvious,' he replied.

A few moments later the car turned left, passing the Texas School Book Depository building. It was about 12.30 pm. Almost at once, shots rang out. Mrs Connally heard them, turned to her right and saw President Kennedy clutch his neck with both hands, then slump down in the seat. Governor Connally thought he identified a rifle shot and in the same instant turned towards the President, fearing an assassination attempt.

In his own words: 'I never looked, I never made the full turn. About the time I turned back where I was facing, more or less straight ahead the way the car was moving, I was hit ... I was knocked over, just doubled over by the force of the bullet ... So I knew I had been hit and I more or less straightened up. About this time Nellie reached over and pulled me down into her lap ... I heard another shot. I heard it hit. It hit with a very pronounced impact ... it made a very, very strong sound. Immediately I could see blood and brain tissue all over the interior of the car and all over our clothes ...'

Mrs Connally thought her own husband was already dead as he fell on to her lap. She heard Mrs Kennedy say, 'They have killed my husband ... I have his brains in my hand.'

On the orders of the Secret Serviceman in charge, the presidential limousine pulled out of the motorcade and drove at speed to the Parkland Memorial Hospital in Dallas. Doctors there found that the President had been hit by two bullets. One had passed straight through his neck (and gone on to wound Governor Connally, sitting immediately in front of him), the other through his head.

Both were fired by Oswald, from the sixth floor of the School Book Depository building; of that there is no official doubt. Sheriff Eugene Boone found the Mannlicher-Carcano rifle with its telescopic sight in a 'sniper's nest', together with three spent cartridge cases. Oswald's palm-print was found on the barrel, as well as on the paper sack he had used to smuggle the gun into the building.

The 1979 Select Committee commented: 'The [Warren Commission] concluded that President Kennedy was struck by two bullets, fired from above and behind him. The Commission based its findings primarily upon the testimony of the doctors who treated the President at Parkland Memorial Hospital in Dallas and the doctors who performed the autopsy on the President at the Naval Medical Center in Bethesda, Maryland. In forming this conclusion neither the members of the Warren Commission, nor its staff, nor the doctors who had performed the autopsy, took advantage of the X-rays and photographs of the President that were taken during the course of the autopsy.' It added that, 'The Commission was concerned that publication of the autopsy X-rays and photographs would be an invasion of the privacy of the Kennedy family.' It adds that since the Warren Report two further inquiries (by a team of forensic pathologists in 1968 appointed by the then Attorney General, and the Rockefeller Commission in 1975) both reached the same conclusion: that the President was struck by two bullets from behind. 'Consequently neither panel ... was able to relieve significantly doubts that have persisted over the years about the location and nature of the President's wounds.'

To assuage those doubts the Select Committee consulted the country's leading experts in forensic pathology, ballistics, photography, acoustics, 'neutron activation analysis and other disciplines'. It also took into account eye-witness evidence, some of it new. And while it agreed that the two bullets which hit the President were fired by Lee Harvey Oswald from the sixth floor of the Book Depository building, it also found that 'the scientific accoustical evidence established a high probability that two gunmen fired at President Kennedy'. That second man fired and missed from a grassy knoll in the Dealey Plaza, below the Book Depository building. And it was this evidence – showing two men in the same area firing on President John F. Kennedy at the same time – that persuaded the Select Committee he was 'probably assassinated ... as a result of a conspiracy'.

The Select Committee also found that the Secret Service was deficient in the performance of its duties; the Department of Justice failed to exercise initiative in supervising and directing the FBI investigation into the assassination; the FBI failed to investigate adequately the possibility of a conspiracy to assassinate the President; the CIA was deficient both in its collection and sharing of information, before and after the assassination; and that the Warren Commission failed to investigate adequately the possibility of a conspiracy to assassinate the President. Nonetheless, all efforts to identify the second gunman and his connection with Oswald failed.

If Oswald allowed himself to be used as 'front man' for a wider conspiracy, what was his personal motive for killing the President? 'It is ... the committee's judgment that in the last five years of his life, Oswald was preoccupied with political ideology. The first clear manifestation of this preoccupation was his defection to the Soviet Union in the fall of 1959 at the age of twenty. The words that accompanied the act went even further. Oswald stated to officials at the American embassy in Moscow that he wanted to renounce his citizenship, and that he intended to give the Russians any information concerning the Marine Corps and radar operations that he possessed. In letters to his brother Robert, Oswald made it clear that in the event of war, he would not hesitate to fight on the side of the Russians against his family or former country. It was also reflected in his attempt to commit suicide when he was informed he would not be allowed to remain in the Soviet Union. It seems reasonable to conclude that the best single explanation for the assassination was his concept of political action, rooted in his twisted ideological view of himself and the world around him.'

Oswald committed a second murder shortly after assassinating President Kennedy. He quickly left the Dealey Plaza area aboard a bus, and when the bus became stuck in a traffic jam took a taxi to his rented room on North Beckley Avenue. He changed his clothes lest they incriminate him and moved out again immediately. When he had walked about a mile he was stopped and challenged by a passing police patrolman named J. D. Tippit. Oswald shot him as he got out of the car – a murder that was witnessed by Jack Tatum. Mr Tatum saw Tippit fall and Oswald step out into the road to stand over his victim, and deliver the 'coup de grace' at point-blank range (altogether he fired four shots). He then went into the Texas Theater Cinema where he was finally overpowered – after a fierce struggle, in which he tried to draw and fire his pistol into the squad of detectives who came after him.

Jack Ruby, the night-club owner who shot Lee Harvey Oswald, was later convicted and jailed. His own version of why he killed Oswald was related to the Select Committee by Ruby's brother Earl, who said Jack telephoned their sister after the assassination of President Kennedy to say how deeply upset he was. Later, after he entered police headquarters at Dallas and watched Oswald led out to address a televised press conference, Jack Ruby lost control of himself and shot Oswald 'because he had a silly smirk on his face' as if pleased with what he had done.

A lawyer representing the Ruby family told the Committee that Jack Ruby later went mad, before dying in prison of cancer in 1967. The lawyer said that after reading the Leon Uris novel *Exodus* Jack Ruby formed the insane belief that all American Jews were being taken to Dallas for extermination on the orders of President Lyndon Johnson. After hearing screams coming from a mental ward near his own prison cell, 'He thought President Johnson was ordering this, and that he was ... the last Jew alive'.

PIERRE, Dale
Black airman responsible for one of the most horrifying multiple murders in Utah's criminal history.

On 22 April 1974 two men entered a hi-fi shop in Ogden, Utah, and held up the store clerks, Stan Walker and Michelle Ansley. They were forced into the basement and tied up. Just then, sixteen-year-old Cortney Naisbitt walked into the shop, to thank Stan Walker for letting him park outside; the youth was also pushed into the basement and tied. The robbers proceeded to take stereo equipment outside to a car. Stan Walker's father came two hours later to look for his son and was made to join the others; then Cortney Naisbitt's mother, Carol, also walked in.

One of the two robbers produced a bottle, which he claimed contained a German drug mixed with vodka, and ordered everyone to drink. It was, in fact, caustic cleaning fluid, as strong as acid. Then the same man – Dale Pierre – shot Mrs Naisbitt in the head, then Cortney Naisbitt, and Stan and Mr Walker. He led Michelle into the next room and spent twenty minutes raping her. After this, she was made to lie down, naked, and shot. When Mr Walker stirred, a ball point pen was placed in his ear and kicked into his head. Then they left.

Cortney succeeded in crawling upstairs and raising the alarm. He and his mother were rushed to hospital. Mr Walker was also still alive. The other two were dead. Mrs Naisbitt died in hospital, but Cortney survived and, after several operations, was finally able to return to his studies; he suffered permanent physical damage.

When news of the killing was released, an airman from the nearby Hill Field base phoned the police to say that he was convinced that Dale Pierre and William Andrews were the killers. Pierre, aged twenty-three, was the leader; Andrews, less intelligent, was willing to do whatever Pierre told him. The two men were arrested. A rental storage agreement found in Pierre's room led the police to a small room full of the missing hi-fi equipment.

Pierre, born in Tobago in 1953, was an ice-cold psychopath,

determined to succeed at any cost. At the time of his arrest he was on bail for three car thefts. He was also suspected of the murder of a black air force sergeant, Edward Jefferson, in October 1973. Jefferson's keys had disappeared when Pierre was in his apartment, taping music. The next day, Pierre reappeared, suggesting that they search again, and the keys were 'found'. Jefferson investigated, and discovered that Pierre had taken the keys to a locksmith and had them duplicated. He changed his locks, and confronted Pierre about it. Two days later, Jefferson was found dead in his apartment, stabbed repeatedly in the face with a bayonet.

Pierre and Andrews were both sentenced to death – although by then the death sentence had been suspended in America. In his book *Victim*, Gary Kinder quotes Pierre as saying that he expects to be released within five years. He also mentions that Pierre spends his time studying books on finance, and intends to be the first man to 'build a corporation with an annual earning capacity of $40 million' while in prison.

One witness at the trial – a cinema attendant – described how he had admitted Pierre to a Clint Eastwood movie, *Magnum Force*, shortly before the hi-fi shop robbery; in this, a pimp forces a prostitute to drink drain-cleaning fluid, and she dies almost immediately. It seems certain that Pierre intended to kill his victims silently – by making them drink the fluid – and was forced to shoot them when he realized this method had failed.

POULIN, Robert
Teenage sex-killer who committed suicide after attempting to kill several classmates.

Eighteen-year-old Robert Poulin lived in the basement of his parents' home in Warrington Drive, Ottawa. When Mrs Mary Poulin, a nurse and lunch-time supervisor, arrived back home in the afternoon, she noticed smoke pouring from the basement, and called the fire brigade. Two firemen, protected by oxygen masks, broke into the basement. They found a charred, semi-naked body lying manacled to a bed, surrounded by burnt books and magazines. The girl had been handcuffed to the bedpost by her left wrist. A post-mortem revealed that she had been stabbed to death and had been raped and sodomized. She was identified as seventeen-year-old Kim Rabot, the daughter of a Sri Lankan family who lived nearby. Robert Poulin had apparently had a 'crush' on her.

In fact, by the time the firemen arrived, Robert Poulin was already dead. After setting his basement on fire, he had gone to St Pius X High School, where he had been a model student, carrying a Winchester pump-action 12-gauge shotgun. At 2.20 pm, he entered a classroom and began to shoot. Within seconds, seven students had been hit (fortunately, none were killed). Someone succeeded in kicking the door shut. There was a shot outside in the corridor, and when Father Bedard went into the corridor, he found a body with its face half blown away, the shotgun lying beside it.

In Poulin's basement, the police found a large collection of girlie magazines, some containing hardcore photographs, and a collection of pornographic books. There was also a blow-up rubber sex doll. His diary gave a detailed account of the build-up to the murder. On 7 April 1975 he had written: 'During my deepest part of my depression a couple of weeks ago I thought of committing suicide, but I don't want to die before I have had the pleasure of fucking some girl. So I decided to order a model gun from an ad in a Gallery magazine. With this I was going to threaten a girl in one of the dark streets around here and rape her. I planned to carry my father's scout knife strapped to the inside of my right leg. If the girl caused any trouble I would kill her, for I was planning to kill myself anyhow, so I had nothing to lose.' Further on in the same entry: 'Recently I went up to Tim's Second-Hand Bookstore and bought all of her back issues of *Playboy*. On Saturday I went back and bought other mags and a couple of these were Nuget [sic] magazines. On the inside of the cover of the first one that I opened I found an ad for Everything Dolls. These are life-like dolls of a girl who has everything. She has a vagina, and it is an electronically operated male-oriented dildo (vibrator): She costs $29.95, and I broke myself ordering her. Now I no longer think that I will have to rape a girl, and am unsure as to whether or not I will still commit suicide.'

A subsequent entry read: 'Everything Doll arrived – a big disappointment.' In September, seven weeks before the murder, he wrote in his journal: 'There are some girls at school that I would love to be good friends with but I know that I am still too shy to go up and talk to any of them. I wish I could overcome this fear of women.'

It emerged that Robert Poulin had been living in the basement room since he was twelve, when a third daughter had been born to the family. He was a typical loner. His father, who had been in the Canadian air force, is known to have wanted his son to be a normal sports-loving boy and encouraged his idea of a military career. A few days before the murder, Robert had been turned down for officer training, and had been deeply disappointed. On the morning of 19 October, shortly after eight o'clock, Kim Rabot and her thirteen-year-old brother John were waiting at a bus stop a few blocks from the Poulin home, and Robert Poulin had approached and asked her to come and have a look at something he had to show her. Probably out of fear of hurting his feelings, she had gone with him. Robert's mother heard him returning home at about 8.15 am. After raping and killing Kim, and placing a plastic bag over her head, Poulin went upstairs at about 10 am and asked his mother to make him a toasted peanut butter sandwich. He then sat watching a quiz show on television until she went out at 11.30. She noticed nothing strange about him.

The inquest revealed that Poulin felt deep hatred for his family, particularly his father, and that he had considered killing them all. His diary revealed that he had made a plan for killing his family, but did not want them to experience the 'true bliss' of death. He decided to burn the house down instead.

PRUDOM, Barry Peter
The 'Cop Killer' who ran amok in northern England in 1982.

By the time he put his ·22 Beretta automatic pistol to his own head and pulled the trigger rather than surrender, Barry Prudom had become known throughout the length and breadth of Britain simply as the Cop Killer. No one knows what triggered off the spate of killing and wounding he indulged in, but it began in midsummer 1982, and it followed a clear pattern. He broke into houses to steal food, petty cash and transport. To all those who turned the other cheek – Prudom was an armed and dangerous man – he displayed a kind of rough compassion. But anyone who dared to stand up to him, be it an innocent householder who tried to defend his life and his property, or a policeman, Prudom maimed or murdered without hesitation.

On 17 June 1982, apparently for no other reason than that he resented the way in which PC David Haigh, a young country bobby, spoke to him in the course of a routine traffic check near Harrogate in Yorkshire, Prudom shot him through the head from point-blank range and drove off, leaving him for dead. There were no witnesses to the shooting. However, in his dying seconds, PC Haigh willed himself to live long enough to write down the registration number of Prudom's green Citroen, KYF 326P, in his notebook. Prudom had already given him a false name (Clive Jones) but his correct date of birth, 18 October 1944; these details were already entered in the blood-stained book. Together they were enough to identify Prudom as the murderer.

KYF 326P was found abandoned in a field near Leeds. An alert policeman who happened to be checking warrants that day spotted an odd coincidence; that the date given for Clive Jones' birth was the same as that listed in a separate warrant – for the arrest of a man called Barry Prudom, who was sought on a wounding charge. An immediate fingerprint check confirmed that Prudom was indeed the real name of the driver PC Haigh had questioned, and the manhunt began.

After abandoning the Citroen which he rightly feared might betray him, Prudom made his way into neighbouring Lincolnshire and broke into a bungalow where an elderly woman lived alone. Now he showed the other side of his complex character. He robbed her of £5, and tied her up before he left – but after he had ascertained she would be found the next morning, when the baker called. She was otherwise unharmed. From Lincolnshire he went to Girton, near Newark-on-Trent in Nottinghamshire, and broke into a house owned by George Luckett and his wife Sylvia. Prudom was after food, cash and above all a car to replace the abandoned Citroen. But because George Luckett made the mistake of trying to defend himself, his wife and their property, Prudom shot him dead and left his wife crippled by putting a bullet into her head, damaging the brain.

On what proved to be the last night of his life, 3 July, Prudom revealed exactly what passed through his mind when he decided on the fate of his separate victims. By then he had taken the Johnson family of three prisoner in their home at Malton, Yorkshire, and was steeling himself for the final shootout with the police whom he knew to be hunting him down.

Of PC Haigh's murder he said, 'I told him I'd been sleeping out in the car, and that I didn't think that was an offence. But he said he was going to take me in, and got stroppy – so I shot him.'

He also told the Johnson family why he shot Mr and Mrs Luckett. He explained how he tied them together by their elbows and then went into the garage to see how much petrol there was in their Rover car. When he came back to the house he peered through some sliding glass doors and saw that George Luckett had freed himself and was holding a gun. 'I shot him with his own gun,' declared Prudom. 'Then I had to shoot her, but I didn't want to kill her.'

On 24 June he drove in the Lucketts' Rover to the Dalby Forest district of North Yorkshire. His intention was to lie low until the hue and cry died down, but he was surprised by dog handler PC Kenneth Oliver. Immediately Prudom blazed off seven rounds at his unarmed adversary before making his getaway. One round clipped PC Oliver's nose, another wounded him in the arm, a third passed clean through his uniform – luckily without hitting him. The constable was later admitted to the intensive care unit at Scarborough General Hospital for emergency heart treatment.

By this time the Cop Killer was headline news. Chief Constable Kenneth Henshaw now had more than 260 policemen armed with a variety of weapons – marksmen's rifles, revolvers, and pump-action shotguns – scouring the North Riding for him. Three thousand more were manning road-blocks, walking the beat in isolated country villages, or operating a network of radio-linked highway patrols: all these were unarmed. 'All showed courage of the highest order,' said Mr Henshaw.

Prudom's next victim was Sergeant David Winter. He and PC Michael Woods, both unarmed, saw a man leave Old Malton post office after buying food there, and the sergeant coolly walked over to question him. PC Woods suddenly shouted 'Watch it, Dave!' but he was too late; Prudom drew the Beretta from his pocket and stalked his quarry as he tried in vain to run for safety. Again he told the captive Johnsons what happened next, and in words to chill the blood.

'I ran after him. The policeman climbed a wall, and I caught up with him. I thought, I'll have this bugger, and shot him. I felt sorry in a way . . . but not really; he was a policeman.' He omitted to tell the horrified family that he shot the unarmed sergeant three times at close range, the last time as he lay unable to move, already at the foot of the wall.

Prudom was finally run to earth in Malton, only a few hundred yards from the police station serving as headquarters in the search for Sergeant Winter's killer. The first vital clue was found by survival expert Eddie McGee, called in by the police to help in the manhunt. He followed a trail in the grass that led to a hide near the local tennis club. The hide was empty, but showed clear signs of recent use. Meantime Prudom, now almost at the end of his tether after more than a fortnight on the run, had broken into a house next to the hide and was holding Mr and Mrs Maurice Johnson, both in their seventies, and their 43-year-old son Brian prisoner. The police had foreseen this possibility and appealed to the public at large to keep a watchful eye on their neighbours, since there were not enough men available to check each house individually. In the absence of any such report, no one had yet checked on the Johnsons.

On the evening of 3 July Mrs Johnson went into her kitchen and turned round – to find Prudom pointing his pistol at her head. He had been hiding behind a chair, and showed himself only when he realized he was confronting an elderly woman. 'You know who I am, don't you?' he said. 'I'm sorry, I don't,' she replied. Fortunately she made no attempt to resist. Prudom marched her into the sitting-room with the Beretta in her back, and bound her and her husband. He cooked eggs and bacon and then, contrary as always, helped his two elderly prisoners to sit up in a more comfortable position. He told them he knew all about them and had been watching their house for three days. Then came the moment Mrs Johnson was dreading, when she heard her son Brian arrive home. Luckily he, too, offered Prudom no resistance.

He told reporters later, 'I got home at half-past six and went into the kitchen. Suddenly I saw this figure looking at me over the table, with a gun pointing straight at my head. I gave a shout and ran into the other room.'

Prudom yelled after him, 'You bloody fool! It's a good job you ran that way or you'd have got a bullet in your head.' He then tied Brian up 'because he was a threat', but untied the parents: and once again his whole attitude changed. As he stood over his three prisoners, wearing a revolver holster at his waist, he asked them if they would like a cup of tea. When they said yes, he observed, 'We all seem to be getting on very well together': and then told them about the people he had killed and wounded in the sixteen days he had been on the run.

Detective Superintendent John Carlton, deputy head of the North Yorkshire CID, commented later: 'It is a known fact that when you get a hostage situation, a close relationship builds up over a period. Initially, until he got to know the Johnsons, he bound them, tied them up ... once this trust between them developed, they were nearly on first name terms.'

Prudom's voluntary confession took a considerable time to complete. Occasionally it was interspersed with quotations from the Bible: but even here he showed the perverse side to his nature by insisting he was not a religious man. Finally he undertook to leave their house by eleven o'clock that night. By this time the Johnsons felt close enough to him to urge him to give himself up, but he refused. 'No. I'll never let the police take me, I'll kill myself first.' He added that he would take at least one more policeman with him before that happened. Then, as if to underline his boast, he asked for another meal and described it as the 'Last Supper'.

Mrs Johnson told the inquest jury of their final goodbyes, not at eleven o'clock as promised but in the early hours of the Sunday morning. 'When we got him standing up . . . we almost escorted him out. He asked if he could stay another night, and said when his foot was better he was going to get away. Outside he had put some wood against a wall for a shelter.' This was the hide Eddie McGee had found. 'I can't understand how the police missed it during their search. He kept apologizing for trespassing, and said he couldn't pay for the food. He said . . . he didn't know there were such nice people in the world.'

Then he limped out to enter the hide where the police found him a few hours later. Chief Inspector David Clarkeson, leading the assault, had no way of knowing if the man in the hide was in fact Prudom. There was only one way to make certain. He moved forward stealthily from the opposite side of the wall and leaned over to push the fencing clear. Prudom fired at him but missed, and the inspector withdrew. 'Before I gave the signal to open fire, I called on the suspect to give himself up. Our intelligence was that he very rarely spoke to police . . . the fact that we heard nothing from him meant nothing.'

With that the shooting began. Two stun grenades were hurled over the wall. A police marksman fired five rifle-shots low into the hide, a chief inspector blazed off four barrels from his pump-action shotgun. Finally Clarkeson advanced on the hide again, holding a shield in front of him. 'I could see through the two-inch-square glass a man wearing a balaclava. He was laid on his lefthand side with a gun in his right hand. It was on his chest, and the muzzle was pointing upward. I didn't know whether he was dead. I held my shield with one hand, drew the gun, stuck it round and fired one shot from my ·38 Smith and Wesson.'

Britain's biggest manhunt was over. Police found seven rounds still in Prudom's automatic – with the safety catch 'on'. But it was found to be so badly worn that experts concluded that the jolt from Prudom's head as he shot himself had caused the catch to slide forward. Dr Sava Savas, a lecturer in forensic medicine, told the inquest jury that in his opinion the bullet which killed Prudom was 'almost certainly' fired from his own gun; the bullet had been fired into the right side of the head and was characteristic of a self-inflicted wound. In addition Prudom had a shotgun pellet wound in his forehead, and twenty-one other injuries caused by pellets. Either of the two head wounds could have caused instant unconsciousness, even death. The jury took only eighteen minutes to agree with Dr Savas that Prudom died by his own hand, firing the same gun that had killed the two policemen and George Luckett.

The one question was – why? There was speculation that he may have been connected to 'overseas organizations', possibly in Northern Ireland, and there were reports of Ministry of Defence security officers making inquiries in Malton. These were based on some coincidences that were never properly explained. Prudom shot PC Haigh near the USAF communications base at Harrogate, where he had earlier worked under the name 'Barry Edwards'. A Volkswagen van Prudom had driven in Britain and abroad was found by police near West Drayton, the RAF communications base. Other reports claimed that he had camped near the NORAD base in Colorado, which in turn is directly linked with the Fylingdales early warning system, only a few miles from where Prudom wounded PC Oliver.

Again, much was made of his SAS training. He had joined the Territorial SAS in 1969, and had been on weekend manoeuvres with them. His former wife Gillian said that he had loved the outdoor life but 'I can't think he was there long enough to learn how to shoot as well as he seems able to. . . . He was upset when he was told he was unsuitable for the SAS and . . . brooded for days.'

Chief Constable Kenneth Henshaw, who directed the manhunt, later told the North Yorkshire Police Committee that Prudom had domestic problems. In 1977 he bought an off-licence to set his wife up in business. However, he needed additional funds so he took a job working as an electrician in the Saudi oilfields. While he was there he learned that his wife no longer wished to remain married to him . . . which must have had a traumatic effect on him. From being a very stable, hard-working man he became morose and irritable.

The former Mrs Prudom was able to give a clue to Prudom's true character; he once said to her, 'I was a bastard, and I'll always be a bastard.' He was extremely jealous and possessive of her, always doubting her fidelity and occasionally hitting her about. She said the only people he loved were his mother and his grandparents. Barry Prudom's mother never married his father, but she often talked of him to Barry and took him to see his father's parents. 'I don't think he ever got over not having a father of his own,' she added.

Whatever the reasons for his cold-blooded series of murders, Prudom's seventeen days on the rampage cost the public £400,000 plus. He was buried in secret seven weeks after his death; the only mourners were his favourite aunt and four other relations. She said, 'The family will always remember him as a dedicated, loving person. He was devoted to his mother, my sister. Something obviously disturbed his mind to such an extent that he just snapped.'

R

RAY, James Earl
Escaped convict thought to have taken on a 'contract' to kill Martin Luther King.

Dr Martin Luther King, Baptist minister and Nobel Peace Prize winner, was the leader of the Negro civil rights movement in America. On 4 April 1968 he came to Memphis, Tennessee, to organize the second mass march in the city that week supporting the local, mainly Negro, dustmen then on strike. He and his campaign staff arrived at the Lorraine Hotel, and at about 6 pm Dr King went on to the balcony of his first-floor room and leaned over the rail to talk to an associate below. A single rifle shot was fired, and he was hit in the neck. He was rushed to hospital, but all attempts to save him failed.

Police investigating the murder quickly found a ·30 Remington Gamemaster rifle on the pavement outside the hotel. Identifiable fingerprints were on it and a warrant was issued on 17 April for the arrest of Eric Starvo Galt, one of Ray's aliases. Three days later, under his real name, Ray was put on the FBI's 'most wanted' list. While the nationwide search for him continued, Ray flew to London using a Canadian passport bearing the name Raymond George Sneyd. A police check established that the real Sneyd was a Toronto policeman, and the hunt for James Earl Ray moved to Europe.

The day after his arrival in London, 6 May, police found that he had cashed in the return half of his ticket and used the money to fly to Lisbon, where he went to ground. Every police force in Europe was alerted by Interpol, and on 8 June, still under the name of Sneyd, Ray was arrested at London airport while in transit for Brussels. He was extradited to stand trial in America. On 10 March 1969, after pleading guilty, he was sentenced to ninety-nine years for the murder of Dr King.

James Earl Ray was born on 10 March 1928, and joined the American army at seventeen, shortly after the end of the war, but was discharged eight months later 'for ineptness and lack of adaptability to service'. He committed a number of armed robberies after his return to civilian life, and was sentenced to twenty years in jail in 1960 for offences committed while on parole. He made two abortive attempts to escape from the Missouri state penitentiary before he finally succeeded in 1967. He was on the run when he committed the murder.

According to a Congressional Select Committee, Ray's motive was probably a combination of avarice and racism; other unidentified conspirators are thought to have been involved, and a 'contract' for Dr King's death was said to be on offer. In 1979 the US Congressional Assassinations Committee found that Ray had almost certainly stalked his prey for some time before shooting him, and decided, 'While the committee recognized the presence of other possible motives – racial or psychological needs – it concluded . . . that the expectation of financial gain was Ray's primary consideration.'

REES, Melvin Davis
Jazz musician and sex-killer.

On 26 June 1957 an army sergeant was driving home for a weekend with a girl-friend, Margaret Harold. They had stopped in a lonely spot near Annapolis, Maryland, when a green Chrysler pulled in front of them. A tall, thin-faced man got out, and identified himself as the caretaker of the property. He asked for a cigarette, then for a lift. Suddenly he pulled out a gun and climbed into the back seat. He demanded money, and wound his fingers into Margaret Harold's hair, pulling her head back. 'Don't give it to him,' she said angrily. There was a shot, and she slumped forward. The sergeant pushed open the door and ran as hard as he could. A mile along the road he found a farmhouse and asked to use the phone. When the police arrived some time later, Margaret Harold was still across the front seat, without her dress. The killer had violated the corpse.

The police searched the area, and found a cinder-block building nearby, with a broken basement window. Inside, the walls were covered with pornographic photographs, and police morgue shots of women who had been murdered. One photograph stood out from the others as normal – it had been clipped out of a college yearbook. The girl in it was finally identified as a 1955 graduate of Maryland University, Wanda Tipson; but she had no recollection of dating any male who corresponded to the sergeant's description of the murderer.

On 11 January 1959 Carrol Jackson was out driving with his wife Mildred and their two daughters, Susan, aged five and Janet, eighteen months. Carrol Jackson was a non-smoker and teetotaler who had met his wife at a Baptist church; she was president of the women's missionary society. As he drove along a road near Apple Grove, Eastern Virginia, an old blue Chevrolet began to overtake, flashing his lights. When Jackson pulled over, the Chevrolet pulled in front and stopped. Jackson screeched to a halt, and was about to lose his temper when a man jumped out of the other car and waved a gun in his face. The tall, thin-faced man with long, ape-like arms and a beetling brow forced the Jackson family to get out of their car and into the boot of his Chevrolet. Then he drove off. Later that afternoon, Mildred Jackson's aunt drove along the same road and recognized her niece's husband's car, abandoned.

The search for the Jacksons revealed nothing. Then another couple came forward to say that they had been forced off the road earlier that afternoon by an old blue Chevrolet. A man had walked back towards their car, but they had quickly reversed and driven away.

Two months later, on 4 March, two men whose car had bogged down on a muddy back road near Fredericksburg picked up armfuls of brush to gain traction, and found themselves looking at the body of a man. It proved to be Carrol Jackson, his hands bound in front of him with a necktie. He had been shot in the skull. Underneath him was the body of his eighteen-month-old daughter, who had simply been tossed into the ditch, and died of suffocation under her father's body. There was no sign of Mildred or Susan Jackson.

On 21 March, boys hunting squirrels close to the spot where Margaret Harold had been murdered noticed freshly dug earth; they brushed some of it aside and saw the blonde hair of a little girl. Police uncovered the bodies of Mildred and Susan Jackson. Mildred had a stocking tied around her neck, but it was loose. Susan had been beaten to death with a blunt instrument. There was evidence that both had been raped. Police theorized that the stocking around Mildred Jackson's neck had been used as a tourniquet to force her to commit some sexual act that disgusted her.

The grave was within a few hundred yards of the cinder-block structure in which the obscene photographs had been found two years earlier. And a quarter of a mile away, the police found a broken-down shack with relatively fresh tyre-marks nearby. Inside, police found a red button from Mildred Jackson's dress.

Again, the investigation came to a halt. But two months later, the police received an anonymous letter that accused a jazz musician called Melvin Davis Rees of the murders of Margaret Harold and of the Jackson family. The man, who said he was a salesman, said that he and Rees had been in a town not far from the spot where Margaret Harold had been murdered, and that Rees had been hopped up on Benzedrine. The writer said he had later asked Rees point-blank if he had killed the Jackson family; Rees had not denied it, but only evaded the question. Police searched for Rees – whose job as a jazz musician kept him travelling – without success. Then, early in 1960, the writer of the letter, who identified himself as Glenn L. Moser, went to the police, to say that he had received a letter from Rees, who was working as a piano salesman in a music shop in West Memphis, Arkansas. An FBI agent went into the store and told Rees he was under arrest. Later that day, the sergeant identified Rees in a line-up as the man who had murdered Margaret Harold.

Detectives hastened to the home of Rees' parents in Hyattsville, armed with a search warrant; in an attic they found a saxophone case containing a ·38 revolver, and various notes describing sadistic acts – including the murder of the Jacksons.

'Caught on a lonely road . . . Drove to a select area and killed husband and baby. Now the mother and daughter were all mine. . . .' He went on to describe a perverted sex act, probably forcing fellatio on her. 'Now I was her master,' he says with relish. He then described killing her slowly in a way that made it clear that his sexual hang-up was sadism.

Maryland police now discovered links between Rees and four other sex-murders of teenagers: two schoolgirls, Marie Shomette and Ann Ryan, had been intercepted in College Park, near the University of Maryland, and shot and raped; the bodies of Mary Fellers and Shelby Venable had been found in Maryland rivers.

Rees was tried in 1961, and executed for the murder of the Jackson family.

People who had worked with Rees (who played the piano, guitar, saxophone and clarinet) found it hard to believe that he was guilty of the crimes, and described him as mild-mannered and intelligent. The girl whose photograph had been found in the hut had, in fact, known him very well, and had given him up because he was married; it just never struck her that the killer of Margaret Harold could be the jazz musician.

Peter Hurkos, the psychic, was called into the case after the disappearance of the Jackson family, and his description of the killer was remarkably accurate – over six feet tall, left-handed, tattooed on the arm, with a walk like a duck and ape-like arms. At the scene of Margaret Harold's murder, Hurkos walked to a bush and plucked off the dead woman's torn skirt which had been there unnoticed since the murder. Hurkos added that the man had committed nine murders. This concurred with the figure the police themselves finally arrived at.

RIJKE, Sjef
Sadistic poisoner sentenced to life imprisonment in 1972.

In January 1971, an eighteen-year-old girl named Willy Maas died after more than a week of stomach pains. Her funeral in Utrecht, Holland, was attended by her grief-stricken fiancé, Sjef Rijke. The symptoms seemed to be those of food poisoning.

Soon after Willy Maas's death, Rijke became engaged to another young girl he had known for several years, Mientje Manders. Towards the end of March, she too was complaining of stomach pains; she died on 2 April 1971. Rijke sat by her bedside, holding her hand, tears running down his cheeks.

The Utrecht police found the coincidence odd, but had no reason to suspect Rijke; he seemed to have no motive for killing his fiancées.

Astonishingly, Rijke was married a mere three weeks after the death of his second fiancée. The marriage lasted only six weeks. Rijke apparently proved pathologically jealous, and he and his eighteen-year-old wife, Maria Haas, had furious fights. She left him and filed for divorce. The police, who had been observing Rijke's affairs with curiosity, interviewed Maria, and inquired whether she had experienced any stomach upsets. Oddly enough, she had – from the moment she was married. Now they had gone away.

Within a short time, another girl had moved into Rijke's house. When she began to suffer from stomach pains, she mentioned the problem to her mother. She ate precisely the same food as her lover, but he seemed perfectly healthy. Her mother inquired whether she ate anything between meals, and the girl admitted to a fondness for peanut butter. They examined the jar, and agreed that it seemed to have an odd metallic taste. The girl suggested taking it down to the public analyst at the health department. The laboratory found that the peanut butter had been laced with rat poison.

Since Rijke seemed to have no motive for poisoning his women, the police looked around for another suspect. His middle-aged cleaning woman had been working for him for several years. Both Rijke and the cleaner were arrested; both vehemently denied any knowledge of the rat poison. But when the owner of a local garden store recalled selling Rijke several lots of rat poison, the investigation concentrated on him. Rijke suddenly broke down and confessed to poisoning Willy Maas and Mientje Manders and attempting the murders of the two other women. He explained that it gave him pleasure to see women suffer; he insisted that it was not his intention to kill. He was found legally sane, and stood trial in January 1972, only a year after the death of Willy Maas. He was sentenced to two terms of life imprisonment.

Sadistic murder by poison is one of the rarest of crimes (see Young, Graham, another of the few recent examples); in Rijke's case, it seems conceivable that it was connected with his pathological jealousy.

ROBLES, Richard
Drug addict who murdered two girls while burgling their apartment.

28 August 1963 was a stiflingly hot day in New York. When Patricia Tolles returned to the apartment on East 88th Street that she shared with two other girls in their early twenties, she was alarmed to find the hall in a state of disorder, and blood in the bathroom. Afraid to enter the bedrooms, she hurried to the telephone to ring Max Wylie, the father of one of her flatmates, Janice Wylie. Wylie went into the bedroom, and found the mutilated bodies of his daughter and of the other girl, Emily Hoffert, tied together with strips torn off the sheet and covered with stab wounds. Emily Hoffert was fully clothed, but Janice Wylie was naked. Medical examination revealed that cream had been smeared between Janice's thighs, obviously in preparation for rape, but this had not been carried out. Janice, an exceptionally beautiful girl who had been hoping to go on the stage, had been receiving obscene phone calls at her office before her death. All attempts to track down the caller were unsuccessful.

In April 1964 a young black, George Whitmore, was arrested and charged with stabbing to death a cleaning woman in the backyard of a Brooklyn house, and of assaulting a night-nurse. The police found a photograph of a girl in his wallet, which he first said he'd found on a junk heap, but later that he got it from 'that building up on East 88th Street'.

He eventually confessed to the murder of the two girls, but at his trial, his lawyer withdrew his confession, saying that it had been forced out of him. When it was shown that the picture was not, as the police believed, that of Janice Wylie, the case against him collapsed.

In 1965 a drug addict named Nathan Delaney was arrested for stabbing a drug pedlar to death, and attempted to do a deal with the police by telling them that he could name the killer of Janice Wylie. On 28 August 1963, he said, a man called Ricky Robles had turned up at his apartment 'looking like a wild man, with his clothes covered in blood' and told him that he needed a shot of heroin because he had 'just iced two dames when I was robbing their apartment on East 88th Street'. Robles told him that when he got in through the service door, he found a naked woman on the bed covering herself with a sheet, and decided to rape her. Before he could do this, Emily Hoffert had appeared, and when she screamed, he stabbed them with kitchen knives with such violence that they broke.

Robles denied the charge, but since he had convictions for burglary and sex offences, and had tied up some of his victims in the same way as Janice Wylie and Emily Hoffert, the police were able to convict him of the two murders. He was sentenced to life imprisonment.

ROSE, Paul and SIMARD, Francis
Joint murderers of the Quebec minister for labour.

In two related acts of terrorism, separatists of the Front de Liberation du Quebec (FLQ) first kidnapped British trade commissioner James Richard Cross on 5 October 1970, and five days later Quebec's provincial minister of labour. The two squads of kidnappers were drawn from independent cells within the FLQ.

James Cross was abducted from his home in Montreal and driven off in a taxi with four armed men. After seizing Cross, those from the 'Liberation cell' announced ambitious terms for his release. They demanded release from jail of twenty-three separatists, payment of $500,000 in gold, and safe passage to Cuba or Algeria for those involved. Lesser demands included reinstatement for some post office workers who had lost their jobs, publication of the separatist manifesto, and the naming of an informer within their ranks who had been aiding the police. After rejecting the demands of the FLQ as a whole, the federal government met them in part by authorizing the Canadian Broadcasting Corporation to read out the FLQ manifesto on television on 8 October. However, at a press conference the same day Robert Lemieux, a lawyer acting as unofficial spokesman for the separatists, accused the government of acting in bad faith and the police of violating the civil rights of suspects taken in for questioning. In a 'final' demand on 9 October, the FLQ warned that unless the twenty-three prisoners were freed by six o'clock the following evening, James Cross would be put to death.

The provincial government's response was read out on TV on 10 October by Quebec's minister of justice Jerome Choquette. It amounted to an exchange, and was far less than the terrorists were seeking, of safe conduct to the country of their choice – if they returned Mr Cross alive. The FLQ answer came within minutes of the 6 pm deadline. Two masked men armed with sub-machine-guns kidnapped Quebec's minister for labour, Pierre Laporte, from his home, drove off with him in a car and threatened to execute him by 10 pm if the demands made earlier by the 'Liberation cell' were not met in full.

The 'Chenier cell' threat was underlined in a note from Minister Laporte to Quebec Premier, Robert Bourassa: 'You ... have the power to decide on my life or my death'. Five minutes before the second deadline expired Bourassa said on television that his government could not meet the separatists' demands until it had positive assurances that both men would be released unharmed.

On 11 October Robert Lemieux was arrested and accused of obstructing the police investigation into the kidnappings. Lemieux complained of government prevarication on the central issue of the release of the prisoners named by the separatists, while the FLQ would go no further than give 'a solemn pledge to the people of Quebec' that it would then release Cross and Laporte. The provincial government wanted each of the two cells involved to surrender one of its members as guarantee of good faith. Lemieux was released on 12 October.

On 15 October students at the University of Quebec occupied administrative buildings in support of the FLQ demands. On the same day, at the urgent request of Bourassa, the federal government ordered Canadian troops to mount guard on public buildings and ministers' homes. Then, in what was said to be the 'final' position, Bourassa rejected FLQ's demand for the release of twenty-three prisoners and offered instead to free five of them, and give the kidnappers safe passage out of the country.

On 16 October – for the first time in Canada's peacetime history – the federal government declared a state of 'apprehended insurrection' in the provinces and invoked wartime emergency powers. These allowed the government to do whatever it deemed necessary in the interests of national security: and under those sweeping powers the FLQ was proscribed, while the police arrested 250 persons in Quebec province.

In a further move next day to defuse the situation, the Quebec government offered immunity from arrest to the kidnappers if they assembled with their two hostages at the Expo 67 site in Montreal. It promised that the area would be regarded as an extension of the Cuban consulate (with appropriate diplomatic immunity) and that Cuban officials would retain custody of Cross and Laporte until the kidnappers themselves landed safely in Havana.

The offer came too late to save Laporte. On 18 October his bloodstained and garrotted body was discovered in the boot of the same car in which he had been kidnapped. On 6 November police arrested nineteen-year-old Bernard Lortie. At a coroner's inquest next day he admitted taking part in Laporte's kidnapping, but denied any involvement either in his murder or in the kidnapping of James Cross.

The hunt for Cross continued, and on 2 December police located and surrounded the house in Montreal where he was held captive. The separatists agreed to negotiate terms for his release, and later handed him over to Cuba's Acting Consul Ricardo Escartin in return for a safe passage out of the country. The hand-over was carried out on the Expo 67 site. Police revealed later that both the house in which Cross was held prisoner and the car in which he was driven to the pavilion were booby-trapped against any surprise attack. A Royal Canadian Mounted Police aircraft flew the three kidnappers, plus four relatives, to Havana. There the Cuban government made it clear that it had allowed them entry solely for 'humanitarian reasons' (i.e. to save Cross) and at the formal request of the Canadian government.

On 28 December, after a nationwide hunt involving thousands of police and troops, the three FLQ men named by Bernard Lortie as his accomplices in the Laporte kidnapping were arrested at a farmhouse near the border with the United States. They were Paul Rose, twenty-seven, his brother Jacques and Francis Simard. All had successfully concealed themselves in a hideaway built below the farmhouse on the three previous occasions it had been searched.

A coroner's inquest in Montreal on 4 January 1971 found the three of them, and Lortie, 'criminally responsible' for the murder of

Laporte. Evidence was given by police that Francis Simard had made an unsigned statement, telling them how Laporte came to be killed. He said the separatists had decided not to execute Cross as he had no connection with Quebec problems, and had seized Laporte as an alternative hostage. On 16 October Laporte had tried to escape from the suburban bungalow where he was held prisoner, but had failed and cut himself on a broken window in the process. This accounted for the bloodstains on his body and clothing. Then 'we decided to strangle him with the chain he had been wearing since his kidnapping. Paul, Jacques and I choked him. We are all equally responsible. We knew what we were doing.'

On 13 March 1971 Paul Rose (who said he was proud to have taken part in Laporte's kidnapping) was sentenced to life imprisonment for his murder. On 30 November he received a second life sentence, to run concurrently, for the kidnapping.

Francis Simard was also convicted of Laporte's murder on 20 May 1971 and jailed for life. Lortie was sentenced to twenty years' imprisonment for kidnapping while Jacques Rose was acquitted of both charges.

In 1974 the three kidnappers given free passage to Cuba in 1970 were allowed to enter France from Czechoslovakia, after what the French authorities described as a 'security error'. It was made plain, however, by other French officials that any Canadian request for their extradition would be denied. Prime Minister Trudeau said that under the terms of their 'safe passage' agreement the three separatists were safe from proceedings unless they re-entered Canadian territory.

SANCHEZ, Ilyich Ramirez
Multinational terrorist leader who masterminded the mass kidnap of OPEC delegates in Vienna.

Sanchez, alias Carlos and the 'Jackal' (from Frederick Forsyth's novel *The Day of the Jackal*), is one of the world's most wanted terrorists. Born in 1949, he was the eldest son of a left-wing Venezuelan lawyer and follower of Lenin. After spending two years with his mother in London in the late 1960s Sanchez went to Moscow to study at the Patrice Lumumba Friendship University. There he befriended various Arab Communist students, joined the PFLP and underwent military training in the Lebanon. He spent some years with the Paris-based cell of the PFLP, then succeeded to international leadership on the death of terrorist Mohammed Boudia (by a car bomb planted by the Israeli secret service).

The raid on the heavily guarded conference hall in Vienna and the kidnap of eighty-one OPEC delegates was ostensibly staged as a protest against the alleged sell-out by influential Arab states, led by President Sadat, to what the PFLP regarded as American imperialism, but also to raise funds for future operations.

The OPEC meeting was in its second day when the gang struck, on 21 December 1975. The six terrorists were Sanchez himself, Gabrielle Krocher-Tiedmann and Hans Joachim-Klein (both West German) and two Palestinians and a Lebanese. After a shootout with Austrian security guards, in which three died and seven were wounded, the gang seized the hostages, including Sheik Yamani and Jamshid Amouzegar, the Irani Minister for the Interior, and forty-one Austrians. The three who died were Youssef Ismirli, the Libyan delegate to the conference, killed by Sanchez, and a policeman and an Iraqi employee, killed by the only woman in the gang.

Responsibility for the attack was claimed via a communique issued in Geneva by an unknown pro-Palestinian group styling itself the 'Arm of the Arab Revolution' – it was in fact the PFLP. Sanchez threatened to execute all Saudi and Iranian officials in the party unless his demands for safe passage out of Austria were met. Klein had been wounded in the attack, and was given emergency hospital treatment before being returned to the gang. Bruno Kreisky, the Austrian Chancellor, together with Algerian Foreign Minister Abdul Aziz Bouteflika and a senior Iraqi diplomat, negotiated with Sanchez for the release of the hostages. For freeing the forty-one Austrians the terrorists were allowed to fly to Algiers with the remaining delegates.

Sheik Yamani and Jamshid Amouzegar, together with 'neutral' hostages from Gabon, Ecuador, Venezuela, Nigeria and Indonesia, were released in Algiers on 22 December. Fifteen Arab hostages were kept aboard the aeroplane and flown on to Tripoli. There they were held captive until King Khaled of Saudi Arabia and the Shah of Iran between them paid over an undisclosed ransom (some estimates put it as high as $50 million). When Sanchez received a coded message from associates outside Libya that the money had been paid, he flew back to Algiers and freed the remaining hostages. Sanchez and his gang were granted six days' political asylum by Algeria, but they did not stay: instead, on 30 December, they flew to an unnamed destination, thought to be Libya again, before returning to their headquarters.

SANDERS, Lindberg
Cult leader whose anti-white group was responsible for the death of a policeman.

Sanders, who described himself as 'the black Jesus', had been in and out of mental hospitals since 1973 and had been diagnosed as schizophrenic. On 7 January 1983 Sanders and nine cult members retreated into a house in the Hollywood section of Memphis, Tennessee, prepared for the end of the world four days later, when the moon would descend and destroy all who did not accept Sanders' teaching. When the moon failed to descend, Sanders persuaded the others that it was because Antichrist had come to earth instead, and that he was personified by white policemen. A phone call was made to police headquarters, asking the police to come to the house for information on a purse-snatcher. Three policemen, including Patrolman Robert Hester, called at the house, to be met by a barrage of gunfire. Two managed to escape – one wounded in the face and hand – but Hester was dragged into the house.

Police surrounded the house and tried to bargain with Sanders over a walkie-talkie, but Sanders answered with obscenities. Many police wept openly as they heard the screams of Hester. Two days later, on 12 January, Hester pleaded, 'Give them whatever they want.' When electronic eavesdropping devices transmitted the comment, 'The devil is dead,' police stormed the house with tear-gas, sub-machine-guns and grenades. Sanders and the six cultists still with him were all killed; the fact that they were in different rooms of the house, and that some had died of a single gunshot wound, raised speculation that some had been executed by the police. Patrolman Hester's body was found with his wrists handcuffed behind him.

SCHMID, Charles Howard
Hero of Tucson's teenagers, many of whom knew he had committed 'thrill killings'.

23-year-old Schmid, the only child of well-to-do parents who ran a nursing home, was a 'Billy Liar' who told incredible stories about his exploits. Despite his short stature he became an athletics champion at school. He wore cowboy boots stuffed with paper to make him taller; this gave him an odd, shambling walk, which he explained by saying he had been crippled in a fight with Mafia hoods. His parents allowed him a small house of his own at the bottom of the garden. There, according to Schmid, he spent his time seducing the teenage girls of Tucson – a university town whose restaurants and drive-ins are usually crowded with students. One girl, Mary French, fell in love with him, and Schmid told her that she had to work for him; he got her a job in his parents' nursing home and made her pay her wages into his bank account.

Like Charles Manson, Schmid seemed to exercise a fascination over teenagers; as a result, his sex life was highly involved – if not as hyperactive as he liked to boast. He claimed that he ran a prostitution ring, and that he had taught his girlfriends a 'hundred different ways to make love'.

In May 1964 he began to feel that mere seduction was repetitive; one evening, in the company of Mary French and a friend named John Saunders, Schmid jumped up shouting, 'I want to kill a girl tonight.' They drove off to the home of fifteen-year-old Alleen Rowe, whose mother was out on night work; Mary French persuaded Alleen to come for a drive. In a desert area near the golf links, Alleen was dragged from the car and raped, then killed with a rock; her body was buried in a shallow grave. Schmid kissed Mary French and told her, 'Remember, I love you.'

In the following year he became involved with a pretty, neurotic seventeen-year-old, Gretchen Fritz, and sobbed wildly when Gretchen rang him from California and told him she had 'gone all the way' with a man she met there. But after a while he told a friend named Richard Bruns that Gretchen was becoming too possessive. On 16 August 1965 Gretchen and her thirteen-year-old sister Wendy went to a drive-in movie then back to Schmid's, where he strangled them both, and dumped their bodies in the desert. Questioned by two Mafia types, who claimed they had been hired by Gretchen's parents to find her, Schmid insisted that they had run away to California.

But, unable to resist boasting, Schmid told Richard Bruns that he had killed the sisters. Bruns thought he was lying, so he challenged Schmid: 'If you killed them, let's go and bury them.' They drove into the desert and located the bodies. After Bruns had helped him bury them, Schmid remarked, 'Now you're in this as deep as I am.'

In San Diego, Schmid was arrested for posing as an FBI agent and questioning bikini-clad girls on the beach. He was becoming increasingly strained, screaming one night: 'God is going to punish me.' Most of the teenagers in Tucson seemed to know that Schmid had killed Alleen Rowe and the Fritz girls, but no one told either their parents or the police. But observing Schmid's neurotic behaviour, Richard Bruns began to fear that the life of his own girlfriend – who had rejected Schmid – was in danger, and began to guard her house at night. Finally, he went to the police, and led them to the bodies of the Fritz girls. Mary French and John Saunders were arrested, together with Schmid, who had recently married a fifteen-year-old girl after a blind date.

The case shocked the parents of Tucson, who had only been dimly aware of how far their children had gone into drugs, alcohol and sex. Schmid was sentenced to two terms of life imprisonment (escaping the death penalty as a result of its suspension in 1971). Mary French received five years; John Saunders, life. In 1972, Schmid and another inmate escaped from the Arizona State Prison, but were recaptured a few days later.

SCHWINDT, Werner
Sex-killer whose victim was his own daughter.

On 25 August 1975 the body of a girl was found in a field near Pforzheim, West Germany. She was lying on her back, naked from the waist down, and her blouse had been pulled open to expose her breasts. Medical examination revealed that she had been a virgin, but had been the victim of rape. Photographs and fingerprints of the girl were sent to all police stations in Germany, and she was quickly identified as Margret Schwindt, who had taken the previous Friday afternoon off from her job in Koellerbach in order to visit her sister in Heidelberg. Her mother, Christel Schwindt, identified her.

Christel Schwindt had been separated from her husband, Werner, since he deserted her when she was pregnant with Margret, but he maintained contact with his children.

The police were unable to discover how Margret had intended to get to Heidelberg, but the likeliest explanation was that she had tried to hitch-hike and been picked up.

Two weeks later, on 4 September, a man walking by Lake Neusidler, not far from Vienna, observed a man lying prone on a park bench. The man was well-dressed, and there was no smell of alcohol on his breath. Suspecting he had suffered a heart attack, his discoverer called the police. When an empty container of sleeping tablets was found under the seat it became obvious that this was a suicide attempt. The man was rushed to hospital, and his stomach pumped out. At a psychiatric clinic in Vienna he identified himself as Werner Schwindt, and explained that he had decided to commit suicide because he was guilty of raping and then strangling his daughter Margret.

Passing through Koellerbach on the day Margret had vanished, Schwindt had called on his daughter and suggested driving her to Heidelberg. When Margret suggested telling her mother where she was going, Schwindt lied that he had already told her. Clearly, he was already contemplating the rape. In a lay-by, he pulled in and asked her if she wanted to go to the toilet; she said perhaps she'd better and went into the bushes. Schwindt followed her, grabbed her as she crouched down, and tore off her knickers. She struggled, then gave in, lying quietly. When it was over, Schwindt panicked at the thought that she would tell her mother, and strangled her. His own evidence made it clear that the whole crime was meditated in advance. He was sentenced to life imprisonment.

SIRHAN, Sirhan Bishara
The Arab fanatic who assassinated Senator Robert Kennedy.

Robert Kennedy, younger brother of President John F. Kennedy, was assassinated while campaigning for the presidency in 1968. Robert Kennedy, who had served as Attorney General in his brother's administration, was forty-two. He had just won the crucial California Democratic presidential primary election, a victory which many felt paved the way for him to become America's second President Kennedy.

The man who murdered him was a Jordanian immigrant, Sirhan Sirhan, aged twenty-four. Sirhan shot him in a Los Angeles hotel kitchen as the news of the California primary was announced, and on the first anniversary of the Six-Day-War in the Middle East in which Israel inflicted a crushing defeat on her Arab foes. The reason: Sirhan was an Arab, Robert Kennedy supported the Israeli cause. Sirhan was sentenced to death for the murder, but had his sentence commuted to life imprisonment when capital punishment was suspended in the United States.

Life imprisonment in California normally means the offender spends a maximum of thirteen years in jail. In 1975 former Parole Board official James Hoover set 1984 as the provisional earliest date when Sirhan would become eligible to apply for parole. When that date was challenged by Los Angeles district attorney John Van de Kamp in 1982, Mr Hoover pointed out that he had merely been following standard California state policy in making the assessment: his role was to evaluate a prisoner's prison behaviour and medical reports, not the importance of his victim. Mr Van de Kamp's deputy told a special parole board hearing at Soledad prison, where Sirhan is held in the maximum security wing, 'If Sirhan's scheduled release is implemented . . . we will risk sending a message throughout the entire world to every misfit, fanatic and political crusader . . . that political assassination in California costs just thirteen years.'

SMITH, Perry and HICKOCK, Richard
Ex-convicts who murdered four members of the Clutter family in Kansas.

Hickock and Smith were convinced that a wealthy farmer, Herbert W. Clutter, kept large sums of money in his home. They had been told this by a former cellmate, Floyd Wells, who had once worked for the Clutters. Smith and Hickock were hoping to retire to an island off the coast of South America, where they could dive for treasure.

Towards midnight on 14 November 1959, they entered the Clutters' home through an unlocked side door. They walked into Herbert Clutter's bedroom, threatened him with a knife, and asked him where he kept the safe. They refused to believe that the $30 in his wallet was all the money in the house. Clutter was made to go and wake his wife, who burst into tears and said, 'I don't have any money.' They then woke up the Clutters' fifteen-year-old son Kenyon. Sixteen-year-old Nancy Clutter came to investigate, and was tied up. Hickock announced his intention of raping Nancy, but Smith ordered him not to. Then all four were killed with a shotgun and hunting knife.

When the bodies were found the next day, the murders caused the same kind of universal fear that the Jack the Ripper murders had caused in London in 1888.

When Floyd Wells heard the news of the murders on the radio in prison, he talked to the authorities, and detective Al Dewey tracked down the two killers in Las Vegas. The investigation and trial dragged on for almost four years, but they were hanged on 14 April 1965.

SOBHRAJ, Charles
Vietnamese confidence man and multiple murderer.

Charles Sobhraj was born in Saigon, South Vietnam, on 6 April 1944. His father was a rich man; his mother was a beautiful peasant girl who had become his mistress. When his father married an Indian girl in Poona, his mother stormed out of the house, and married a sergeant in the French army. The four-year-old boy resented the sudden drop in living standards. He saw a great deal of violence in his early years, including two explosions that killed many people. At the age of nine he was taken to France, but he hated Europe, and was a persistent bed-wetter. He was unhappy at a Catholic boarding

297

school in a Paris suburb, and was the butt of racist jokes. At the age of fifteen he was described as undisciplined, unwilling and lazy. When his stepfather found him a job in a garage, he was sacked for reversing the wires on a transformer and almost burning the place down. He ran away from home to try to return to his father in Saigon, but his stepfather tracked him down. Then he stowed away on a ship at Marseilles bound for Vietnam, but was again caught and sent back.

Sobhraj's father came to Paris and promised to send for him when he returned to Saigon. When the ticket failed to arrive, Sobhraj bought a gun and tried robbery. He was caught after his second attempt, but the woman withdrew her complaint. Sobhraj finally made the trip to Saigon, but the relationship between father and son deteriorated after he overturned his father's car, and he was sent to India. He ran away from relatives in Poona and again stowed away on a ship and returned to Saigon. His father, now furious, sent him back to France.

Imprisoned for stealing a car, Sobhraj escaped shortly before he was due for parole, and was transferred to a more secure jail. He went on hunger strike and refused to speak. Befriended by a prison visitor, Alain Benard, he was finally paroled, and obtained a job selling fire extinguishers. He met a beautiful girl named Chantal and asked her to marry him. She was with him when, fleeing from police in a stolen car, he crashed into a telegraph pole; he was sentenced to six months. While there, he practised strenuous physical exercises to keep in trim. On his release, he married Chantal and took a regular job. It bored him. He stole his sister's cheque book, forged a cheque for 6,000 francs, and tried to make a quick fortune in a gambling casino; he lost, and was soon back in prison. His sister withdrew her complaint.

After Sobhraj had raised some 30,000 francs by writing dud cheques, he and Chantal fled to Bombay. Here he developed into a 'fixer' and confidence man of extraordinary ability. He made a considerable income from diamond smuggling, currency deals, and the sale of luxury goods acquired with dud cheques. Sobhraj felt he deserved a life of ease and wealth, and was willing to take risks to get them. He befriended American dropouts, stole their passports, and used them in his complicated business deals. But an ambitious jewel robbery in Delhi led to his arrest. Granted bail – in spite of an escape attempt – in 1972, he and his wife fled to Kabul, where they were jailed for failing to pay the hotel bill, stealing a car and attempting to cross the border illegally. Again, Sobhraj escaped, returned to France, and kidnapped his baby daughter from his mother-in-law, leaving the latter locked in a hotel room in a drugged stupor. It was on his way back to India that he committed his first murder – although, since it was unintentional, it could be described as manslaughter. He drugged the driver of a hired car, put him in the boot, and drove towards Teheran. The driver died of suffocation, and the body was dumped in a river.

In Teheran, he was arrested by the Shah's secret police; he was carrying a briefcase full of forged passports, and they suspected he was aiding the anti-Shah movement. He spent a year in jail. Chantal, after six months in prison, returned to France and sued for divorce. She went to America with another man.

In Istanbul in November 1973, Charles was joined by his younger brother Guy, whom he taught how to rob rich tourists. He made the acquaintance of a middle-aged couple, spiked the man's drink with a laxative, designed to upset his stomach, then persuaded the man to swallow more pills to cure it. The two brothers took the man for a night on the town, and returned him to his hotel heavily drugged. While Guy made conversation with the wife, Charles searched the man's bedroom. The man woke up, but was too heavily sedated to do more than shout. The brothers grabbed the woman, and Charles injected her buttock with a drug. When she was unconscious he took the room key to the desk, asked the clerk to open the safe, and removed the man's valuables. He and Guy decamped with valuables and several thousand dollars. In Athens, Guy drugged and robbed a Lebanese businessman. Unfortunately the businessman recognized Guy later at the airport, and the two brothers were arrested. In the following April Sobhraj made a brilliant escape from a guard's van on the island of Aegina. He used to say to Guy, who remained in prison, 'Always remember that their desire to keep me locked up is no match for my desire to be free.' It never struck him that he could avoid being locked up if he turned his very considerable abilities to making money honestly.

Back in Delhi, Sobhraj met a beautiful Canadian girl, Marie-Andrée Leclerc. They lived together for a time, then she returned to Quebec, and Charles went on 'business trips' to Bombay and Hong Kong. She flew back to live with him in Bangkok, where Sobhraj had taken a flat at Kanit House. There he became involved in the heroin business. He gained his inside knowledge from a drug trafficker named André Breugnot, whom he drugged, then bullied into telling everything. Afterwards, Sobhraj gave him more drugs, and drowned him in the bath. The death was listed as an accident.

Flat 504 in Kanit House witnessed an endless procession of guests, many of them dropouts from Western society. Sobhraj made use of them as drug couriers, and continued to deal in gems.

On 13 October 1975, a young American girl from Seattle, Teresa Knowlton, came to Sobhraj's flat. Later, with the aid of an Indian henchman called Ajay, Sobhraj killed her, forcing her to take a drug, then ordering Ajay to dump her in the sea. The motive for killing her is not clear – Sobhraj seems to have suspected she was a drugs courier who was holding out on him. He later said that a major drugs syndicate in Hong Kong had hired him to 'make an example' of amateur couriers. The next 'amateur' they set out to discourage was a Turk from Ibiza named Vitali Hakim. Sobhraj and Ajay drugged him, beat him into revealing names and addresses, then killed him by breaking his neck. The body was dowsed with petrol and burned. Hakim had revealed that his next contact would be a French girl named Stephanie Parry. She arrived in Bangkok and was met by Sobhraj. She was drugged and strangled.

The next victims were a young Dutch couple, Cornelia Hemker and Henricus Bitanja who had saved up for five years for a round-the-world trip. Sobhraj befriended them in Hong Kong and invited them to stay at his flat in Bangkok. They arrived there on 11 December. Two days later they were both 'sick' – Sobhraj having administered some of his pills. On 16 December, Sobhraj and Ajay drove them to a lonely spot in the countryside; both were now heavily drugged. They were strangled, then petrol was poured on the bodies and set alight. Sobhraj told other house guests that the Dutch couple had gone to hospital for treatment. But one of these guests, Dominique Rennelleau, disbelieved the story; he himself suspected that 'Alain Gautier' (as Sobhraj called himself) had been drugging him. Two neighbours, Remy and Nadine Gires, also began to have their suspicions.

Shortly before Christmas, two more burnt bodies were found near Katmandu, where Sobhraj was staying at the time; they were Connie Jo Bronzich of Santa Cruz and Laurent Carrière of Manitoba. Sobhraj was using the passport of the murdered Dutchman, Bitanja, and staying in the hotel under his name. Sobhraj was questioned by the police, and asked to wait in Katmandu until their investigations were completed; but he took the first opportunity to slip out of Nepal.

At Varanasi in northern India, Sobhraj met an Israeli named

Allen Aren Jacobs. When Sobhraj, Ajay and Leclerc moved on to Goa, the Israeli was found dead in bed. Sobhraj later remarked that this had been an accident: 'We only wanted his passport.' Since Sobhraj had become a professional killer, such accidents happened easily.

In Goa they met a party of three Frenchmen and became friendly. On 9 January 1976 they all drove south together. The three Frenchmen were drugged and thrown into their van; then the van was crashed against a tree. Fortunately, the Frenchmen survived, although their money and passports vanished into Sobhraj's briefcase. Next stop was Hong Kong, where they drugged a schoolteacher, Allen Gore, and cashed his letter of credit, worth $8,000.

Meanwhile, back in Bangkok, a Dutch diplomat named Herman Knippenberg was investigating the disappearance of the Dutch couple – their charred corpses had been wrongly identified as Australians. When he was able to identify the corpses as those of the missing tourists, Knippenberg had taken a major step towards trapping Charles Sobhraj. He discovered the connection with 'Alain Gautier', and visited Kanit House. Remy and Nadine Gires voiced their suspicions about their neighbour. When the Thai Drugs Squad burst into Sobhraj's flat, Sobhraj assured them he was Allen Gore, the school-teacher he had robbed in Hong Kong. In spite of the piles of false passports, the police allowed Sobhraj to leave Bangkok. The local community talked knowingly of a huge bribe. Knippenberg was allowed to search the flat, and found various items that had belonged to the Dutch couple. And with Sobhraj out of the country, the Bangkok newspapers were openly speaking about the 'web of murder, robbery and forced druggings', printing photographs of five of the eight victims.

Sobhraj's career was far from over. He and Leclerc flew to Penang, where he drugged and robbed three Australian tourists. He was arrested for trying to cash stolen traveller's cheques but talked his way out of it. Ajay flew to join him in Penang, bringing Roong, a beautiful Thai girl whom Sobhraj had seduced with a promise of marriage. Later, Sobhraj and Leclerc flew to Paris, where he took an office and displayed gems to local jewellers. He went to call on a high-ranking police official he had met in Singapore – and learned for the first time that he was now a wanted man. Again, he talked his way smoothly out of it, explaining that it was a story concocted by jealous business rivals . . .

When he lost $200,000 in a Rouen casino, Sobhraj decided that he needed to carry out an ambitious crime. He went back to Bombay and proceeded to recruit accomplices for a series of big jewellery robberies in Delhi and Agra. Money for immediate expenses was obtained by drugging and robbing travellers. One of the accomplices decided it would be easier to decamp with Leclerc's handbag, containing all their money. Sobhraj had to replan the big jewel robberies from scratch. He drugged a French traveller, Luke Solomon, and stole his money, but he administered too much of the drug and the man died in hospital. Sobhraj made the acquaintance of a group of sixty French engineering students in Agra, and promised to meet them all in Delhi. There, a few days later, he gave them all tablets 'to prevent dysentery'. But he had again miscalculated the dose. Large numbers of the students began groaning and collapsing; twenty of them were laid out in the hotel foyer. Sobhraj's plan to steal their passports was going awry. Two policemen arrived and began to question him. But before he could talk his way out of this corner, Deputy Superintendent Naranda Nath Tuli, who had been hunting Sobhraj, arrived at the hotel. The drugging of tourists had alerted him that Sobhraj might be in Delhi. Now he looked at this young man, who claimed his name was Daniel, and knew the hunt was over. He ordered the police to handcuff Sobhraj. It was 5 July 1976. Sobhraj's career of crime had lasted ten years; in that time he had been responsible for at least ten deaths.

Other accomplices were arrested, including Marie-Andrée. Her relationship with Sobhraj had long ago deteriorated into a non-stop quarrel, and she lost no time in testifying against him. Ajay had vanished. Two other women, Barbara Sheryl Smith and Mary Ellen Eather (who had smuggled in the hacksaw with which he escaped from imprisonment in Greece) were also charged. For the killing of Luke Solomon Sobhraj received a seven-year sentence of hard labour, and for the drugging of the engineering students, two years in jail. 'He will never get out of jail,' said Superintendent Tuli. 'There are still five more cases against him.'

To Richard Neville, co-author of *The Life and Crimes of Charles Sobhraj*, he talked openly about his career, as if anxious to have full details of his crimes recorded. This book, which obviously consolidated the case against Sobhraj, in no way diminished either his confidence in ultimate victory over the courts or his range of criminal activities while in Tihar jail. Using hidden tape-recorders he blackmailed warders into giving him freedom within the prison precincts, allowing him long 'conjugal' visits from two girls who had fallen in love with him on reading his biography (he obligingly proposed marriage to both of them) and a cell filled with luxuries. In the High Court Sobhraj won a case for the removal of leg irons and shackles, which benefited all other prisoners and assured his popularity, and an appeal against the sentence of hard labour which, together with the conviction of murder, was quashed.

In 1982 he was taken under heavy guard to Varanasi to answer the charges of murdering Allen Jacobs. He defended himself with great publicity, sacking his lawyer and staging theatrical protests against the prosecution witnesses. Sobhraj, together with Leclerc, was sentenced to life but intends this time to 'get out of jail by legal means'. He was then taken on to Agra to face robbery charges, which were dropped. The threat of his return to Tihar jail caused an uproar among prison officials who had been congratulating themselves on having got rid of their most troublesome prisoner. In the meantime, Thailand and Nepal join the queue of countries waiting to extradite him.

SOLIS, Magdalena
Monterey prostitute and priestess of a murderous sex cult.

Some time in the early months of 1963, two Mexican brothers, Santos and Cayetano Hernandez, discovered an easy and pleasant way to make a living in the remote village of Yerba Buena. They convinced the villagers that the Inca gods of the mountain were willing to give up their treasures to those who offered them worship and sacrifice. The sacrifices included money and the use of their bodies for sexual purposes; the 'high priest' Cayetano preferred the men, while his brother Santos was interested in women. (The peasants were apparently unaware that the Incas had lived in Peru, and that their own ancient deities would probably be Aztecs.)

However, the villagers became restive when no treasure was forthcoming; the priests silenced them by assuring them that the two chief gods of the Incas would shortly appear among them. The brothers went to Monterey and persuaded a brother and sister – Eleazor and Magdalena Solis – to return with them to impersonate the gods. Magdalena, a blonde, was a prostitute, and her brother was her procurer. Magdalena was lesbian, while Eleazor, like Cayetano, was homosexual.

The Hernandez brothers stage-managed a scene in which Magdalena and her brother made a dramatic appearance; while the cult members were hacking at the walls of the mountain cave in which they performed their religious ceremonies, a handful of flash powder was thrown on to the brazier, and the god and goddess appeared amid the smoke. The peasants assumed that Eleazor was St Francis of Assisi, and he was happy to accept this identity. The beautiful Magdalena began to conduct the religious ceremonies, to everyone's satisfaction. A pretty teenage girl named Celina Salvana had already been recruited as a chief acolyte by the Hernandez brothers, and she was regularly 'purified' by sexual contact with the priest Santos. Now she was shared by Santos and the goddess Magdalena. When Magdalena became jealous, Santos relinquished Celina to her. Meanwhile, Eleazor and Cayetano regularly purified the farmers and able-bodied peasant lads. The only villager who knew what was going on was a man called Jesus Rubio, who had doubted the sanctity of the Hernandez brothers from the beginning, and who had been taken into their confidence and given a share of the takings.

The treasure still failed to materialize, so (according to the account of the case in Brad Steiger's *The Mass Murderer*), Magdalena Solis told the faithful that her fellow gods and goddesses required the villagers to 'sacrifice' the unbelievers among them. The two chief dissenters were promptly beaten to death, and their blood added to the chicken blood that was drunk from a sacrificial bowl. During the next two months, six more unbelievers were killed at the ceremonies. Several others escaped to neighbouring villages.

Celina Salvana began to long for the masculine embraces of the 'high priest' Santos; and when Magdalena heard that she had been defiling herself in the arms of a male, she flew into a murderous rage. At the next meeting of the sex cult, on 28 May 1963, the pretty teenager was bound to a sacrificial cross, knocked unconscious by Magdalena, then beaten to death by the assembled worshippers. All this was witnessed by a fourteen-year-old boy named Sebastian Gurrero who happened to be passing. The boy hoped to become a doctor, and walked every day seventeen miles to the schoolhouse in Villa Gran, which was why he had not heard about the cult in his own village. Now he witnessed with horror the girl being beaten to death, then saw the worshippers pile brush around her body and set it alight. Too frightened to move, he saw Magdalena point out yet another unbeliever, a farmer, who was hacked to death with machetes. Then, in a state of hysteria, he rushed to Villa Gran and reported what he had seen at the police station. The police were inclined to be sceptical. A patrolman named Luis Martinez volunteered to drive over to Yerba Buena to check on the story.

Martinez and Sebastian Gurrero never returned. On 31 May the police in Cuidad Victoria, capital of the state of Tamaulipas, were notified of their disappearance. Police and soldiers descended on the village of Yerba Buena. They found the hacked corpses of the patrolman and the schoolboy; the patrolman's heart had been cut out.

As they approached the cave they were met with rifle fire. Three policemen were wounded, but the soldiers' response soon induced the besieged cultists to surrender. Santos Hernandez was killed by a bullet. His brother Cayetano had vanished. The cultists told the police that the Inca gods would strike them dead for blasphemy. In fact, the Inca gods were both in a deep sleep induced by marijuana. Both were arrested.

Jesus Rubio finally admitted that he was responsible for the disappearance of Cayetano; he had killed him, intending to take his place as high priest.

Magdalena and her brother, together with twelve other cult members, were brought to trial on 13 June 1963, and all received sentences of thirty years in jail.

SPECK, Richard
Killer of eight nurses in a Chicago hostel.

Around midnight on 13 July 1966 there was a knock on the door of a young Philippino nurse, Corazon Amurao, in the nurses' hostel at Jeffrey Manor, Chicago. Sleepily, she opened the door, and found herself confronting a rather good-looking, pock-marked young man who smelt strongly of alcohol; he was pointing a gun at her. He ordered the nurse down the hall to another bedroom, where three nurses were sleeping, made them get up, then herded the four into yet another bedroom, where there were two more. The man kept assuring the nurses that he had no intention of hurting them, but that he needed money to go to New Orleans. He sliced up sheets with a knife, and bound and gagged each girl, asking them where they kept their money. At 12.30 three more nurses entered the dormitory; the man pointed the gun at them and tied them up. When he had collected all the money, and nine bound and gagged girls, all aged between twenty and twenty-three, lay on the floor, the man sat on the bed fingering his knife. Then he took one of the girls out into the next room. A few minutes later, another one. Corazon Amurao, certain his intention was rape, began struggling to free herself, suggesting they should all attack him; another Philippino, Merlita Gargullo, agreed with her, but the others seemed to feel that rape was preferable to provoking the man to violence. Seeing that no one was prepared to act, Miss Amurao rolled under a bunk bed. She could hear a tiny scream as each girl was taken into the next room. Finally, only one – Gloria Davy – was left. The man came back and removed her jeans, and raped her for about twenty-five minutes, asking her at one point, 'Would you mind putting your legs around my back?' Then he took her out too.

At 5 am Miss Amurao was alone, and the killer seemed to have left. She rolled out from under the bed, and looked into the next room. What she saw sent her running on to the balcony, shouting: 'All my friends are dead!'

A man and a woman, walking a dog, heard her and ran underneath the balcony. 'Just wait there. Don't jump!'

They summoned the police, who entered the hostel by the back door, and found a naked, mutilated girl on a couch. It was Gloria Davy. Another corpse lay half out of the window of an upstairs bathroom. In one bedroom there were three more corpses, the place covered in blood. The remaining three bodies were in another bedroom. The man had behaved exactly like a fox in a poultry farm, killing for the joy of killing. The only nurse who had been raped – and sodomized – was Gloria Davy. Merlita Gargullo had been killed by one deep stab in the neck. Mary Jordan was stabbed in the heart, neck and left eye. Susan Farris had been mutilated, stabbed nine times, and strangled. Pat Matuske had been strangled only. Pam Wilkening had been stabbed in the heart. Nina Schmale had been slashed in the neck and strangled. Valentina Pasion had been stabbed four times and strangled.

Corazon Amurao was able to describe the killer; she had noticed a tattoo on his arm bearing the words 'Born to raise hell'. There were other clues. The hands of the girls had been tied with the palms together, the way a policeman handcuffs his prisoners; that suggested an ex-convict. The square knots were the kind tied by seamen. The man had spoken of returning to New Orleans.

Half a block away from the hostel was the hiring hall of the seaman's union; police quickly learned that a pock-marked man with a tattoo had been inquiring about a ship to New Orleans two days earlier, and had returned on Wednesday – the day of the murders –

to fill in an application form. He had left his name, Richard F. Speck, and his sister's telephone number. The police also learned that Speck had heard that the nurses often sunbathed in the backyards of their hostels, and he had been wandering around the park behind Jeffrey Manor, hoping for a glimpse of naked girls.

The police rang the number of Speck's sister, declaring that a job was now available. Speck rang back, and promised to be along in half an hour, but failed to turn up. The police knew he was their man; Corazon Amurao had identified his photograph – clipped to the application form – as the killer.

Detectives began combing the kind of lodging houses that sailors stayed in. They found a hotel on North Dearborn street with Speck's name in the register – but he had checked out half an hour ago. They found a hotel where Speck had been seen the evening after the murders. He had been with a prostitute named Mary, and then later picked up and left with another prostitute. It seemed he had an insatiable sexual appetite. He had paid one of them $30. Yet on the previous day, they discovered, he had been drinking so heavily that he had been forced to switch from beer to cheap wine.

On 15 July a policeman was called to another small hotel on Dearborn Street, at the complaint of a prostitute, who said that the man she had spent the night with had a gun. Probably Speck had jokingly pointed it at her; the previous evening, he had grabbed a bartender round the throat and pressed a twelve-inch hunting knife against him, claiming that it had killed several people. The bartender had told him to quit horsing around. The policeman confiscated Speck's gun and ammunition, but as the name of the suspect had not yet been released, he had no reason to arrest him. A few hours later, detectives were surrounding the hotel – only to be told again that they had just missed Speck.

The following day the man in charge of the case, Superintendent Wilson, announced on television that the man they wanted to interview was Richard Speck, and the camera focussed on Speck's photograph.

Speck had registered in a small room in the Starr Hotel, West Madison Street, under the name of B. Brian. But he had spent all the money he had taken from the nurses, and badly needed a drink. He pestered his next-door neighbour for one several times. At midnight, he again knocked on the door, and when the neighbour – George Gregrich – opened it, fell into the room, bleeding from slashed wrists. Twenty minutes later, Speck was at the Cook County

Hospital. Dr LeRoy Smith, the resident surgeon, noticed the tattoo 'Born to raise hell'. He had seen an item about it in the evening paper. He ordered the nurse to ring the police. The man asked in a whisper: 'Do you collect the $10,000, doc?'

Speck had been born in Kirkwood, Illinois, on 6 December 1941, and at twenty had married a fifteen-year-old girl; they had a daughter. Speck and his wife had separated, and he bore her a deep grudge, declaring that he would go back to Texas and kill her if it was the last thing he did. Significantly, his wife resembled the only nurse who had been sexually attacked, Gloria Davy. In 1965, while still living with his wife, Speck had been arrested for pressing a carving knife against the throat of a woman who was parking her car in her garage. A neighbour heard her screams, and Speck ran away. He was caught, and sentenced to 490 days in jail; he was released shortly before the authorities in Huntsville were able to catch up with him as a parole violator.

In March 1966 he had returned to the town where he had been brought up, Monmouth, Illinois; Speck's brother still lived there, and he found Speck a job as a carpenter. But his brother was not a satisfactory employee. He spent a lot of time drinking heavily, was obsessed by sex, and boasted about his conquests and his toughness – he had lived for years on the ore barges on the Great Lakes. Girls would talk to him – Corazon Amurao even described him as gentle-looking – but seemed to have no desire to get to know him better. He had pestered a divorcee, Mary Pierce – who worked in a bar – for a date, but she declined. On 10 April she disappeared. Her naked corpse was found three days later in a hog house behind the bar. Five days later, a 65-year-old woman reported that she had been raped and robbed, and the rapist sounded like Speck; when police arrived to question him, he had disappeared to the ore boats again. On 3 May he had to be rushed into hospital for an appendectomy, and made friends with a nurse. On 23 June Speck took her swimming and dancing. She observed that he had a lot of hatred in him – he said there were two people in Texas he would kill if he got the chance. On 27 June Speck again went on an ore boat, but was dismissed in Indiana Harbour five days later. That day, in nearby Dunes Park, three girls vanished, leaving clothes behind them in the car. They had obviously been wearing swimsuits. Their bodies were never found. And when police investigating the murder of the eight nurses learned about this, they also discovered that there had been another mass murder in Benton Harbour, Michigan, about fifty miles from Indiana Harbour, in February; the ages of the females who had been stabbed to death ranged from seven to sixty. Speck had recently arrived in the area, en route to Monmouth.

In prison, Speck was interviewed by a psychiatrist, Dr Marvin Ziporyn, who gave it as his opinion that Speck was in a trance on the night he killed the nurses. He had taken various pills as well as huge quantities of alcohol. He may have intended only to rob the women, until the sight of Gloria Davy triggered a mechanism of violence. Speck had been neurotic since childhood – he had once hit himself on the head with a hammer, in anger with his father, and had later suffered more head injuries in a brawl. His normal manner was anything but homicidal – a man who knew Speck described him as 'a charmer'.

Speck was sentenced to more than six hundred years in jail. In 1976, an appeal for parole was refused.

STÜLLGENS, Robert Wilhelm
Compulsive German sex-killer.

On 12 June 1980 neighbours of the Deck family, who lived in a block of flats at 12 Tussmannstrasse, Düsseldorf, asked the police to check on their apartment, since no one had heard or seen them for two days. In the apartment, police found the naked body of Margret Deck, and her children, Thomas, two, and the baby, Christian, six weeks old. All three had been stabbed to death. Her husband, Wilhelm Deck, was missing.

A few days later, checking on a report from another neighbour, the police broke into a flat in the building which had been occupied by a man called Stüllgens. There they found the body of Wilhelm Deck, who had been stabbed in the back.

A check with police records revealed that Robert Stüllgens, aged thirty, had been released from prison only a few months previously. He had been serving a term for raping a young mother in a park and attempting to rape the child. He had explained at the time that he was unable to control himself.

Stüllgens was arrested in Essen, where his mother lived, and taken back to Düsseldorf where he admitted to the murders of the Deck family. He had seen Margret Deck in the basement of the block of flats, and immediately felt a compulsive need to have sex with her. He had waited for her husband to come home from work, and asked him to help move some furniture. As soon as the husband was in

Stüllgens' flat, he was stabbed to death. Stüllgens then took his keys, let himself into the Deck apartment, and waited for Margret to come home with the children. He forced her to strip and to perform an act of fellatio on him, before stabbing her and the two children to death.

He was sentenced to life imprisonment.

SUTCLIFFE, Peter
The Yorkshire Ripper.

The reign of terror by the man who became known as the Yorkshire Ripper began on 29 October 1975, with the murder of Wilma McCann, and ended on 2 January 1981, when Peter Sutcliffe was arrested in Sheffield with a prostitute who was almost certainly intended as his fourteenth murder victim.

The attacks on Yorkshire women began on 5 July 1975, when a woman named Anna Rogulskyj was struck on the head with a hammer. On 15 August Olive Smelt was knocked unconscious by a hammer blow from behind. The attacker slashed both women – Mrs Smelt's buttocks were cut. Both recovered after brain surgery.

On 29 October Wilma McCann, a Scotswoman who had separated from her husband and taken to prostitution, left her four children to go on a pub crawl in Leeds. In the early hours of the following morning, she was struck on the head from behind with a ball-headed hammer, then dragged into a playing field. Here the killer pulled up her dress, and inflicted injuries on the stomach, chest and in the genital area with a knife and, possibly, other tools.

From then on, the murders followed in regular succession. The Ripper's next victim, Emily Jackson, was a housewife who had three children. Her husband was a roofing specialist who often worked in the evenings; his wife would drive him to the job and collect him a few hours later. What Sydney Jackson did not know was that during those hours his wife supplemented her income by soliciting from the van she drove. On the evening of 20 January 1976 she failed to return for him and he took a taxi home. The following morning, his wife's body was found in a narrow passageway in Leeds, the head battered unrecognizably, and with fifty stab wounds in her chest.

More than a year passed before the Ripper struck again. Irene Richardson was separated from her husband; her two children lived with foster parents. She was not a professional prostitute, but had 'fallen on hard times' and hung around street corners. The Ripper picked her up on the evening of 5 February 1977 and drove her to Roundhay Park, Leeds. Her body was found the following morning by a jogger; she was lying near the sports pavilion.

A Bradford prostitute, Tina Atkinson, picked up the Ripper on 23 April and took him to her flat in Oak Avenue. The following morning a male friend found the door unlocked. Tina Atkinson was dead in bed; a police surgeon said she had been battered unconscious and been the victim of a 'frenzied sexual attack' – although she had not been raped.

Sixteen-year-old Jayne MacDonald was an unusually pretty girl who spent the evening of 25 June 1977 dancing at the Hofbrauhaus in the centre of Leeds, and was not far from her home, near Roundhay Park, when the Ripper knocked her unconscious, dragged her behind a fence, and stabbed her again and again. Possibly he mistook her for a prostitute – she lived only six doors from Wilma McCann in the notorious Chapeltown area.

On 27 July Maureen Long was walking through central Bradford when the Ripper drew up in his car and propositioned her. Soon afterwards, he was dragging the unconscious woman away from the street lights. But something disturbed him, and he left her there and hurried away. She recovered after a brain operation, and was able to say that her assailant had been driving a white Ford Cortina. She said he had blond hair – a detail that was discovered to be inaccurate when Sutcliffe was arrested four years later.

The Ripper crossed the Pennines, and claimed his next victim in Manchester on 1 October. During the early morning he encountered a twenty-year-old Scots girl, Jean Jordan, and took her to the Southern Cemetery. There he killed her with exceptional violence, stripping her naked and mutilating the body. Her clothes were scattered all around. She was the common-law wife of a chef, Alan Royle, who had picked her up on his way home from work five years earlier when she had just run away from her home in Motherwell. The couple had two children, but they had begun to drift apart not long before her death, and she spent her evenings away from home with 'friends'. She had, in fact, worked as a prostitute and taken clients back to her flat while her husband was at work. The body was not found until nine days later, when the medical examination revealed that the murderer had killed her with eleven blows to the head, and stabbed her twenty-four times. Eight days later, he had returned to the body and torn off all the clothing then stabbed and slashed her several times more, tearing open the abdomen and making a long wound from the left shoulder to the right knee.

In this case, the police at last found a clue. In Jean Jordan's handbag there was a new £5 note, which had been issued at Shipley, Yorkshire, only four days before the murder. It seemed probable that the killer had handed it to her. The police traced the batch of notes to the depot where Sutcliffe worked as a lorry-driver, and questioned him. Since there appeared to be no evidence to connect him with the murders, he was cleared.

By early 1978 the hunt for the Ripper had become one of the largest police operations ever mounted in northern England. George Oldfield, the assistant chief constable in charge of the case, gave colleagues the impression that his search for the Ripper had become a personal crusade. Police work on the case was exhaustive; the police were willing to pursue any lead, no matter how tenuous.

The Ripper decided to move to Huddersfield to find his next victim: he felt that police activity in Leeds was becoming too intensive. Helen and Rita Rytka were eighteen-year-old twins, and much of their lives had been spent in the care of the social services. In 1977 they decided that prostitution was an easier way of making a living than factory work, and they would wait to be picked up by cruising cars. On the evening of 31 January Helen was picked up by a car shortly after nine, and Rita soon after. When Rita was dropped off later, there was no sign of Helen. And when Helen had still not returned by the next morning, Rita began to fear the worst. Later that morning, a lorry-driver noticed a pair of black lace briefs near a timber yard close to the flat shared by the twins. The yard foreman hung them up on a nail 'for the lads to laugh at'. Two days later Rita Rytka went to the police and reported that her sister had disappeared. The police immediately suspected another Ripper killing, and searched the timber yard. Helen's body was found underneath an archway, screened by timber, and lying under a piece of corrugated asbestos. She was naked, and had been battered unconscious, then stabbed in the chest area. Medical evidence showed that on this occasion, the killer had had sexual intercourse with her – probably after knocking her unconscious but before stabbing her.

By this time the police suspected that the Ripper was responsible for another disappearance. Ten days before Helen Rytka was killed, Yvonne Pearson had set out to ply her trade around Bradford's city centre; she left her two small children at home with a baby sitter. She never returned. Two months later a man crossing a piece of waste ground noticed a human arm protruding from under an abandoned settee. The head had been battered so violently that the skull had shattered into twenty-one fragments. Stuffing from the settee had been rammed down her throat, presumably to stifle screams or groans. Lack of stab wounds left some doubt whether this was another Ripper victim. Sutcliffe later admitted that he had been disturbed when another car drew up alongside.

In Manchester, on 16 May, a forty-year-old prostitute named Vera Millward was expecting a regular client who failed to turn up; so, leaving her two children in the charge of her common-law Jamaican husband, she went off in search of another client. At 1.15 am a man visiting the Royal Infirmary heard three screams and a cry for help, then silence. The next morning, Vera Millward's body was found lying near a flower bed – a favourite site for prostitutes. The blows to her skull had been so violent that it had virtually disintegrated. She had also been stabbed many times.

So far, all the victims but Jayne MacDonald had been prostitutes, and it seemed probable that the Ripper had mistaken her for one. But the next victim, nineteen-year-old Josephine Whitaker, was clearly not a prostitute. She had spent the evening of 4 April 1979 watching television at her grandparents' home in Halifax, then walked home towards midnight. The Ripper had attacked her as she was crossing Savile Park, fracturing her skull from ear to ear. Then he stabbed her frenziedly with a rusty screwdriver which had been specially sharpened. He pulled up her clothes and stabbed her in the vagina several times. The police found traces of oil on the body, and inferred – correctly – that the killer worked in an engineering factory.

It seemed clear that the killer was now prepared to murder any woman when the urge was upon him. The next victim was a student at Bradford University, Barbara Leach, who had spent the evening of 1 September at the Mannville Arms, not far from the university. She left at about 1 am, and told her friends she wanted a breath of air before going to bed at her flat in Grove Terrace. Her body was found a day later against a dustbin in a back alley, close to the spot where she had been last seen. She had been covered with old carpets held down with bricks. She had been stabbed repeatedly with a pointed weapon – the same rusty screwdriver that had killed Josephine Whitaker.

By this time there had been a new development in the case. In 1978 and 1979 the police had received three letters signed 'Jack the Ripper' threatening more murders. Then on 26 June 1979 the police received a cassette – addressed in the same handwriting as the three letters – containing the voice of the Ripper. Speaking with a slow Geordie accent, obviously reading aloud, the voice taunted George Oldfield for failing to catch him: 'You can't be much good, can you?' He promised to strike again, and warned that if the police got too close he would probably 'top' himself (commit suicide). The tape was treated seriously – although after Sutcliffe's arrest it became clear that both tape and letters were from a hoaxer – and the police wasted much time looking for the letter-writer in the Wearside area. In July George Oldfield became ill from overwork on the case, and suffered a heart attack.

On 20 August Marguerite Walls, a civil servant in the Department of Education at Pudsey, worked late until 10.45, and was making her way home to Farsley when she encountered the Ripper. He knocked her unconscious with a blow on the head, then dragged her into a garden and ripped off most of her clothes. He then knelt on her ribs – breaking three of them – and strangled her with a piece of rope (Sutcliffe later explained that he did not have his knife with him). Then he covered the body with grass cuttings.

The next two victims survived. In October 1979 Sutcliffe walked up behind Dr Upadhya Bandara, from Singapore, who was returning home from a course in the Nuffield Centre in Leeds, and threw a rope round her neck. He hit her on the head and dragged her down the road, then changed his mind – he later claimed to have apologized – and left her. A few weeks later, on 5 November, he came close to being caught when he attacked sixteen-year-old Theresa Sykes near her home in Huddersfield. Her boyfriend heard her screams and ran to her aid. The Ripper had knocked her to the ground, but he ran away.

Possibly it was this close shave with capture that made Sutcliffe decide to lie low for a while. His final murder took place more than a year later. Twenty-year-old Jacqueline Hill, a Leeds University student, had attended a meeting of voluntary probation officers on 17 November 1980, and caught a bus back to her lodgings soon after 9 pm. An hour later, her handbag was found near some waste ground by an Iraqi student, and he called the police. It was a windy and rainy night and they found nothing. Jacqueline Hill's body was found the next morning on the waste ground. She had been battered unconscious with a hammer, then undressed and stabbed repeatedly. One wound was in the eye – Sutcliffe later said she seemed to be looking at him reproachfully, so he drove the blade into her eye.

This was the Ripper's last attack. On 2 January 1981 a black prostitute named Olive Reivers had just finished with a client in the centre of Sheffield when a Rover car drove up, and a bearded man asked her how much she charged; she said it would be £10 for sex in the car, and climbed in the front. He seemed tense and asked if she would object if he talked for a while about his family problems. When he asked her to get in the back of the car, she said she would prefer to have sex in the front; this may have saved her life – Sutcliffe had stunned at least one of his victims as she climbed into the back of the car. He moved on top of her, but was unable to maintain an erection. He moved off her again, and at this point, a police car pulled up in front. Sutcliffe hastily told the woman to say she was his girlfriend. The police asked his name, and he told them it was Peter Williams. Sergeant Robert Ring and PC Robert Hydes were on patrol duty, and they were carrying out a standard check. Ring noted the number-plate then went off to check it with the computer; while he radioed, he told PC Hydes to get into the back of the Rover. Sutcliffe asked if he could get out to urinate and Hydes gave permission; Sutcliffe stood by an oil storage tank a few feet away, then got back into the car. Meanwhile, the sergeant had discovered that the number-plates did not belong to the Rover, and told Sutcliffe he would have to return to the police station. In the station, Sutcliffe again asked to go to the lavatory and was given permission. It was when the police made him empty his pockets and found a length of clothes-line that they began to suspect that they might have trapped Britain's most wanted man.

To begin with, Sutcliffe lied fluently about why he was carrying the rope and why he was in the car with a prostitute. It was the following day that Sergeant Ring learned about Sutcliffe's brief absence from the car to relieve himself, and went to look near the oil storage tank. In the leaves, he found a ball-headed hammer and a knife. Then he recalled Sutcliffe's trip to the lavatory at the police station. In the cistern he found a second knife. When Sutcliffe was told that he was in serious trouble, he suddenly admitted that he was the Ripper, and confessed to eleven murders. (It seems odd that he got the number wrong – he was later charged with thirteen – but it is possible that he genuinely lost count. He was originally suspected of fourteen murders, but the police later decided that the killing of another prostitute, Jean Harrison – whose body was found in Preston, Lancashire – was not one of the series. She had been raped and the semen was not of Sutcliffe's blood group.)

315

A card written by Sutcliffe and displayed in his lorry read: 'In this truck is a man whose latent genius, if unleashed, would rock the nation, whose dynamic energy would overpower those around him. Better let him sleep?'

The story that began to emerge was of a lonely and shy individual, brooding and introverted, who was morbidly fascinated by prostitutes and red-light areas. He was born on 2 June 1946, the eldest of five children and his mother's favourite. His school career was undistinguished and he left at fifteen. He drifted aimlessly from job to job, including one as a grave-digger in the Bingley cemetery, from which he was dismissed for bad timekeeping. (His later attempt at a defence of insanity rested on a claim that a voice had spoken to him from a cross in the cemetery telling him he had a God-given mission to kill prostitutes.)

In 1967, when he was twenty-one, he met a sixteen-year-old Czech girl, Sonia Szurma, in a pub, and they began going out together. It would be another seven years before they married. The relationship seems to have been stormy; at one point, she was going out with an ice-cream salesman, and Sutcliffe picked up a prostitute 'to get even'. He was unable to have intercourse, and the woman went off with a £10 note and failed to return with his £5 change. When he saw her in a pub two weeks later and asked for the money, she jeered at him and left him with a sense of helpless fury and humiliation. This, he claimed, was the source of his hatred of prostitutes. In 1969 he made his first attack on a prostitute, hitting her on the head with a sock full of gravel. In October of that year, he was caught carrying a hammer and charged with being equipped for theft; he was fined £25. In 1971 he went for a drive with a friend, Trevor Birdsall, and left the car in the red-light area of Bradford. When he returned ten minutes later he said, 'Drive off quickly,' and admitted that he had hit a woman with a brick in a sock. Sutcliffe was again driving with Birdsall in 1975 on the evening that Olive Smelt was struck down with a hammer.

In 1972 Sonia Szurma went to London for a teacher's training course and had a nervous breakdown; she was diagnosed as schizophrenic. Two years later, she and Sutcliffe married, but the marriage was punctuated by violent rows – Sutcliffe said he became embarrassed in case the neighbours heard the shouts, implying that it was she who was shouting rather than he. He also told the prostitute Olive Reivers that he had been arguing with his wife 'about not being able to go with her', which Olive Reivers took to mean that they were having sexual problems. Certainly, this combination of two introverted people can hardly have improved Sutcliffe's mental condition.

Sutcliffe's first murder – of Wilma McCann – took place in the year after he married Sonia. He admitted: 'I developed and played up a hatred for prostitutes . . .' Unlike the Düsseldorf sadist of the 1920s, Peter Kürten, Sutcliffe never admitted to having orgasms as he stabbed his victims; but anyone acquainted with the psychology of sexual criminals would take it for granted that this occurred, and that in most of the cases where the victim was not stabbed, or was left alive, he achieved orgasm at an earlier stage than usual. The parallels are remarkable. Kürten, like Sutcliffe, used a variety of weapons, including a hammer. On one occasion when a corpse remained undiscovered, Kürten also returned to inflict fresh indignities on it. Sutcliffe had returned to the body of Jean Jordan and attempted to cut off the head with a hacksaw.

It was when he pulled up Wilma McCann's clothes and stabbed her in the breast and abdomen that Sutcliffe realized that he had discovered a new sexual thrill. With the second victim, Emily Jackson, he pulled off her bra and briefs, then stabbed her repeatedly – he was, in effect, committing rape with a knife. Sutcliffe was caught in the basic trap of the sex criminal: the realization that he had found a way of inducing a far, more powerful sexual satisfaction than he was able to obtain in normal intercourse, and that he was pushing himself into the position of a social outcast. He admitted sobbing in his car after one of the murders, and being upset to discover that Jayne MacDonald had not been a prostitute (and later, that her father had died of a broken heart). But the compulsion to kill was becoming a fever, so that he no longer cared that the later victims were not prostitutes. He said, probably with sincerity, 'The devil drove me.'

Sutcliffe's trial began on 5 May 1981. He had pleaded not guilty to murder on grounds of diminished responsibility, and told the story of his 'mission' from God. But a warder had overheard him tell his wife that if he could convince the jury that he was mad, he would only spend ten years in a 'loony bin'. The Attorney-General, Sir Michael Havers, also pointed out that Sutcliffe had at first behaved perfectly normally, laughing at the idea that he might be mentally abnormal, and had introduced the talk of 'voices' fairly late in his admissions to the police. On 22 May Sutcliffe was found guilty of murder, and jailed for life, with a recommendation that he should serve at least thirty years.

T

TERRORISM
The world's most sinister growth industry.

1981 was a vintage year for terrorism, which knows no frontiers. It began on 1 January with the bombing, still unresolved, of the Norfolk Hotel in Nairobi with the loss of sixteen lives. There was no established motive, no claim for responsibility, only suspicion. The hotel is Jewish owned. A German-speaking woman and her companion (travelling on a Maltese passport) who left the hotel shortly before the attack and have not been traced since, point to the likelihood of yet another combined Arab-West German terrorist operation.

In June 'counter-revolutionary' terrorists supporting the deposed President Bani-Sadr set off a time-bomb in Tehran which killed seventy-four people, and decimated the ruling Islamic Republican Party. In August a second 'counter-revolutionary' bomb, smuggled this time into the prime minister's private office, killed him and the new president outright. In October, the same month as the IRA strike at London, terrorists from the little-known 'Front for the Liberation of Lebanon from Foreigners' exploded a car bomb outside the offices of the PLO in Beirut and slaughtered a hundred people. Yet perhaps the most desolate terrorist attack of all in 1981 came on 13 May, with the attempted assassination of Pope John.

Although he was hit by five bullets fired at almost point-blank range, the Pope survived; other than its known connection with terrorism the attempt – mercifully – has no place in this encyclopaedia. That connection, however, gives rise to the question most people asked on hearing the news, regardless of religious denomination: who would want to murder such a patently good man? What could have been the motive? Although nothing has been finally established, reports leaked to the press say that Mehmet Ali Agca, the 'Grey Wolf' Turkish terrorist who pulled the trigger, did so at the behest of the Bulgarian secret service: which of course is directly linked with the KGB. The theory is that the order was given to kill the Pope because the Western-based Catholic Church holds too much sway in Poland, the weakest link in the Communist chain. All such reports are strenuously denied by Russia and Bulgaria.

By definition, no *Encyclopaedia of Modern Murder* could be reckoned complete without reference to this 'most sinister growth industry' – a *Times* headline in 1981 – whose by-product is murder. During the 1970s there were more than 2,600 bombings and explosions, 700 cases of arson and firebombing, kidnappings and hijackings galore. The most sinister growth rate of all came in selective assassination, which soared from seventeen cases in 1971 to an astronomical 1,169 in 1980. While there is space only to review a handful of terrorist killings in detail, the fact is that terrorist murder now forms part of our daily news throughout the Western world. No official details are available of terrorist activity, if any, within the Soviet Union or its satellite countries.

In Northern Ireland it is as commonplace for a person to be killed or maimed by terrorist attack as it is for a child to be born. Not even the sick in hospital are spared. On mainland Britain men and women with only a passing interest in politics – far less influence over events in Ulster – may find themselves at risk window-shopping in Oxford Street, sipping a pint of beer in a Birmingham pub, or even listening to the band in Regent's Park on a sunny afternoon. Death from a terrorist bullet or bomb can come just as easily and as unprovoked elsewhere in Europe; to Italian families waiting to board a train at Bologna, to Jewish families attending service at any synagogue in France, to air travellers changing planes at Athens – a favourite hunting ground for Arab terrorists – and to every policeman on duty in Spain. And the chances of being killed by terrorists (or counter-terrorist activists) are infinitely greater for all who live in the Central American republics, such as El Salvador, Guatemala and Nicaragua, and Namibia, Angola and Zimbabwe in Africa. There are terrorist organizations fighting some cause or other from Morocco to the Philippines, from West Germany to South Africa, in Tokyo as well as Belfast, and right through the Americas from Argentina to Canada. In 1977 Captain Frank Bolz, New York City's police department specialist in terrorism, reckoned there were 140 'clearly defined' terrorist groups then active in the world. That number has since grown, and there are proven links between some of the more militant organizations.

Japanese Red Army terrorists, acting on behalf of the Arab PFLP (Popular Front for the Liberation of Palestine) carried out the attack on Lod airport in 1972 (see Okamoto, Kozo), but this was clearly no one-off mercenary arrangement. It took months of careful international co-operation to bring about. The three Japanese involved were first given the specialist training required to carry out a Middle East/European operation at Arab guerrilla camps in the Lebanon and Jordan; flown out via Beirut to Rome, where they were met by other terrorists who arranged their hotel accommodation, issued them with Soviet-made Kalachnikov automatic rifles and grenades and – presumably – false passports and onward flight tickets to Tel Aviv. The weapons were packed in suitcases and sent aboard as baggage-hold cargo, thus ensuring that the gunmen themselves would pass normal screening tests. Their instructions at Lod international airport were to await the arrival of an El Al flight, due ten minutes after their own touchdown, before opening fire 'so as to kill as many Israelis as possible'. In the event these were either ignored or misunderstood by the Japanese. At his trial Okamoto said, 'We did all this in co-operation with the PFLP. We did it in partnership with them.' Such meticulous planning, which took Israeli security – reckoned to be the best in the world – completely by surprise might have come straight from the pages of a novel.

In October 1977 four Arab terrorists from the PFLP returned the compliment, by attempting to win freedom for thirteen members of the Baader-Meinhof gang awaiting trial in West Germany. They hijacked a Lufthansa plane and murdered the pilot at Dubai before they moved on to Mogadishu, where they were overwhelmed by a combat team of West German commandos (see Baader-Meinhof Gang). Three of the PFLP terrorists were killed outright, the fourth – a woman – was wounded. In 1978 the PFLP organized an attack in London on unarmed aircrew from El Al, the Israeli airline. That operation was reportedly financed from ransom money paid out by the OPEC countries for the safe return of the eleven delegates kidnapped in Vienna in 1975 (see Sanchez, Ilyich Ramirez).

Mr Charles Russell of the US Air Force Directorate of Counter-Intelligence said in 1978 that 'the largest number of foreign terrorists who have co-operated with the Palestinians during the last nine years came from West Germany,' and added 'probably . . . more Germans have been involved than Palestinians'. He also said that the PFLP had received assistance from 'one or more terrorists from the Netherlands, Brazil, France, Venezuela, Britain, Colombia, Turkey, Algeria, Egypt, Libya, Jordan, Lebanon and Italy'.

While all individual terrorist organizations raise funds by kidnapping, robbery, blackmail and private subscription (for instance,

NORAID, the Irish Northern Aid Committee, which raises cash in the United States for the IRA), the man generally acknowledged to act as unofficial banker for world terrorism is Colonel Gaddafi. On 5 August 1977 US Senator H. John Heinz II declared, 'Perhaps the nation most responsible for aid to terrorism is Libya. In recent years, Libya has been the resting and planning place for several international terrorists; Ilyich Ramirez Sanchez, better known as Carlos, mastermind of the 1975 raid on the OPEC ministers conference in Vienna; the Japanese Red Army attackers of the American consulate in Kuala Lumpur; Hans Joachim Klein, a member of the Carlos attack team at Vienna; and Wilfred Bose, another Carlos associate, killed last June by Israeli soldiers during the rescue of hostages in Entebbe, Uganda. The Libyans, however, supply much more than asylum to their "guests". Libya is . . . the traditional armourer and financier of terrorist groups.'

That is not simply an unofficial viewpoint. In a letter to Senator Jacob Javits in 1978, the US State Department accused four countries – Libya, Iraq, South Yemen and Somalia – of assisting terrorists. The State Department said Libya had provided refuge for terrorists on eight occasions, including the Black September squad responsible for the Munich Olympics massacre and the attack on a TWA airliner in Athens in 1973. Of Iraq it said: 'To what degree Baghdad provides financial, military, logistical or training support is unclear, but it appears that a substantial degree of support goes to one renegade Fatah group and the Waddi Haddad wing of the PFLP, both of which carry out international terrorist activities.' It also accused South Yemen (formerly the British colony of Aden) of giving sanctuary to terrorists, and Somalia of involvement in the kidnapping of the French ambassador at Mogadishu in 1975 plus the hijacking of a school bus in Djibouti a year later.

In 1977 Chancellor Helmut Schmidt of West Germany warned that terrorism could trigger off a new world war. He was delivering the annual Alastair Buchan lecture at London's Institute of Strategic Studies, and called for a united front against those terrorists, 'whose sole aim is to destroy the fabric of our liberal society . . . The world can no longer make light of terrorist violence as the work of people who have simply been led astray by allegedly political motives.'

While terrorism in one form or another has been with us for centuries, it has never before been so widespread and concerted. In the splendidly detailed *Political Terrorism* the authors remind us that '. . . Latin America in the 1960s was the home ground of several prominent theorists of political violence – for example, Ernesto (Che) Guevara, Carlos Marighella, General Alberto Bayo – as well as the scene in which their theories were put into practice. In this period and the years that followed, such developments as attacks on diplomats and hijackings of aircraft began to give terrorism in Latin America an increasingly international colouration – and made it increasingly a matter for international concern. . . .'

Few South American countries have been so plagued by terrorists as Argentina. Between 1958 and 1960 alone it suffered an estimated five thousand terrorist incidents. Then, after a period of comparitive calm, a new wave of terrorism began in 1970, coinciding with the revival of the movement for the return of Peron. Twenty were shot dead and three hundred wounded in the huge crowd which greeted him on arrival at Ezeiza airport. By the time his widow assumed the presidency following his death in 1974, terrorism from both rightist and leftist groups was rampant throughout the country. By early 1976 it was estimated that one kidnapping every twenty minutes took place somewhere in Argentina.

Best organized, biggest and most militant of the Argentinian terrorist organizations was the Trotskyist ERP (Peoples Revolutionary Army). A typical operation on 21 March 1972 was the kidnapping of Oberdan Sallustro, president of the giant Fiat combine. ERP demanded a $50 million ransom from Fiat for his safe return, together with the release of fifty political prisoners. Fiat were said to be willing to pay, but General Lanusse, the Argentine president, refused to negotiate with the kidnappers. When police finally found the suburban house in Buenos Aires where Sallustro was held prisoner and forced their way in, he had already been executed by his captors. The one terrorist caught was interrogated and tortured. As a result twenty-six more ERP terrorists, more than half of them women, were brought to trial. Some of the allegations of torture were upheld by the judge: three of the accused were jailed for life, seven others given prison sentences ranging from one to twelve years.

In a combined operation on 10 April 1972 ERP and a second leftist group called FAR (Revolutionary Armed Forces) assassinated General Carlos Sanchez, commanding the 2 Corps anti-guerrilla drive in the Rosario sector north-west of the capital. Eight months later FAR gunmen shot dead anti-terrorist intelligence co-ordinator Rear Admiral Emilio Berisso near Buenos Aires. In April 1973 Colonel Hector A. Iribarren, head of intelligence in 3 Army Corps, was killed by Montoneros (Peronist left-wing) terrorists in Cordoba.

In a spectacular kidnap bid they rammed his car but shot him dead when he attempted to run for it. In a revenge attack the same month, ERP gunmen murdered Rear Admiral Hermes Quijada as he drove through Buenos Aires: he had been chairman of the Joint Chiefs of Staff when prison guards at Trelew, in the south of the country, shot and killed sixteen of their comrades when they allegedly tried to escape in 1972. After Quijada's assassination the military government declared a state of emergency in the five main provinces of Buenos Aires, Santa Fe, Cordoba, Mendoza and Tucuman, but the order was soon rescinded and acts of terrorism continued unabated.

Diplomats and foreign businessmen were kidnapped, ransom money totalling millions of dollars was paid out, politicians, government officials and military leaders were assassinated in the widespread unrest. In two days in May 1974, there were thirty bombings in Buenos Aires and Cordoba. In 1976 the Junta outlawed the leftist organizations. Their members, together with non-terrorists suspected of left-wing sympathies, were then hunted down in a new reign of terror by right-wing 'death squads' such as the AAA (Argentinian Anti-Communist Alliance). 'Death squad' was the collective name given to groups composed of off-duty police and military whose prisoners mostly 'disappeared'. By the end of the decade the army of 'the Disappeared' in Argentina was believed to number up to thirty thousand.

On 28 April 1983 the Argentine junta published a report saying that all the 'Desaparecidos' – the Disappeared – must now be regarded as dead. The report stated: 'Many of the casualties in confrontation with the legal forces did not have any identity documents, or had false papers. In many cases their fingerprints were erased. In these cases, bodies were not reclaimed and because of the impossibility of identifying them, they were . . . legally buried as NN (no name).' The report offered no explanation for the erasure of the victims' fingerprints, and added that the soldiers and policemen involved were following orders, and their actions were 'considered as acts of (military) service'.

There was widespread terrorist violence in Chile, too, in the 1960s and 1970s. Again it was essentially a struggle between left and right. President Allende was elected to office on 24 October 1970. Two days beforehand General Rene Schneider, the C-in-C of the Chilean army, was shot and fatally wounded by an unknown gunman. Schneider was a patriot who publicly pledged that his troops would support whichever presidential candidate was legally elected; and his murder was seen as part of a wider plot by the extreme right to stop Allende, a Marxist, assuming office.

Acts of terrorism by the left followed Allende's victory. In June 1971 Edmundo Perez Zujovic, a far-right Christian Democrat, was assassinated by terrorists in the capital, Santiago. His daughter Maria, who was in the ambushed car with her father, identified one of his killers as a prominent member of the Marxist 'Organized Peoples Vanguard' group. More prominent right-wingers from the 'Fatherland and Liberty' organization were rounded up and arrested in March 1972. Others were detained later and charged with conspiracy to murder President Allende and of plotting to free an army general awaiting trial for complicity in the Schneider assassination.

By 1973 the whole country was plunged into near anarchy, and talk of civil war. Amid widespread disorder the four members of the junta – General Augusto Pinochet Ugarte, head of the army; General Gustavo Leigh Guzman, air force; Admiral Jose Castro, navy; and General Cesar Mendoza, national police – acted in concert to topple Allende and seize power for the right. According to the police, he took his own life rather than surrender power to the junta; most neutral observers remain convinced that he was murdered. General Pinochet was sworn in as president on 13 September 1973.

His own regime has in its turn been accused of savage repression and torture. Senator Carlos Altamirano claimed in January 1974 that 15,000 persons had been murdered and 30,000 more imprisoned for their political beliefs, with 200,000 sacked from their jobs and 25,000 students expelled from Chilean universities.

On 21 September 1976 Orlando Letelier, a former ambassador to the United States and Allende's defence minister at the time of the coup, was killed by a car bomb as he drove to his office at the Institute for Political Studies in Washington. A woman aide with him was killed; her husband, travelling in the same car, escaped unhurt. Letelier, who had been deprived of his Chilean citizenship only eleven days before the bomb explosion and was an outspoken critic of the Pinochet regime, was thought to have been murdered by agents of DINA, the Chilean secret police. The *Washington Post* reported that the bomb was planted by Cuban rightists in DINA pay; Senator Edward Kennedy condemned the killing as 'political terrorism'.

Political terrorism has claimed thousands of lives in tiny Guatemala over the past twenty years. In the early 1960s the Guatemalan army suffered heavy losses at the hands of left-wing terrorists. In

325

1967 right-wing paramilitary groups, armed with weapons supplied under the US military aid programme, hit back. American diplomats and military advisers came under direct attack by terrorists from the FAR (Revolutionary Armed Forces) Communist group. At one stage the entire foreign diplomatic corps in Guatemala City felt itself threatened, and called for increased protection.

On 16 January 1968 two US military aides, Colonel John D. Webber Jr, head of the military mission, and navy advisor Lieutenant Commander Ernest A. Munro, were shot dead as they drove to their embassy. Two of their American staff travelling with them were wounded. FAR claimed responsibility and said the attack was retaliation for the murder by rightists of Miss Guatemala of 1950, who was suspected of being an FAR sympathizer. On 28 August the same year John Gordon Mein, the US ambassador to Guatemala, was assassinated. Two carloads of FAR terrorists ambushed his car en route to the embassy and tried to kidnap him. (Their intention had been to hold him to ransom for the release of FAR leader Camillo Sanchez.) Mein tried to escape and was shot down: his chauffeur was left unharmed. He was the first US ambassador to be assassinated on duty.

On 31 March 1970 FAR kidnapped West German ambassador Count Karl von Spreti and demanded freedom for seventeen political detainees in exchange for his safe return. As soon as their terms were rejected by the government, they raised the bidding: now they demanded freedom for twenty-two terrorists plus payment in cash of $700,000 in return for von Spreti's life. Guatemalan President Julio Cesar Mendez Montenegro came under intense pressure to give in to the terrorists: West German special envoy William Hoppe arrived with a secret offer from Bonn to pay the ransom, if Guatemala would free the prisoners; Chancellor Brandt sent a personal plea; a delegation of foreign diplomats called on Foreign Minister Alberto Mohr. As well as asking him to save von Spreti, they demanded increased personal protection for all diplomats serving in the country. President Montenegro refused to give way and Count von Spreti's body was found on 5 April 1970.

West German reaction was bitter. Chancellor Brandt publicly confirmed his government's willingness to pay the ransom and charged the Guatemalans with inability to provide his accredited diplomatic representative with proper protection. The Guatemalan response was to reveal that four of the terrorists named in the exchange deal had confessed to taking part in Mein's assassination.

And they added that their own lives, as well as the government's credibility, were at stake.

Unofficial reaction was more positive. A right-wing paramilitary group known as 'Le Mano' (the Hand) shot dead Cesar Paniagua, one of the leaders of the outlawed Communist Guatemalan Labour Party, on 6 April. They executed two more members of the party three weeks later. And on 5 May police found the bodies of three other prominent left-wingers with a note pinned to each: 'An eye for an eye'. A new wave of counter-terrorist activity began. Georgie Anne Geyer reported in *New Republic* on 4 July 1970 that FAR had become 'a fractured, blood-let group of urban guerrillas for whom terrorism had largely become an end in itself'. Seven years later Amnesty International said that twenty thousand people had been executed or had disappeared in Guatemala since 1966.

On 24 March 1980 the Central American republic of El Salvador lurched close to civil war with the assassination of Archbishop Romero, champion of the poor and oppressed. The archbishop, who was sixty-two, was shot by an unknown gunman as he celebrated mass in San Salvador. Thirty people died and some four hundred others were injured in the street fighting which followed the assassination. The murder – five months after President Romero's overthrow and exile – was seen by many as the penalty for the archbishop's refusal to endorse the 'moderate' military junta in power. The junta, led by Colonels Jaime Abdul Gutierrez and Adolfo Majano, had promised the people land reform, free elections, and a return to law and order. Instead El Salvador suffered further terrorism and bloodshed, and Archbishop Romero had continued to denounce extremists both of the right and left. Many threats were made both on his life and those of his clergy. In February 1980 he vowed, 'I am prepared . . . to offer my blood for the redemption and resurrection of El Salvador.' One month later, the unknown gunman took him at his word.

Anastasio Somoza Debayle, dictator of Nicaragua and one of the most feared and hated men in all Central America, was finally deposed on 17 July 1979 by the country's left-wing Sandinista rebels. His resignation and exile ended nearly half a century of rule by the Somoza dynasty. The long battle to oust him is said to have cost Nicaragua fifty thousand dead, many more wounded, and to have left half a million people homeless.

Somoza's father ruled Nicaragua for twenty years until his assassination in 1956. When the new President Somoza took office in 1967

– after a period of interim rule by his brother and a puppet administrator – he was already commander in all but name of the all-powerful Nicaraguan National Guard. His own regime became a byword for repression, feeding on graft and brutality – repression which increased with each military success by the Sandinista rebels until the United States government, which had long backed the anti-Communist Somoza dynasty, finally accused him of violation of human rights.

Among countless other acts of violence, President Somoza's security forces were held responsible for the assassination in Managua in January 1978 of newspaper editor Pedro Joaquin Chamorro, a long-term opponent of the dynasty. Chamorro was much respected outside Nicaragua for his stand against the Somozas, and his murder became a *cause célèbre*. Following his National Guard's military defeat by the Sandinistas President Somoza fled to Miami, taking with him a personal fortune put at $100 million. It bought him only a few more months of life. From Miami he moved on to the Bahamas, and thence to Paraguay, where on 17 September 1980 he was ambushed by a terrorist squad in Asunción; they killed him in a hail of bazooka and sub-machine-gun fire, then made off. No one doubted who was responsible, and Paraguay promptly severed relations with the newly installed Sandinista regime in Nicaragua.

Several Mediterranean countries, including Cyprus and the islands of Corsica and Sicily have – like the nations of South America – been plagued for many years by terrorism. Again, there is space only for a résumé of certain selected incidents.

On 20 December 1973 Admiral Luis Carrero Blanco, prime minister of Spain, was murdered in the heart of Madrid by terrorists from the ETA (Basque nation and freedom) separatist organization. It took weeks to plan. Posing as sculptors, the assassination squad first rented a room overlooking a street along which the Prime Minister passed regularly each morning. They then dug a tunnel leading under the middle of the road, and between them carried 100 lbs of plastic explosive to the site – divided into a number of Christmas-wrapped parcels to avoid rousing suspicion – to construct a massive bomb. On the morning of the murder, two men 'from the electricity company' ran a cable over a wall and a hundred yards along the street to connect it with the explosive device. It was then detonated by remote control minutes after the Prime Minister left the Jesuit church nearby, where he had attended mass. He, his chauffeur and police bodyguard were all killed outright. The violent blast hurled their car high into the air, injured several passers-by, ripped off sections of balcony all along the street and damaged a further twelve vehicles.

The terrorists timed the explosion to coincide with the opening of Spain's most important political trial for many years. It concerned ten persons accused of membership of the proscribed left-wing 'Workers Commissions' trade union movement, and was known to Spaniards as the '1001 trial' (from the number of the docket on the Madrid Public Order Court). The trial was hurriedly adjourned, then surprisingly re-opened seven hours late. In the meantime a queue of five thousand persons waiting for seats was forcibly dispersed by police, who made several arrests.

On 4 November 1982 General Victor Lago, the officer commanding Spain's crack Brunete armoured division, was shot dead in Madrid by ETA motorbike terrorists. General Lago was on his way to his headquarters in an army car flying his two-star pennant. As it neared the Arch of Triumph on the western outskirts of the city the two motorcyclists drew alongside and opened fire with sub-machine-guns. The general died almost immediately. His army driver was wounded, but survived. General Lago, who was born in 1919, fought for Franco in the Spanish Civil War, and as a member of the Spanish Blue Division which served alongside Hitler's troops in Russia in World War II. His death brought the tally of army officers killed by terrorists in Spain between 1977 and 1982 to twenty-nine, eight of them generals.

On 23 December 1975 a 'hit squad' of three masked men ambushed and shot dead Richard S. Welch, head of station for the American CIA network in Greece, outside his home in Athens. Political extremists from both right and left immediately claimed responsibility, but the Greek authorities remained sceptical. A reward of $200,000 for information failed to bring any serious response and some sources felt Welch had been 'eliminated' by rival foreign intelligence agents.

The identity of every individual head of station overseas becomes known, eventually, to all other intelligence agencies: but since such knowledge is reciprocal, no further action (other than surveillance) is acceptable. In the case of Mr Welch, however, he was first publicly identified in a Greek newspaper as a CIA operative, a disclosure which automatically made him a potential target for every political extremist and crank in the country.

The official total of persons arrested in Turkey for 'terrorist offences' in the two years following the armed coup on 12 September 1980 was *in excess of 56,000*. By the time the figures were released in October 1982, nearly 25,000 of those were still detained; 17,000 were on or awaiting trial and 6,500 were serving prison sentences. 143 had been executed.

There are several terrorist organizations operating today, both inside Turkey and abroad. The latter include the organization responsible for the assassination attempt on Pope John, and an Armenian group responsible for the murders in 1983 of senior Turkish diplomats.

On 17 May 1971 four gunmen from the TPLA (Turkish Peoples Liberation Army), a left-wing organization which has links with the PFLP, forced their way into the Istanbul residence of Israeli consul-general Ephraim Elrom. They bound and gagged the twelve people inside, kidnapped the diplomat when he arrived home for lunch, and executed him five days later when the Turkish authorities rejected their demands to free 'every revolutionary under arrest in the country'. Mr Elrom's body was found on 23 May a few hundred yards from his consulate. He had been shot three times in the head at close range. Three suspects were arrested and the description of nine others circulated. After a prison breakout one year later, one of the arrested terrorists was shot dead. A second, recaptured alive, was sentenced to death for his role in the Elrom murder.

On 26 March 1972 three NATO technicians working at the secret radar base at Unye, on Turkey's Black Sea coast, were kidnapped and later murdered by the TPLA. Two, Gordon Banner and Charles Turner, were British; the third, John Stewart Law, came from Canada. All three were executed by their terrorist kidnappers when the Turkish authorities refused to free three TPLA prisoners in exchange – including the man under sentence of death for complicity in the Elrom murder. Turkish security forces stormed the terrorist hideout after sounds of shooting were heard, and themselves shot dead all ten terrorists inside. A note was found saying the TPLA terrorists considered it their 'basic right and debt of honour' to execute 'English agents of the NATO forces occupying Turkey'.

Responsibility for the assassination in 1983 of Galip Balkar, Turkey's ambassador in Belgrade, was claimed by an Armenian group calling itself 'the Justice Commandos of the Armenian Genocide'. Mr Balkar was their twenty-fourth victim in a ten-year campaign against Turks abroad, mostly diplomats. Their aim is twofold: the establishment of an independent Armenian state, and to avenge the alleged massacre of some 1.5 million Armenians in Eastern Turkey, their original homeland, during World War I. Ambassador Balkar was shot in the head in an ambush and died in hospital without regaining consciousness. A Jugoslav student who tried to intervene was killed and the ambassador's Turkish chauffeur and a passing Jugoslav colonel were both wounded. Two men were arrested and will stand trial in Belgrade.

Among earlier terrorist incidents, two Turkish ambassadors were murdered in Europe in October 1975. On 22 October, three men walked into the Turkish embassy in Vienna and killed ambassador Danis Tunaligilm with sub-machine-guns. All three escaped. On 24 October two terrorists waiting in ambush in Paris opened fire with sub-machine-guns on the car carrying Ismail Erez, killing both the envoy and his chauffeur. Again the assassins escaped. In both instances responsibility was claimed by different terrorist organizations. One call to the Agence France Presse office in Beirut claimed they were the work of the 'Secret Armenian Army'. Other calls to the Associated Press office in Vienna, and to Radio Station Europe 1 in Paris, claimed responsibility on behalf of Eoka-B, the Greek-Cypriot terrorist organization.

In January 1973 Mehmet Baydar, Turkish consul-general in Los Angeles, and Bahadir Demir, his deputy, were both shot dead as they attended lunch at the Biltmore Hotel in Santa Barbara, California. Their assassin was Armenian Gourgen Yanikian, who surrendered to the authorities.

Years of simmering unrest which followed the Balfour Declaration of 1917 ('to facilitate the establishment in Palestine of a national home for the Jewish people') were followed by a full-scale Arab terrorist campaign in the Middle East in the four years leading up to World War II. From 1936–9 Arab terrorists attacked Jewish settlements in Palestine (a British mandate under League of Nations charter), murdered the immigrants, burned their farms, laid culvert mines and ambushed convoys. After the war it was the turn of the Jews to wage a terrorist campaign – this time against the British, who continued to restrict Jewish immigration to assuage mounting Arab hostility. British troops were shot, kidnapped and hanged, police patrols ambushed, merchant shipping threatened by frogmen in Haifa harbour and British military headquarters blown up in Jerusalem before the mandate ended in mid May 1948, and the new state of Israel proclaimed. From that day on the Israelis have been subjected to an even more bitter and bloody terrorist campaign, which has claimed countless lives and was in part responsible for each of the Arab-Israeli wars of the last three decades.

The Arab terrorist organizations as they are known today originally operated under a single high command, that of the Palestine Liberation Organization. The PLO itself was a creation of the Arab summit conference in Cairo in 1964. It is a political body which represents the homeless Palestinian Arabs. Its official base is in Damascus, Syria, but until the Israeli invasion of the Lebanon in 1982 it also maintained an operational HQ in Beirut. It has a three-tier structure consisting of a thirteen-man executive committee (six guerrilla leaders and six professional/intellectual Palestinian representatives, under the chairmanship of Yasser Arafat): a consultative council (forty-three members), and a National Council or Lower House (172 members).

The two main guerrilla organizations are El Fatah, led by Yasser Arafat, which has six thousand members and the PFLP, a Marxist-Leninist group which has a smaller active membership but is even more militant. In recent years the PFLP has broken away from PLO leadership and now conducts independent terrorist operations as senior representative of the self-styled 'Rejectionist Front', which is opposed to any kind of political settlement with the common enemy Israel. Smaller groups include As Saiqa (sponsored by Syria, two thousand strong); the PDFLP, or Popular Democratic Front for the Liberation of Palestine (a PFLP splinter group, still Marxist but more moderate); the PFLP-General Command (another splinter group, also Marxist but radical); and the Arab Liberation Front (sponsored by Iraq). Together with the PFLP, these last two terrorist organizations, PFLP-GC and Arab Liberation Front, make up the Rejectionist Front. Another militant terrorist group called 'Black September' – which was responsible for the Munich Olympics massacre in 1972 and the attack on the Saudi Arabian embassy in Khartoum in 1973, among a host of other incidents – recruited its members from the ranks of both El Fatah and the PFLP. Confusingly however, the PLO denies any official link with Black September.

Arab terrorists and Israelis have fought each other on land, sea and air. The first aerial hijacking of the Middle East 'war' was carried out on 23 July 1968. Three gunmen from the PFLP seized an El Al Boeing 707 with forty-one passengers and crew aboard over Italy, and forced the pilot to fly to Algiers. It was a relatively low-key operation in which no one was injured, but it started a trend soon to become odiously familiar to air travellers the world over.

In this first operation the Algerian government, which denied all knowledge of the plot, promptly released nineteen non-Israeli passengers and flew them to Paris. Ten Israeli women, children and air hostesses were freed four days later and taken to Geneva. The PFLP then asked the International Red Cross to supervise the exchange of the remaining Israeli male passengers and crew for an unspecified number of guerrillas held in Israel. The Israeli prisoners and the Boeing were returned to Tel Aviv, and on 2 September Israel informed the Red Cross she would free sixteen Arabs captured prior to the 1967 desert war.

On 21 February 1970 a Swissair plane bound from Zurich to Tel Aviv caught fire in mid air following an explosion in the baggage hold and crashed fifteen minutes after take-off, killing everyone aboard. In a statement from Beirut the PFLP claimed responsibility, saying (incorrectly) this was its 'first operation abroad'. Western reaction was uniformly hostile and within hours a statement by El Fatah denied PLO involvement. Yasser Arafat later repeated the denial, saying its policy was 'against endangering civilians, wherever they are'. But, he warned, 'the unified command . . . is now seriously reviewing the entire question of attacks on international airlines'.

On 10 June 1970 Major Robert Perry, the US military attaché in Amman, Jordan, was murdered by unknown Arab terrorists firing automatic weapons through the door of his home in the capital. His murder came after a wave of hijackings, and losses among the terrorists during clashes with Jordanian regular troops. Sixty tourists – mostly British and American – were held hostage by the PFLP in two hotels in Amman, in order to put pressure on the Jordanian troops to stop shelling their bases inside Palestinian refugee camps. All the hostages were released unharmed two days after Major Perry's murder, but Dr George Habbash, the PFLP leader, told them: 'Believe me – and I am not joking – we were determined to blow up both hotels with you in them if we had been smashed in our camps.'

Jordanian Prime Minister Wasfi Tell was assassinated during an official visit to Cairo on 28 November 1971 by members of the Black September terrorist splinter group. He was caught in a hail of crossfire as he returned to his hotel from a meeting of the Joint Defence Council of the Arab League – convened, ironically, to discuss joint strategy against Israel. Jordan's foreign minister Abdullah Saleh was slightly wounded in the same attack, an Egyptian bodyguard more seriously. Four men were arrested. Three months later they were released on bail (put up by the PLO) after a ballistics report was submitted which suggested that the bullets which killed Wasfi Tell had not been fired from their guns.

At 4.30 am on 5 September 1972 a commando squad of Black September terrorists scaled a high-wire fence and broke in to the Munich Olympic Village quarters housing the Israeli team. Their aim was to take the whole team hostage against the release of the two hundred Arab terrorists then detained in Israel. Two Israeli athletes were shot dead because they raised the alarm, enabling six others to escape. The remaining nine were overpowered and bound.

After day-long negotiations with the West German authorities the terrorists agreed to leave with their hostages, and to be ferried by bus and helicopter to the military airfield at Fürstenfeldbruck. There a Boeing 707 was to stand by to fly them all to Cairo. The first part of the move passed without incident. On arrival at Fürstenfeldbruck, two of the terrorists left their helicopter and checked the interior of the Boeing before allowing the others to board.

What happened next is still uncertain, but reports at the time said hidden German sharpshooters tried to pick off the two terrorists as they walked back across the tarmac to report to their comrades. They missed – and a gun battle began. A terrorist exploded a hand grenade in one helicopter, killing himself and four of the hostages and wounding the pilot. Fire broke out in the machine, but German firemen who tried to put it out were driven off by terrorist automatic fire, and the helicopter was burned out. Five Israeli athletes in the second helicopter were all killed before the battle ended half an hour later. Fifteen died at Fürstenfeldbruck: nine hostages, five terrorists and one West German policeman. The two athletes killed earlier brought the overall total to seventeen. Three wounded Black September terrorists were taken prisoner.

On 14 September the Executive Committee of the PLO put out a statement saying it was not responsible for Black September's actions, adding that its own objective was 'aimed only at pressuring Israel to release detained guerrillas from Israeli jails'. On 29 October two more Black September gunmen hijacked a Lufthansa Boeing 727 flying from Beirut to Ankara. They threatened to blow it up with all twenty passengers and crew aboard if their three comrades arrested at Munich were not released. After two refuelling stops they remained airborne over Zagreb in Jugoslavia until a second aircraft, supplied by West Germany, landed with the three men. Rescuers and rescued were then flown in the Boeing 727 to Tripoli where they landed in triumph. The Israeli government condemned the West German decision to free the three terrorists, saying, 'Every capitulation . . . encourages them to continue their demands.'

On 2 March 1973 Arab terrorists travelling in a Land Rover bearing diplomatic plates seized the Saudi Arabian embassy in Khartoum, where a reception to honour the departing US chargé d'affaires, Mr George C. Moore, was in progress. No Sudanese police were on duty at the gates as the eight terrorists drove in, firing machine-pistols and revolvers. Some diplomats escaped by climbing over the embassy wall; others hid and got away later. US ambassador Cleo A. Noel Jr was wounded in the ankle and Mr Guy Eid, Belgian chargé d'affaires, shot in the leg. They were bound, along with Mr Moore, and beaten up. Other diplomats taken prisoner included the host, Saudi ambassador Sheik Abdullah el Malhouk with his wife and four children, and the Jordanian chargé d'affaires.

The intruders, who all claimed to be Black September terrorists, then threatened to kill six of their hostages unless certain demands were met. Those demands included: the release of leading El Fatah guerrilla Abu Daoud, imprisoned in Jordan with several others for plotting to assassinate King Hussein; the release of Sirhan Sirhan, the man who assassinated Bobby Kennedy; the release of certain members of the Baader-Meinhof gang under arrest in West Germany, and freedom for every Arab woman prisoner detained by Israel. Sudan's Minister of the Interior, who carried out negotiations on behalf of the countries concerned, told them the next day that the Jordanian government rejected their demand out of hand. The terrorists withdrew two demands only, the release of the Arab women prisoners in Israel and the release of the Baader-Meinhof gang (they had failed to capture the West German ambassador, who had left the reception early). On all the others they stood firm.

President Nixon spelled out America's response at a press conference. He said firmly that while the United States would do all it could to try to secure the release of the hostages 'it would not pay blackmail'. A few hours later, Ambassador Noel, his chargé Mr Moore and the Belgian chargé, Mr Eid were taken down to the basement of the Saudi embassy and murdered. Their killers refused to hand over the bodies for burial until they were guaranteed safe conduct. The Sudanese response was to order them to surrender by dawn next day or face the consequences. The terrorists surrendered, and the siege was lifted.

One of the terrorists confessed that the attack had been planned and directed not by Black September but by El Fatah headquarters in Beirut. All eight stood trial, were found guilty of murder and jailed for life by a Sudanese court on 24 June 1974. President Numeiry immediately commuted the sentences to seven years apiece, and said they would be handed over to Yasser Arafat (who denied complicity) for punishment. Next day they were released to the PLO and flown to Cairo. No details of their punishment, if any, were revealed. El Fatah terrorist Abu Daoud was freed under the terms of a general amnesty proclaimed in Jordan six months later. In 1977 he was arrested in Paris on suspicion of having masterminded the Olympic Village kidnappings. The French courts, however, rejected demands from both West Germany and Israel for his extradition: instead he was freed, deported and flown to Algeria.

The other side of the Arab-Israeli terrorist 'war' emerged on 21 July 1973 when Ahmed Bouchiki, a Moroccan suspected by the Israeli secret service of being a Black September terrorist leading an operation in Scandinavia, was shot dead in Lillehammer, Norway. Police in Oslo later arrested six persons of varying nationality – but all Jewish – in connection with the murder. At their trial the prosecution said that Bouchiki had been mistaken for a Palestinian. According to the Oslo newspaper *Aftenposten*, his killers were members of an Israeli counter-terrorist group known as 'the wrath of God' and an offshoot of the militant Jewish Defence League. *Aftenposten* said the group had been infiltrated by two Israeli secret service undercover agents, who remained in contact with Israeli diplomat Yigal Eyal in the Oslo embassy. They were said to have killed Bouchiki in order to foil a terrorist plot to hijack an El Al plane landing in Denmark.

On 17 December 1973, in a repeat of the Lod airport massacre, five PFLP terrorists attacked a Pan American Boeing 707 about to take off from Rome for Beirut and Tehran. After raking the hull with bullets, they lobbed incendiary grenades inside and set it ablaze. All twenty-nine persons on board were killed, including fourteen American oilmen and four Moroccan government officials.

The terrorists then hijacked a Lufthansa plane, after seizing five Italian hostages and shooting dead a sixth who tried to escape. Another was shot on the runway and died before he reached hospital. The hijacked plane flew first to Beirut with the terrorists, hostages and German crew, but was refused permission to land. It finally put down in Athens next morning, 18 December. The hijackers then demanded the release of two Black September gunmen serving life imprisonment for the attack at Athens airport four months earlier.

As they waited for a response the terrorists fired their guns into the air, to trick the pilot into thinking they had carried out their threat to shoot the hostages. He urged the authorities to accede, but they refused. The PFLP terrorists then shot one hostage and dumped his body on the tarmac, before ordering the pilot to fly them on to Damascus. From Damascus they went on to Kuwait, where they freed the remaining hostages in return for a promise of safe passage to a country of their choice. That promise was not kept. The Kuwaitis handed them over to the PLO 'for trial' when it condemned the hijacking and promised to do 'all in its power' to prevent future incidents.

As airlines and airports everywhere tightened security, the guerrillas switched tactics to attack 'soft' targets inside Israel. On 11 April 1974 three PFLP terrorists crossed from Lebanon into the Israeli frontier settlement of Kiryat Shmona. They broke into some apartments in a four-storey housing block and murdered eighteen people, including women and children. Sixteen others were wounded. All three terrorists died later. Their haversacks, said to be filled with explosives, blew up under fire (according to Israeli sources).

On 15 May 1974 three PDFLP (Popular Democratic Front) terrorists forced their way into a school at Maalot, five miles inside the border from Lebanon, where ninety Israeli school-children lay asleep. Seventeen of the children and three teachers escaped by leaping from windows, the rest were taken hostage. The terrorists then demanded the release of twenty Arab prisoners, and set a deadline. Israeli troops stormed the school when negotiations broke down, but were too late. They found sixteen children already executed, and another five died later of wounds. A family of three was murdered in a separate incident. All three terrorists and one Israeli soldier died in the assault.

Feeling in Israel ran high following the two attacks and fighter-bombers carried out reprisal raids on targets in the Lebanon.

On 27 June 1976 an Air France plane bound from Tel Aviv to Paris with 258 passengers was hijacked in Athens by armed terrorists and forced to fly to Entebbe, Uganda. Passengers and crew were then held to ransom for the release of fifty-three terrorists detained in five different countries: Israel (forty), West Germany (six), Kenya (five), France and Switzerland one apiece. The hijackers issued an ultimatum saying if all fifty-three were not flown to Entebbe by 1 July, they would blow up the plane with their hostages in it.

Two of the hijackers were West German, five Arab. They jointly claimed responsibility in the name of the PFLP, although the group denied responsibility. Among the prisoners they hoped to free were Kozo Okamoto, the Japanese Red Army gunman who led the attack on Lod airport in 1972; Archbishop Hilarion Capucci, convicted of gun-running in 1974; and six members of the Baader-Meinhof gang and its ally, the June 2 Movement. Israeli intelligence named Wilfried Bose, a member of the Baader-Meinhof gang and associate of Ilyich Ramirez Sanchez ('Carlos'), as the ringleader. The other West German terrorist, a woman, was never positively identified.

Mrs Dora Bloch, a 73-year-old grandmother who held joint British-Israeli citizenship, was taken ill during the hijack and admitted to Kampala hospital for observation once negotiations started. Although obviously sympathetic to the terrorists, Idi Amin's Ugandan government officially denied complicity in the hijack plot. On 28 June General Amin, together with the French ambassador to Uganda, persuaded the hijackers to move the hostages out of the threatened plane into the transit lounge at Entebbe. Two days later forty-seven women, children and elderly passengers were released unharmed and flown to Paris: ominously, none of the hundred Israelis aboard were included. On 1 July a further ten passengers were freed. Again, none were Israeli. Suddenly – in what was thought to be a complete reversal of its customary hardline policy – the Israeli government announced its willingness to negotiate 'with a readiness to release' an unspecified number of Arab prisoners in exchange for the hostages.

As the hijackers celebrated their victory, two hundred Israeli commandos landed at Entebbe on 3 July under cover of darkness and stormed the main airport building. Every move was carried through with precision timing. The four terrorists guarding the hostages in the transit lounge were killed outright. Two more who hid near the control tower were found and shot dead: the seventh was pursued and killed in another wing of the building. Then while one commando unit led the hostages aboard the Israeli transport planes, a second unit destroyed the entire Ugandan fighter force – ten MiGs parked on the runways – to forestall any attempted pursuit. A third commando unit fought a brief, bloody battle with Ugandan troops to gain control of the airfield and hold it against counter-attack, killing twenty Ugandan soldiers in the process.

Two transports took off with the hostages while the third commando remained on the ground at Entebbe as rearguard. Finally all three transport met up and refuelled at Nairobi en route to Tel Aviv and safety. The Israeli casualties totalled one dead (Lieutenant Colonel Yehonathan Nethanyahu, aged thirty, commanding one of the assault teams) and two hostages wounded. The entire operation, rearguard action included, was over in ninety minutes and remains a classic example of Israeli professionalism – and ruthlessness – when protecting its own.

The one passenger left behind was Mrs Bloch in Kampala hospital. She was visited next day by Mr Peter Chandley, second secretary from the British High Commission. She was then guarded by two Ugandans. When Mr Chandley returned an hour later he was denied access to her. After four days of procrastination by the authorities, Britain's High Commissioner James Hennessy called personally on Amin to demand news of Mrs Bloch. The general's reply – that he had no knowledge of her whereabouts – was described as 'totally unacceptable' by the Foreign Office in London. Next day an enterprising Israeli reporter phoned General Amin direct, who maintained that Mrs Bloch had been taken to Entebbe on the day of the raid and 'returned to Israel with the others'. She was never seen alive again.

On 13 July 1976 the Nairobi newspaper *Daily Nation* quoted a Ugandan newly-arrived in Kenya as saying that he had seen what he took to be Mrs Bloch's body (it had been partly burned) in a forest near Kampala on 5 July.

The bodies of Entebbe airport's three Ugandan radar operators were lying nearby, he said. They too are believed to have been executed, for their failure to pick up the incoming Israeli transports on the night of the raid.

On 11 August 1976 a squad of four terrorists hurled grenades and fired sub-machine-guns on passengers waiting in the transit lounge at Istanbul airport to board an El Al flight to Tel Aviv. Four persons were killed and thirty wounded. Two Arab terrorists, who confessed under questioning to membership of the PFLP, were captured. Both were later sentenced to death by a Turkish court, but had their sentences commuted to life imprisonment.

Among the dead was American Harold W. Rosenthal, an aide to US Senator Jacob Javits. Two were Israelis. The fourth, a Japanese, was found to be carrying a gun; police assumed him to be one of the terrorist gang. The other terrorist involved escaped in the confusion. The two Arabs who were captured said the attack was a reprisal for the Entebbe raid. Predictably, PFLP headquarters in the Lebanon denied all knowledge of the attack.

On 11 March 1978 a team of heavily armed El Fatah (PLO) terrorists landed by dinghy south of Haifa and killed thirty-five persons, with another seventy wounded, in a series of attacks down the coast road to Tel Aviv. Their objective was to seize a holiday hotel and hold the guests to ransom in exchange for five top terrorists held by the Israelis. Among them – inevitably – was Kozo Okamoto, of the Japanese Red Army: each guerrilla organization was now vying with the others for the honour of securing his release.

Gail Rubin, aged thirty-nine, an American photographer, was walking on the beach when the terrorists landed. As soon as she told them where they were, they murdered her and pressed on. After shooting a number of other unarmed civilians the terrorists hijacked a bus and ordered the driver to take them to Tel Aviv. On the way they shot up several vehicles – including a second bus, from which they took a large number of hostages, including children. They were finally halted just seven miles from Tel Aviv, at a hastily erected barrier thrown up by troops and police flown in by helicopter. In the ensuing battle the hijacked bus exploded and burst into flames, killing 'at least' twenty-five of the hostages. Nine El Fatah terrorists were killed and two taken alive. Israeli ground, sea and air forces hit back at targets in the Lebanon three days later, inflicting heavy casualties. At the same time their troops set up a six-mile-deep security zone along the northern border with Lebanon.

Finally, goaded beyond endurance by years of hijacking, ground infiltration and rocket attacks on border settlements, Israel took the ultimate reprisal. Using the attempted assassination of her ambassador in London as pretext, Israeli forces invaded the Lebanon in 1982 to crush the PLO. Few professional armies of comparable size could have stopped them: the Arab guerrillas who tried were simply brushed aside. Civilian casualties in areas controlled by the PLO were severe. An estimated eleven thousand Arab suspects and PLO sympathizers were detained. In addition a PLO armed force numbering about seven thousand men, under the command of Yasser Arafat, was trapped inside Beirut by Israeli troops. The city was then systematically pounded, despite increasing Western concern. The guerrillas eventually withdrew, with their personal weapons but without their families, under UN protection.

Hopes of a lasting settlement were wrecked almost immediately by two major incidents. First Lebanon's Christian president-elect,

Bashir Gemayel, was assassinated by Muslim extremists. Then his murder was followed by the slaughter of some two thousand Palestinians by pro-Israeli Christian militia in the Beirut refugee camps (and former PLO strongholds) of Sadra and Shatila.

Bashir Gemayel, the man on whom the Israelis pinned their hopes of restoring authoritative government to the Lebanon, was killed by a car bomb on the eve of assuming office. Israeli troops then entered West Beirut 'to prevent further bloodshed'. Instead they allowed heavily armed Lebanese Christian militia to pass through their lines in battalion strength, and fired parachute flares to light the area as the militia systematically butchered the men, women and children living inside the camps. No one will ever know for certain how many died: the bodies had to be quickly disposed of through fear of pestilence. Estimates varied from five hundred to two thousand. Yasser Arafat put the total later at five thousand. What is uncontested is that the killing went on for over forty hours, between 16 and 18 September 1982: and during that time the watching Israeli troops made no attempt to intervene.

Whatever Western sympathy remained for the Israeli position in Lebanon evaporated with the mass murders. Mr Morris Draper, senior American envoy in Beirut at that time, sent a telegram of protest to Israeli defence minister Ariel Sharon saying, 'You must stop this horrible massacre. I have an officer in the camps who is counting the bodies. The situation is terrible. They are killing children. You should be ashamed. You have absolute control of the area and you are therefore responsible for what is happening there.'

An official inquiry later in Israel also put much of the blame on Ariel Sharon, and called for his dismissal from office. He *was* replaced as defence minister – but retained cabinet rank as minister without portfolio, which nullified much of the good that the fair and impartial inquiry had done. Worse still, in the opinion of most observers, the one sure outcome from Bashir Gemayel's murder and the camp massacres is that the seeds of future terrorist activity in the Middle East have already been sown.

TRUBER, Manfred
Delinquent teenage gang-leader whose reign of terror in Vienna lasted just over two months.

On 28 June 1974 a housewife turned a corner near the Vienna City Hall and found an elderly man lying on the ground, his face bloody. He was Johann Kuehn, and he had died of a ruptured spleen. Some ribs were broken, and the bruising on his head indicated that he had been kicked as he lay on the ground. The Vienna police immediately suspected that he was the latest victim of a gang of three youths who had been committing attacks during the past two weeks. They had knocked down a seventy-year-old woman, kicked her unconscious, and ripped off her underwear – although there was no sexual assault. They also knocked down an elderly man and stole his money and wristwatch. Johann Kuehn was the third victim.

On 4 July the gang grabbed a twenty-year-old girl and dragged her into the bushes. When she tried to run away, one of them almost severed her ear with a knife. Cowed, she took off her clothes; then the leader lay on his back and made her perform sexual intercourse sitting astride him. She had to do the same for the other two. They were kicking and beating her when a policeman heard her screams and they ran away. She described them as looking neat and well-dressed, 'nice boys', with long hair, all rather young.

Robberies of elderly people continued but, fortunately, none were seriously hurt. On the night of 13 July two Jugoslav construction workers had settled down to an evening of drinking when one of them, Milo Groznic, noticed that his friend was no longer with him. He found Kalya Ramis lying on the pavement, his nose almost severed from his face. Police later determined that he had been stabbed twenty-seven times. Three young men had been seen in the area around the time of the murder.

On the afternoon of 7 August, another young girl was grabbed in the Ausgarten Park and raped by three youths; her description made it clear that they were again the 'nice boys'. Their score now totalled two murders, two rapes and eighteen attacks. They had not been contented with raping the girl in the park; they had continued to inflict pain and humiliation on her for an hour afterwards. Because there were people around, they forced her to lie still, threatening to kill her with a knife; the police felt reasonably certain that she *would* have been killed if the place had been more solitary.

Four more robberies and attacks followed during the next three weeks. Then, on 30 August, an elderly widow was walking through a deserted alleyway at 4.30 pm when three young men stepped out of a doorway. One of them punched her on the side of the head. The woman was outraged. She swung her handbag into his face, knocking him to the ground, then kicked him hard; the blow landed in his throat. She kneed one of the boys in the groin and hit the other in the face, scratching him. The two fled. The boy on the ground tried to get up, and she again kicked him in the face. Moments later, police had arrived; when they realized that they had probably caught the leader of the 'nice boys', they radioed for help, and the area was soon surrounded by patrol cars. The two who had fled were cornered in a basement. They proved to be Peter Filipovits, aged seventeen, and Walter Wallner, nineteen. The leader – who had been knocked down by the angry widow – was Manfred Truber, seventeen. A carving knife found on Truber was subjected to laboratory tests, and proved to be the knife that had killed Kalya Ramis.

Under the Austrian laws dealing with under-age criminals, all three received only short prison sentences. The Austrian woman who dealt with the gang single-handedly was sixty-eight years old.

W

WHITMAN, Charles
Sniper who killed eighteen people in a morning.

Charles Whitman was apparently normal until he was twenty-five; then, in March 1966, his mother decided to leave his father, with whom she lived in Florida, and move to Austin, Texas, to be near Charles and his wife Kathleen. His father has been a harsh, authoritarian man, and had often beaten both his children and his wife.

Whitman suffered from increasingly erratic behaviour after his mother moved to Austin. He was studying architectural engineering at the University of Texas. On 29 March he went to see the campus psychiatrist to discuss the manic rages that swept over him, occasionally leading him to assault his wife. He also mentioned that he fantasized about taking a deer rifle up the tower of the university and sniping at passers-by. The psychiatrist noted that Whitman seemed full of aggression and hostility. Whitman cancelled his next appointment, saying that he had decided to 'fight it out alone.'

On 31 July Whitman wrote a note – virtually a suicide note – saying that he could not understand his violent impulses and that he intended to murder his wife. He was interrupted by friends, and spent the next few hours talking quite normally with them. Then, at midnight, he went to his mother's apartment and stabbed her to death. He left a note saying that he loved his mother with all his heart.

In the early hours of the following morning he returned to his own apartment and stabbed his wife to death as she lay in bed. He concluded his suicide note by saying that he hated his father, and that life was not worth living.

He packed a duffel bag – dating from his days in the marines – with a veritable arsenal of weapons. On 1 August he rented a 'dolly' – a small push-cart – and bought more guns. He loaded the dolly with his weapons, went to the university, and went up to the observation deck. There he encountered the receptionist, Edna Townsley; he shattered her skull with a blow of the rifle butt. A young couple appeared just after he had dragged Mrs Townsley's body behind a desk. The girl grimaced in disgust at the pool of blood on the floor, but neither of them wondered how it had got there. They smiled at Whitman; he smiled back, and they walked out unharmed.

Nineteen-year-old Mike Gabour walked into the room; Whitman killed him with a shotgun blast, and then directed the gun at two women who were behind the youth. He killed the boy's aunt, Marguerite Lamport, and wounded his mother. The husbands of the two women, walking close behind them, realized that they were confronting a maniac, and succeeded in dragging the bodies back down the stairs.

At 11.48 am Whitman began shooting from the tower.

Claire Wilson, who was pregnant, fell with a bullet in her stomach (she survived but the baby was killed). Nineteen-year-old Thomas Eckman knelt beside her, and was killed outright. Within twenty minutes, nine people had died, and eight were wounded. The bell tower was surrounded by police, and a light plane went up with a marksman to try to shoot the mad sniper. Whitman's deadly accurate fire drove the plane away.

An hour and a half after he had started shooting, Whitman was riddled with bullets by three policemen who burst into the observation tower. He had killed twenty-one since midnight, and wounded another twenty-eight.

The autopsy revealed a brain tumour the size of a walnut. It was probably this, pressing on the amygdaloid nucleus – the brain's aggression centre – that caused the uncontrollable rages and the final slaughter.

WILLIAMS, Wayne
The Atlanta murderer who was suspected of killing twenty-eight young blacks.

On a hot Sunday in July 1979, two bodies were found close to Niskey Lake, Atlanta, Georgia; one had been blasted by a shotgun, the other so decomposed and mauled by wild dogs that it was impossible to say how death came about.

They were later identified as two black teenagers: Edward Smith and Alfred Evans. The killings caused little stir in a city with a high murder rate. Neither did the disappearance in September of another black teenager, Milton Harvey.

On 21 October a neighbour asked nine-year-old Yusuf Bell to fetch her a box of snuff. Yusuf, the son of an ex-civil rights worker, Camille Bell, was an unusually gifted child whose hobby was mathematics, and who read encyclopaedias for recreation. He also disappeared. This time, the event caused some excitement, since Camille Bell was a well-known figure in the Mechanicsville neighbourhood where she lived. A week later, a decomposed corpse was found near College Park; it proved to be the missing Milton Harvey. Yusuf's body was found stuffed into the crawl-space in an abandoned elementary school. He had been strangled. Although he had been missing for ten days, it was clear that he had not been dead for more than half that time. His clothes had been cleaned, and the body washed. At the same time another nine-year-old, Jeffrey Mathis, vanished; a girl said she had seen him climbing into a blue and white car.

In early March 1980 a twelve-year-old black girl, Angel Lanier, was found tied to a tree, her briefs stuffed down her throat; she had been raped. But it was difficult to decide whether this was related to the other killings, since the assumption was that the killer – now known to black children as 'the Man' – was homosexual.

The vanishing continued. In late May, Eric Middlebrooks was found bludgeoned and stabbed to death. In early June, Christopher Richardson disappeared on his way to a swimming pool. Soon after this Aaron Wyche was found under a railway bridge; police said he had died of an accidental fall, but his parents insisted he was terrified of heights; a second autopsy concluded he had died violently. An eight-year-old girl, LaTonya Wilson, vanished from near her home in late June. By the beginning of July, the murders had continued for a year, and seven black children had been murdered and three had vanished.

Blacks all over the country were convinced that a white racialist was responsible. The police pointed out that this was unlikely; the children had disappeared mostly from black neighbourhoods, where a white would stand out. Camille Bell and the parent of another murdered child, Mary Mapp, decided to form a group of parents who had lost children, and in early July they called a press conference to protest at police inaction, arguing that even if the killer was a black, the police were still dragging their feet because the victims were not white children. On 30 July Earl Terrell disappeared; on 30 August Clifford Jones disappeared, and was found the next day, strangled. A special police task force was increased from five members to twenty-five. Civic groups raised a $100,000 reward for the killer, and a scheme set up of athletic and cultural programmes to keep young blacks off the streets. Later, a curfew on children would be imposed. Some blacks held a theory that the killer was a policeman, but the police argued that he was more likely to be a black teenager, who would be trusted by others. The belief that the killings were racially motivated was strengthened by the fact that, with the exception of Angel Lanier, none of the victims had been sexually assaulted.

On 14 September Darron Glass disappeared; on 9 October Charles Stevens; his body was found the next day, suffocated. Nine days later, a search of woodland area revealed the body of LaTonya Wilson, but the body was too badly decomposed for the cause of death to be determined. By then, the Atlanta police chief George Napper was admitting that all leads had been exhausted. When the suffocated body of Aaron Jackson was found on 2 November, there was still no clue to the identity of the killer. On 4 January 1981 Lubie Geter disappeared from a shopping mall. Five days later, police found the badly decomposed bodies of two missing children in a wood south of Atlanta – Christopher Richardson and Earl Terrell. Lubie Geter was found in early February. By March 1981 twenty bodies had been found, leaving one still missing. By mid May, the count of victims had risen by six.

On 22 May came the break. Police close to a bridge on the Chattahoochee River heard a splash, and saw a man climb into a station-wagon. They stopped it, and found that it was driven by a plump young black who identified himself as Wayne Williams, aged twenty-three; he said he was in the music business, working as a promoter. He was questioned, but the police could see no reason to detain him, so he was allowed to go, and placed under constant surveillance. Two days later, the body of 27-year-old Nathaniel Cater, the oldest victim, was found floating in the river. Dog hairs found on the body matched those found in Williams' station-wagon and his home. One witness testified to seeing Williams leaving a theatre hand in hand with Cater just before his disappearance. Another witness testified to seeing Williams in the company of another of the victims, Jimmy Payne, also found in the river. A young black who knew Williams well testified that Williams had offered him money to perform oral sex, and another described how, after he had accepted a lift, Williams had fondled him through his trousers, then stopped the car in secluded woods; the teenager had jumped out and run away. He also said that he had seen Williams with Lubie Geter. When laboratory examination established that fibres and dog hairs found on ten more victims were similar to those found in Williams' bedroom, the police decided to arrest him. He was charged only with the murders of Cater and Payne.

Wayne Williams was the only child of two schoolteachers, Homer and Fay Williams, in their mid-forties when he was born. He was a brilliant and spoiled child. He studied the sky through a telescope and set up a home-built radio station. When his transmitter was powerful enough to reach a mile, he began selling advertising time. He was featured in local magazines and on TV. When he left school at eighteen he became obsessed by police work and bought a car that resembled an unmarked police car. The prosecution later described him as a 'Manichean' personality (the Manichees were world-haters): intelligent, literate and talented, but a pathological liar, a frustrated dreamer and a man who felt himself to be a failure. He was obsessed by a desire for quick success, and first became a photographer, studying television camera work. He claimed to be a talent scout, trying to set up a pop group to sing soul music. He seemed to hate other blacks, according to several witnesses, referring to them as niggers. Yet he distributed leaflets offering blacks between the age of eleven and twenty-one 'free' interviews about a musical career. One of the victims, Patrick Rogers, was a would-be singer.

The evidence was, as the prosecutor conceded, entirely circumstantial, and it was with some reluctance that the judge allowed it to be strengthened by details relating to other murders besides those with which Williams was charged. His trial began in January 1982, and ended in March when, after twelve hours' deliberation, the jury found him guilty of the two murders. He was sentenced to two consecutive life terms. Although doubts have been expressed about the other murders, it has been pointed out that the 'crime wave' stopped after Williams' arrest.

WRIGHT, Blanche
America's first hit woman.

On 21 January 1980 there was a knock on the door of Felipe Rodriguez, a Colombian drug dealer in the Bedford Park district of the Bronx, New York; it was a young black woman who said she wanted to buy drugs. As Rodriguez opened the door, a black man who had been standing pressed against the wall pushed his way in. Rodriguez was thrown to the floor at gunpoint, and handcuffed. His common-law wife, Martha Navas, pleaded for his life; the man dragged her into the next room and shot her three times in the head with a gun equipped with a silencer. Then he shot Rodriguez in the head. He and his companion looted the apartment, taking $8,000 in cash and narcotics. They were disturbed by a knock at the door – a neighbour, Luis Martin, had come to see what the commotion was about. He too was shot, and his pockets rifled. The killers left after shooting Rodriguez once more in the head; but somehow, Rodriguez survived to describe his attackers.

Only two weeks later, another drug dealer named Marshall Howell was leaving his expensive apartment in Diplomat Towers, Mount Kisco, New York, accompanied by his bodyguard Sam Nevins, apparently prepared to do business, for he carried $6,500 in his pockets. A young Negro couple walked past them, looking into one another's eyes. As soon as they had passed the two men, the man released his hold on the girl, drew a 9 mm automatic, and fired at Marshall Howell. But as he pulled the trigger a second time, the gun jammed. The bodyguard turned, pulled out his own gun, and shot the gunman in the chest. At this, the girl drew a gun and began shooting. Nevins began to run, and Howell sank to the pavement. The girl walked up to him, put the gun against his head, and shot him.

In the murdered man's apartment police found nearly a quarter of a million dollars in cash, and vast quantities of cocaine.

Papers in the pocket of the dead gunman identified him as Joseph Morales, although the address on them proved to be non-existent. Four days after his death, a woman who identified herself as his aunt, Lupe Ocasio, asked for his effects and for his body; it was sent to the Bronx mortuary, near her home.

Fingerprints from the corpse revealed that his real name was Robert Young, and that he had escaped from the Matteawan State Hospital for the Criminally Insane in a mass breakout in May 1977.

Young had a long criminal record which included two murders, rape and sodomy. In 1974 he had been interrupted when burgling the apartment of a nurse in the Bronx; he had shot her then committed sodomy on the body. He was also wanted for sodomizing an eleven-year-old girl, and investigation of this case had uncovered the gun that had killed the nurse. He had been sentenced to eighteen years in prison, but sent instead to the asylum for the criminally insane. Recaptured in St Louis, he had escaped again.

Police called on Young's aunt the day after she had reclaimed his body, and were admitted by an attractive young black girl. She told them she was Blanche Wright, aged twenty-one, and that she lived in the same building. She answered the description of the hit woman, and in her apartment, police found a gun. At first, Wright insisted she knew nothing whatever about the killings. But when the police suggested that she had let down her partner in crime by not firing sooner, she became indignant, and retorted that it was her bullets that had killed Marshall Howell.

She also admitted that she and her lover, Robert Young, were contract killers. They had been hired to kill Howell because he had failed to pay up on a drugs deal. They had also been responsible for the attempted murder of Rodriguez and the murder of his common-law wife and their neighbour, and for the contract killing of another drugs dealer, Carlos Medina, in November 1979. Wright insisted that her lover had forced her to take part in the killings. The daughter of an alcoholic woman, she had been sexually abused since she was seven – a foster father had died of a heart attack while trying to rape her. Her trial was delayed when she was found to be pregnant; but after the birth of the baby, the case was resumed. She was sentenced to eighteen years to life for the shooting of Marshall Howell, and fifteen years to life for her part in the murder of Martha Navas and Luis Martin.

X

X, Michael
Black power leader executed in Trinidad for ordering two murders.

Michael X was born Michael de Freitas, the son of a Portuguese planter and a black girl, in Trinidad on 17 August 1933. He came to London and lived in the Notting Hill area, where he married, and drifted into the protection racket, working for the notorious slum landlord Peter Rachman.

In the 1960s de Freitas became fascinated by the black power movement in the United States, particularly by the black Muslim power leader, Malcolm X. He founded the Racial Adjustment Action Society and made violent racialist speeches. Many whites who knew him well said that de Freitas was not a racialist but that he recognized there was a place for him as England's own Malcolm X (who was murdered by fellow black Muslims in Harlem in 1965).

It was a speech in which he declared that any white man seen with a black woman should be shot that led to his prosecution in 1967 under the new Race Relations Act, and to a sentence of a year in jail. Out in 1968, he landed in further trouble with the police, accused of robbery; in 1969 he jumped bail, and went to Trinidad in 1970. There he moved into a $45,000 house in Christina Gardens, Arima, a smart suburb occupied by professional people. How he acquired the house is not known, but he had many wealthy friends, including John Lennon, Muhammad Ali, Sammy Davis Jnr, and millionaire Nigel Samuel. He was known and liked by many writers, including Alexander Trocchi and John Michell, who saw no justification in Michael X's description as a 'hate-filled racialist'.

The authorities in Trinidad soon had reason for regretting the return of Michael X (or Abdul Malik, as he now called himself, having converted to Mohammedanism) for he turned to revolutionary activities. There were black power marches – much of Trinidad was violently anti-white – and these led to an army mutiny and a siege of the police headquarters. The mutiny was suppressed and Michael X found it difficult to maintain his position as leader. He was short of money and was being pressed to complete the purchase of his house. He returned to the criminal activities he had followed in England, prostitution racketeering, arms smuggling and robbery.

In November 1971 an American black called Allen Donaldson but who changed his name to Hakim Jamal, came to Trinidad with his beautiful white girlfriend, Gale Benson, who had met Jamal in London while Michael X was still there. She divorced her husband, became Jamal's mistress and adopted the Muslim name of Hale Kigma. She was fascinated by Jamal but totally dominated by Michael X, whose black power group she joined. She seems to have had a powerful masochistic streak and Michael X described how he once tied her naked to a bed and beat her until he was tired.

Another of Michael X's followers was a young barber named Joseph Skerritt. When Skerritt disobeyed an order to raid a police post Michael X decreed his execution. On 8 February 1972 Skerritt was told to join a group digging a trench 'to facilitate drainage'. He was then attacked with knives and cutlasses, and Michael X himself delivered the blow that almost severed the head from the body. The trench was filled in, and lettuces planted in the freshly turned earth. Soon afterwards Steve Yates, a follower, disappeared during a bathing excursion to Sans Souci Bay.

Gale Benson also vanished; she had not been seen since 2 January. Hakim Jamal reported her disappearance to the police, but later claimed that nobody seemed interested. He had left Trinidad for the United States on 20 January, before the murder of Skerritt.

Ten days after the murder of Skerritt, Michael X left Trinidad with his wife and four children; he claimed that he had been invited by the government of Guyana to celebrate its Republic Day; the Guyana government later denied this. That night – 19 February 1972 – Michael X's bungalow burst into flame; by dawn, it was gutted. Michael X was informed of the fire while staying in Georgetown, Guyana; his immediate response was to wire his lawyer to get an injunction to prevent anyone visiting the premises. But he was too late. Acting on a tip – probably from the rival gun-running organization that had burned the house – the police began to dig in the garden. The search took three days, but they finally found the spot where Joseph Skerritt had been buried. The hacked body, almost decapitated, was uncovered. The police were now looking for Gale Benson, and earth-moving machinery was brought in to help. After two more days, they found her body. Keith Simpson, a leading pathologist, was brought from London to examine it. She had a cutlass wound down her throat, which indicated that someone had thrust it into her neck, probably as she was trying to struggle out of her grave. Particles of soil in her lungs showed that she had been buried while still alive and had died of suffocation.

Hakim Jamal was located in Massachusetts and allegedly broke down when he heard of the finding of the body. He indicated that he had left Trinidad because he felt his own life was in danger. The black militants had resented Gale Benson because she was white, and Jamal for bringing her there. There was also a suggestion that Gale Benson was trying to cause a break between Jamal and Michael X.

Three of Michael X's followers were arrested and charged with the murders. They were Edward Chadee, aged twenty, Stanley Abbott, thirty-four, and Adolphus Parmasser, twenty-one. Parmasser turned state's evidence, so only the other two stood trial. Parmasser later described how Steve Yates, the man who had disappeared, had lured Gale to the pit that had been dug and pushed her in; then she was hacked with a machete and a cutlass until she collapsed and could be buried alive.

Police who went to Georgetown, Guyana, to bring Michael X back for questioning found only his wife; Malik had vanished into the jungle. On 1 March he tried to hitch a lift, and was reported as being in the area of Gold Hill, sixty miles from Georgetown. He was found asleep in a woodman's hut and arrested.

In May 1973 Hakim Jamal was shot down by five gunmen in front of his family, in Boston. Inevitably, it was believed that Michael X had ordered the killing from his prison in Trinidad. Michael X and his two lieutenants were all sentenced to death. He appealed several times, but the sentence was upheld, and he was hanged in November 1974.

Y

YOUNG, Graham
The man who poisoned purely for the sensation of power it gave him.

Graham Young's mother died a few months after his birth in September 1947. Graham was a solitary child, a loner, who admired the Nazis and argued that Hitler was a great man. His intelligence made him scorn his environment and acquaintances. With his chemistry set he made explosives; he admired the Victorian poisoner William Palmer.

In the winter of 1961, he began administering small doses of antimony tartrate to his family, and watching the symptoms with fascination. His elder sister Winifred noticed that her stomach seemed to be permanently upset, and she was once violently sick in the street. On one occasion, Young ate the wrong food by mistake and was himself sick. His stepmother died in April 1962. Young apparently loved her sincerely, but his curiosity about the action of poisons was uncontrollable. His sister began to suspect something when her tea tasted bitter one morning – she spat out the mouthful – and she began to feel dizzy later in the day; a hospital diagnosed belladonna poisoning. As his father grew steadily weaker, Young continued to administer antimony tartrate. A hospital diagnosed his illness as arsenic poisoning – to Graham's disgust. 'How ridiculous not to be able to tell the difference between arsenic and antimony poisoning!' The family finally became suspicious, and Young was arrested. Bottles of antimony tartrate found tucked inside his shirt made it clear that he was guilty. He confessed to the poisonings, and was sent to Broadmoor, the prison for the criminally insane.

He was released in February 1971, after nine years. While he was in custody, a fellow prisoner had died of poison under mysterious circumstances. At twenty-three, Young took a job with John Hadlands, a photographic firm in Bovingdon, Hertfordshire. Within a few weeks, Bob Egle, the head storeman, developed violent back and stomach pains; he died on 19 July 1971. Young was selected by the manager to attend the cremation. After the service, Young talked in a superior tone of voice about the causes of Egle's death, showing an unusual medical knowledge.

So many of Young's fellow workers began to suffer from mysterious stomach upsets that they coined the term 'Bovingdon bug' for whatever was causing it. In October 1971 Fred Biggs, the man in charge of another store, became ill. Young was lacing his tea with thallium; on 30 October Young wrote in his diary, 'I have administered a fatal dose of the special compound to F.' Thallium causes gradual paralysis of the nervous sytem. Doctors who studied Fred Biggs in hospital were baffled. Nineteen days later, he died, after a grim fight for life.

Two more men at Hadlands began to suffer stomach upsets and pins and needles in the feet; both also began to lose their hair. On 12 November, a team of doctors was invited to Hadlands to try to track down the 'bug'. They decided to invite all the staff together to ask questions. To the surprise of Dr Robert Hynd, the Medical Officer of Health, Young asked a number of searching medical questions, including whether the symptoms were consistent with thallium poisoning. As suspicion began to settle on him, as yet vague and unsupported, the management decided to start a routine check on all members of staff. Young was the most recent arrival, and in due course, Scotland Yard received an inquiry about him. Their answer electrified the management at Hadlands. Within hours, Graham Young had been arrested on suspicion of murder. His diary was found, and Young explained it as notes for a projected novel. The thallium was found in his pocket – a dose meant for himself if he was caught. He finally confessed to the poisoning of Bob Egle and Fred Biggs, and was sentenced to life imprisonment. In her book *Obsessive Poisoner* his sister Winifred speaks of his 'craving for publicity and notice'. Young undoubtedly felt that he was more intelligent than other people and that he deserved to become known. His secret poisonings gave him a sense of power – he liked to describe himself as 'your friendly neighbourhood Frankenstein'. But his sister also described how, not long before his arrest, he came to see her in a state of deep depression, explaining that he was lonely. When she suggested various forms of socializing, he replied: 'Nothing like that can help. You see, there's a terrible coldness inside me.' It could be the epitaph of most psychopathic killers.

YOUNG, Thomas Ross
Glasgow mass rapist and murderer, sentenced to three life terms.

On 27 June 1977 a farmer from Glenboig, near Glasgow, noticed a sickening smell coming from undergrowth beside a farm track; he pulled aside the undergrowth and saw the decomposing body of a woman, naked from the waist down, with her hands tied behind her. Her briefs had been stuffed into her mouth. When the find was reported, a Glasgow woman was able to identify the victim as Frances Barker, who had vanished on 10 June. After an evening with her brother-in-law she had taken a taxi home, discovered she had left her keys behind, and began to walk back, through the Maryhill area of Glasgow. Somewhere en route she met her murderer.

Police soon discovered that there was a rapist at large in the Maryhill area; a number of women, among them several prostitutes, told of being attacked, sometimes at knife-point; many were savagely beaten – one girl had her hearing permanently damaged when a man rained blows on her and tried to drag her into a car. Only the intervention of a passer-by saved her.

The break in the case came sooner than expected. A sixteen-year-old girl complained that she had been repeatedly raped by a lorry driver named Thomas Young. She had called at 71 Ashley Street on 24 June looking for a friend. A powerfully built man had dragged her into the house, where he held her for the next ten hours, beating and raping her. When police called at the address, Young had left – obviously in a hurry. They called on his wife, from whom he was separated; she said she had not seen him recently. But the police felt she was nervous, and kept a discreet watch on the house. Not long after, Young was sighted at the kitchen window; police rushed in and arrested him. On their previous visit he had been lying in a hideout under the floorboards. They discovered a number of items in the hideout, including a powder compact that was identified as belonging to Frances Barker. Hairs found in the cab of Young's lorry were identical with those of the corpse. Faced with this evidence Young admitted to the rape and murder.

He had been in trouble with the law since he was nine, when he was arrested for theft. At thirteen he was sent to an approved school for indecent assault. In 1962 he was jailed for house-breaking, and in 1963 received three months for failing to maintain his children. In 1967 he was jailed for eighteen months for raping a girl in

Shropshire; then in 1970, he received eight years for raping a girl of fifteen in the cab of his lorry.

In 1967 Young had also been questioned about the disappearance of Pat McAdam. She had spent the night of 18 February at a party in Glasgow; the following day, she set out with a girl-friend to hitch-hike back to her home in Dumfries. They were picked up by a lorry driver who bought them a meal, and the friend later dozed in the cab as the driver kissed and cuddled Pat in the back of the lorry. The friend was dropped off at Annan, and Pat was never seen again. Thomas Young was identified, and he insisted that he had made love to Pat in a lay-by, then dropped her off near her home. His lorry had been seen parked on a quiet country road – well off his route – not far from a bridge; but no sign of Pat McAdam's body could be found.

A BBC team interviewed the Dutch clairvoyant Gerard Croiset about the disappearance; holding Pat's Bible, Croiset stated that she had been beaten to death with some heavy tool like a wrench. His description of the bridge and the place where the lorry had been parked was weirdly accurate, even to the small detail of a car without wheels parked in a front garden, with a wheelbarrow tilted against the back.

But why should Pat have been killed? The motive was supplied by her friend, who mentioned that Pat had refused to sleep with someone after the party because she was menstruating that weekend; she presumably tried to discourage Young with the same reason.

When Young was released from prison after serving two-thirds of his sentence, he went on a rampage of rape that continued for two years, until his arrest. He boasted to police that he had had sex with more than two hundred women in the cab of his lorry, and had raped those who refused to submit voluntarily. Even after the murder of Frances Barker, he took a woman back to the same place and tried to rape her.

It became apparent at his trial that Young was a man whose sex urge was so violent and compulsive that he became virtually insane when the desire came upon him; the rape of the sixteen-year-old girl revealed a complete indifference to the consequences.

ZODIAC
Californian mass murderer who, at the time of writing, is still unidentified.

Between 20 December 1968 and 11 October 1969 'Zodiac' committed five known murders, and seriously wounded two more victims.

The first was discovered by a woman driving between Vallejo and Benica, near San Francisco, who saw a parked station-wagon and two bodies lying nearby. Police hurried to the spot, and found a teenage boy lying dead near the vehicle – he had been shot behind the left ear. Some distance away was the body of a girl who had been shot in the back several times, probably as she ran from the killer. The dead boy was identified as David Farraday, a high school student and the girl was Bettilou Jensen; the spot where they were found was known as a lover's lane. The killings appeared to be motiveless – the boy's wallet was still intact in his pocket and the girl had not been sexually assaulted.

On 5 July 1969 a man with a gruff voice rang the Vallejo police department. 'I want to report a double murder,' he said. 'If you will go one mile east on Columbus Parkway to a public park, you will find the kids in a brown car. They are shot with a 9 mm Luger. I also killed those kids last year. Goodbye.'

The police found the car as the man had described it. In it they found a seriously wounded man, Michael Mageau, and a dead girl, Darlene Ferrin, mother of a young child. Mageau was later able to tell the police that he and Darlene Ferrin had driven into the parking lot when a car drove up and halted beside them. It drove away but returned ten minutes later. Someone shone a searchlight, blinding them both, then walked over and, without a word, started shooting. Mageau described the figure as stocky, about five foot eight, round-faced with wavy light-brown hair, aged between twenty-five and thirty. Witnesses had seen the killer's car driving away very fast.

On 1 August the Vallejo *Times-Herald* and two San Francisco newspapers received letters signed with a cross over a circle, the sign of the zodiac; the letters described the killings in a detail that would have been impossible for anyone who had not committed them. The letters also contained several lines of some kind of code or cipher. The writer stated that if the ciphers in all three letters were put together, his identity would be known. The man threatened to 'go on the rampage' if his letters were not published, and said he would kill a dozen people. A code expert deciphered the lines and read, 'I like killing people because it is so much fun it is more fun than killing wild game in the forest because man is the most dangerous animal of all to kill something gives me the most thrilling experience it is even better than getting your rocks off with a girl the best part of it is when I die I will be reborn in paradise and all I have killed will become my slaves I will not give you my name because you will try to slow down or stop my collecting of slaves for my afterlife.'

Publication of the letters produced more than a thousand leads from people who thought they might know the killer's identity. None of these led anywhere.

On 27 September a man with a gruff voice rang the Napa police department, and said that he wanted to report a double murder. Police hurried to the shores of Lake Berryessa and found a man and woman both bleeding from stab wounds. In a sports car parked nearby the police found scrawls which included the zodiac sign. The two victims, Cecilia Shepard and Bryan Hartnell, were both students at Pacific Union College. Hartnell was still alive, and was able to tell the police how they had been accosted by a man wearing a hood with eye slits cut in it and the sign of the zodiac marked in white. He carried a pistol and a knife, and asked for money. Through the eye slits, Hartnell could see the dark frames of spectacles and light-brown hair. Hartnell described him as 'paunchy'. The man bound the two students, then said, 'I am going to stab you people', and did so repeatedly.

On the telephone, close to the Napa police headquarters, from which the man had made his call, the police were able to lift three fingerprints. But they failed to lead to the killer. Two weeks later, on 11 October, the killer shot a taxi driver, Paul Stine, in the back of the head on the top of Nob Hill in San Francisco, then walked off, taking the driver's wallet and a fragment torn from his shirt. The bullet was found to have come from the same gun that killed Darlene Ferrin. The next day the San Francisco *Chronicle* received another Zodiac letter, enclosing a bloody fragment of shirt. The writer complained of the inefficiency of the police and went on, 'Schoolchildren make nice targets. I think I shall wipe out a school bus some morning. Just shoot out the tyres, then pick off the kiddies as they come bouncing out.'

The murder of the taxi driver proved to be the last known Zodiac killing. On 21 October a caller claiming to be Zodiac rang the Oakland police station, and declared that he would be willing to give himself up if he could be represented by a famous lawyer – he said his first choices were F. Lee Bailey and Melvin Belli. He also asked that time should be reserved for him on an early morning talk show on television. This was done, and it was announced on the television station. Thousands of people in the area watched the Jim Dunbar Show when it started at 6.45 am. At 7.41 a caller came on the line with a soft boyish voice and identified himself as Zodiac. He called back fifteen times, and talked to Melvin Belli about his murders and about the headaches he suffered from. He ended by agreeing to meet Belli in front of a store in Daly City, but failed to turn up.

Three people who heard Zodiac's voice – Bryan Hartnell, a woman telephone operator, and a patrolman, said that the voice of the caller bore no resemblance to that of the killer they had heard. On the other hand, two months after the telephone call, Melvin Belli received a note in the same handwriting as the earlier Zodiac notes, enclosing another piece of the taxi driver's shirt. The note claimed that he had killed eight people so far, and intended to kill a ninth soon. If the caller on the television show had been an imposter, it seems certain that this letter would have denounced him.

In March 1971 the Los Angeles *Times* received another letter saying, 'If the blue meanises [menaces] are ever going to catch me, they had best get off their fat asses and do something.' It concluded: 'The reason I am writing to the *Times* is this, they don't bury me on the back pages like some of the others.' It was signed with the circle and a cross, and the number 17 followed by a plus sign.

In 1974 the San Francisco police department received another Zodiac letter claiming that he had now killed thirty-seven people, and that he would do 'something nasty' unless he received more newspaper publicity. Again, police said that the handwriting was the same as in the previous letters. And that was the end. In the last nine years nothing more has been heard of Zodiac.

In many ways, the killings bear an interesting resemblance to those of New York's Son of Sam (see Berkowitz, David) and on the television programme he identified himself as 'Sam'. It seems possible that the same psychological profile applies – a shy man who is afraid of women, and who consequently resents courting couples.

ZON, Hans van
Mass murderer who lived in a fantasy world and killed totally without motive.

Born in Utrecht, Holland, in 1942, van Zon was a typical mother's boy. His mother resented his father's low status as a workman and inspired her son with the idea of being a somebody. He was a quiet, lethargic child, noted for his politeness to adults; he always preferred to play with younger children, and seemed rather autistic and uninterested in anything outside himself. On leaving school, he was dismissed from a succession of jobs for petty dishonesty. He seemed to live in a fantasy world. At sixteen he went to Amsterdam, bought himself expensive clothes, and began living by his wits, describing himself as a student – the very word student had a fascination for him. He borrowed money from a Catholic priest, promising to go to a Catholic institute in Doorn; he kept his promise, but ran away almost immediately. He was good looking and had many love affairs, not always with girls. In July 1964 he committed what was probably his first murder. He had taken a girl named Elly Hager-Segov out for the evening, and experienced a sudden urge to kill her. Late at night he went to her room and claimed that he had missed his last train home; she allowed him to stay. When she refused to allow him to make love a second time, he strangled her, undressed her, then cut her throat with a bread knife.

In 1965, according to a confession (which he later withdrew) he was responsible for the death of a homosexual film director, Claude Berkeley, in Amsterdam. He married Caroline Gigli, persuading her to support him by working as a chambermaid in hotels. In early 1967, she accused him of planning to kill her, and the police kept him in jail for a month, since he was on probation for a minor offence. After his release, his wife took him back. In April that year he murdered Coby van der Voort, with whom he had been having an on-off affair for some time. After lovemaking, he placed a pink powder on his tongue and swallowed it, telling her it was a sexual stimulant. It was pink icing. She asked to try some, and he gave her a knock-out drug, after which he killed her with a piece of lead piping. He undressed her, stabbed her with a bread knife, and tried to have intercourse with the body.

Soon afterwards, when drunk, he made the mistake of boasting about her murder in front of a convict known as Oude Nol, who blackmailed him into committing more crimes. An eighty-year-old firework-maker was selected as a victim; on 31 May 1967 van Zon went to Jan Donse's shop and killed him with the same piece of lead piping that he had used on Coby van der Voort. In August, he murdered a farmer, Reyer de Bruin, who lived alone at Heeswijk, striking him with the lead pipe, then cutting his throat. But when van Zon went to kill and rob a widow named Woortmeyer (whom Oude Nol had once courted) he failed to put enough force into the blow. She woke up, found a large sum of money missing, and called the police. Van Zon was arrested and implicated Oude Nol, who received seven years; van Zon received life.

SELECT BIBLIOGRAPHY

Ambrister, Trevor *Act of Vengeance, The Yablonski Murders and Their Solution* (Barrie and Jenkins, London, 1976)

Becker, Jillian *Hitler's Children, The Story of the Baader-Meinhof Gang* (Michael Joseph, London, 1977)

Bugliosi, Vincent and Gentry, Curt *Helter Skelter, The True Story of the Manson Murders* (W. W. Norton, New York, 1974)

Cheney, Margaret *The Coed Killer (Edmund Kemper)* (Walker and Company, New York, 1976)

Clark, Tim and Penycate, John *Psychopath, The Case of Patrick Mackay* (Routledge and Kegan Paul, London, 1976)

Critchley, T. A. *Conquest of Violence: Order and Liberty in Britain* (Constable, London, 1970)

Deeley, Peter and Walker, Christopher *Murder in the Fourth Estate (The Hosein Brothers)* (Gollancz, London, 1971)

Fawkes, Sandy *Killing Time (Paul Knowles)* (Hamlyn, London, 1978)

Flackes, W. D. *Northern Ireland: A Political Directory 1968–79* (Gill and Macmillan, Dublin, 1980)

Foot, Paul *Who Killed Hanratty?* (Jonathan Cape, London, 1971)

Frank, Gerald *The Boston Strangler (Albert DeSalvo)* (New American Library, New York, 1966) (In England: Pan Books, London, 1973)

Gaute, J. H. H. and Odell, Robin *The Murderer's Who's Who* (Harrap, London, 1979)

Gaute, J. H. H. and Odell, Robin *Murder 'Whatdunit'* (Harrap, London, 1982)

Goodman, Jonathan *Trial of Ian Brady and Myra Hindley* (David and Charles, Newton Abbot, 1973)

Green, Jonathan *The Directory of Infamy, The Best of the Worst* (Mills and Boon, London, 1980)

Hawkes, Harry *Murder on the A34 (Raymond Morris)* (John Long, London, 1970)

Helpern, Milton and Knight, Bernard *Autopsy: The Memoirs of Milton Helpern* (Harrap, London, 1979)

Kennedy, John F. *Report on the Select Committee on Assassinations,*

SELECT BIBLIOGRAPHY

US House of Representatives (US Government Printing Office, Washington, 1979)

Keyes, Edward *The Michigan Murders (Norman Collins)* (Reader's Digest Press, New York, 1976)

Kidder, Tracy *The Road to Yuba City: A Journey into the Juan Corona Murders* (Doubleday, New York, 1974)

Klausner, Lawrence D. *Son of Sam (David Berkowitz)* (McGraw-Hill Book Company, New York, 1981)

Livsey, Clara *The Manson Women: A 'Family' Portrait* (Richard Marek, New York, 1980)

Lucas, Norman and Davies, Phil *The Monster Butler (Archibald Hall)* (Arthur Barker, London, 1979)

Lunde, Donald T. *Murder and Madness* (San Francisco Book Company, San Francisco, 1976)

Lunde, Donald T. and Morgan, Jefferson *The Die Song (Herb Mullins)* (W. W. Norton, New York and London, 1980)

Michaud, Stephen G. and Aynesworth, Hugh *The Only Living Witness (Ted Bundy)* (Simon and Schuster, New York, 1983)

Morris, Terence and Blom-Cooper, Louis *A Calendar of Murder* (Michael Joseph, London, 1964)

Nash, Jay Robert *Murder, America* (Harrap, London, 1981)

Nash, Jay Robert *Bloodletters and Badmen: A Narrative Encyclopaedia of American Criminals* (Evans and Company, New York, 1973)

Neville, Richard and Clarke, Julie *The Life and Crimes of Charles Sobhraj* (Jonathan Cape, London, 1979)

Olsen, Jack *The Man With the Candy: The Houston Mass Murders (Dean Corll)* (Simon and Schuster, New York, 1974)

Rule, Ann *The Stranger Beside Me (Ted Bundy)* (W. W. Norton, New York and London, 1980)

Schwarz, Ted *The Hillside Strangler: A Murderer's Mind* (Doubleday, New York, 1981)

Sereny, Gitta *The Case of Mary Bell* (Eyre Methuen, London, 1972)

Sifakis, Carl *The Encyclopaedia of American Crime* (Facts on File, New York, 1982)

Sobel, Lester A. *Political Terrorism, Vols 1 and 2* (Clio Press, Oxford, 1975)

Valentine, Steven *The Black Panther Story (Donald Neilson)* (New English Library, London, 1976)

Issues of *True Detective* and *Master Detective* magazines, 1960–83.

CLASSIFIED INDEX

NAME INDEX